Collected Essays on Economic Theory
Volume II

MONEY, INTEREST AND WAGES

John Hicks

Money, Interest and Wages

Collected Essays on Economic Theory
Volume II

Harvard University Press
Cambridge, Massachusetts
1982

Library of Congress Cataloging in Publication Data

Hicks, John Richard, Sir, 1904–
    Money, interest, and wages.

    (Collected essays on economic theory; v. 2)
    Includes index.
    1. Economics – Addresses, essays, lectures.
2. Keynesian economics – Addresses, essays, lectures.
I. Title. II. Series.
HB171.H6346 1982   330   81-82476
ISBN 0-674-58425-2   AACR2

Contents

Abbreviations

Books by the author

The Theory of Wages (1932)	*TW*
Value and Capital (1939)	*VC*
A Contribution to the Theory of the Trade Cycle (1950)	*TC*
Capital and Growth (1965)	*CG*
Critical Essays in Monetary Theory (1967)	*CEMT*
A Theory of Economic History (1969)	*TEH*
Capital and Time (1973)	*CT*
The Crisis in Keynesian Economics (1974)	*CKE*
Economic Perspectives (1977)	*EP*
Causality in Economics (1979)	*CE*

Journals

Economic History Review	*EHR*
Economic Journal	*EJ*
Journal of Economic Literature	*JEL*
Journal of Political Economy	*JPE*
Oxford Economic Papers	*OEP*
Quarterly Journal of Economics	*QJE*

Preface

The essays I have chosen for this second volume are those concerned with what used to be called *economic dynamics*. I do not nowadays care for that description, since the mechanical analogy is not one which I would want to emphasise. And it seems to have gone out of fashion. Its place has been taken by *macro-economics*, but I do not care for that either. There is much that is 'macro' (relating to the whole of a closed, or national economy) which does not belong here; the social income papers in volume I are obvious examples. And there are some things which do belong here, as for instance the theory of portfolio selection, which are not 'macro' at all. So that won't do either.

I am sure that there will be readers who will want to describe the theme of this volume as *Keynesian economics*. It is true that there are some papers which occupy a central place and which are directly concerned with Keynes's *General Theory*; there is nevertheless an element in the work here presented, running through it all from the earliest to the latest, which is not at all Keynesian. I fully recognise that I have taken a great deal from Keynes, but I am not at all interested in the orthodoxy of what I have taken. I have been trying to see what I myself could make of it; it does not trouble me if some of the things I find myself making of it have no more than a distant relation to anything he said.

So the title I have chosen does make an acknowledgement to Keynes; but it is Keynes's turned the other way up. It is the simplest I can find which comes near to being appropriate.

As was done in volume I, the essays in this volume are arranged chronologically, nearly in the order in which they were written. The reason for adopting that arrangement here is, however, rather different. The 'welfare' essays formed a natural sequence, the later work being built on the earlier. The sequence was fairly self-contained; it was not necessary, after the first steps had been taken, to make much reference to writings outside it, by myself or by others, and what references had to be made could be fully explained. The sequence in this volume is by no means so self-contained.

In the first place, as I have often had occasion to emphasise, monetary theory is 'in history'; it is influenced by the course of events in the 'real world', in a way in which other departments of economic theory are less influenced, or less continually influenced. So here it does have to be remembered that the earlier of these essays were written in an atmosphere still dominated by the Depression of the 1930s; that a later group were prompted by problems of post-war reconstruction; and that the inflation of the 1970s is a background to the latest work. Then, in the second place, there are many of these papers which in substance are reviews, prompted accordingly by the work of others; though I hope it will be found that they have some value in themselves, it is in relation to a series of notable writings by others that they have to be read. Thirdly, and perhaps most seriously, it is no more than a fraction of my own work in this field which can here be presented. The rest is scattered over a large number of books, written at various dates over half a century; and it is in these books that a more satisfactory statement of the arguments of these essays will often be found. Several of them are indeed no more than first sketches for the books which were to follow them. They need to be looked at in relation to those books if they are to be assessed.

So it will be seen how it is that the papers fall into four groups.

Part I (1931–5) consists of those that were written before I saw the *General Theory*. I am quite proud of these papers; but I am sure that to the modern reader they require a bit of explanation. This I have tried to provide in an introductory essay (1) written specially for this volume.

Part II (1936–46) consists entirely of reviews. It begins with reviews of the *General Theory* itself, the well-known '*IS–LM*' paper being the second of them. The rest are reviews of writings by Keynes's contemporaries and 'opponents', from whom I am glad to be able to show that I remained capable of learning. What is perhaps the most important of these is a review of a book by Charles Rist, a book which to Keynesians (if they read it) must have seemed quite horrifying. I was myself more concerned to understand it than to attack it.

Part III (1947–55) apart from a review of Harrod, which was to lead on to my book on the Trade Cycle (1950), consists of papers suggested by post-war problems. Though in origin they are topical, the topical issues are treated in such a way as to open up general issues. Some of these general issues are still with us.

Part IV (1956 to the present) covers a long period, and covers it very thinly. This had to be, because most of the work I have done in this field – quite a lot of it, when it is taken together – has appeared elsewhere, in a whole series of books, no less than seven of them. It is quite surprising when one counts them up. There must be very few people who have read them all. What was to be done about them? Two of these books[1] were themselves collections of essays, and some of those essays might have been extracted; and there was another[2] which might have been included as a whole. But from the other four[3] it would not have been possible to have extracted the relevant passages without a lot of explanation; and one would not have got far along that tack before one had constructed a new volume, not much shorter than the present. This would clearly not have fitted into the present plan.

Nevertheless this work is important; it is the work to which the rest of this volume has been leading up. It must have some representation. It could, I decided, be partially represented by half-a-dozen papers, written during those years, which had not gone into the previously collected volumes; these might go some way towards filling the gap. I have put them in, but there would still be something missing. I have therefore written two new papers, here numbered essay 19, parts III and IV, which will be found to contain a brief description of some of the other ideas which have come to me in this last phase – my post-Keynesian, or (as it has turned out) neo-Wicksellian phase. For in the end I have had to go back to Wicksell, to Wicksell and his Swedish successors (chiefly but not only Myrdal), from whom, as will be seen in the earlier essays, I had started. I have had to do that in order to get a theory which would be wide enough to be appropriate, not only to the old problems, but also to the new ones which have afflicted us, in many countries, in these last years.

I make no pretence that it can give us ready answers. No blueprint for a solution will be found in these pages. There will be found some reasons for rejecting the pseudo-solutions, which have made such a noise in the world, since they have been advertised as easy ways out. I do not believe that there is any easy way out. So it is wrong to enlist in any of the economic 'parties'. To go too far in one direction leads to one sort of breakdown; too far in another to another sort. It is essential to find a way of maintaining some degree of monetary stability, but it cannot be done by monetary means alone.

---

[1] *CEMT* (1967); *EP* (1977).
[2] *CKE* (1974).
[3] *CG* (1965); *TEH* (1969); *CT* (1973); *CE* (1979).

Acknowledgements

I would like to thank Dieter Helm, of New College, Oxford, for his assistance in the preparation of this volume.

The following have kindly given permission to reprint the more recently published papers: *Economic Inquiry* (for the reconstructed version of essay 3), Lexington Books (for essay 21), *The Economic Record* (for essay 22), *The Journal of Post Keynesian Economics* (essay 23), Stirling University (for essay 24).

Part I
Premonitions

1

Introductory: LSE and the Robbins Circle

This is an introduction to the first five of the following essays (2-6), which were written at the London School of Economics, where I was teaching from 1926 to 1935. They were all of them written during the last six of those nine years, after the advent of Lionel Robbins, as professor and head of department, in the autumn of 1929. He gathered around him a group of young economists, among whom these papers circulated, and to whom, at his seminar, most must have been read. What I owed to those discussions is reflected in them.

We seemed, at the start, to share a common viewpoint, or even, one might say, a common faith. Some of us, especially Hayek, have in later years maintained that faith; others, such as Kaldor, Abba Lerner, George Shackle and myself, have departed from it, to a greater or less extent. We took different routes in departing from it; the particular route which I took myself is revealed in these essays.

The faith in question was a belief in the free market, or 'price-mechanism' – that a competitive system, free of all 'interferences', by government or by monopolistic combinations, of capital or of labour, would easily find an 'equilibrium'. (We were not, at that stage, very interested in the welfare characteristics of that equilibrium; 'equilibrium is just equilibrium', as Robbins[1] said.) Hayek, when he joined us, was to introduce into this doctrine an important qualification – that money (somehow) must be kept 'neutral', in order that the mechanism should work smoothly. That, as will be seen, was to cause us quite a lot of trouble.

But Hayek did not join us until 1931. There is a pre-Hayek stage which can be identified, and which (from my point of view) is important. At this stage the focus was on non-monetary matters, on other kinds of 'interference'. To this stage my own *Theory of Wages* (1932) belongs. There was some influence from Hayek in the latest

---

[1] *The Nature and Significance of Economic Science* (1932), p. 127.

stages of writing it, but most of it is pre-Hayek. I had certainly started to write it even before 1929.

I must here insèrt a bit of personal background,[2] to show how it was that I became involved. I had taken my first degree, at Oxford, in 1925. When I arrived at Oxford, I had been trained as a mathematician; and I took the first part of the course for a degree in mathematics. But I had too many interests outside mathematics; so I changed over to 'philosophy, politics and economics', a new course which had just been established. It was really too early to take PPE; the teaching required for it had not yet taken shape. I was well taught in philosophy and in politics (or contemporary history); but the economics I got at that stage was worth nothing at all. I was nevertheless advised to turn to economics, as it was (rightly) thought that in that direction I should find it easiest to get employment. But I had to learn my economics after I had graduated. I had one postgraduate year, in which I was set to write a thesis on wage-differentials in two trades (building and engineering); that was the way in which Oxford (then) thought one should begin to study economics. I was lucky, with no more than that to my credit, to get a job at LSE, at first on probation; what I learned at LSE gradually became enough for me to hold it down.

When I arrived at LSE, the economics department was in an interregnum – between the long reign of Edwin Cannan, and that of Robbins, which was to be even longer. I think that that is the right way of putting it, though the gap was filled by two distinguished figures: Hugh Dalton, who was acting head in 1926-7, and Allyn Young, who was professor little more than a year, before his sudden death at the beginning of 1929. They did not last long enough to upset the Cannanite influence.[3] The economics which I found 'in the air' at the School was Cannanite. It was from Cannan that the LSE 'free market' tradition descended.

Robbins himself had been a pupil of Cannan, and one aspect of the programme he had set before himself was a restoration of Cannanism. The new appointments which he was able to bring about, after returning, were of old Cannanites, such as Arnold Plant and Frederic Benham. I was myself, at that time, quite sympathetic to their viewpoint; it was indeed some conversations I had had with

[2] This is described at more length in a recent paper 'The Formation of an Economist' (*Banca di Lavoro Quarterly*, 1979). It will be reprinted in Volume III.

[3] Young had a great influence on Kaldor, who was his pupil. I did not see much of him. I suppose that he thought of me as a descriptive economist, working on detailed problems of the labour market. He had no reason to think of me as a theorist.

Plant[4] which had been particularly effective in turning me in a free market direction. But if this had been all, I don't quite see how I could have fitted in.

It was not all. Cannan's economics had been very insular; Robbins, when he came, was already widely read in what had been written in other countries. There were two places, in particular, where he felt that he had found allies. One was Chicago (Knight and Viner); the other Vienna (at this stage principally but not only Mises). It should be emphasised that hardly any economics books in foreign languages were then available in English translation. I was just beginning to read German, though I have never caught up with Robbins' reading in German. But one of the smatterings I had got at Oxford was a reading knowledge of French and Italian; I enjoyed reading books in those languages so when the LSE library became available to me, I turned to Pareto[5] and Walras. Though my maths were getting rusty, I found that I had plenty with which to cope. When Robbins found that I had been doing this reading, he set me to lecture on General Equilibrium, hoping, no doubt, that here there would be another alliance.[6]

He also set me to lecture on Risk, starting of course from Knight. I was rash enough to write up what I had been saying in those lectures, after the very first time I had given them. The crude thing

---

[4] During a visit that I paid, in 1928, to South Africa. I taught for a term at the University at Johannesburg; Plant was then professor at Cape Town. Quite apart from these conversations, what I saw in South Africa changed my view of Trade Unions. Up to then, I had been looking at them through the pink-coloured spectacles that I had acquired from my Oxford teachers, such as G. D. H. Cole. The South African unions, then, and for long afterwards, purely white unions, could not be regarded as instruments for the advancement of labour as a whole, as I had been taught that the British Trade Unions were. To look on them as monopolists, the effects of whose actions were similar to those of other monopolists, fitted them much better. So when I came to write *TW*, it was that interpretation of union behaviour which had become dominant. Nevertheless I retained an impression from my earlier work, that the working of the labour market could not be just like the working of other markets – that the labour market could not be (as I would now say) a flexprice market. This does appear in chapter 4 of *TW*, on 'The Working of Competition'. I still stand, after all, by what I said in that chapter.

The effect of conversations with W. H. Hutt, who travelled with me to South Africa (no air passages in those days!), and who became Plant's successor in Cape Town, should also be acknowledged.

[5] It was Dalton who, already in my first year at LSE, had sent me to Pareto. He had learned Italian when with the British army in Italy in 1918, and had got some interest in Italian economics.

[6] Since it was from this angle that I was then approaching Pareto, I took no interest in his normative theory. I am sure that in these early lectures there was no mention of the 'Pareto optimum'.

which resulted appears here as essay 2. It has some bearing on what was to follow, but I place it here as representative of my work at that stage, after the coming of Robbins, but before the coming of Hayek.

Hayek's *Prices and Production* lectures were given at LSE in February 1931. In the following autumn he came to LSE as professor, and may thereafter be said to have been a fairly regular member of our group. But already, after the February, what he had said in the lectures was a major topic of discussion. It was immensely exciting, but also very puzzling. There were bits of it one could use, as I did in the latest parts of *TW*;[7] but there was a central mystery which escaped one. As soon as *TW* was off my hands, I had to get down to it.

I remember Robbins asking me if I could turn the Hayek model into mathematics – providing, I suppose, the mathematical appendix it seemed to require. I couldn't do it. I first thought that the reason for my failure must be my inexpertness at difference equations, or differential equations; I had once known something about them, but had forgotten what I had known. Then it began to dawn on me that, before such techniques could be applied, the model must be better specified. It was claimed that, if there were no monetary disturbance, the system would remain in 'equilibrium'. What could such an equilibrium mean?

This, as it turned out, was a very deep question; I could do no more, in 1932, than make a start at answering it. I began by looking at what had been said by those economists who seemed to have taken most care in the specification of their models – Pareto and Wicksell (with whose *Lectures* I was by that time familiar). Their equilibrium was a static equilibrium, in which neither prices nor outputs were changing, since no one had an incentive to do anything, that was open to him, to change it. In Wicksell's case, in view of his special interest in capital theory, it must be a state in which there was no incentive to accumulate or decumulate, a stationary state. That, clearly, would not do for Hayek. His 'equilibrium' must be a progressive equilibrium, in which real wages, in particular, would be rising; so relative prices could not remain unchanged.

The next step, in my thinking, was to pick up a hint that I had found in Knight[8] – equilibrium with perfect foresight. Investment of capital, to yield its fruit in the future, must be based on expectations, of opportunities in the future. So there would be a sense of equili-

---

[7] Published in the autumn of 1932, so must have been completed quite early in that year, about twelve months after I had attended the Hayek lectures.

[8] F. H. Knight, *Risk, Uncertainty and Profit*, pp. 172-3; also p. 194. See below, p. 34.

brium, according to which it would exist if these expectations were right, so that plans which were based upon them could be carried through without amendment. When I put this to Hayek, he told me that this was indeed the direction in which he had been thinking. He gave me a copy of a paper on 'intertemporal equilibrium', which he had written some years before his arrival in London; the conditions for a perfect foresight equilibrium were there set out in a very sophisticated manner.[9] But having done that, he had just rushed on to his *monetary* disturbances. Surely, I could not help feeling, there must be many ways, other than monetary, in which a perfect fore-sight equilibrium might get disturbed. There ought to be some way in which in a model they could be allowed for.

And more was to come. I had before me that passage in Knight. He asserted much more than Hayek asserted; he said that in an equilibrium with perfect foresight there would be no place for money! Not just misbehaving money, even well-behaving money! So there should have been a stage in the model-building, in which money as such was brought in; this had just been jumped over by Hayek. One must introduce uncertainty, before one can introduce money.

That was really the main thing I had to say in my 1933 paper (essay 3). I was not afraid to introduce uncertainty, since I had already done some work in that field (as has been seen). But I was not yet able to do more than take the first steps. I saw that the demand for money, being a stock demand, must proceed in terms of a balance-sheet theory, so I was led on to the spectrum of assets, of which I was to make much more later. But this took me away from the Hayek problem which I had been set. I tried to get back, in the last pages of my paper, without much success.

In spite of the questions which I had asked – very searching questions they turned out to be – I saw as yet no need to abandon the Hayek construction, though it clearly needed to be reformulated. Two things, in particular, needed to be done. It would clearly be necessary to devise a better concept of equilibrium, one which would serve to isolate specifically monetary disturbance, but which was not burdened by that terribly unrealistic *perfect foresight*. And it would clearly be necessary to devise a better theory of the behaviour of an economy which was not in equilibrium. These were the directions in which one was called to proceed, but it took some time before I made progress in either of them.

[9] See below, pp. 31–2.

If I had had more contact with what was then going on at Cambridge, in the 'Keynes circle' and otherwise, I might have got help from that quarter; but I knew very little of what was going on. The *Treatise on Money* was of course available to me; there are some references to it in what I had written;[10] but I found the *Treatise* very hard to understand. Though I was echoing some passages in it, its method as a whole was to me uncongenial. I had no notion that at that very time Keynes himself was giving it up.

The first help I got was not from Cambridge, but from Sweden. I read Myrdal's *Monetary Equilibrium* in German and wrote a review of it, which here appears as essay 4. I now feel that I wrote that review too soon, since it does not yet show how much I learned, and was to learn, from Myrdal. I had not yet absorbed the importance of what he said about sticky prices; I had not fully seen that this was the direction in which I must look for a solution of my problem about equilibrium. I ought to have seen it more quickly, in view of the work I had already done on the working of the labour market.[11] But it took some time to sink in, and perhaps did not do so at all fully until after I had absorbed the *General Theory*, and had even taken some steps towards emancipating myself from it.

It must have been very shortly after I wrote that review, that I wrote the 'Suggestion for Simplifying the Theory of Money' (essay 5). The centre of this was an elaboration of the balance-sheet theory which I had just roughed out the year before. Though it bears a relation, as Keynes himself told me it did,[12] to his theory of Liquidity Preference (of which as yet I knew nothing), and though its relation to what he had said in the *Treatise* is explicitly recognised, the advance from what I said in essay 3 had a quite different origin. My main occupation, in the time which elapsed between the writing of the two papers, had been with demand theory – the 'Reconsideration of the Theory of Value' which I had written in conjunction with Roy Allen.[13] It was obvious, when coming back to money after working

---

[10] Pp. 37–8 below. These references, there, are quite superficial; they did not get in at all until the main lines had been laid down. This is proved by a first draft which is printed in 'Recollections and Documents' (*EP*), in which there are references to Hawtrey, but none to Keynes at all. It was after this draft had been circulated, to some of my friends, that my attention was drawn to some similarities between what I was saying and what Keynes had said in the *Treatise*.

[11] See n. 4 above.

[12] When I sent him a proof of my article, he wrote 'I agree with you that what I now call Liquidity Preference is the essential concept for Monetary Theory'. That was dated December 24th, 1934.

[13] Volume I of this Collection, essay 1.

on consumer demand, that there was a parallel; the same technique that we had been using in demand theory could be used in this other context. The former indeed was a flow problem, while this was a stock problem; the role of uncertainty here was far more important than it was there. But these differences were no obstacle to the use of a similar method.

I have, to this day, a much higher opinion of 'Simplifying' than of any other of these early papers; I would still stand by what I said in it, so far as it goes. It is no more than a statement of what might now be called the 'micro-foundations' of monetary theory; but these are stated very clearly and I believe correctly. By themselves, they are no more than a beginning; but to begin with them is the right way to begin. One can then show, straight off, as I think I did show, that the use of money is enough in itself to make a free market system potentially unstable; and that the higher the degree of development, or sophistication, that it exhibits the greater does the danger of instability become. Monetary institutions (not just Central Banks, but all the variety of legal arrangements which have been used, at one time and another, as supplements to, or substitutes for, central banking control) can then be introduced as means of checking, or moderating, the instability. When they are introduced in this way, not brought in at the start (with the particular institutions and regulations that exist in one's own time being taken for granted), one can see that they must be imperfect safeguards against instability, and are themselves liable to be infected by it. It is a 'psychological' instability, not a mechanical, which is in question; so it cannot be remedied by the application of a formula, as so many, both then and in later days, have been tempted to suppose.

I sometimes feel, looking back, that it ought to have been my duty, after writing 'Simplifying', to have abandoned all other interests, and to have devoted myself entirely to pushing forward along the road on which I had taken first steps. As it was, nearly thirty years had passed before I got back to it.[14] I allowed myself to be distracted, first by the writing of *Value and Capital* (on which I had already begun to work when I wrote the 'Simplifying' paper) and then by the *General Theory* of Keynes.

Keynes's Liquidity theory was so near to mine, and was put over in so much more effective a way than I could hope to achieve, that it seemed pointless, at first, to emphasise differences. Sometimes, indeed, he put his in such a way that there was hardly any difference.

---

[14] The first signs of return are in the paper originally entitled 'Liquidity' (1962) which appears, in an abridged form, as essay 19, part I, below.

But, as time went on, what came to be regarded, in many quarters, as Keynesian theory was something much more mechanical than he had probably intended. It was certainly more mechanical than I had intended. So in the end I had to go back to 'Simplifying', and to insist that its message was a Declaration of Independence, not only from the 'free market' school from which I was expressly liberating myself, but also from what came to pass as Keynesian economics.

There is one further paper which belongs to this early group: 'Wages and Interest: the Dynamic Problem' (essay 6). This was published in the *Economic Journal* in the month that I moved to Cambridge (September 1935), but must certainly have been written before I left LSE. Though the *General Theory* was not available to me when I wrote it, I must certainly have heard that Keynes was determining the rate of interest by the supply of money. I was curious to test out this doctrine on the model with which I was working, an early version of that which was to be elaborated in *VC*. The 'static' part of that book (which carries on from my General Equilibrium lecture and from the Hicks–Allen article) must already have been well advanced; I was beginning to work on the 'dynamic' side. The idea of a model of very short-run equilibrium had come to me from Sweden, partly from Myrdal's book, and partly from conversations with Lindahl, who had been visiting London on several occasions during this period. The relations between this model and Keynes's, and Lindahl's, all of which have to be distinguished, are explored in later essays in this volume.[15]

I have one more thing to say about these early essays, looked at together. I have explained how the problems that were considered in them were forced upon my attention, in the first place, by Hayek; and I have shown that the position I was taking at the end of the sequence was much nearer to Keynes's than to his. I could see that, then; but now, from a longer perspective, I can see that one reason, at least, for my divergence from him was that I had become more interested in short-run problems, which were Keynes's problems, and less in the problems of the longer run, of the 'cycle', which were his concern. In these terms there did not need to be any opposition; an all-round economist should have attended to both. How I got back to the longer-run problems (at first under the influence of Robertson, and then of Harrod, who even in the thirties, were trying to look at both sorts of problems together) will appear later on.[16]

[15] Especially essays 18 and 23.
[16] In essays 10 and 15.

2

Uncertainty and Profit

This was published in *Economica* in May 1931, but was certainly written in 1930, since I have a note from Keynes, dated December 1930, rejecting it for the *Economic Journal*. I put it here, in spite of its immaturity, since it shows the background from which I began on the things which follow – F. H. Knight's *Risk, Uncertainty and Profit* (1921) – not yet even the Austrians. I have no doubt that one of Keynes's reasons for rejecting it was its crude view of probability, and there I would now be on his side (see chapter 8 of my *Causality in Economics*, 1979). That choices involving uncertainty can be usefully analysed, up to a point, in terms of numerical probabilities has nevertheless been abundantly shown in later work. It may be that this is the first place where that line of attack was sketched out (as has been stated by K. J. Arrow).[1] But even in these terms it falls far short of an adequate discussion because of its implicit assumption that the shares and bonds that are in question cannot be re-sold. So there is no place for Liquidity. Two years later, in the essay which follows this, I had begun to get a glimpse of the liquidity problem.

No doubt because of its immaturity, this essay is very prolix; so I have spared the reader some opening paragraphs, which do no more than give the reference to Knight, and claim that the numerical probability assumption (rejected by Knight) can still be used as an instrument of analysis. I have also cut out a concluding section, which adds very little.

I

The first proposition in any modern theory of profit must be that which maintains the inevitable connection between profit and uncertainty. In a market in which the course of future events was entirely foreseen, profit could not exist. All services would be

[1] In *Econometrica* (1951), p. 411.

remunerated at rates fixed in advance according to the value of their marginal products, allowance being made for changes in these values during the periods for which the contracts were to run. There would be no 'residue'; a firm need not take the form of one group paying wages to another group, but might as well be a co-operative association, of which all, capitalists and labourers, were equally members, and from which all drew their remuneration in the same familiar way.[2]

Nevertheless, although there can be no profit without uncertainty, in an organised society profit is not the only form of income that arises from uncertainty; still less is it the only economic symptom of it. If we were 'isolated men', this indeed might not be the case. For an isolated man, the economic uncertainty that is relevant to his activities is the chance that the result of his labours (and waitings) will fall short of his expectations or will exceed them. Every operation in which he engages will be subject to more or less of this kind of uncertainty, and his total income is thus uncertain, since it depends not only on his own exertions and on the known qualities of his land and his tools, but on their unknown qualities and his own unknown qualities, the chance of earthquake, accident or disease. According to the definition which I shall subsequently recommend, his income would be a profit-income, albeit of a rudimentary kind.

But even in his case, not quite all the uncertainty to which his operations are exposed will exert a direct effect on the size of his income. His income is made up of the returns to separate operations, and in each of these operations there is a chance, which may be large or small, of any given divergence from the most probable result. But if we are measuring his income over a fairly long period of time, it is probable that the uncertainty will be somewhat reduced by the mere number of separate returns of which his income is composed. Of course, since the operations are not independent (if Robinson got a touch of malaria it would affect them all adversely) this reduction will not be very considerable. But I find it difficult to believe that there will not be *some* grouping and *some* setting-off, so that if we

---

[2] In this fundamental principle, Knight was anticipated by Hawley and, to some extent, by Mangoldt. Cf. Hawley, 'The Risk Theory of Profit' (*QJE*, VII, 465): 'The circumstance that no single concrete example can be cited in which the entire elimination of risk is not coincident with the elimination of the residue of the product is conclusive of the element of risk being the fundamental characteristic of the entrepreneur function.' And H. Mangoldt (*Lehre von Unternehmergewinn*, p. 36): 'Nicht in der Verbindung verschiedener Produktionsmittel, sondern in deren Anwendung auf eigene Gefahr liegt das Wesen der Unternehmung.' But what in these is largely intuition, in Knight is demonstration.

supposed, for argument, that the chance of each operation falling short of the expected return by a given percentage was the same (p), the chance of the whole income falling short by the same percentage would be less than p – however small the difference might be.[3]

In organised society, we have to take account not only of a much more extended tendency to the reduction of effective risks, but also of an institutional mechanism whereby the remaining effective risks can be borne in one of two ways. I mean the institution of hiring in advance. A man may perform services, or provide other forms of resources for use in production; and he may do this either for a fixed payment, agreed on before he performs his share in the bargain, or for a payment which depends in some agreed way on the result of the productive process, whatever that result may be. There are thus three main ways by which, in organised society, risks may be dealt with.

(1)   As a result of economic organisation, the risks inhering in particular processes may be reduced.
(2)   The resultant or *effective* risks may be borne by certain persons in return for a fixed payment.
(3)   The effective risks may be borne for a payment whose amount will vary with the return given by the operation in question.

In order to lay bare the essentials of the theory of profit, we must first examine carefully the nature of these three alternatives, and then discuss in what manner the risks inherent in production will be divided between them. We shall find that the last of these classes alone engenders what is entitled to the description of profit, but the nature of profit and the causes determining its magnitude can only be conveniently discussed as part of the wider problems here proposed.

II

With the development of organised co-operative production, the reduction of risks also develops on a scale far beyond the reach of an isolated man. Reduction of risks is not the only, or indeed the main cause which leads to co-operation and specialisation; but production on a larger scale does nevertheless have a tendency to reduce risks.

[3] Of course, a particular operation may not only fail to yield the expected return, but result in a net loss. The fire may not merely fail to roast the pig satisfactorily, but also burn down the house. Even in this case 'grouping' will usually diminish the risk, in so far as the operations are independent. But in the case of an isolated man that will not be very far.

What matters to a firm is not the risk of failure or imperfect success in any one of its particular operations or processes, but the chance of a considerable divergence from the most probable number of successes over the whole output. And, by a simple application of the law of large numbers, it can be shown that this chance diminishes rapidly as the number of operations increases. If the chance of failure in a given operation is $\frac{1}{5}$, then it is clear that the chance of total loss might be great enough to deter many people from undertaking it. But if 1,000 exactly similar operations were undertaken, then although we still could not say that the result of the whole enterprise was *certain*, there would be a practical certainty of at least 750 successes. The risk would not be abolished, but it would be considerably reduced. And as the number of operations increased, the nearer we should get to absolute certainty.[4]

This is by far the most important way in which the natural growth of industry reduces risks; but it may be observed that other ways are possible. There is a certain class of events which are unfavourable for some types of production, but favourable for others. Of these the most important are variations in the weather, and price changes. Certain kinds of technical development may bring together under the same control these complementary operations. In such cases the risks will offset one another, and the total risk will be reduced.

Lastly, any change in the means and ends of production will affect the causes of those favourable or unfavourable events whose occurrence is uncertain but possible, and which are liable to affect the success of an undertaking. The use of plate-glass windows increases the risk of window-slashing; the use of electric light diminishes the risk of fire. Whether the use of advanced methods of production diminishes or increases risks on the whole, is a difficult question. But in any case the head of a firm will have to face the risks inherent in the kind of production and the methods of production he has chosen to adopt.

For any given technique and any scale of production, there is thus a corresponding amount of uncertainty incurred. There is a chance

---

[4] In practice, this tendency loses a certain amount of its effectiveness (1) because the separate operations performed in a business are not usually exactly similar, (2) because they are not completely independent. One workman makes more mistakes than another; and on the other hand, certain kinds of accidents not merely result in a failure of the particular process being worked at the time, but by damaging labourer or machine or by starting a conflagration, reduce the firm's total resources over a long or short period. Nevertheless, so long as there is some basis of similarity and some degree of independence, increase of the scale of a business will reduce most kinds of risk to some extent.

that the business will be completely destroyed with all the resources used in it; there are varying chances of lesser degrees of failure, and at the same time chances of all sorts of degrees of success. This 'scheme' of chances will depend, as we have seen, on the technique and the scale of operations, and although it is unlikely that these will be chosen mainly from a consideration of the risk they involve, it is nevertheless clear that by varying them, a business can vary to some extent the risk it runs. We may find the head of a business hesitating between two schemes of production, of which one is more efficient than the other, but also more risky. It may be worth while to sacrifice some efficiency in order to acquire greater security. The chance of total loss will be diminished, and so, perhaps, will the chance of partial loss; yet since his costs are greater, the chance of any given amount of net gain is also reduced. The principles on which such a decision will be based are derived from considerations that we have yet to examine. Here it is only necessary to point out that such decisions are made. One way of dealing with the uncertainty involved in a given undertaking is to reduce that uncertainty by changing the scale and technique of production. But how far this will be done clearly depends on the availability of other methods.[5]

[5] It will be observed that here and throughout this paper I speak of 'reduction' of risks, and not, as Professor Knight sometimes does, of 'elimination'. Professor Knight's doctrine of 'measurable risks' is one of the parts of his teaching that I am quite unable to accept, at any rate in the uncomprising form in which he first states it (*Risk, Uncertainty and Profit*, pp. 43ff.). It is quite true that there are certain kinds of risk that are practically eliminated in a business of reasonable size – Mangoldt's 'Champagnerfabrikant' with his broken bottles is the classical example of this. Experience has shown that the chance of failure is expressible by a definite fraction. But even here the possibility of elimination depends on the size of the business. It will not necessarily be desirable to extend a business beyond what would from other points of view be the optimum size in order to eliminate completely a small risk. Nor will it necessarily be worth while to eliminate such a risk by insurance. Insurance involves costs of administration and it is once more a question of balancing advantages whether these costs should be insured or not.

Further, the grouping of measurable risks is simply a limiting case, and not a very important one, of the general principle of reduction. Reduction is applicable even when experience does not give us sufficient ground for a knowledge of the exact chances. Even Professor Knight himself admits this (*ibid.*, p. 239) and the whole case has been admirably stated by Professor Hardy: 'All applications of the law of averages rest on a grouping of things, unlike in many respects, into classes, on the basis of certain similarities; if cases nearly alike are infrequent, we must do our grouping on the basis of less homogeneous classes. If the classification is crude, or if the cases are not numerous, the statistical method loses its accuracy. But these cases certainly shade off into Professor Knight's "true uncertainties" by imperceptible degrees, the margin of error getting larger as the evidence gets more scanty.' (*Risk and Risk-bearing*, p. 55)

It is neither completely true to say that all 'measurable risks' will be reduced by grouping, nor that only measurable risks will be reduced, though indeed it is only measurable risks

III

Assume, then, for the present, that the form and scale of our firm are given. How will the remaining effective uncertainty be borne? Who will suffer the losses and pocket the gains which result from the varying fortunes of the enterprise?

There seem to be two possible ways of dealing with the remaining uncertainty. (1) Certain specific risks can be transferred to outside parties; (2) the remainder must be borne by those actually co-operating in the firm, bringing their labour or their capital or both. In what follows we shall be mainly concerned with the second of these alternatives. The first (including insurance, in a broad sense, and speculation) is in many ways closely related to the technical adjustment of risks already discussed. But it is also in part a distribution of risks among those most willing to bear them, and the operation of that we shall proceed to illustrate in a more general case. When this has been done, the analysis of insurance will present few difficulties, and for the sake of brevity will be omitted in this paper.

A conceivable form of economic structure would be one in which all the parties to a firm shared in the same way in the risks of enterprise. Labourers and capitalists would form a co-operative association, each participating in the 'ownership' of the business, and each consequently drawing his remuneration in the form of an agreed proportion of the firm's income. But in practice such a scheme is highly exceptional. Partly for historical reasons, but partly, as we shall see, on account of its usually superior efficiency, enterprise has generally taken another form. The co-operating parties are divided into two groups, one only of which receives a remuneration depending on the firm's success (that is to say, receiving a share of profits). The members of the other receive a remuneration which is not directly contingent on the result of the operations in which they collaborate, but which is fixed before the act of collaboration is performed. The first group receives profits, the second receives wages, interest, or rent.[6]

---

that can be eliminated. If it is maintained that the doctrine of measurable risks gives a fair approximation to the truth, that may be admitted; but an approximation is of little use when it is no simpler and less illuminating than the truth itself.

[6] This definition of profit (originally due to R. Cantillon) has been revived by Professor E. Cannan (*Reviews of Economic Theory*, p. 311). It has in its favour the powerful consideration that it gives the exact sense in which the term is used in practical business; as other definitions most palpably do not. And I think we shall find that it leads us to a rather deeper knowledge of the nature and causes of profit than other definitions do.

The slightest consideration of the history of industrial structure will show that although this division has nearly always existed, it has by no means always, or even usually, coincided with the traditional division of the factors of production. In some stages of industrial development it has been nearly true to say that while labour receives wages, capital receives profits; but it has never been quite true. At other times it has seemed appropriate to identify the receiver of profit with the provider of some particular sort of labour, i.e. management or organisation; but hardly had organisation been promoted to the rank of a separate factor of production when the growth of the salaried manager deprived this scheme of its plausibility. Today we must surely admit that the decision whether any factor of production is to be paid by a share of profit or by a previously fixed reward does not depend on the nature of the service rendered. Profit is not in any sense correlative with wages and interest. The distinction between wages and interest does depend on the nature of the service; the distinction between them and profit depends on the way the service is remunerated.

The division between the two groups is in fact a scheme for the distribution of risks; but it is not a simple scheme whereby all risks are transferred from one group to the other. The group whose payment is fixed in advance does retain some risks, in particular, the risk that when the service has been performed, the payment will not be made. Legal provisions have reduced this risk to a minimum, but they cannot abolish it altogether, since it is always possible that the enterprise will yield a return which is insufficient for the firm to cover its commitments. This is in fact practically the only risk which is left to the capitalist who invests in fixed-interest-bearing securities; but to the labourer who is being paid in what is logically the same way, it is much less important than the risk that the service that he performs will involve him in some danger to life and limb, for which Workmen's Compensation will most inadequately compensate. In the cases of both labour and capital, then, it is impossible for the party who is engaged at a fixed payment to be relieved of all risks – but the risks are very considerably reduced, and the kind of uncertainty borne is very considerably changed.

The difference between the kinds of uncertainty borne by the two groups can be easily illustrated by the method of frequency curves.[7] Along *OX* we plot sums of money; along *OY* fractions expressing chances. Suppose the chance that a particular unit of capital or

[7] First, I think, used for this sort of problem by Professor A. C. Pigou (*Economics of Welfare*, Appendix A).

labour will bring to him who supplies it a gain of £50, is $\frac{1}{6}$. Then we shall plot $OM = 50$ (£'s) and $PM = \frac{1}{6}$. In this way the whole uncertainty of the result of a particular investment can be expressed in the form of a curve and we can read off from the curve the chance that the investment will give any particular result.[8]

Where resources are hired for a fixed payment, but there is a possibility that the payment will not be made (or not made in full) or that some incidental misfortune will overtake the lender as a result of the investment, then the uncertainty-curve will take the form shown in Fig. 2.1. When resources are exposed to uncertainty, and the reward is to be a share in the net return, *whatever it is*, the form of the curve will be as in Fig. 2.2. In many cases the curves will be much less dissimilar than those shown in the diagrams, but so long as there is a maximum possible reward, and the chance of that maximum being paid is relatively large, the case falls into the first class. (In either case, of course, there may or may not be the chance of a negative return.)

When the first method of hiring resources is used, the question is simply one of demand and supply at various promised rates of payment. Supply will, of course, be considerably affected by the confidence of lenders in the realisation of their expectations. Where the

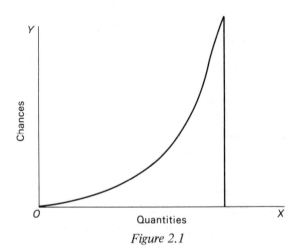

Figure 2.1

[8] This statement is, of course, not quite accurate. But anyone acquainted with the theory of statistics can make the necessary emendation, and refinements in this direction would be out of place here.

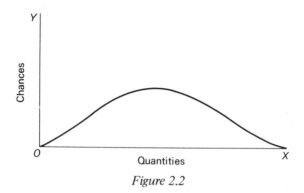

Figure 2.2

second method is used, however, we can no longer treat the problem as one of equilibrium at a rate. Yet for any given set of terms (or uncertainty-curve) there will be a certain supply of any given kind of resources (including the resources furnished by the 'entrepreneur' himself if we are dealing with a private business). Similarly, as we shall see, there will be a certain demand. In either case, a change in the terms offered will change the form of the uncertainty-curve, and this change will react on the demand and supply of the resources in question. By changing the terms, demand and supply can thus be brought into equilibrium as in ordinary price-theory. But whereas in price-theory, the adjustable index is a numerical ratio, here it is a relation or function, and to complete our comprehension of the nature of this equilibrium we must examine how changes in the function react on demand and supply.[9]

---

[9] Let p be the chance that a return of £x will be secured from the investment of one unit of a certain kind of resources.

Then various schemes of uncertainty can be represented by functions

$$p = \phi_1(x), \quad p = \phi_2(x).$$

If Z_1, Z_2 represent the quantities supplied when the anticipations of reward are ϕ_1, ϕ_2, the conditions of supply can be represented by the function $Z = f(\phi)$. Similarly the conditions of demand can be represented by $Z' = F(\phi)$.

If Z' is greater than Z, it will be necessary to revise the terms in favour of the lender. A scheme ϕ' must be proposed, so that

$$f(\phi') > f(\phi).$$

It must therefore next be examined how changes in the form of the function ϕ will affect the demand and supply of resources.

IV

What, then, will be the effect of a change in the chances of reward on the supply[10] of resources for a given employment? The simplest possible assumption would make everything depend on the 'expectation' of reward, in the sense in which that word is used in the theory of probability – the sum of the products of chances and quantities of return anticipated.[11] Of two alternatives the investor would go to that one where the expectation of reward was higher, and thus if the expectation was increased, the supply offered would increase too.

If this assumption were correct, and if the estimates of investors were either accurate or showed no bias in either direction, then we should arrive at the interesting conclusion that no net share in the National Dividend was to be attributed to anyone for the bearing of risk. In the long run, and over large groups of people, successes and failures would balance, so that the return received by the whole body would be the same as if their investments had carried no risk at all.

But this conclusion, in many ways so convenient, is not really consistent with observed facts. For it also follows from this assumption that *any* two schemes of uncertainty, where the expectation was the same, would be indifferent to the lender. And this as a general rule seems highly unlikely. It would mean that people would be equally ready to invest in an undertaking that promised a safe £100, in one which promised equal chances of £200 or nothing, and in one which promised nine chances of £110 to one of £10. It seems fairly safe to say that this is not the case.

Attempts have been made to arrive at a more satisfactory principle by means of the law of diminishing marginal utility. On this basis, the indifference of two uncertainty-schemes would not imply equal expectations. That scheme which has the greater proportion of chances of low returns must have a higher expectation, i.e. it must also have a greater proportion of high returns and this must more than counterbalance arithmetically the low ones. It is the expectations of subjective satisfaction, not the expectations of money returns, which must be equal if the two schemes are to be indifferent.[12]

Such a theory is certainly more satisfactory than the crude view which bases everything on money expectation, but it is improbable

---

[10] Supply comes logically first, for demand is mainly derived demand.

[11] Thus, if the chance that a given operation will yield £50 is $\frac{1}{4}$, £70 is $\frac{1}{2}$, and £80 is $\frac{1}{4}$, the expectation is £67 10s.

[12] Perhaps the most elegant application of diminishing marginal utility to this problem is to be found in J. B. Clark, 'Insurance and Business Profits' (*QJE*, October 1892).

that it contains the whole truth. We may accept diminishing marginal utility as a practically universal law when it is applied to actually realised satisfactions. The things which a man can buy with a second £100 are rarely as essential to him as those which he buys with his first. But although it would follow from this – if man were a completely rational being – that his desire for £200 would be less than twice as strong as his desire for £100, can we be certain that it does really follow, in view of the known peculiarities of the human species?

And there is one peculiarity which does suggest a powerful tendency in the other direction – the taste for gambling. There is no doubt that under certain conditions men are willing to exchange a certainty for a scheme of uncertainties the value of whose expectation is considerably less than the value of the certainty they abandon. But this scheme of uncertainties is nearly always of one type. When the scheme includes a small chance of a very large gain, 'rational conduct' (based on the law of diminishing marginal utility) would estimate the value of this chance as very small indeed. Practice, however, does just the reverse. The philosopher who acted up to his principles would never be willing to give even £1 for a $\frac{1}{1000}$ chance of winning £1,000. But men can always be found who will give a good deal more. Whether this is due to an unconscious 'blind eye' to the chances, or to a conscious preference, may be left to the psychologist. I suspect the latter. But economics need only concern itself with the fact, and the fact is undeniable.

Some writers[13] show a rather amusing indignation at the suggestion that the 'alert business man' is in any way affected by an inclination to so ignoble a vice as gambling. Yet when we observe that our second type of uncertainty-curve does very often approximate quite closely to the type assumed with such alacrity by the gambler, it becomes difficult to believe that persons with a tendency in that direction can be altogether excluded from the market.[14]

If the gambling motive almost certainly affects the supply of resources when the uncertainty accepted is of the second type, it is much less likely to be important when the payment offered is fixed. In that, our first case, there are no 'dazzling prizes', and rational

[13] Such as Mr Hawley, 'Reply to Final Objections' (*QJE*, August 1901). Mangoldt and Professor Knight, however, incline to the view expressed here.

[14] Nor can I agree with Mr Hawley that such persons will be excluded by 'the survival of the fittest'. It is possible to go a long way in the under-estimation of risks without finishing in the bankruptcy court. The over-optimistic will get smaller incomes than they might have done, but they need not get no incomes at all. Even if the most reckless do often come to a bad end, Nature seems to have great powers for the manufacture of their like.

utilitarianism will often give us a good picture of the action of large groups of men. Even here (particularly in the case of labour) there is indeed some tendency to see the reward and not the risks which have made it high; but with schemes of the second type it is probably much stronger. With them there can be little doubt that resources are frequently available somewhat more cheaply than they would be if men were guided by purely rational motives.

We are now in a position to describe more definitely the effects of uncertainty on the supply of any factor of production. Although the reactions of different people towards uncertainty will necessarily vary, in theory we can nevertheless draw up a scale of market preferences. We can arrange uncertainty-schemes in an order which will indicate what lenders as a group prefer; and we shall find them showing their preferences in a practical manner by increasing the amount they supply when the terms offered rise in the scale. There is thus a definite relation between any given uncertainty-scheme and the quantity of the factor of production in question which will be elicited by it. One uncertainty-scheme can, of course, elicit only one quantity of the factor; but the same quantity may be equally well secured by an indefinite number of different uncertainty-schemes. Any variation in an uncertainty-scheme will either increase or diminish the resources offered, excepting in the case when the variation is composed of two separate movements which compensate and thus leave the supply unchanged. What rules can we lay down about the effects on supply of changes in the scheme offered?

(1)   Any change which takes the form of moving the whole uncertainty-curve to the right, without changing its shape, will increase the amount of resources offered.[15] This may be taken as self-evident.

(2)   By a process of compensation, carried out in accordance with the principles of diminishing marginal utility and 'gambling over-estimate' (as discussed above) a curve of any given form can always be found which is equivalent to another given curve, and which would elicit the same supply in response to it.

By a combination of these propositions, it can always be discovered whether one uncertainty-scheme would be preferred to another, or whether the two are equivalent.[16]

---

[15] That is to say, $p = \phi(x + h)$ will always be preferred to $p = \phi(x)$. A simple vertical movement of the uncertainty-curve is, of course, impossible.

[16] I fear this is hardly simplicity itself, but it must regretfully be admitted that in order to analyse the situation in question completely, even further complications would be neces-

V

Our separate discussions of the various factors affecting the disposal of resources where uncertainty is present can now be brought together fairly easily.

The demand of a business for any factor of production can be regarded as dependent on the success which is anticipated for the whole enterprise, and on the terms on which other resources are available. It is a resultant of the process of adjustment whereby the various factors are fitted into their places – the places where they best suit the purpose of the head of the firm.

The relation of uncertainty to this adjustment can best be seen if we begin with the case of a private business, controlled by a single head, who brings certain supplies of capital and labour of his own, and seeks to secure as large a profit as possible on that capital and labour.

Let us begin by supposing his technical methods to be chosen already. Then the risks to which his hired labour and capital will be exposed will be mainly decided already, and in consequence the quantity of each kind he can get will depend chiefly on the rates he is prepared to pay. If the amounts of resources he considers to be necessary are available at such rates as leave the anticipated return on his own capital and labour as favourable to himself (i.e. the resultant uncertainty-scheme as high up on his own scale of preferences) as he considers it possible to make it, then he will rest content. On the other hand, if he is dissatisfied with the return he thus anticipates for himself, several kinds of adjustments are open to him.

If the rates he has to pay for his resources are so high as to leave the expectation of return on his own capital and labour considerably below that which he could get elsewhere in relatively secure investments (it is not impossible that he will be content with a return somewhat below) then his most obvious course is to contract the scale of his business. But without adopting so drastic a measure, other adjustments can be made.

---

sary. For when uncertainty is present, we cannot expect the same terms to be reached in equilibrium throughout a perfect market. Therefore the supply we have been discussing can only be taken as the supply elicited by the demands of a single firm, and that depends not only on the factors considered above, but on the terms offered by its competitors. Also the difference in investors' preferences will sometimes make it possible for a firm to raise resources on better terms (in the aggregate) by offering a series of different schemes, appealing to different classes of investors. But the complete analysis of these possibilities would lead us far afield, and the discussion in the text will perhaps suffice for the purposes of this paper.

(1) He may put more capital and labour (effort) of his own into the business. This will both enable him to be content with a smaller quantity of hired resources, and, by giving the resources he does hire better security, enable him to get them on better terms.

(2) He may change his technical methods, either in order to use less of a particular kind of resources whose owners are particularly sensitive to the risks they run, or in order to reduce certain kinds of risks, and so become able to get resources on better terms.

(3) He may pass on specific risks to persons who do not directly co-operate in the concern, but who are more willing to bear these risks than those who do, usually because they have special means of risk-reduction. It may thus be possible to get better terms from those who actually bring labour or capital by relieving them of certain risks (reducing their chances of small or negative return) although it would not be worth the employer's while for him to bear these risks himself. But they can be borne by the outsiders with special facilities to the advantage of both parties. The main methods of passing-on are, of course, insurance and hedging.

Thus by some or all of these methods the balance-sheet of the firm may be varied so as to render the chances of return on the employer's own resources more favourable to him.

In the converse case, when the rates offered by lenders are lower than those which would make the employer's chances most favourable, adjustments can be made in the contrary direction. He can expand the business, he can use less of his own resources, he can change his technique, or he can reduce his insurance. As in the former case, but by adjustments in the contrary direction, equilibrium can be reached.

Now it will probably be observed that some of these adjustments, though always theoretically possible, nevertheless in practice get little scope in a small firm. In particular, a small private entrepreneur has little opportunity of adjusting risks by changing his own investment in the business. And this is a serious weakness of the private business. As long as that form of organisation is persisted in, only those employers with large capital resources of their own can expand effectively to meet increasing opportunities. The small employer cannot expand his business, for the security he can give both to capitalists and labourers is so small that the rates he would have to pay would rise very steeply indeed. And it is only to a very limited extent that he can provide security for them by technical change or by insurance.

Expansion is definitely stopped by the deficiency of his own resources.

Under these circumstances, he can only push the prospects of return on his own resources to the most favourable point by following a line of development which inevitably involves the sacrifice of private independence. Conversion of the firm into a joint-stock company enables him to acquire new resources by the second method and cease to rely entirely on his own supply. Such resources, as we have seen, will often be available on relatively favourable terms, and expansion will be able to proceed to a point higher on his scale of preferences.

When conversion has taken place, the same problems of adjustment will, of course, arrive at later stages. But here the test is no longer the preferences of one man. The single entrepreneur has perhaps retired from the business, or has taken his place as one of a board of directors. These directors may indeed take their own preferences as sole guide. But the structure usually secures that this guide will not be far removed from the interests of shareholders generally, and the theory that directors act for their shareholders has the power to control action in a large proportion of cases.

VI

The main forces governing equilibrium are those described, but in the case of the joint-stock company and particularly in regard to the transition from private firm to company, new considerations arise. These are associated with the problem of control.

That problem has been excluded from our previous discussion. It has been excluded because of a tacit assumption which we have hitherto been making, but which is not really warranted. We have assumed that once an investment is made, the chances of its success or failure depend on causes outside human control. To a considerable extent they do, not outside potential control, perhaps, but outside any control that is actually feasible. Yet not altogether. The chances of success of a given investment (whether of capital or labour) depend on the efficiency with which all those who work in the same firm co-operate with the factor in question. The fact of this dependence, and investors' necessarily imperfect knowledge of its nature, are powerful causes deterring investment. Where the dependence can be lessened, or where investors' knowledge of co-operating factors can be increased, resources will be provided more readily than where this is not the case.

The force of competition will thus stimulate the development of methods for satisfying these requirements. Of these the 'first method' of our previous discussion – contractually fixed payment – is certainly one. That method is a protection to the investor, since the chance that the firm will fail completely is much less than the chance that it will do badly, and it is also a chance that is easier to estimate. But the same method is also a protection to the resources that co-operate with the factor in question. The hiring of a labourer (and labour is the only factor whose efficiency is in doubt) by a contractual payment fixed in advance is a protection to everyone else engaged in the business, for it is possible to dispense with any worker (including manager) whose performance does not come up to expectations.[17]

When resources are remunerated by the second method, that of a share in the surplus (and since the return to the whole business is necessarily uncertain, some must always be rewarded in this way), another form of protection must be sought. In practice, we can trace three different kinds of protection which are used to meet this difficulty.

(1)   Those resources which take their share as profit may actually belong to that person or those persons who take the most important decisions. This is the case of the 'one-man business' or private partnership.

(2)   The owners of the resources may choose persons in whom they have confidence to take decisions for them. This is the theory of the joint-stock company, actually realised only in some cases.

(3)   Although the shareholders' choice of directors may in fact be only nominal, they may nevertheless possess sufficient confidence in the management of the company to be satisfied with the position. In extreme cases, even nominal selection may be absent. There can be no doubt that it is simply on confidence of this kind that the institution of the joint-stock company really rests.

Where none of these conditions are present, a business will find it impossible to acquire resources on the second plan in competition with others who offer one or other of these advantages. And it may

---

[17] It may indeed fairly be claimed that in practice the method of hiring lower grades of labour over-protects the investor of capital. This is owing to the short period for which the contract runs. The labourer may be nearly certain of getting his stipulated reward for the week for which he is engaged. But in order to be available for that week's work, he is involved in commitments which extend far beyond the week.

be guessed that even if such competition were absent, the supply of resources in the absence of confidence would be very small.

The bearing of control on the adjustment discussed in the previous question should now be clear. If the head of a private business wishes to acquire resources by the second method – and we have found that circumstances may arise when this is highly desirable – then he can rarely do so by going to the open market as he would ordinarily do when hiring resources for a fixed return. Unless his abilities and character are extremely widely trusted, he will not be able to get resources in this way. It will be necessary for him to sacrifice some independence and submit perhaps to a considerable measure of control by others. This in many cases he may be unwilling to do. To him, as to his prospective shareholders, the right of ultimate control is an asset, not a liability, and it may well be that the advantages of conversion will have to be very great before he is willing to agree to sacrifice his single control.

If he does decide to convert his firm into a company, the degree of control offered to shareholders is then another adjustable factor affecting the supply and demand of resources. The methods by which such adjustments can be made – the manipulation of voting rights – are familiar. The same problem arises if the extension of a firm, which is already a company, involves a new issue of shares.

3

Equilibrium and the Cycle

This paper has had a curious history. It was written to be translated into German; it appeared, in German, under the title 'Gleichgewicht und Konjunktur', in the Vienna *Zeitschrift für Nationalökonomie*, no. 4 of 1933. The English original had been circulated, to Keynes and to Robertson, as well as in LSE; but in later years it got lost. The present version is a re-translation, partly by myself and partly by Dr Barry Schechter (who had been asked to undertake it by Robert Clower, in order that it should be published in *Economic Inquiry*, the economic journal of the University of California, Los Angeles, where it appeared in November 1980). I think that it is a fairly accurate reproduction of the lost original.

The circumstances in which it was written have been explained on pp. 6–7 above. The 'new theory of money and the cycle' which is spoken of in the opening paragraph is of course Hayek's; it was from Hayek that I began – where I got to will be seen. Even at the end, I was minimising my differences from Hayek. I could do so because, as I have elsewhere explained (*Economic Perspectives*, p. 141n), I still thought, like Pigou and Robertson, and Hayek, but by that time unlike Keynes, that 'we were talking about *fluctuations*, which, since they did not result in complete collapse or complete explosion, could not have engendered an expectation of going on forever. Booms could then be considered as times of high prices, slumps as times of low prices – with regard to some norm, which throughout the fluctuations would not be changed, or not much changed'. When I came to reviewing the *General Theory* (essay 7 below) I found that this sheet-anchor had been abandoned; and that was the thing about it which, on a first impression, I found it hardest to take.

The great advances that have been made in recent years in our understanding of the Trade Cycle have consisted chiefly of the successful application of economic theory (and especially of monetary theory) to the problem of fluctuations. This application was itself both the cause and the consequence of new developments in the field of pure theory; for one of the chief things that had to be done was to bring monetary theory into a closer relation with general (non-monetary) economics. The development in our knowledge of the Cycle was thus, from one point of view, a purely theoretical development. It took the form of the construction of a theory of Money that finds a place inside general economic theory rather than outside it.

The object of the present paper is to make a small contribution to this theoretical development by enquiring into the place that is to be occupied in the new theory of Money and of the Cycle by the central notion of pure economics: the concept of equilibrium. I begin with a discussion of the equilibrium concept as it is found in Pareto, partly because it is by that route that I myself came to the ideas that I shall be discussing. I believe, however, that this approach has some advantage in itself, since it is the Lausanne school that has been most concerned with the concept of equilibrium and has interpreted it, on the whole, in the strictest manner.

I. The Generalisation of the Concept of Equilibrium

Although it is in Pareto that we find the strictest application of the equilibrium concept, it is in vain that we look in his work for a precise definition. 'Economic equilibrium', he says in the *Manuel*, 'is a state which would be maintained indefinitely if there were no change in the conditions under which it is observed.'[1] Now this is an ambiguous, in the light of earlier discussions, indeed, one might almost say deliberately ambiguous definition.

The ambiguity comes out most clearly if one simply looks at the theory of exchange. The equilibrium concept can then be applied to two quite different situations. First, we might assume that people are coming to the market with given quantities of goods and are exchanging them among themselves until a point is reached at which no further voluntary exchange is possible between any two parties. This point may well be described as 'a state which would be maintained indefinitely'. Marshall,[2] however, had already shown that such an equilibrium is not unconditionally determined. The quantities that will be exchanged depend upon the initial prices at which

---

[1] V. Pareto, *Manuel d'économie politique*, p. 153.
[2] A. Marshall, *Principles*, Appendix on Barter.

exchange begins; these prices can vary quite considerably, though within limits. There are several ways, indeed, of getting round this difficulty. Perhaps the best is that of Edgeworth, who assumes that initial transactions are only provisional, so that it is open to any party to re-contract if a better offer is later available to him.[3]

A second interpretation of Pareto is more to the point. Here we assume a continuing market, in which on every day new bargains for the supplies of that day are made. We then ask the question: What are the maintainable prices, i.e. what prices under unchanging conditions of demand and supply can be maintained indefinitely, so that no one needs to sell tomorrow at prices different from those attained today?(Though this problem is rightly regarded as the central problem of economic statics, it is already in one sense a dynamic problem. Its mechanical counterpart is to be found in Newton's First Law of Motion – the body 'moving at constant speed in a straight line'.)

The impression can hardly be avoided that a chief reason why Pareto failed to make a proper distinction between these two interpretations was his desire to concentrate attention upon those principles that can be interpreted in either sense. Such an endeavour explains the extreme generality of many of his results, but it is also responsible for some of their limitations. Most importantly, it is responsible for the fact that he never produced a satisfactory theory of capital.

There is one section in the *Manuel* that seems to indicate that in essentials Pareto accepted the theory of capital and interest due to Böhm-Bawerk. Interest is for him the 'price of transformation over time'.[4] But this notion was never fully worked out and incorporated into his system – though the incorporation would not have presented any particular difficulty once it had been decided that equilibrium was to be interpreted in the second sense – that of the ongoing market.

Such an extension of the Paretian system, to cover Production that takes Time, would nevertheless have had one most significant limitation. The extended equations would only have been applicable

[3] F. Edgeworth, Papers, vol. II, pp. 311–12. This way out, and indeed the whole distinction between the two concepts of equilibrium, is already expressed in essence in *Mathematical Psychics* (1881). 'Thus an auctioneer having been in contract with the last bidder (to sell at such a price if no higher price) re-contracts with a higher bidder. So a landlord on expiry of lease, re-contracts, it may be, with a new tenant' (*ibid.*, p. 17).

See also, on this problem, H. Mayer, in *Wirtschaftstheorie der Gegenwart*, II, esp. pp. 196–7; and my own paper, 'Edgeworth, Marshall, and the Indeterminateness of Wages' (*EJ*, 1930), to be reprinted in Volume III.

[4] *Manuel*, pp. 311–12.

to the conditions of a Stationary Equilibrium – the equilibrium of an economy in which there is no net saving. This is obvious as soon as one considers that the conditions of equilibrium in Period II, in an economy with net saving, cannot be the same as they were in Period I; so the prices ruling in Period II cannot be the same.[5] A precise formulation of the conditions of Stationary Equilibrium is a useful achievement; but it must be admitted that on this interpretation the Paretian system is much further removed from reality than its creator supposed it to be. The Lausanne equations become no more than an exact formulation of what Marshall called the 'famous fiction' of the Stationary State.[6] As such, they are not a description of reality. At most, they are a tool for its analysis – a tool that would be much more effective if it were sharpened further.

One step in that direction has already been shown to be possible.[7] As soon as we suppose that people engage in processes of production that take time, we ought to take account of the influence of future (expected) as well as current prices on their behaviour; for it is with an eye to the future prices of their products that people will embark upon 'indirect' or 'roundabout' methods of production. So long as we are confining attention to Stationary Equilibrium, we can set future prices and present prices equal to one another, and so make the equilibrium determinate. Supplies and demands for goods and services and for free capital give us $n + 1$ equations to determine n prices and the rate of interest.[8]

Once we drop the the assumption of Stationary Equilibrium, present and future prices are no longer equal. We have (apparently) $n + 1$ present prices and countless future prices, with still no more than $n + 1$ equations. There are not enough equations to determine all prices. This, however, is a difficulty that can be got around in the

[5] This, as of course one now realises, is not strictly correct. I was doubtless thinking, as I believe I generally did in the 1930s, of the accumulation of capital in an economy with a fixed supply of labour.]

[6] A. Marshall, *Principles*, p.366ff.; see also L. Robbins, 'On the Conception of a Stationary Equilibrium' (*EJ*, 1930). I am not questioning that such a formulation, in spite of the high degree of abstraction that it entails, is of fundamental importance.

[7] F. H. Knight, *Risk, Uncertainty and Profit*, ch. 5; F. A. Hayek, 'Das intertemporale Gleichgewichtssystem' (*Weltwirtschaftliches Archiv*, 1928); J. Tinbergen, 'Ein Problem der Dynamik' (*Zeitschrift für Nationalökonomie*, 1932).

[8] The necessity for such a capital equation among the conditions of Stationary Equilibrium may appear surprising; it has indeed often caused trouble. But it is clear, on close examination, that it is necessary – in order to make sure that the same amount of capital as is set free by the completion of old processes is reinvested on the initiation of new processes.

following way. Suppose that we place ourselves at a point of time *A* and consider a given period of time over which wants and resources (the economic data) change in a manner that is foreseen. This whole period can be divided into *m* subperiods, each so short that the movement of prices *within it* can be neglected. This gives us $m(n+1)$ prices to be determined.[9] If we merely impose the condition that *present* supplies and demands are to be equal, the problem remains unsolved. But if we seek to discover what prices, in each subperiod, will equate supplies and demands in each subperiod, the problem is solvable; for we then have $m(n+1)$ equations to determine the $m(n+1)$ prices. Naturally, *n* can be made as large as we like, so the whole Period can be made as long, and the subperiods as short as we like to make them.

What would such a system of equations signify? Just this: that however the economic data vary, there will always be a set of prices which, if it is foreseen, can be carried through without supplies and demands ever becoming unequal to one another and so without expectations ever being mistaken.[10] The condition for equilibrium, in this widest sense, is Perfect Foresight. Disequilibrium is the Disappointment of Expectations.

Such a 'dynamic equilibrium' is obviously still far from being a description of reality. It does nevertheless serve as a model of a *perfectly working* economic system, which is much more usable as a standard of comparison than is the model of Stationary Equilibrium. Because of ignorance of future changes of data (and still more of the consequences of changes of data – not only of future or present changes, but also of those that have already occurred in the past) such a perfect Equilibrium is never attainable. A real economy is always in disequilibrium.[11] The actual disequilibrium may be compared with the idealised state of dynamic equilibrium to give us a way of assessing the extent or degree of disequilibrium. Some

[9 It will be noticed that the question of the horizon, as it has since been called, is here neglected.]

[10 As, of course, one now realises, this is very much of an overstatement; at the best it is only true for variations in data within limits. (Only the first steps towards Activity Analysis had been taken at the time of writing; I had had no opportunity to make myself familiar with them.)]

[11] After Dr Hayek, in the first part of the above-cited article, has constructed an 'intertemporal' equilibrium, very much on the lines I have here been describing, he proceeds, in the second part, to maintain that a change in the effective volume of monetary circulation is to be regarded as an independent cause of disequilibrium. I cannot accept this in its literal sense, though I am prepared to agree that in a world of imperfect foresight monetary changes are very likely to lead to acute disequilibrium (see below).

changes of data can be left out of our reckoning, since they cause no significant disequilibrium of prices; they are too small or are offset by countervailing changes. In the same way there may be other changes that have serious effects in limited fields but remain confined in their general effects. Such changes may cause the most violent partial disequilibria, but their effects are limited to particular sections of the economy. There are changes, finally, that do have general effects; they cause unexpected variations in many if not in most prices. Cyclical fluctuations are clearly of this last type. For such general disequilibria we may be justified in assuming that the disturbances occur in those structural elements that have the most general direct effect on prices – the rate of interest and the value of money.[12] (This applies whether or not the original cause of disequilibrium was of this character.)

II. Equilibrium and Money

Money as medium of indirect exchange plays no part in the Lausanne equilibrium.[13] Money as standard of value does, of course, play a part; for of the $(n + 1)$ goods and services, one is chosen to act as standard (or '*numéraire*') in terms of which the prices of the other n goods and services are measured. But this says nothing about the demand for money in its use as money; the tacit assumption of perfect foresight deprives the *numéraire* of any monetary function.

To see how this is, begin by assuming that there is in the economy a stock of some money material that is used in the usual way as a means of payment but which, for the rest, is not a commodity in the economic sense; i.e. it has no non-monetary use. It is necessary that at every instant the money stock should be divided among the individuals composing the economy in proportions that depend upon their requirements for it. But what is the source of this requirement for money? Simply the need for it as a means of making future payments. For making present payments one does not hold it; one pays it out. It is only for future payments that one needs to hold a stock of money.

[12] The whole of this paragraph, and n. 11, is, of course, an olive branch to Hayek.]

[13] L. Walras did indeed make a serious attempt to treat money as a means of payment (see his *Théorie de la Monnaie*; also A. W. Marget, 'Leon Walras and the Cash-balance approach to the Problem of the Value of Money', *JPE*, 1931). But the ambiguity in the equilibrium concept is in Walras' sheer confusion (much more than it is in Pareto); the outliers of his system – his capital theory as well as his monetary theory – are seriously damaged by it. [Even after reading Patinkin, I would not altogether withdraw this note.]

But it must be noticed that it is only to meet uncertain future payments that a stock of money is necessary. If the date and amount of future payments are absolutely certain, money does not need to be held in order to meet it; it is more profitable to lend it out, until the date when the payment has to be made. If instead money were held for this purpose, the individual would be doing something that would not be to his benefit; so the position would not be one of equilibrium.

Against this drastic conclusion it may perhaps be objected that an assumption has slipped in: that money can be profitably lent out for any period, however short. But this is indeed what in fact happens. Money is lent out through a middleman – the banker.[14]

A further possible objection is also rejected: that a certain minimum amount of money must be accumulated before it is lent out, in order that the inconvenience of continual lending and encashment should be overcome, or that the time taken by acts of payment sets an irreducible minimum to the demand for money from the whole economy. The first of these difficulties can be overcome (in the conditions supposed) by using the borrowers' promise to pay as a substitute for cash, while the use of cheques and bills is a long-established means of overcoming the second. Thus we cannot escape the conclusion that if the future course of economic data (and the corresponding future course of prices) were exactly foreseen, there would be no demand to hold money as money. People would lend out all their money holdings – either through the banks or through some corresponding mechanism. It is clear, too, that under the same assumption, the Bank itself would need to hold no cash reserve.[15]

If the demand for money is zero, the price level will be indeterminate – though relative prices may be perfectly determined. As long as people hold cash, the position is not one of equilibrium, since it will be to everyone's benefit to increase future income by lending out present money holdings. This difficulty may indeed be overcome to a

[14] Cf. K. Wicksell's concept of the 'virtual velocity of circulation' (*Lectures*, vol. II, pp. 67ff.). Banking is of course no more than the application of the law of large numbers to the reduction (but never to the elimination) of this kind of risk. For the rest, banks just play the part of intermediaries in the process of 'lending out' (though the importance of this function is of course not to be denied). Accordingly it seems to me that the practice of modern monetary theorists, of treating their problem as a banking problem, bank deposits being reckoned as money, while its practical convenience is evident, tends on the whole to obscure the true nature of the matter.

[15] Cf. Knight, *op. cit.*, p. 194: 'with all forms of friction eliminated, there would seem to be hardly a limit to the substitution of credit for any sort of commodity as a medium of exchange and a stable value-standard would apparently be impossible to establish.'

certain extent if we treat as money a commodity with a non-monetary utility. Equilibrium can then (formally) be established. But the prices that will be determined in this way by the Lausanne equations have little relation to those that would be established in fact. For, in fact, people always demand money as money – not because it has a direct utility to them, but because it is to be used in the making of future payments. In addition to the demand for money as a commodity, there is a demand that arises directly out of ignorance of the future.

If one accepts this argument, the following consequences emerge.

(1) Monetary theory, in the strict sense, falls outside equilibrium theory.[16] Since the use of money is closely connected with imperfect foresight, it needs to be analysed in association with the theory of Risk. Velocity of circulation, in its most important aspect, is a risk-phenomenon.

(2) The Trade Cycle is a 'purely monetary phenomenon' in one sense only: that every large change in economic data affects risk and hence affects the velocity of circulation of money. It has additional real effects through its monetary repercussions. Whatever the *causa causans* of an economic crisis, it is bound to have a monetary aspect.

(3) Cyclical fluctuations have nothing necessarily to do with monopolistic or political interference, though they may be aggravated by such interference. Even a system of pure *laisser faire* would be subject to monetary disturbances. On the other hand it is clearly possible that a banking monopoly may be used as a means of diminishing the violence of fluctuations.[17]

III. Risk and Money in the Trade Cycle

When the risk factor is present, it will have an extremely significant influence on the way in which a person holds his assets. In times of utter chaos and mutual mistrust, an individual will desire to hold all his assets in the form of immediately disposable purchasing power

[16] 'The laws of exchange contain nothing in themselves, which can determine the absolute level of money prices' says Wicksell (*Interest and Prices*, p. 39). This is quoted (but not confuted) by L. Mises (*Théorie des Geldes*, p. 99).

[17] Since it is impossible for any banking system to control all possible means of increasing the velocity of circulation of money, such a monopoly – like other monopolies – will have to beware of competition from substitutes. Whether or not its profits are diminished by such competition, its power of control is bound to be affected.

(i.e. of money). (This assumes, of course, that the general mistrust does not go so far as to extend to money itself.) With rather greater confidence, the individual will be content to hold some assets in rather less disposable forms. In times of greater confidence, a higher proportion of assets will be locked up in forms not at all immediately available because the individual does not take seriously the chance that he will need them immediately.

In advanced communities, a representative individual may be considered to hold his assets in innumerable different forms which may, however, be broadly classified: Cash, Call loans, Short-term loans, Long-term loans, Material property (incl. shares). Broadly speaking, there is an increasing risk-element as we go from left to right; and again, broadly speaking, there is a higher promise of return in the same direction to compensate for increased risk. The distribution of assets among these forms is governed by relative prospects of return and by relative risk factors.

Any rise in the promised rate of return will shift capital towards the right; any rise in the anticipation of risk will shift it towards the left. (It must indeed be admitted that different kinds of risk are relevant at different points of the sequence. Nevertheless it seems to be shown by experience that general shifts, going broadly in the same direction all along the sequence, are both frequent and significant.)

It accordingly follows that any grand shock to confidence will have the effect of a general leftward shifting of assets.[18] Cash holdings will pile up; entrepreneurs will cease to invest capital in marginal uses. The supply of capital in the short-term money market may increase or diminish; it is not surprising that it generally seems to increase, for that only shows that the shocks we experience are not the worst shocks conceivable.

It is extremely pertinent to enquire at this point whether such a state of affairs can be expected (in the absence of further exogenous shocks and under the assumption of free competition) to be self-liquidating, or whether it sets up a cumulative tendency. There are obviously some ways in which the effect is cumulative. Sales of securities by one set of investors impose losses (and consequent shocks) on another set; forced sales of commodities also transmit losses. And anticipation of such losses will lead to purely speculative sales; that is to say, the anticipation of further price falls stimulates the leftward drive.

---

[18] So long as it is not accompanied by lack of confidence in the future value of money or by an expectation of higher interest rates. These, however, will almost inevitably go together.

Nevertheless, so long as the nominal yield on securities remains the same, a fall in their prices raises the actual return on any capital that is tempted to move rightwards. When securities and property of all kinds can be bought very cheap, there must come a time when the actual yield is so high that some investors are tempted back – even though they have to stand the risk of possible further falls in price.[19]

Thus, if nominal yields stay constant, there is a compensating tendency; but in fact the losses imposed on businesses are likely to reduce nominal yields. The fall in prices will have raised wages (and other fixed charges) relative to these other prices; profit will therefore fall. Under our assumption of free competition, long-run costs will probably fall; but in the case of wages, it cannot be assumed that the reduction will be at all immediate.[20] In the meantime the fall in profits will check the reflux into securities and (what is more serious) will make it unprofitable for firms to borrow at rates that are high enough to tempt the timid investor.

So long as this condition holds, the economy is in a state of Depression; when Depression has taken root, and expressed itself in a sequence of business losses, the natural way out is by a reduction in costs.[21] I do not mean to imply that every Depression must end that way; a favourable change in data may make it unnecessary. But a reduction in costs is the only step that arises naturally out of the process and that is favourable to recovery. Under free competition, such a reduction will occur – in the end; but if the labour market is not freely competitive – wage-reductions being resisted by Trade Unions – the position is doubly difficult. The period of adaptation is lengthened while risk is increased by labour unrest.

But this is not our problem for the moment; sticking to the assumption of competitive markets, we can go on to the point where the acute stage of the Depression is over. The reflux of assets is then sufficient to stem the increase in idle cash holdings but insufficient to restore the earlier asset-distribution. What will be the general appearance of the economy after this point is reached?

There will, first of all, be a significant gap between rates of interest on long and short loans. The former will be high, the latter very low. And (at least up to the point when the wage-reduction has been fully worked out) there will be a further gap between the return on

[19] Cf. J. M. Keynes's analysis of the 'Excess-bearish factor' (*Treatise on Money*, esp. vol. I, pp. 141–3).

[20] Cf. *TW*, pp. 51–6; and for the *real* effects of this kind of disequilibrium, *TW*, chs. 9–10.

[[21] As will be evident to the reader, the argument at this point takes a very un-Keynesian twist, which (later on) I would not have defended.]

capital, physically invested in enterprises, and the return that can be obtained by investing in financial assets on the stock exchange. This will inhibit the raising of new capital by businesses; they will have to content themselves with short borrowing or (perhaps) with the issue of debentures. In a situation such as we are considering, which still conceals important elements of mistrust and insecurity, the demand for capital is likely to remain strictly limited. Until new borrowing can take place more freely there is unlikely to be full recovery.

How is this gap between rates of interest to be reduced? Wage reductions themselves will work in the right direction, but they are perhaps not the only way by which this object may be attained. It becomes profitable for business capital to be reinvested, not within the business, but in financial assets. Though this 'unnatural' movement temporarily increases unemployment, it makes a future expansion of business more feasible by driving up the prices of securities. On the other side, current savings will also contribute to the rise in security prices.

Neither of these means, however, is simple or reliable. For saving during a Depression leads to complications of the kind that have been described by Keynes.[22] In terms of the preceding analysis, his argument seems to come out as follows. To the saver, the act of saving represents an increase in his net assets – an increment which (as we have seen) may be held in various forms between which important distinctions have to be made. The simplest assumption (for normal times) is that the saver will distribute his saving between various groups of assets in much the same proportions as he has distributed his previous capital. But if this holds, it follows that in normal times saving has some deflationary bias; to offset this bias, saving must be accompanied by some reduction in the 'risk-factor'. In times of prosperity this is no doubt what actually happens, but in times of depression the leftward bias of saving is liable to reinforce deflation.

Besides, even if the saving is solely directed to the purchase of securities, it does not necessarily follow that the gap will narrow. For though on one side the prices of securities rise (so that it is easier for businesses to borrow) there is on the other side a fall in commodity prices through reduced consumption, which makes borrowing harder. It may well be that more damage is done by saving, via reduction in profits, than is amended via raising of security prices. However this

---

[22] *Treatise on Money, passim.* [As will be evident from the two paragraphs that follow, my studies in the *Treatise* had not yet gone very deep.]

may be, once a rise in security prices has begun, it will be reinforced by a 'rightward' movement of assets, seeking a speculative gain from the rise of price. Businesses can then obtain more capital and employ more labour. The way to general upswing is then open.

It is perfectly possible that such a recovery may be choked off by a shock to confidence of a purely exogenous character; or alternatively that it may be somewhat checked by a fall in interest rates due to increased saving. In some ways the latter will be the easiest route into a phase of comparative (but not excessive) stability; for excessive stability, leading to a continual rightward movement of assets, is dangerous.

I do not think I need elaborate this here, since this is an area that has recently been thoroughly investigated by others.[23] Some remarks may nevertheless be added as a suitable way of concluding the present paper.

There seems to be no general theoretical reason that makes it impossible for a rightward shift of asset distribution to occur in such a way as not to lead to a crisis.

Let us go back to our 'dynamic equilibrium', assuming (for the moment) as we must then do, that the money commodity is not a means of payment but simply a numeraire or standard of value. It is then evident that the changes in the structure of production that occur as a result of a rightward shift are the same as those that would occur, under the former assumptions, if there was a fall in the 'utility' of the money commodity in its non-money use. Surely a price-system (varying over time appropriately) could be found into which this change in data could be absorbed without inducing any disequilibrium.

It is indeed obvious that the foresight required to avoid such a disequilibrium would be extraordinarily difficult. It would be necessary for entrepreneurs to be able to distinguish between the new capital made available by the rightward shift, and that which is set at their disposal by new saving.[24] The rightward shift will indeed increase the amount of available capital[25] and will therefore reduce the rate of interest; but it will not reduce it as much as it would have

---

[23] I allude, of course, in particular to Hayek's *Prices and Production*. What follows is simply a commentary on Dr Hayek's analysis.

[24] This is what I seem to have written in 1933; but even within the general structure of my argument, it is surely an over-statement. Entrepreneurs – not even the entrepreneurs of one's models – do not have to be economists; so long as they have the right expectations (or more or less the right expectations) it does not matter *why* they have them.]

[25] Because of the change in income distribution, which such a shift necessarily brings with it.

been reduced by true saving. For the analysis of the resulting situation there are *three* rates of interest to be distinguished, and not (as generally supposed) two. There is: *A* the rate of interest that would have been necessary for dynamic equilibrium if there had been no rightward shift; *B* the rate of interest that is established as a result of the shift, and *C* the rate that will maintain equilibrium *in spite of the shift*. Of these, *A* corresponds more or less to Wicksell's 'natural rate' (though it seems to be implied in the Wicksellian concept that prices are expected to remain unchanged – a condition which, in general, is not consistent with dynamic equilibrium). *B* is Wicksell's 'market rate of interest'. As for the relation between *A* and *C*, the increase in the capital supply on the loan market will tend to diminish *C* relative to *A*, but the expectation of higher prices will tend to raise *C*; it is therefore uncertain whether *C* or *A* will be the higher. But in every case *C* will be higher than *B*, assuming, that is, that there is a failure to distinguish between true saving and the rightward shift. The divergence between *B* and *C* is responsible for the malinvestment. For whereas with true saving the demand for new capital comes predominantly from the 'higher stages' of production – from firms, that is, that are actively engaged in the introduction of more 'indirect' (or capital-intensive) methods – the corresponding demand, in the case of a mere rightward shift, will come to a considerable extent from firms in the 'lower stages'. These latter firms begin to borrow as soon as they anticipate the higher costs to which they will be exposed as the higher stages begin to compete with them more intensively for labour. If equilibrium is to be maintained in this second case, a higher rate of interest will be required than in the first.[26]

If we assume that entrepreneurs fail to make the necessary distinction – and I maintain that they will usually fail to do so – it will

---

[26] One must, I think, interpret Dr Hayek's argument (*Prices and Production*, pp. 51ff.) when taken literally, as referring to a single credit expansion (or rightward shift) of given amount. The immediate consequence of such an expansion is a rise in the prices of producers' goods, while the prices of consumers' goods remain unchanged. If it is assumed that producers expect the prices, corresponding to this necessarily impermanent situation, to maintain themselves in the future, there must be disequilibrium; this is not an assumption that we have to make, but I would concede that it is very plausible to make it. Then, in the long run, producers' good prices must fall and consumers' good prices rise (if there is no further increase in monetary circulation). Entrepreneurs in the higher stages will make losses, for their selling prices will have fallen below their costs [which depend, in Hayek's view, on consumer-good prices].

The basic trouble is the difficulty of economic calculation *over time*, when the value of money is unstable. [The reading of Hayek's argument which I was trying to express is, I think, rather better put in this note than it is in the text.]

follow that the rightward shift will bring with it an element of potential disequilibrium. As a consequence of a given rightward shift, business transactions will be undertaken, which eventually will be shown to be unprofitable if this shift persists. It must nevertheless be recognised that over a great part of the Boom forces are at work that tend to accelerate the shift. Once prices have begun to rise, profits will rise with them. At a high level of profits it will be hard for even the most thoughtless venture to make losses – so risk will be reduced. With higher profits and lower risks, the shift itself will tend to accelerate. And the acceleration will cover up what would otherwise have appeared as malinvestment; investments that would otherwise have produced losses will survive to make a modest profit. The Tempo of the boom gets faster and faster, but it can be maintained only if it continues to accelerate.

If the money material has a non-monetary use, such acceleration must ultimately become impossible. If it has no such use, indefinite acceleration must ultimately lead to a breakdown of the monetary system. But in either case it is probable that the boom will be interrupted earlier. As soon as the abnormality of the situation becomes apparent, the capitalist will begin to have doubts; the velocity of the shift will begin to decline and the extent of malinvestment will begin to be uncovered. This naturally leads to a loss of confidence and a shift of assets in the opposite direction.

That economic fluctuations arise, is sufficiently explained by Imperfect Foresight, that they take the form that they do so is to be explained largely by the close connection between imperfect foresight and the use of a Means of Payment.[27]

[27 I suppress a quotation from Marco Fanno with which I concluded. It hardly seems to bear translating from Italian.]

4

A Review of Myrdal

This was a review (published in *Economica*, November 1934) of the German version of G. Myrdal's book, *Monetary Equilibrium*, which had been included in a collected volume *Beiträge zur Geldtheorie* (edited by F. A. Hayek). It was there bound up with three other works, which are nowadays of less interest. The review was no more than a first impression; though I praised the book highly, I have come to feel that I did not praise it highly enough. (See above, p. 8.) But it has to appear in this place, since it registers the first impact on my thinking of contemporary Swedish work. I was lucky that I had the Myrdal so early; Keynes did not read it until the English translation appeared in 1939. It is clear, from some remarks recorded by Kahn ('On Re-reading Keynes', *British Academy Proceedings*, 1974, p. 374) that when he did read it he was quite impressed.

Professor Myrdal's essay seems to me quite the most exciting work on monetary theory which has appeared since Mr Keynes's *Treatise* and Professor Hayek's *Prices and Production*. Whether his conclusions are right or wrong (and some even of his major conclusions still leave me afflicted with grave doubts), there can be no question at all that his work marks a very definite step in advance. It is even one of those books one feels loath to criticise, for fear that one's criticisms may perhaps deter some reader from examining the book itself – and that would be a disaster.

Professor Myrdal's subject is twofold. On the one hand, he is concerned to submit the argument of *Geldzins und Güterpreise* to the searching criticism which the latter parts of that book have so obviously long needed; here, then, he is only concerned with restating Wicksell's argument in a form in which it shall be rigorously true. But, on the other hand, he is also concerned with the more ambitious attempt to restate it in a form in which it shall be capable of being used as a criterion of practical monetary policy; so that we shall not only be able to say, after the trouble has occurred, that the natural rate must have got out of equilibrium with the market rate, but shall be able to detect incipient trouble and so prevent the disease from developing. It is hardly surprising that the intellectual powers which acquit themselves so brilliantly in the negative criticism of Wicksell, possibly achieve a less certain victory in the second and much harder task.

Wicksell, it will be remembered, had put forward three conditions of monetary equilibrium: (1) that the market rate of interest should equal the natural rate (i.e. the technical marginal productivity of real capital); (2) that the capital market should proceed as if 'real capital were lent *in natura*'; (3) that the price-level should remain unchanged. Professor Myrdal takes each of these conditions in turn and submits them to searching examination. He finds, as others have found, that (1) and (2) are consistent, but that the fulfilment of conditions (1) and (2) does not necessarily imply the simultaneous fulfilment of (3). So far, indeed, he is in substantial agreement with other writers; but beyond this he diverges sharply.

In chapter IV, devoted to the first Wicksellian condition, he begins by showing that the purely technical character imputed by Wicksell to the natural rate is due entirely to the simplicity of Wicksell's assumptions – one finished good and one original factor of production. (An argument made familiar to us in England by Mr Sraffa.) Once we allow for the multiplicity of finished goods, the natural rate can only be interpreted as an expected rate of yield, in monetary terms. But this interpretation not only makes the natural rate dependent on psychological elements (the expected course of prices), but it also raises serious difficulties about 'maintaining capital intact'. At the end of a long argument (too long, in spite of its great importance, to be even summarised here), Professor Myrdal concludes that the first Wicksellian condition can only be interpreted as implying equality between the value and cost of production of new capital goods (whether or not they are 'replacement' goods – the distinction between new and replacement goods is abandoned). He recognises that both terms of this new equation must be regarded as dependent upon the market rate of interest, a change in which will react upon both.

Chapter V is concerned with the second Wicksellian condition, which is reinterpreted as meaning equality between savings and investment. By an argument parallel to that of Mr Keynes (though much greater care is taken over the question of replacement), Professor Myrdal shows that this condition reduces to substantially the same thing as the value-cost equation which resulted from the first condition.

But (and this is of the first importance in connection with the application of the doctrine), such a difference between savings and investment will never be capable of detection by statistical inquiry after the event. For the difference between investment and savings (or, what comes to the same thing, the difference between value and cost of capital goods) is always taken up by *profits* and *losses* which are not distinguishable *ex post*. It is only *ex ante*, in the anticipations of entrepreneurs, that a difference between investment and savings may show itself.

In chapter VI, which deals with the third Wicksellian condition, Professor Myrdal's conclusions are even more radical. His reinterpretation of the natural rate as a monetary concept involving psychological elements, makes it necessary for him to abandon not only the price-stabilisation of Wicksell but also the correlation of price-level and productivity, deduced by *neutral money* theorists. It is theoretically conceivable, he begins, that *the* condition of monetary equilibrium, which had emerged from his previous analysis, might be satisfied with any trend of the price-level, provided interest rates were properly adjusted to that trend. In fact, however, the possible movements are limited by the existence of particularly *sticky* prices (long-term contracts, wage rates, etc.), so that a policy which sought to preserve monetary equilibrium would in fact aim at stabilising such relatively sticky prices. But although it would aim at this sort of stabilisation, the means of stabilisation could only be found by a maintenance of the value-cost or savings-investment relation previously described, since the stickiness of the sticky prices ensures that there would be no tendency for them to move until monetary equilibrium had already been disturbed, and the damage therefore already done.

These three chapters contain the core of Professor Myrdal's work. There is much in the remainder of his essay which is of intense interest; the complications due to risk, to monopoly, to international trade, are each examined; statistical methods for testing the existence of monetary equilibrium are discussed. But these questions really arise only if we have first accepted the reasoning of the crucial three chapters; it therefore seems hardly possible to discuss them in a notice like the present.

It thus seems best to conclude with a very tentative criticism of that central argument. If one accepts Professor Myrdal's criticism of

Wicksell (and most of it, in my view, one must accept), the question remains, 'What is monetary equilibrium for?' Wicksell (and usually Mr Keynes) would equate the market rate of interest to the natural rate in order to stabilise the price-level; Professor Hayek would keep money neutral in order to prevent distortions of the productive process; these are at least moderately clear aims. But what is the point of Professor Myrdal's monetary equilibrium? Certainly not to attain any particular end which he himself regards as socially desirable; he is very careful to explain this. The only clue which he gives is a reference back to Wicksell – that monetary disequilibrium implies the setting in of a 'Wicksellian cumulative process'. But, at the stage he has reached, has he the right to refer back to Wicksell any longer? Just what is the precise difference between such a cumulative process and the sort of inflation which he would consider, theoretically at least, as consistent with monetary equilibrium? One gets certain vague ideas from his book, but nothing definite enough; and nothing which altogether convinces one that the concept, in the form in which he has left it, remains an essential part of monetary theory.

If this criticism is entirely misplaced (which seems very likely) Professor Myrdal's essay may be taken at its face value as a contribution of the first importance towards the control of the Trade Cycle; if it is not, his work remains as a hardly less significant turning-point in the development of monetary theory.

5

A Suggestion for Simplifying
the Theory of Money

A paper read at the Economic Club, November 1934, and printed in
Economica, February 1935. Meetings of the Economic Club were
held at LSE, and provided an opportunity for discussion, between
LSE economists and other economists working in London – including
those (at that date quite few) who were working in the Civil Service
or in the City, in finance houses or as financial journalists. (Hawtrey
was one of those who attended most regularly.) It had got about, on
this occasion, that I had something to say, so there was an unusually
large attendance.

I have little to say as preface to this essay, beyond what was said
on pp. 8–9 above. Its weakest point is its neglect of the liabilities
side, dismissed, much too casually, in n. 6. I don't now think that the
stricture I passed on it myself, at the end of the first of my 'Two
Triads' papers (*Critical Essays in Monetary Theory*, p. 16) is really
valid. It was not proper, in view of the attention given to costs of
investment, to say that it is 'over-voluntarist'. I shall return to this
matter in essay 19, part III.

I

After the thunderstorms of recent years, it is with peculiar diffidence
and even apprehension that one ventures to open one's mouth on the
subject of money.[1] In my own case these feelings are particularly
intense, because I feel myself to be very much of a novice at the
subject. My education has been mostly in the non-monetary parts of
economics, and I have only come to be interested in money because
I found that I could not keep it out of my non-monetary problems.
Yet I am encouraged on reflection to hope that this may not prove a

[1] The reader is asked to bear in mind the fact that the paper was written to be read
aloud, and to excuse certain pieces of mischief.

bad approach to the subject: that some things at least which are not very evident on direct inspection may become clearer from a cross-light of this sort.

It is, of course, very largely by such cross-fertilisation that economics progresses, and at least one department of non-monetary economics has hardly emerged from a very intimate affair with monetary theory. I do not, however, propose to resume this particular liaison. One understands that most economists have now read Böhm-Bawerk; yet whatever that union has bred, it has not been concord. I should prefer to seek illumination from another point of view – from a branch of economics which is more elementary, but, I think, in consequence better developed – the theory of value.

To anyone who comes over from the theory of value to the theory of money, there are a number of things which are rather startling. Chief of these is the preoccupation of monetary theorists with a certain equation, which states that the price of goods multiplied by the quantity of goods equals the amount of money which is spent on them. This equation crops up again and again, and it has all sorts of ingenious little arithmetical tricks performed on it. Sometimes it comes out as $MV = PT$, and once, in its most stupendous transfiguration, it blossomed into

$$P = \frac{E}{O} + \frac{I' - S}{R}$$

Now we, of the theory of value, are not unfamiliar with this equation, and there was a time when we used to attach as much importance to it as monetary theorists seem to do still. This was in the middle of the last century, when we used to talk about value being 'a ratio between demand and supply'. Even now, we accept the equation, and work it, more or less implicitly, into our systems. But we are rather inclined to take it for granted, since it is rather tautologous, and since we have found that another equation, not alternative to the quantity equation, but complementary with it, is much more significant. This is the equation which states that the relative value of two commodities depends upon their relative marginal utility.

Now, to an *ingénu*, who comes over to monetary theory, it is extremely trying to be deprived of this sheet-anchor. It was marginal utility that really made sense of the theory of value; and to come to a branch of economics which does without marginal utility altogether! No wonder there are such difficulties and such differences! What is wanted is a 'marginal revolution'!

That is my suggestion. But I know that it will meet with apparently crushing objections. I shall be told that the suggestion has been tried out before. It was tried by Wicksell, and though it led to interesting results, it did not lead to a marginal utility theory of money. It was tried by Mises, and led to the conclusion that money is a ghost of gold – because, so it appeared, money as such has no marginal utility.[2] The suggestion has a history, and its history is not encouraging.

This would be enough to frighten one off, were it not for two things. Both in the theory of value and in the theory of money there have been developments in the twenty or thirty years since Wicksell and Mises wrote. And these developments have considerably reduced the barriers that blocked their way.

In the theory of value, the work of Pareto, Wicksteed, and their successors, has broadened and deepened our whole conception of marginal utility. We now realise that the marginal utility analysis is nothing else than a general theory of choice, which is applicable whenever the choice is between alternatives that are capable of quantitative expression. Now money is obviously capable of quantitative expression, and therefore the objection that money has no marginal utility must be wrong. People do choose to have money rather than other things, and therefore, in the relevant sense, money must have a marginal utility.

But merely to call that marginal utility X, and then proceed to draw curves, would not be very helpful. Fortunately the developments in monetary theory to which I alluded come to our rescue.

Mr Keynes's *Treatise*, so far as I have been able to discover, contains at least three theories of money. One of them is the Savings and Investment theory, which, as I hinted, seems to me only a quantity theory much glorified. One of them is a Wicksellian natural rate theory. But the third is altogether much more interesting. It emerges

---

[2] A more subtle form of the same difficulty appears in the work of Marshall and his followers. They were aware that money ought to be subjected to marginal utility analysis; but they were so dominated by the classical conception of money as a 'veil' (which is valid enough at a certain level of approximation) that they persisted in regarding the demand for money as a demand for the things which money can buy – 'real balances'. As a result of this, their invocation of marginal utility remained little more than a pious hope. For they were unable to distinguish, on marginal utility lines, between the desire to save and the desire to hoard; and they necessarily overlooked that indeterminateness in the 'real balance' (so important in some applications of monetary theory), which occurs when the prices of consumption goods are expected to change. On the other hand, I must admit that some versions of the Marshallian theory come very close to what I am driving at. Cf. F. Lavington, *English Capital Market*, ch. VI.

when Mr Keynes begins to talk about the price-level of investment goods; when he shows that this price-level depends upon the relative preference of the investor – to hold bank-deposits or to hold securities. Here at last we have something which to a value theorist looks sensible and interesting! Here at last we have a choice at the margin! And Mr Keynes goes on to put substance into our X, by his doctrine that the relative preference depends upon the 'bearishness' or 'bullishness' of the public, upon their relative desire for liquidity or profit.

My suggestion may, therefore, be re-formulated. It seems to me that this third theory of Mr Keynes really contains the most important of his theoretical contribution; that here, at last, we have something which, on the analogy (the appropriate analogy) of value theory, does begin to offer a chance of making the whole thing easily intelligible; that it is from this point, not from velocity of circulation, natural rate of interest, or Saving and Investment, that we ought to start in constructing the theory of money. But in saying this, I am being more Keynesian than Keynes; I must endeavour to defend my position in detail.

II

The essence of the method I am proposing is that we should take the position of an individual at a particular point of time, and enquire what determines the precise quantity of money which he will desire to hold. But even to this simple formulation of the problem it is necessary to append two footnotes.

1. *Point of Time*. We are dealing with an individual decision to hold money *or* something else, and such a decision is always made at a point of time. It is only by concentrating on decisions made at particular points of time that we can apply the theory of value to the problem at all. A very large amount of current controversy about money seems to me to be due to the attempt, superficially natural, but, in fact, highly inconvenient, to establish a close relation between the demand for money and *income*. Now the simple consideration that the decision to hold money is always made at a point of time shows that the connection between income and the demand for money must always be indirect. And in fact the whole conception of income is so intricate and beset by so many perplexing difficulties, that the establishment of any connection with income ought only to be hoped for at a late stage of investigation.[3]

[3] Cf. E. Lindahl, 'The Concept of Income' in *Essays in Honour of Gustav Cassel*.

2. *Money*. What sort of money are we considering? For the present, any sort of money. The following analysis will apply equally whether we think of money as notes, or bank deposits, or even metallic coins. It is true that with a metallic currency there is an ordinary commodity demand for the money substance to be considered, but it is relatively unimportant for most of our purposes. Perhaps it will be best if we take as our standard case that of a pure paper currency in a community where there are no banks. What follows has much wider application in reality. Only I would just ask you to keep this standard case in mind, since by using it as a basis for discussion, we may be able to save time a little.

An individual's decision to hold so much money means that he prefers to hold that amount of money, rather than either less or more. Now what are the precise contents of these displaced alternatives? He could reduce his holding of money in three ways:

(1)   by spending, i.e. buying something, it does not matter what;
(2)   by lending money to someone else;
(3)   by paying off debts which he owes to someone else.

He can increase his holding of money in three corresponding ways:

(1)   by selling something else which he owns;
(2)   by borrowing from someone else;
(3)   by demanding repayment of money which is owed by someone else.

This classification is, I think, complete. All ways of changing one's holding of money can be reduced to one of these classes or a combination of two of them – purchase or sale, the creation of new debts or the extinction of old.

If a person decides to hold money, it is implied that he prefers to do this than to adopt any of these three alternatives. But how is such a preference possible?

A preference for holding money instead of spending it on consumption goods presents no serious difficulty, for it is obviously the ordinary case of a preference for future satisfactions over present. At any moment, an individual will not usually devote the whole of his available resources to satisfying present wants – a part will be set aside to meet the needs of the future.

The critical question arises when we look for an explanation of the preference for holding money rather than capital goods. For capital goods will ordinarily yield a positive rate of return, which money does not. What has to be explained is the decision to hold assets in the form of barren money, rather than of interest- or profit-yielding securities. And obviously just the same question arises over our second and third types of utilisation. So long as rates of interest are positive, the decision to hold money rather than lend it, or use it to pay off old debts, is apparently an unprofitable one.

This, as I see it, is really the central issue in the pure theory of money. Either we have to give an explanation of the fact that people do hold money when rates of interest are positive, or we have to evade the difficulty somehow. It is the great traditional evasions which have led to Velocities of Circulation, Natural Rates of Interest, *et id genus omne.*[4]

Of course, the great evaders would not have denied that there must be some explanation of the fact. But they would have put it down to 'frictions', and since there was no adequate place for frictions in the rest of their economic theory, a theory of money based on frictions did not seem to them a promising field for economic analysis.

This is where I disagree. I think we have to look the frictions in the face, and see if they are really so refractory after all. This will, of course, mean that we cannot allow them to go to sleep under so vague a title.

III

The most obvious sort of friction, and undoubtedly one of the most important, is the cost of transferring assets from one form to another. This is of exactly the same character as the cost of transfer which acts as a certain impediment to change in all parts of the economic system; it doubtless comprises subjective elements as well as elements directly priced. Thus a person is deterred from investing money for short periods, partly because of brokerage charges and stamp duties, partly because it is not worth the bother.

The net advantage to be derived from investing a given quantity of money consists of the interest or profit earned less the cost of investment. It is only if this net advantage is expected to be positive (i.e. if the expected rate of interest ± capital appreciation or depreciation, is greater than the cost of investment) that it will pay to undertake the investment.

---

[4] I do not wish to deny that these concepts have a use in their appropriate place – that is to say, in particular applications of monetary theory. But it seems to me that they are a nuisance in monetary theory itself, that they offer no help in elucidating the general principles of the working of money.

Now, since the expected interest increases both with the quantity of money to be invested and with the length of time for which it is expected that the investment will remain untouched, while the costs of investment are independent of the length of time, and (as a whole) will almost certainly increase at a diminishing rate as the quantity of money to be invested increases, it becomes clear that with any given level of costs of investment, it will not pay to invest money for less than a certain period, and in less than certain quantities. It will be profitable to hold assets for short periods, and in relatively small quantities, in monetary form.

Thus, so far as we can see at present, the amount of money a person will desire to hold depends upon three factors: the dates at which he expects to make payments in the future, the cost of investment, and the expected rate of return on investment. The further ahead the future payments, the lower the cost of investment, and the higher the expected rate of return on invested capital – the lower will be the demand for money.

However, this statement is not quite accurate. For although all these factors may react on the demand for money, they may be insufficient to determine it closely. Since the quantity of available money must generally rise to some minimum before it is profitable to invest it at all, and further investment will then proceed by rather discontinuous jumps for a while, we shall expect to find the demand for money on the part of private individuals, excepting the very well-to-do, fairly insensitive to changes of this sort. But this does not mean that they are unimportant. For among those who are likely to be sensitive, we have to reckon, not only the well-to-do, but also all business men who are administering capital which is not solely their own private property. And this will give us, in total, a good deal of sensitivity.

IV

Our first list of factors influencing the demand for money – the expected rate of interest, the cost of investment, and the expected period of investment – does, therefore, isolate some factors which are really operative; but even so, it is not a complete list. For we have also to take into account the fact, which is in reality of such enormous importance, that people's expectations are never precise expectations of the kind we have been assuming. They do not say to themselves 'this £100 I shall not want until June 1st' or 'this investment will yield 3.7 per cent'; or, if they do, it is only a kind of short-hand. Their expectations are always, in fact, surrounded by a certain penumbra of doubt; and the density of that penumbra is of immense importance for the problem we are considering.

The risk-factor comes into our problem in two ways: first, as affecting the expected period of investment; and second, as affecting the expected net yield of investment. There are certain differences between its ways of operation on these two lines; but, as we shall see, the resultant effects are broadly similar.

Where risk is present, the *particular* expectation of a riskless situation is replaced by a band of possibilities, each of which is considered more or less probable. It is convenient to represent these probabilities to oneself, in statistical fashion, by a mean value, and some appropriate measure of dispersion. (No single measure will be wholly satisfactory, but here this difficulty may be overlooked.) Roughly speaking, we may assume that a change in mean value with constant dispersion has much the same sort of effect as a change in the particular expectations we have been discussing before. The peculiar problem of risk therefore reduces to an examination of the consequences of a change in dispersion. Increased dispersion means increased uncertainty.

If, therefore, our individual, instead of knowing (or thinking he knows) that he will not want his £100 till June 1st, becomes afflicted by increased uncertainty; that is to say, while still thinking that June 1st is the most likely date, he now thinks that it will be very possible that he will want it before, although it is also very possible that he will not want it till after; what will be the effect on his conduct? Let us suppose that when the date was certain, the investment was marginal – in the sense that the expected yield only just outweighed the cost of investment. With uncertainty introduced in the way we have described, the investment now offers a chance of larger gain, but it is offset by an equal chance of equivalent loss. In this situation, I think we are justified in assuming that he will become less willing to undertake the investment.

If this is so, uncertainty of the period for which money is free will ordinarily act as a deterrent to investment. It should be observed that uncertainty may be increased, either by a change in objective facts on which estimates are based, or in the psychology of the individual, if his temperament changes in such a way as to make him less inclined to bear risks.

To turn now to the other uncertainty – uncertainty of the yield of investment. Here again we have a penumbra; and here again we seem to be justified in assuming that spreading of the penumbra, increased dispersion of the possibilities of yield, will ordinarily be a deterrent to investment. Indeed, without assuming this to be the normal case, it would be impossible to explain some of the most obvious of the observed facts of the capital market. This sort of risk, therefore, will ordinarily be another factor tending to increase the demand for money.

V

So far the effect of risk seems fairly simple; an increase in the risk of investment will act like a fall in the expected rate of net yield; an increase in the uncertainty of future out-payments will act like a shortening of the time which is expected to elapse before those out-payments; and all will ordinarily tend to increase the demand for money. But although this is what it comes down to in the end, the detailed working of the risk-factor is not so simple; and since these further complications have an important bearing upon monetary problems, we cannot avoid discussing them here.

It is one of the pecularities of risk that the total risk incurred when more than one risky investment is undertaken, does not bear any simple relation to the risk involved in each of the particular investments taken separately. In most cases, the 'law of large numbers' comes into play (quite how, cannot be discussed here), so that the risk incurred by undertaking a number of separate risky investments will be less than that which would have been incurred if the same total capital had been invested altogether in one direction. When the number of separate investments is very large, the total risk may sometimes be reduced very low indeed.

Now in a world where cost of investment was negligible, everyone would be able to take considerable advantage of this sort of risk-reduction. By dividing up his capital into small portions, and spreading his risks, he would be able to insure himself against any large total risk on the whole amount. But in actuality, the cost of investment, making it definitely unprofitable to invest less than a certain minimum amount in any particular direction, closes the possibility of risk-reduction along these lines to all those who do not possess the command over considerable quantities of capital. This has two consequences.

On the one hand, since most people do not possess sufficient resources to enable them to take much advantage of the law of large numbers, and since even the large capitalist cannot annihilate his risks altogether in this manner, there will be a tendency to spread capital over a number of investments, not for this purpose, but for another. By investing only a proportion of total assets in risky enterprises, and investing the remainder in ways which are considered more safe, it will be possible for the individual to adjust his whole risk-situation to that which he most prefers, more closely than he could do by investing in any single enterprise. It will be possible, for example, for him to feel fairly certain that in particular unfavourable eventualities he will not lose more than a certain amount. And, since, both with an eye on future commitments with respect to debt, and future needs for consumption, large losses will lay upon him a proportionately heavier burden than small losses, this sort of adjustment to the sort of chance of loss he is prepared to stand will be very well worth while.

We shall, therefore, expect to find our representative individual distributing his assets among relatively safe and relatively risky investments; and the distribution will be governed, once again, by subjective preference for much or little risk-bearing.

On the other hand, those persons who have command of large quantities of capital, and are able to spread their risks, are not only able to reduce the risk on their own capital fairly low – they are also able to offer very good security for the investment of an extra unit along with the rest. If, therefore, they choose to become borrowers, they are likely to be very safe borrowers. They can, therefore, provide the safe investments which their fellow-citizens need.

In the absence of such safe investments, the ordinary individual would be obliged to keep a very considerable proportion of his assets in monetary form, since money would be the only safe way of holding assets. The appearance of such safe investments will act as a substitute for money in one of its uses, and therefore diminish the demand for money.

This particular function is performed, in a modern community, not only by banks, but also by insurance companies, investment trusts, and, to a certain (perhaps small) extent, even by large concerns of other kinds, through their prior charges. And, of course, to a very large extent indeed, it is performed by government stock of various kinds.

Banks are simply the extreme case of this phenomenon; they are enabled to go further than other concerns in the creation of money substitutes, because the security of their promises to pay is accepted generally enough for it to be possible to make payments in those promises. Bank deposits are, therefore, enabled to substitute money still further, because the cost of investment is reduced by a general belief in the absence of risk.

This is indeed a difference so great as to be properly regarded as a difference in kind; but it is useful to observe that the creation of bank credit is not really different in its economic effects from the fundamentally similar activities of other businesses and other persons. The significant thing is that the person who deposits money with a bank does not notice any change in his liquidity position; he considers the bank deposit to be as liquid as cash. The bank, on the other hand, finds itself more liquid, if it retains the whole amount of the cash deposited; if it does not wish to be more liquid, but seeks (for example) to restore a conventional reserve ratio, it will have to increase its investments. But substantially the same sort of thing happens when anyone, whose credit is much above the average, borrows. Here the borrowing is nearly always a voluntary act on the part of the borrower, which would not be undertaken unless he was willing to become less liquid than before; the fact that he has to pay interest on the loan means that he will be made worse off if he does not spend the proceeds. On the other hand, if the borrower's credit is good, the liquidity of the lender will not be very greatly impaired by his making the loan, so that his demand for money is likely to be at least rather less than it was before the loan was made. Thus the net effect of the loan is likely to be 'inflationary', in the sense that the purchase of capital goods or securities by the borrower is likely to be a more important affair than any sale of capital goods or securities by the lender, made necessary in order for the lender to restore his liquidity position.

Does it follow that all borrowing and lending is inflationary in this sense? I do not think so; for let us take the case when the borrower's credit is very bad, and the lender is only tempted to lend by the offer of a very high rate of interest. Then the impairment of the lender's liquidity position will be very considerable; and he may feel it necessary to sell rather less risky securities to an even greater capital sum in order to restore his liquidity position. Here the net effect would be 'deflationary'.

The practical conclusion of this seems to be that while *voluntary* borrowing and lending is at least a symptom of monetary expansion, and is thus likely to be accompanied by rising prices, 'distress borrow-ing' is an exception to this rule; and it follows, further, that the sort of stimulation to lending, by persuading people to make loans which they would not have made without persuasion (which was rather a feature of certain phases of the world depression), is a dubious policy – for the lenders, perhaps without realising what they are doing, are very likely to try and restore their liquidity position, and so to offset, and perhaps more than offset, the expansive effects of the loan.

VI

It is now time for us to begin putting together the conclusions we have so far reached. Our method of analysis, it will have appeared, is simply an extension of the ordinary method of value theory. In value theory, we take a private individual's income and expenditure account; we ask which of the items in that account are under the individual's own control, and then how he will adjust these items in order to reach a most preferred position. On the production side, we make a similar analysis of the profit and loss account of the firm. My suggestion is that monetary theory needs to be based again upon a similar analysis, but this time, not of an income account, but of a capital account, a balance sheet.We have to concentrate on the forces which make assets and liabilities what they are.

So as far as banking theory is concerned, this is really the method which is currently adopted; though the essence of the problem is there somewhat obscured by the fact that banks, in their efforts to reach their 'most preferred position' are hampered or assisted by the existence of conventional or legally obligatory reserve ratios. For theoretical purposes, this fact ought only to be introduced at a rather late stage; if that is done, then my suggestion can be expressed by saying that we ought to regard every individual in the community as being, on a small scale, a bank. Monetary theory becomes a sort of generalisation of banking theory.

We shall have to draw up a sort of generalised balance sheet, suit-able for all individuals and institutions. It will have to be so general-ised that many of the individual items will, in a great many cases, not appear. But that does not matter for our purposes. Such a generalised balance sheet will presumably run much as follows.

Assets	*Liabilities*
Consumption goods – perishable	
Consumption goods – durable	
Money	
Bank deposits	
Short term debts	Short term debts
Long term debts	Long term debts
Stocks and shares	
Productive equipment (including goods in process)	

We have been concerned up to the present with an analysis (very sketchy, I am afraid) of the equilibrium of this balance sheet. This analysis has at least shown that the relative size of the different items on this balance sheet is governed mainly by anticipation of the yield of investments and of risks.[5] It is these anticipations which play a part here corresponding to the part played by prices in value theory.[6]

Now the fact that our 'equilibrium' is here determined by subjective factors like anticipations, instead of objective factors like prices, means that this purely theoretical study of money can never hope to reach results so tangible and precise as those which value theory in its more limited field can hope to attain. If I am right, the whole problem of applying monetary theory is largely one of deducing changes in anticipations from the changes in objective data which call them forth. Obviously, this is not an easy task, and, above all, it is not one which can be performed in a mechanical fashion. It needs judgment and knowledge of business psychology much more than sustained logical reasoning. The arm-chair economist will be bad at it, but he can at least begin to realise the necessity for it, and learn to co-operate with those who can do it better than he can.

---

[5] As we have seen, these risks are as much a matter of the period of investment as of the yield. For certain purposes this is very important. Thus, in the case of that kind of investment which consists in the starting of actual processes of production, the yield which is expected if the process can be carried through may be considerable; but the yield if the process has to be interrupted will be large and negative. Uncertainty of the period for which resources are free will therefore have a very powerful effect in interrupting production. Short-run optimism will usually be enough to start a Stock Exchange boom; but to start an industrial boom relatively long-run optimism is necessary.

[6] I am aware that too little is said in this paper about the liabilities side of the above balance sheet. A cursory examination suggests that the same forces which work through the assets side work through the liabilities side in much the same way. But this certainly requires further exploration.

However, I am not fouling my own nest; I do not at all mean to suggest that economic theory comes here to the end of its resources. When once the connection between objective facts and anticipations has been made, theory comes again into its rights; and it will not be able to complain of a lack of opportunities.

Nevertheless, it does seem to me most important that, when considering these further questions, we should be well aware of the gap which lies behind us, and that we should bring out very clearly the assumptions which we are making about the genesis of anticipations. For this does seem to be the only way in which we can overcome the extraordinary theoretical differences of recent years, which are, I think very largely traceable to this source.

VII

Largely, but not entirely; or rather a good proportion of them seem to spring from a closely related source, which is yet not quite identical with the first. When we seek to apply to a changing world any particular sort of individual equilibrium, we need to know how the individual will respond, not only to changes in the price-stimuli, or anticipation-stimuli, but also to a change in his total wealth.[7] How will he distribute an increment (or decrement) of wealth – supposing, as we may suppose, that this wealth is measured in monetary terms?

It may be observed that this second problem has an exact counterpart in value theory. Recent work in that field has shown the importance of considering carefully, not only how the individual reacts to price-changes, but also how he reacts to changes in his available expenditure. Total wealth, in our present problem, plays just the same part as total expenditure in the theory of value.

In the theory of money, what we particularly want to know is how the individual's demand for money will respond to a change in his total wealth – that is to say, in the value of his net assets. Not seeing any *a priori* reason why he should react in one way rather than another, monetary theorists have often been content to make use of the simplest possible assumption – that the demand for money will

[7] The amount of money demanded depends upon three groups of factors: (1) the individual's subjective preferences for holding money or other things; (2) his wealth; (3) his anticipations of future prices and risks. Changes in the demand for money affect present prices, but present prices affect the demand for money mainly through their effect on wealth and on price-anticipations.

be increased in the same proportion as total net assets have increased.[8] But this is a very arbitrary assumption; and it may be called in question, partly for analytical reasons, and partly because it seems to make the economic system work much too smoothly to account for observed fact. As one example of this excessive smoothness, I may instance the classical theory of international payments; as another, Mr Harrod's views on the 'Expansion of Bank Credit' which have recently been interesting the readers of *Economica* and of the *Economist*.[9] It would hardly be too much to say that one observed fact alone is sufficient to prove that this assumption cannot be universally true (let us hope and pray that it is sometimes true, nevertheless) – the fact of the trade cycle. For if it were true, the monetary system would always exhibit a quite straightforward kind of stability; a diminished demand for money on the part of some people would raise the prices of capital goods and securities, and this would raise the demand for money on the part of the owners of those securities. Similarly an increased demand for money would lower prices, and this would lower the demand for money elsewhere. The whole thing would work out like an ordinary demand and supply diagram. But it is fairly safe to say that we do not find this straightforward stability in practice.

The analytical reason why this sort of analysis is unsatisfactory is the following: the assumption of increased wealth leading to a proportionately increased demand for money is only plausible so long as the value of assets has increased, but other things have remained equal. Now, as we have seen, the other things which are relevant to this case are not prices (as in the theory of value) but anticipations, of the yield of investment and so on. And since these anticipations must be based upon objective facts, and an unexpected increase in wealth implies a change in objective facts, of a sort very likely to be relevant to the anticipations, it is fairly safe to assume that very many of the changes in wealth with which we are concerned will be accompanied by a change in anticipations. If this is so, the assumption of proportionate change in the demand for money loses most of its plausibility.

---

[8] Of course, they say 'income'. But in this case 'income' can only be strictly interpreted as 'expected income'. And in most of the applications which are made, this works out in the same way as the assumption given above.

[9] The above was written before reading Mr Harrod's rejoinder to Mr Robertson. As I understand him, Mr Harrod is now only maintaining that the expansion of bank credit *may* work smoothly. With that I am in no disagreement.

For if we assume (this is jumping over my gap, so I must empha-sise that it is only an assumption) that an increase in wealth will very often be accompanied by an upward revision of expectations of yield, then the change will set in motion at least one tendency which is certain to diminish the demand for money. Taking this into account *as well as* the direct effect of the increase in wealth, the situation begins to look much less clear. For it must be remembered that our provisional assumption about the direct effect was only guess-work; there is no necessary reason why the direct effect should increase the demand for money proportionately or even increase it at all. So, putting the two together, it looks perfectly possible that the demand for money may either increase or diminish.

We are treading on thin ice; but the unpleasant possibilities which now begin to emerge are sufficiently plausible for their examination to be well worth while. What happens, to take a typical case, if the demand for money is independent of changes in wealth, so that neither an increase in wealth nor a diminution will affect the demand for money?

One can conceive of a sort of equilibrium in such a world, but it would be a hopelessly unstable equilibrium. For if any single person tried to increase his money holdings, and the supply of money was not increased, prices would all fall to zero. If any person tried to diminish his money holdings, prices would all become infinite. In fact, of course, if demand were so rigid, the system could only be kept going by a continuous and meticulous adaptation of the supply of money to the demand.

Further, in such a world, very curious results would follow from saving. A sudden increase in saving would leave some people (the owners of securities) with larger money balances than they had expected; other people (the producers of consumption goods) with smaller money balances. If, in their efforts to restore their money holdings, the owners of securities buy more securities, and the producers of consumption goods buy less consumption goods, a swing of prices, consumption goods prices falling, security prices rising, would set in, and might go on indefinitely. It could only be stopped, either by the owners of securities buying the services of producers, or by the producers selling securities. But there is no knowing when this would happen, or where prices would finally settle; for the assumption of a rigid demand for money snaps the connecting link between money and prices.

After this, we shall be fairly inured to shocks. It will not surprise us to be told that wage-changes will avail nothing to stop either an inflation or a deflation, and we shall be able to extend the proposition for ourselves to interference with conventional or monopolistic prices of any kind, in any direction. But we shall be in a hurry to get back to business.

VIII

These exercises in the economics of an utterly unstable world give us something too mad to fit even our modern *Spätkapitalismus*; but the time which economists have spent on them will not have been wasted if they have served as a corrective to the too facile optimism engendered by the first assumption we tried. Obviously, what we want is something between the two – but not, I think, a mere splitting of the difference. This would give the assumption that an increase in wealth always raises the demand for money, but less than proportionately; if we had time, it might be profitable to work out this case in detail. It would allow for the possibility of considerable fluctuations, but they would not be such absurd and hopeless fluctuations as in the case of rigid demand.

However, I think we can do better than that. The assumption which seems to me most plausible, most consistent with the whole trend of our analysis, and at the same time to lead to results which at any rate look realistic, is one which stresses the probable differences in the reactions of different members of the community. We have already seen that a considerable proportion of a community's monetary stock is always likely to be in the hands of people who are obliged by their relative poverty to be fairly insensitive to changes in anticipations. For these people, therefore, most of the incentive to reduce their demand for money when events turn out more favourably will be missing; there seems no reason why we should not suppose that they will generally react 'positively' to changes in their wealth – that an increase in wealth will raise their demand for money more or less proportionately, a fall in their wealth will diminish it. But we must also allow for the probability that other people are much more *sensitive* – that an increase in wealth is not particularly likely to increase their demand for money, and may very well diminish it.

If this is so, it would follow that where the sensitive trade together, price-fluctuations may start on very slight provocation; and once they are under way, the rather less sensitive would be enticed in. Stock Exchange booms will pass over into industrial booms, if industrial entrepreneurs are also fairly sensitive; and, in exactly the same way, stock exchange depressions will pass into industrial depressions. But the insensitive are always there to act as a flywheel, defeating by their insensitivity both the exaggerated optimism and the exaggerated pessimism of the sensitive class. How this comes about I cannot attempt to explain in detail, though it would be an interesting job, for one might be able to reconcile a good many apparently divergent theories. But it would lead us too deeply into Cycle theory – I will only say that I think the period of fluctuation turns out to depend, in rather complex fashion, upon the distribution of sensitivity and the distribution of production periods between industrial units.

Instead, I may conclude with two general reflections.

If it is the insensitive people who preserve the stability of capitalism, people who are insensitive (you will remember) largely because for them the costs of transferring assets are large relatively to the amount of assets they control, then the development of capitalism, by diminishing these costs, is likely to be a direct cause of increasing fluctuations. It reduces costs in two ways: by technical devices (of which banks are only one example), and by instilling a more 'capitalistic' spirit, which looks more closely to profit, and thus reduces subjective costs. In doing these things, capitalism is its own enemy, for it imperils that stability without which it breaks down.

Lastly, it seems to follow that when we are looking for policies which make for economic stability, we must not be led aside by a feeling that monetary troubles are due to 'bad' economic policy, in the old sense, that all would go well if we reverted to free trade and *laisser faire*. In so doing, we are no better than the Thebans who ascribed the plague to blood-guiltiness, or the supporters of Mr Roosevelt who expect to reach recovery through reform. There is no reason why policies which tend to economic welfare, statically considered, should also tend to monetary stability. Indeed, the presumption is rather the other way round. A tariff, for example, may be a very good instrument of recovery on occasion, for precisely the reason which free-traders deplore; that it harms a great many people a little for the conspicuous benefit of a few. That may be just the sort of measure we want.

These will be unpalatable conclusions; but I think we must face the possibility that they are true. They offer the economist a pretty hard life, for he, at any rate, will not be able to have a clear conscience either way, over many of the alternatives he is called upon to consider. His ideals will conflict and he will not be able to seek an easy way out by sacrificing either.

6

Wages and Interest:
the Dynamic Problem

PREFATORY NOTE

There are several paradoxes about this paper (the 'Bread' paper I
have been in the habit of calling it); the place which it occupies in
the present volume is not the least of them. It is an odd paper; but its
position here is rather central. It looks back to *The Theory of Wages*
(1932) and forward to *Value and Capital* (1939). And it is looking
sideways at Keynes. I had not seen the *General Theory* when I wrote
it. (It was published in the *Economic Journal* in September 1935,
three months before the appearance of Keynes's book.) But I knew
that something was on the way, and I had heard some rumours of
what it would contain. So the fact that I had the 'Bread' paper
behind me explains some of the things which I said in the reviews of
the *General Theory* which follow (essays 7 and 8). The connection
between them is worked out in some detail in a quite recent paper
(essay 23).

There is this link with Keynesian theory; yet the main question
that is asked in 'Bread' is one which, on the strictest Keynesian
principles, one ought not to ask; one is indeed instructed not to ask
it. Trade Unions, one is told, may affect money wages, but they have
no power over real wages (the level of real wages); a general rise in
money wages, with money interest constant, will simply result in
higher prices, so that the real wage is unchanged. Thus to ask about
the effect of a change in real wages, on employment, on real capital
formation, and on the real rate of interest, is a nonsense question.
There was much force in this, and for many years I was inclined to
accept it. But, as time went on, and the power of Trade Unions
increased, and the ingenuity of their bargainers increased, this strict
Keynesian position became less defensible. The Keynesians seemed
to be reduced to screaming that wages must not be indexed; those
less committed could not, by that time, help asking: what if they are,
formally or informally, indexed? One then came back to the

question of real wage changes, such as I had discussed in *TW* and in 'Bread'.

That was the point I had reached, in my own thinking, in the early sixties; I decided as a consequence to let *TW* be reprinted (it had long gone out of print, and I had resisted demands for a second edition). In that second edition (1963) I appended to the old text a reprint of 'Bread' and also a 'Commentary', which included a discussion of the relation between the two treatments (*TW*, 1963 edition, pp. 354–71). But this brought me face to face with another paradox.

I knew that what I had said on a crucial issue, in the one place and in the other, was quite different. In the book I had made interest fall when wages rose, but in 'Bread' I made interest rise. I was convinced, when writing 'Bread' that what I was saying there must be correct; so I accepted that what I had said in the book (chapters 9–10) must be wrong. I said this explicitly, as will be seen from n. 14 below. But when I came back to the issue, in 1963, I had at my disposal a variety of growth models (on one of which I was myself currently working, to appear in *Capital and Growth*, 1965) which seemed to confirm the analysis of the book, not that of 'Bread'. So I had to admit that in the 'Bread' paper the other analysis had been too hastily rejected.

The way out, I said in the Commentary, was to insist that 'what was being discussed in the "Bread" paper (and also what was being discussed by Keynes) was a short-period, or impact effect. But that, quite certainly, was not what I was discussing in *TW*. All I was doing there (all that I could be doing with the tools that were then at my disposal) was to examine how things would work out in the long run' (*TW*, 1963 edition, p. 362). Having made that distinction, I could go on, as I did in the Commentary to justify what I had said in the book, at least to the extent of showing its consistency with the theory of growth equilibrium, or steady state equilibrium, which was so fashionable in the sixties, at the time when I was writing.

That was all very well, and since it was *TW* on which I was writing a Commentary, I did not at that point need to go any further. But here it is 'Bread' on which I am commenting, so there is something more on that side which needs to be added. It is not quite enough to say (as I did say in the Commentary, p. 367) that it was the *impact* effect of the rise in real wages which would result in a rise in the real rate of interest. Why should there be a rise in that rate? The reason I gave (in 1963, and much less clearly in 1935) was that there would be *lags* in adjustment. 'The full effect on employment does not exert itself at once; the full effect in reducing capitalists' consumption does not exert itself at once; thus while output is declining, there may well be a shortage of "bread", which ... would be reflected in a rise in the "bread" interest rate.' But the reader might still have asked why.

The argument can be sharpened if we say that in the current week the output of bread, being largely determined by what has been done in the past, will be much the same as it would have been otherwise (i.e. if the real wage had not risen). Since employment has not yet fallen, much, the demand for bread from the labourers will have risen, above what it would have been otherwise. The capitalists have to expect diminished future incomes, but this may not yet have much effect on their current consumption, and it would need to be a big effect if it were to offset the increased demand from the labourers. Taking these things together, there would seem to be an excess demand for bread. There is in the model no other price which can move, to eliminate this excess demand, but the rate of interest. There is nevertheless still the question: why should it be that a *rise* in the rate of interest would tend to eliminate this excess demand? There is something more there which needed to be examined.

I don't think that one need lay any stress upon the 'classical' effect of a rise in interest – to encourage saving; whether or not that is a significant effect, in general, it can hardly be significant in the case supposed. What the rise must do, in the case supposed, is to increase the pressures on both parties – on labour, by accelerating the decline in employment, and on capitalists, by increasing the capital losses which they would (admittedly) be incurring even without it. That there should be any rise in interest which would be sufficient to restore (temporary) equilibrium within a 'week' is no doubt implausible; but the 'week' need not be taken too seriously. The essential point, that the impact effect of a rise in real wages is to raise the real rate of interest, still stands.

Now this is not at all an un-Keynesian doctrine. It can be re-stated in much more Keynesian terms. The Keynesian would say that an *indexed* rise in wages, beyond what is consistent with high employment, must result in indefinite inflation; it must certainly do so if no monetary steps are taken to check it. That is the same thing as is being said here. The real rate of interest must rise; if the money rate is kept unchanged, there is (Wicksellian) cumulative inflation – Wicksell and Keynes come together. My 'Bread' paper is the link between them.

And when this 'Bread' paper is taken in conjunction with the long-period analysis (of *TW* and of the growth models) it throws up a burning issue. How does one get from the impact situation, in which (as has been shown) the real rate of interest rises, to the long-period situation, in which (as has also been shown) it must fall? That, I believe, is a theoretical expression of the central issue which, in these latter days of cost inflation, is perplexing economists, Keynesians and monetarists alike. There will be much later essays in this collection (essays 20 and 24) where I shall come back to it. I do not claim to have a solution.

I

Very much the most difficult and awkward part of the theory of wages is that which abuts on the theory of capital and interest. It is impossible to have an adequate theory of the determination of wages – at least in the short period – without having an adequate theory of capital and interest; and up to the present that has not been generally available.

Most modern theories of capital fall into one or two classes. On the one hand, there is the 'timeless' type of theory, which treats capital as a factor of production like any other. Such a theory is that of J. B. Clark. In practice, it assimilates capital to land, treating it as the inexhaustible provider of a regular stream of resources. On the other hand, there is the 'period of production' theory of Böhm-Bawerk and Wicksell. This treats capital as 'stored-up labour' – labour stored up *in the past.*[1]

In spite of the controversies which have gone on between the adherents of these two theories, they both fall under the same condemnation. They are both 'stationary' theories, built upon the hypothesis of a stationary state, quite satisfactory under that hypothesis, but incapable of extension to meet other hypotheses, and consequently incapable of application. In a stationary state they

---

[1] In my book, *The Theory of Wages,* I employed an unhealthy amalgam of these two theories; and for this, at least, I was very properly rebuked by Mr G. F. Shove (*EJ,* 1933, pp. 470-2).

The present paper, which seeks to explore a better path, owes something to I. Fisher's *Theory of Interest*; and more to those few works of Professors Lindahl and Myrdal which are accessible to one who does not read Swedish (E. Lindahl, 'The Concept of Income', in *Essays in Honour of Gustav Cassel*; G. Myrdal, 'Der Gleichgewichtsbegriff', in *Beiträge zur Geldtheorie*). I have also had the advantage of reading some unpublished writings by Mr A. G. Hart, of Chicago, and Mr V. Edelberg, of London, which bear closely upon my subject.

are both correct. The 'timeless' theory is correct, because capital, in stationary conditions, must always be renewed in exactly the same form as that in which it wore out; even if it is technically exhausted, it is economically inexhaustible. Böhm-Bawerk's theory is correct, because the amount of labour employed in producing new capital instruments must always be exactly the same as that which had been employed in the past in producing a similar quantity of those instruments which are now in use. But once we leave stationary conditions, these convenient equalities disappear, and theories based upon them cease to be applicable.

To found a theory upon an assumed equality, which is not a real equality, is a most dangerous thing to do; for the more complex the theory becomes, the more specialised it becomes. The blinkers grow, until they shut out nearly all the landscape. One distinction blurred over breeds another, until we have in the end only a special case of a special case of a special case.

If we must simplify (and of course we must – to take into account all the complexities at one bound would be ridiculous), it seems much better to simplify in another way. I propose in this paper to employ all the ordinary simplifications of economic theory – those simplifications which we can employ comfortably, because we have some idea of how to remove them – but not to employ the dangerous simplification of a stationary state.

The first advantage of leaving stationary conditions is that it imposes upon us a new responsibility about time. In a stationary state, one moment of time is much like another, and it is possible to be very careless about time without going far wrong. But in dynamic conditions, the events of one moment are ordinarily different from the events of another, so that we are warned to mark them off clearly if we want to avoid confusion.

One consequence of this seems to be that in dynamic analysis the assumption of continuity, which is so convenient in statics, becomes highly inconvenient. We are accustomed to thinking of economic magnitudes as continuous 'flows', but the convenience of this is limited to the static case, when the flows are constant through time. A flow which varies through time is very difficult to handle. Consequently it seems best to cut up the varying flows into short sections, each of which can be treated as constant. We can do this by supposing changes to take place, not continuously, but at intervals.[2]

---

[2] It seems quite as legitimate to treat the continuous variable time as if it were discontinuous, as it is to treat the discontinuous demand schedule as if it were continuous.

Bearing these things in mind, let us draw up a set of simplifying assumptions.

(1) We shall assume a community which is wholly engaged in the production of a single homogeneous good, which we shall call Bread.

(2) Bread is made by the co-operation of labour (assumed homogeneous) with capital goods (not homogeneous) which we shall call Equipment. Equipment may include land, buildings, machinery, raw materials, and half-finished goods.

(3) Since every part of time has characteristics of its own, we cannot manage the analysis of more than a finite period of time. In particular, the period of time under consideration must have a beginning. Everything which takes place before that beginning is a datum.

(4) At the beginning there exists a certain amount of Equipment, and a certain stock of finished Bread. The Bread and the Equipment are owned by entrepreneurs; but against these assets, the entrepreneurs have Debts, owed either to the labourers or to rentiers. The amounts of initial Bread, initial Equipment, and initial Debts are the necessary result of what has gone before, and are therefore all data.

(5) In order to avoid monetary complications, we shall provisionally assume that all prices (including Debts) are reckoned in terms of Bread. The rate of interest is a 'bread' rate of interest; it arises out of a contract to supply so much bread in the future in return for so much bread now.

(6) Transactions take place discontinuously. Let us say that the market is only open on one day in the week (Monday); on that day labour is hired, labour is paid, and on that day loans are made. (Equipment, on the other hand, is not exchangeable.) We shall also assume here that all loans are made for the week, and can be repaid if either party desires on the following Monday. This is a more dangerous assumption than most, since it implies that all loans are short. It is not, however, the sort of assumption which is very difficult to remove.

(7) Lastly, I assume perfect competition in the market for labour, in the market for loans, and consequently in the market for bread.

II

In our simplified economy there are thus two prices: a rate of wages and a rate of interest. On each market day these two prices have to be determined, the rate of wages at that level which will equate the demand and the supply for labour on that day, the rate of interest at that level which will equate the demand and the supply for loans. Now these demands and supplies are simply the resultants of the actions of individual entrepreneurs, labourers and rentiers; so that in order to discover the principles governing them, we have to examine the position of a representative entrepreneur, a representative labourer, and a representative rentier respectively.

The representative rentier finds himself on the first Monday with certain debts due to him (debts which include accrued interest, that being also a 'bygone'). He has to decide how much of this sum to consume, and how much to reinvest. His decision will depend, in the general case, upon his relative preferences for present consumption, and for consumption at various future dates; upon the current rate of interest and upon the rate of interest which he expects to rule in future weeks. These are the things, that is, which he may take into account; it makes no difference to our analysis if he is, in fact, much less circumspect, and bases his decision (say) only upon the current rate of interest, and his desires to possess certain capital values at the end of the first week.

If we could assume that the labourer cannot vary the amount of labour which he is willing to perform in any particular week, then the position of the labourer would be substantially similar to that of rentier. He receives a certain claim to bread on the first Monday (either in respect of past services or as an advance on future), and he has to decide how much to consume now and how much (if any) to invest. The only difference would be that his decision may be affected by his anticipations of future rates of wages.

If we must assume that the labourer can vary the amount of labour he performs, so that he has to choose how much labour to perform now, a rather more difficult problem emerges. But although it could be dealt with by the general methods of this paper, it seems unnecessary to consider it here.

The representative entrepreneur has to consider how much labour to employ now, and how far he will increase (or diminish) his debts. This last will depend partly upon his relative preferences for present and future consumption (in which matter he behaves just like a rentier), but partly also upon his estimates of the profitability of production. His demand for labour will depend wholly upon his estimates of the profitability of production – that is to say, upon the particular production plan he chooses to adopt.

A production plan can be regarded, on the basis of our simplifying assumptions, as a series of outputs of bread in successive weeks, together with the series of inputs of labour necessary to obtain those outputs.[3] For the entrepreneur has actually to determine, not only how much labour he will employ in the first week, but how he will employ that labour, whether in the production of bread for the next market day, or in the production of bread for the more distant future (activity which, a week after, will only have resulted in the production of equipment). He has a choice between a wide variety of production plans, but not an unlimited variety, since his choice is conditioned by the amount of equipment which is in his possession at the beginning. The fact that his initial equipment is given imposes *one* relation on the stream of outputs and inputs. Thus, if all the inputs are given, and all outputs but one, we can tell what is the maximum output which can be obtained on that remaining date; if all the outputs are given, and all inputs but one, we can tell what is the minimum input necessary on the remaining date. This relation may be called, by analogy with static theory, the *production function.*

Since he works under his limitation, the entrepreneur will only be able to increase his output at any specified date in the future, if he either diminishes his output at some other date, or increases his employment of labour at some date or other. He cannot increase the output of any period without either diminishing some other output or increasing some input.

Of the various possible plans, that one will be chosen which maximises the present value of the entrepreneur's net assets.[4] His estimation of this value depends partly upon the current rates of wages and interest, partly upon the wages and interest rates which he expects to rule at relevant dates in the future.[5] These latter rates

---

[3] Each output to be reckoned at the date when it is sold, each input at the date when it is paid.

[4] This depends upon the assumption that he can borrow or lend freely at fixed rates of interest (perfect competition). The entrepreneur's preferences about consumption at different dates do not affect the choice of a production plan. For any increase in the present value of his assets will always make it possible for him to reach a preferred consumption plan by suitable borrowing or lending.

[5] More strictly, the *probable* rates. Cf. A. Marshall, *Principles*, 8th edition, p. 858 – the last sentence in the book.

are pure estimates, but on these estimates both the present value of his assets and the production plan adopted will depend.

Present value will be maximised when it is impossible to increase it by any variation in the production plan. Three kinds of variation are technically possible: (1) output of one date may be substituted for output of another date, (2) input of one date may be substituted for input of another date, (3) one output and one input may be simultaneously increased or diminished. Examination of the third type of change gives us a set of marginal productivity conditions; and it will appear that when these conditions are satisfied, changes of the first two types cannot be profitable either.

Change of the third type will be unprofitable if the cost of any unit of future labour (discounted back to the present) or current labour (undiscounted) equals the discounted value of every alternative output that could be got from it. That is to say, the anticipated rate of wages in any period must equal the marginal product of that labour in any subsequent period (discounted back to that period), or to the marginal product of that labour in any previous period (accumulated on to that period).[6] Once these conditions are satisfied, it follows that a small change of the third type must leave present value unchanged. But a small change of the first or second type can always be reduced to two changes of the third type; if these leave present value unchanged, their sum must do so as well. The marginal productivity conditions are therefore enough to determine the production plan.

But although these marginal productivity conditions are sufficient to determine the production plan, there is no need to put the conditions into this form if it is not convenient. We can, if we like, derive conditions from the first type of change – the substitution of one output for another. This would give us conditions analogous to Wicksell's equation – the rate of interest equals the relative marginal productivity of 'time'.[7] Unlike Wicksell, however, we have to take

[6] It should be observed that in general the labour of any period has as many marginal products as there are periods under consideration, for it will be possible, by employing extra labour at any particular date, to increase output at any other period we choose. Future labour even has a marginal product in the periods before it is actually applied; for the output of bread in the near future might be increased at the expense of the deterioration of equipment – which could be made good at a later date. (I owe this last point to Mr Edelberg.)

[7] K. Wicksell, *Lectures on Political Economy*, Vol. I, pp. 172–84.

into account the possibility that the expected rate of interest may be different at different future dates.[8]

III

Like the marginal productivity conditions of static theory, our present marginal productivity conditions are only a means to an end. What we want to discover from them is the way in which the firm's production plan (and in particular its demand for current labour) will be affected by changes in the prices and price-anticipations which govern it. This we may now proceed to examine; but it is very important to be clear first of all that the changes with which we are concerned are purely hypothetical changes. We are still on our first Monday; we are examining the differences between the production plan actually adopted and that which would have been adopted if prices or price-anticipations had been different.

The only current prices which enter into the problem are the current rate of wages and the current rate of interest; the only anticipated prices the rates of wages and rates of interest which the enterpreneur expects to rule in subsequent weeks. How will changes in these rates affect the current demand for labour?

A fall in the current rate of wages (unaccompanied by any fall in expected rates of wages, or by any change in interest) will ordinarily increase the demand for labour in two ways. On the one hand, it will cause current labour to be substituted for future labour; on the other hand, it will reduce the marginal cost of output at various dates in the future. Consequently, it will be profitable to plan an expansion of future output, in whose production more current labour, at any rate, is likely to be used.

---

[8] Like the ordinary static marginal productivity theory, the above analysis assumes that the production function is continuous. This assumption has caused trouble even in static theory (witness the disputes about 'constant coefficients' or 'fixed proportions') and it is much more dubious here. For there can be no doubt that a good many output–input pairs will be quite *unrelated*, in the sense that a small increase in input at date t_1 could not facilitate any increase in output at date t_2, while a small diminution in input at t_1 could not leave all other outputs unchanged, even if output at date t_2 were abandoned altogether.

The difficulty could be overcome by replacing our 'marginal products' by 'marginal net products' in the manner of Marshall, but it seems hardly worth while to work that out here. For the reader will observe that in the following section we never need to assume that *any* input–output pair is capable of variation; we shall only use the marginal productivity conditions to give us the laws of adjustment for those pairs which are capable of being adjusted.

A fall in the current rate of interest (unaccompanied by any fall in expected interest rates, or by any change in wages) will have exactly similar effects. It will raise the discounted values of all future receipts and future outpayments relatively to that of current labour; and this comes to the same thing, in its effects on the production plan, as a cheapening of current labour.

A fall in the rate of wages which is expected to rule at some future date (current rates, and all other expected rates, remaining the same) is less certain in its effects. It is natural to suppose that the labour of this future period would tend to be substituted for current labour, and therefore the demand for current labour would be diminished. But this is not certain; for it is conceivable that the labour of the two periods may be technically complementary, so that the new production plan, although it is adopted because it uses more labour at the future date (when labour is expected to be cheap), may also demand the employment of more current labour as well.

A fall in the rate of interest expected to rule during some future period (once more, other rates being equal) is most likely to increase the demand for current labour. For it raises the discounted values of all the outputs subsequent to the future period in question, and also raises the discounted cost of all subsequent inputs. It thus becomes more profitable to produce certain outputs, and this will normally increase the demand for labour of any period; but at the same time late applications of labour have become more expensive, so that the increased demand is likely to fall mainly upon the labour of earlier periods. Among these is current labour, and the demand for current labour is therefore likely to rise.[9]

These four cases give us the elements of our present problem; for all possible changes in wages and interest can be reduced to combinations of these four cases. Some particular combinations, however, are so important that it may be useful if we work them out in detail.

We have to recognise that the expectations of the future course of wages (and interest) are largely based on current rates; consequently a change in current rates is very unlikely to leave expected rates unchanged. When this is taken into account, we evidently ought to inquire what is the effect of a change in current wages (or interest)

---

[9] Against this must be set the empirical fact (on which Marshall based his analysis of the 'short period') that initial equipment is likely to be fairly specific. This implies that the technically possible production plans are likely to vary more widely in the opportunities they offer for the employment of future labour (particularly labour of the more distant future) than in the opportunities they offer for current labour. In the present application, therefore, it would seem that the increased demand for labour is more likely to exert itself upon future labour (though labour of an earlier date than that at which the fall in interest is due) than upon current labour itself.

which induces a proportionate change in expected wages (or interest) in the same direction.

A general fall in wages (current and expected) will diminish the marginal cost of output at all dates, and must therefore lead to an expansion of output. This expansion may be general (at all dates), but it is not inevitable that it should be so. (Technical conditions may concentrate the increased output upon particular periods.) In order to produce the increased output, more labour will be needed; but how this increased demand for labour will be divided between current labour and future labour cannot be determined *a priori*. It is conceivable, though not perhaps very probable, that there might be no increased demand for current labour at all.[10] Since future labour is unchanged in cost relatively to current labour, there will be no direct substitution of one for the other.[11]

A general fall in interest (current and expected) will lead to a more complicated change. It is now not merely a matter of future labour becoming dearer relatively to present; future labour of every period becomes dearer relatively to all earlier labour (current and future), cheaper relatively to all future labour of a later date. There will therefore be a slight incentive to substitute current labour for labour of the near future, and at the same time a much stronger incentive to substitute it for labour of the distant future. Taking these together, it looks as if there would be a very definite increase in the demand for current labour.[12]

[10] Compare the preceding note.

[11] Since the amount of labour employed will tend to increase relatively to the initial equipment, we may say, if we like, that there is *substitution* of current labour for past labour. But this is rather misleading, as the amount of past labour is embodied in the initial equipment, and is a *datum*. The use of such expressions in chapter IX of my *Theory of Wages* misled many readers, and to some extent the author himself.

[12] Even this might conceivably be offset by queer forms of complementarity. Take the following special case. A fall in the rate of interest for all periods raises slightly the discounted cost of labour to be performed in three weeks' time, and raises much more the discounted cost of labour to be performed in 20 weeks' time. The important substitution will therefore be against labour performed in 20 weeks' time – in favour of current labour, and labour performed in three weeks' time. Now it is possible that labour performed in three weeks' time may be much more easily substituted for the distant future labour; so that this substitution would be effective, while the substitution of current labour for the distant future labour (on account of technical conditions) would be relatively ineffective. Further, if this was so, it would be possible for current labour to be complementary with the distant future labour; so that the marginal product of current labour might be diminished, by the diminution in the planned employment of labour in 20 weeks' time, more than enough to offset its own increased relative cheapness. Whence the demand for current labour might be diminished.

This is perhaps improbable, but it is not inconceivable. It is given here as an example of the things not dreamed of in the philosophy of Böhm-Bawerk and Wicksell.

But this is not all. The discounted values of all future outputs would be raised by an amount which would increase as the output date receded into the future. This would be a further factor tending to increase the demand for labour, which would exert itself upon labour of all periods; but particularly upon those applications of labour which are appropriate for the production of increased output in the more distant future. There can be little doubt that this would be a further factor tending to increase the demand for current labour.

Six cases are, perhaps, enough. They seem to show that any fall in wages or interest is likely to increase the current demand for labour, excepting a fall in the expected future rates of wages, unaccompanied by a fall in current rates. This is, on the whole, what we should expect; so far then our analysis has done no more than uncover a few (doubtless improbable) exceptions to a common-sense conclusion.

IV

These things, then, determine the firm's demand for labour on the first Monday; what determines its demand for loans? Strictly, what we want is the extent to which it will desire to increase or diminish its debts; and this increase or diminution is the difference between its expenditure (on input and entrepreneurs' private consumption) and its receipts from output. The demand for loans thus depends very largely upon the demand for labour, and this dependence can be a source of great confusion if it is not treated very carefully.

There is, however, a way by which this difficulty can be avoided. The market for loans will be in equilibrium on the first Monday (demand will equal supply) if the extent to which entrepreneurs desire to increase (or diminish) the debts owed by them is exactly matched by the extent to which labourers and rentiers desire to increase (or diminish) the debts owed to them. Rentiers will desire to diminish the debts owed to them by an amount equal to their present consumption;[13] labourers to increase (or diminish) the debts due to them by an amount equal to the difference between their wages and their present consumption. Therefore, if the loan market is to be in equilibrium, we must have

Wages + Entrepreneurs' consumption − Output of bread
$$= \text{(Wages − Consumption of labourers)}$$
$$- \text{Consumption of rentiers.}$$

[13] It will be remembered that these debts include accrued interest.

∴ Entrepreneurs' consumption + Rentiers' consumption
+ Labourers' consumption = Output of bread.

∴ Demand for bread = Supply of bread.

An obvious result, so it would appear! But it conveys the less obvious message, that in order to determine the rate of interest, we need not examine that elusive thing, the 'capital market'; for if the market for labour is in equilibrium, and if the market for bread is in equilibrium, the market for loans must be in equilibrium too.

The reason why we can refer back to the bread market in this way is that we have taken bread as our standard of value. There are two prices to be determined – a rate of wages and a rate of interest; and three equations to determine them – equations of supply and demand for labour, loans and bread. Of these three equations (as in the system of Walras) one follows from the other two. But it is completely indifferent which of the three equations we strike out in this way; convenience seems to dictate that we should strike out the equation relating to loans.

As an example of the sort of analysis which now becomes open to us, let us take the case of Trade Union action. Suppose that in our first Monday the labourers form a Trade Union, and insist (successfully) upon a higher wage than they would otherwise have got. What will be the effect on employment? That is to say, what will be the difference between the number of labourers employed under these conditions and the number who would have been employed at the same date if there had been no combination?

The analysis of the last section enables us to answer this question, so long as we can assume that the rate of interest is unaffected. It will depend to some extent upon the length of time for which the rise in wages above the competitive level is expected to last; but in any case the demand for labour on the first Monday will probably fall – though, in view of the specificity of equipment, not much.

Is it necessary to make any correction of this result for a change in the rate of interest? We can investigate this by inquiring whether the higher rate of wages will affect the supply or the demand for bread. The supply of bread is (mostly) a datum, due to decisions which have been made in the past; so it is only the demand for bread which may be seriously affected. Now, since the receipts of the labourers will have been increased, and they are not likely to desire to save all their gains, their demand for bread will probably rise. There is no reason why the demands of the rentiers should be affected. The only hope of preventing a rise in the total demand for bread, therefore, comes from the entrepreneurs.

As a result of the rise in wages, the total value of the entrepreneurs' assets (measured in terms of bread) must have been reduced. Consequently, on the basis of their present expectations, they will have to plan a reduction in consumption either now or in the future. If they are quick to adjust their consumption habits, they may choose to consume less now; in which case the total demand for bread may be unaffected. But if they are not quick, the total demand for bread will rise, and the rate of interest will rise.

The effects of a rise in the rate of interest can be worked out on the same lines as before. It generally gives a secondary fall in the demand for labour in addition to the primary fall.[14]

V

This analysis of the effects of Trade Union action is, I believe, formally correct: that is, it is correct on its own assumptions. But it is not an analysis which can be applied to the real world in a rough-and-ready fashion – though it is capable of being extended in such a way as to make it applicable.

For the world we have been analysing is a world in which wages are paid in bread, and the rate of interest is a 'bread' rate of interest; in the real world wages are paid in money, and the rate of interest is a money rate. This affects our analysis in two ways.

On the one hand, since the enterprise does its calculations in money, and the price of its product in terms of money is not fixed, we have to take into account, when analysing the production plan, not only current and expected rates of wages and interest, but also the current price of the product, and the expected movement of that price. This means that when we are analysing the effects of a rise in money wages, we have another set of indirect influences to take into account – indirect influences through the prices of products.

On the other hand, since money is now taken as the standard of value, it is the equation of demand and supply for money which is

---

[14] The distinction, made in chapter IX of my *Theory of Wages*, between unemployment due to the direct effects of a rise in wages, and unemployment due to indirect effects through 'capital consumption', was therefore valid; but the analysis of both effects was very faulty.

The whole of that chapter ought to be withdrawn. Böhm-Bawerk was no substitute for mathematics!

available to determine the rate of interest. The 'consumption–good' equation which we used before is now no longer available, for it is fully occupied in determining the prices of consumption goods. This means that the reactions through interest are monetary reactions, and will depend in practice on the monetary system.

Thus, in order to analyse the effects of a rise in money wages, we ought (1) to examine the effect on the production plans, assuming unchanged (current and expected) interest rates and prices of products; (2) to allow for the effect on product prices of any expenditure of the increased wages;[15] (3) to examine the secondary effect on employment by this route, still assuming interest rates unchanged; (4) to examine the effect on the demand for money of these previous adjustments (interest still unchanged); (5) if we decide that the demand for money will be increased, to inquire whether that increased demand can be satisfied without a rise in the rate of interest. To answer these last questions will be a matter for monetary theory – but they do not look unanswerable.

Finally, it should be observed that in all our investigations we have never got beyond our first Monday. There is no reason why theory should be becalmed at that point; and it is clear that in order to give a complete answer to the problems we have raised, we ought to go on to see what happens on Monday week. However, time must go in its own order; and Monday week will have to be another story.

---

[15] It is possible that very little of the increased wages may be spent before Monday week. If this is so, then (at this stage) the capital value of the entrepreneurs' assets will be reduced, unless they expect an increased demand from the labourers later. And such a reduction might induce them to economise.

Part II
Reactions

7

The General Theory:
a First Impression

PREFATORY NOTE

This was a review article, published under the title 'Mr Keynes's Theory of Employment' in the *Economic Journal*, June 1936. (I chose that title, as a hint that I had some suspicions about 'generality'.) I had just three months in which to write it, since the book had only come into my hands on its publication in January, and it was required that my piece should be submitted by some date in April. I could hardly do more than give an impression, in so short a time. Nevertheless, on re-reading what I said, for the purpose of this collection, I feel fairly happy about it. There is hardly anything of substance in it which I would now wish to withdraw.

I could do as well as I did, at such short notice, because the 'method of expectations' as I called it here was already familiar to me. It was the same kind of method as I had been using myself (see the preceding essay). I had myself been insistent that the proper application of it was to short-period problems. Keynes was mainly using it for short-period problems (though his period was longer than mine); so long as he was using it for short-period problems I could follow him closely. When he tried to push it forward into a longer-period analysis, I found myself having misgivings; and I still have misgivings about that, even to this day.

After my piece had been published, Keynes wrote to me about it, and I replied. (The letters have been published in his *Collected Writings*, Vol. XIV, pp. 70–9.) Most of the issues discussed between us concerned the outliers of his theory – his concept of 'income' (the user cost deduction), and the 'own rates of interest'. My view that these outliers were unnecessary seems, in later years, to have established itself. Few modern 'Keynesians' pay much attention to them.

A much more substantial issue was the 'elasticity of supply of consumption goods' where I had clearly dissociated myself from a strict Keynesian position. Keynes was able to show me, in our correspondence, that he had (formally) safeguarded himself on this matter; but I remained of the opinion that more than a formal safeguard was required. I do not pretend that I was thinking of a possible constraint in the supply of natural resources, such as, in modern days of oil squeezes, has proved to be the Achilles heel of the Keynesian revolution. That, in 1936, was far in the future. What did look like being actual, in 1936, was the old cyclical trouble. Unemployment is concentrated in a few industries; transference from those industries, to others where labour is scarce, may not be easy. I did not win Keynes's acceptance of this in our correspondence; but I think he did come to accept it, for it was only a few months later, in those famous letters to the *Times*, that he was expressing apprehension about the economy becoming over-heated, when there was still 10 per cent unemployment, as officially reckoned. (For the evolution of Keynes's ideas on these practical issues, see G. C. Peden, 'Keynes, the Treasury and Unemployment in the Later Nineteen-Thirties', *OEP*, March 1980.) 1936 was the year of the Jarrow marchers, as Mr Peden reminds us; I still don't find it useful to say that those people were 'voluntarily' unemployed.

I

The reviewer of this book is beset by two contrary temptations. On the one hand, he can accept directly Mr Keynes' elaborate disquisitions about his own theory, and its place in the development of economics; praising or blaming the alleged more than Jevonian revolution. Or, on the other hand, he can concentrate upon investigating these disquisitions, and tracing (perhaps) a pleasing degree of continuity and tradition, surviving the revolution from the *ancien régime*. But it seems better to avoid such questions, and to try to consider the new theory on its merits.

First of all, then, what is the new theory about? It is presented to us, primarily, as a theory of employment; but before the book is ended, both author and reader are convinced that it is not only a theory of employment. It is sometimes presented as a theory of 'output in general'; sometimes as a theory of 'shifting equilibrium'. And the reader, at least, will take some time to get out of the habit of regarding it as a theory of money, for it is evidently a further development and superior re-formulation of those original ideas which tantalised and vexed us in the *Treatise*.

It may be suggested that the relation between these different aspects is as follows. The new theory is a theory of employment, in so far as the problem of employment and unemployment is the most urgent practical problem to which this sort of theoretical improvement is relevant. It is a theory of output in general *vis-à-vis* Marshall, who took into account many of the sort of complications which concern Mr Keynes, but took them into account only with reference to a single industry. It is a theory of shifting equilibrium *vis-à-vis* the static or stationary theories of general equilibrium, such as those of Ricardo, Böhm-Bawerk or Pareto. It is a theory of money, in so far as it includes monetary theory, bringing money out of its isolated position as a separate subject into an integral relation with general economics.

Probably the most striking, to a casual reader, of the theoretical doctrines of this book is that which proclaims the necessary equality of Savings and Investment. This looks like a decided recantation of one of the most fundamental principles of the *Treatise on Money*, but inspection shows that it is nothing of the sort. It is merely a change in definition – but a change in definition which marks a very important change in point of view.

In the *Treatise*, Mr Keynes was still to a considerable extent under the influence of the traditional approach to problems of the Trade Cycle. Ordinary (static) economic theory, so the old argument went, explains to us the working of the economic system in 'normal' conditions. Booms and slumps, however, are deviations from this norm, and are thus to be explained by some disturbing cause. Such theories therefore ran in terms of deviations: deviations between market and natural rates of interest, deviations between the actual money supply and some neutral money, forced saving, deviation between saving and investment.

The present theory breaks away from the whole of this range of ideas. It is no longer allowed that ordinary economic theory can give a correct analysis of even normal conditions; the things it leaves out of account are too important. But if there is no norm which we have understood, it is useless to discuss deviations from it. The changing, progressing, fluctuating economy has to be studied on its own, and cannot usefully be referred to the norm of a static state.

The new definitions of saving and investment reflect this new point of view. They are defined with reference to the changing economy itself, and have no element of normal profits hidden away in them.

They are equal because – and this takes us near the heart of Mr Keynes's method – even in a changing economy, supplies and demands are equal. They are equal so long as we define supply as that amount of a commodity which sellers are willing to offer at a particular date in the market conditions of that date; unsold stocks being unsold because sellers prefer selling them later to selling them at a lower price now. These stocks being reckoned as part of future supply, not current supply, it follows that current supply and current demand must be equal – just because every transaction has two sides.

We can even reckon prices as being determined by current demand and supply, so long as we emphasise the word *current*, and exclude goods held over for the future. Current supply is then largely determined by people's willingness to hold goods over for the future, and that depends upon their expectations of the future.

There thus emerges a peculiar, but very significant, type of analysis. If we assume given, not only the tastes and resources ordinarily assumed given in static theory, but also people's anticipations of the future, it is possible to regard demands and supplies as determined by these tastes, resources and anticipations, and prices as determined by demands and supplies. Once the missing element – anticipations – is added, equilibrium analysis can be used, not only in the remote stationary conditions to which many economists have found themselves driven back, but even in the real world, even in the real world in 'disequilibrium'.

This is the general method of this book; it may be reckoned the first of Mr Keynes's discoveries. It is, as a matter of fact, not altogether a new discovery, for several lines of inquiry have been pointing this way in recent years. One may refer, perhaps, to the writings of the econometrists,[1] who have enlarged the validity of their equations by explicitly introducing anticipations. And an even closer analogy to Mr Keynes's work is to be found in the methods which have been common in Swedish economics for several years.[2] But this is only to say that he has had his forerunners, and that there are not a few centres of economic thought where this book will meet with a very sympathetic reception.

From the standpoint of pure theory, the use of the method of expectations is perhaps the most revolutionary thing about this book; but Mr Keynes has other innovations to make, innovations directed towards making the method of anticipations more usable.

[1] E.g. C. F. Roos, *Dynamic Economics.*

[2] E. Lindahl, 'Prisbildningsproblemets uppläggning' (*Ekonomisk Tidskrift*, 1929), *Penningpolitikens medel* (1930); G. Myrdal, 'Der Gleichgewichtsbegriff als Instrument der Geldtheoretischen Analyse', in *Beiträge zur Geldtheorie* (1933). My own article, 'Wages and Interest', essay 6 above, was written to some extent under Swedish influence.

That there was a great need for these latter innovations, no one will deny who has considered the great complexity of the factors determining output in general even under static assumptions – complexity which is likely to be increased when the assumptions are generalised. A great part of Mr Keynes's work may be regarded as an endeavour to cut through this tangle, by grouping complex factors together into bundles. This process is one of drastic simplification, but it is necessary if the theory is to become an instrument of practical thought.

Before going on to these simplifications, we may, however, insert some remarks about the general method of expectations, remarks which apply not only to Mr Keynes's work, but also to all other uses of the method, which have been made or may be made in the future.

The point of the method is that it reintroduces determinateness into a process of change. The output of goods and the employment of labour, together with the whole price-system, are determined over any short period,[3] once the stock of goods (goods of all kinds, including capital goods) existing at the beginning of the period, is given, and once people's expectations of future market conditions are given too. Further, we can deduce, by ordinary economic reasoning, what the outputs, employment and prices would be if expectations were different, capital equipment different, tastes different, and so on. But all that this reasoning gives us is hypothetical results; we can deduce what the system of prices and production would be *at this date*, if the fundamental determining factors were different. The method is thus an admirable one for analysing the impact effect of disturbing causes; but it is less reliable for analysing the further effects.

It is, indeed, not impossible to say something about further effects; for we can deduce what the stocks of goods will be at the end of the period if the decisions are carried out, and this gives us a basis for the analysis of a second period. But it is probable that the change in actual production during the first period will influence the expectations ruling at the end of that period; and there is no means of telling what that influence will be. The more we go into the future, the greater this source of error, so that there is a danger, when it is applied to long periods, of the whole method petering out.

---

[3] The period being taken short enough for us to be able to neglect changes in expectations within it. Its length will therefore depend upon the degree of precision we are aiming at.

This source of trouble, it should be observed, comes in from the first. It is unrealistic to assume that an important change in data – say the introduction or extension of a public works policy – will leave expectations unchanged, even immediately. But this generally means only that there is a psychological unknown, affecting the magnitude of the impact effect. As more time is allowed, more and more scope is allowed for such variations, both in degree and kind. We must not expect the most elaborate economic analysis to enable us to see very far ahead.

Mr Keynes is usually very careful in allowing for this sort of difficulty. But it has to be recognised that, for this reason, his analysis does not settle nearly as many questions as we might hope. Even if his theory is generally accepted, there will still be room for wide differences of opinion about the consequences of particular policies.

II

I have thought it desirable to mark a division between my general discussion of the method of expectations, on the one hand, and what I have to say about Mr Keynes's more special theory on the other. For distinctly different issues are raised under these two headings. We can discuss the legitimacy of the method of expectations as a matter of pure theory, in the abstract manner proper to pure theory. When, however, we come to Mr Keynes's special theory, the question mainly is whether the grouping he adopts is a convenient grouping; and that is mainly a question of judgment, depending upon our estimates of the relative importance of particular causes in particular situations.

Here we must remind ourselves that Mr Keynes's main object – though sometimes he turns aside from it – is to provide a theory of employment; and it is for its efficacy in illuminating the problem of employment that his classification ought to be judged. It may very well be that it is the best framework to use for that problem, and yet that for other problems a different framework is to be preferred.

For example, it is a fundamental postulate of Mr Keynes's special argument that the expectations of entrepreneurs can be divided into two types – 'short term' and 'long term'. Short-term expectations are 'concerned with the price which a manufacturer can expect to get for his "finished" output at the time when he commits himself to start the process which will produce it'; long-term expectations are 'concerned with what the entrepreneur can hope to earn in the shape of future returns if he purchases (or, perhaps, manufactures) "finished" output as an addition to his capital equipment' (pp. 46–7).

Now, long-term expectations, as Mr Keynes shows convincingly in one of his most brilliant chapters, are wayward things. It is almost impracticable to make good estimates of the state of the market years ahead, and yet this is what an entrepreneur has to try to do. Further, those professional speculators who have often been looked upon as specialised forecasters do not find it to their interest to look more than a little way ahead.

Long-term expectations are therefore best regarded as independent variables; but short-term expectations are more closely connected with current receipts. Mr Keynes therefore determines to neglect any possible divergence between short-term expectations and current prices.

This enables him to classify industries into two types, capital goods (or investment) industries, whose activities depend mainly upon the wayward long-term expectations; and consumption goods industries, whose activity depends upon current receipts. So far as the consumption goods industries are concerned, it is thus possible to apply the familiar Marshallian analysis. They are considered all the time as being in equilibrium, save that, of course, the demand for their products comes partly from people engaged in the investment industries, and will thus be affected by the activity of those industries.

Assuming now that we start from a position where there is a considerable amount of unemployment, and assuming for the present that money wage-rates can be taken as fixed; then if there is an increase in employment in the investment industries, due to an upward revision of long-term expectations, this will induce an increased demand for consumption goods. This increased demand will lead to a secondary expansion of the consumption goods trades; by how much?

This question, obviously of great importance for the theory of employment, is dealt with by Mr Keynes in a manner which may perhaps be paraphrased as follows. Let us look upon the consumption goods industries, and the people engaged in them, as a unit, a 'country'. This 'country' experiences an increased demand for its exports; what is to happen to its balance of payments? The increased exports cannot be matched by imports (for the new capital goods are not ready yet, they are only being begun); apart from money transfers, there must therefore be lending. But how is the lending to be induced?

The traditional answer would evidently have been – a rise in the rate of interest, but Mr Keynes, like many other economists, is doubtful about the direct effect of a rise in the rate of interest in diminishing consumption. Are we, however, obliged to believe that the people in the consumption goods trades, because they become better off, consume less? Mr Keynes thinks not; he believes that the explanation is to be found in an increased production of consumption goods, which so improves the position of these people that they are able to consume more than before, and yet have an increased surplus to satisfy the needs of the investment industries.

Granted a high elasticity of supply in the consumption goods industries, this does not seem an improbable outcome; and if things do work out this way, it is perfectly intelligible that the increased demand for loans from the investment industries should encounter an increased supply, so that there is no reason for the rate of interest to rise. Thus the effect on total employment of an increase in investment can be taken as depending mainly upon the extent to which the production of consumption goods has to increase in order to make an adequate margin between the production of consumption goods and the consumption of them in the consumption goods industries. This will depend upon the way increased wealth reacts on the demand for consumption goods – Mr Keynes's 'Propensity to Consume', the relation between demand for consumption goods and income.[4]

---

[4] Mr Keynes expresses income in terms of 'wage-units' (p. 41); but this makes no difference so long as we assume money wage-rates fixed.

It should be understood that the above is a very free paraphrase of Mr Keynes's argument. His own method of stating it is rendered exceedingly complex by his use of a very peculiar concept of 'income'. To discuss this concept fully would require an article in itself, so I must confine myself to one or two remarks. It is true that Mr Keynes's 'income' is the quantity which the entrepreneur maximises, but he can equally well be thought of as maximising the present value of his planned stream of outputs and inputs – the latter gives the same results, so Mr Keynes's concept is not necessary here. Nor does it seem to me that it escapes from the conventional vagueness detected in the concept of 'net income' (about which there is no difference of opinion, neither about its usefulness, nor about its trickiness); for the entrepreneur's estimate of user cost will depend upon his estimate of the likelihood of involuntary losses. Expected involuntary losses surely influence voluntary decisions. Finally, a concept of income, which depends, as Mr Keynes's does, upon the degree to which industry is integrated, seems hardly happy.

I have therefore endeavoured to see whether Mr Keynes's substantial arguments necessarily involved his concept of income. My conclusion has been that they do not. The only thing which he seems to gain from this concept is an apparent simplification of the doctrine of the multiplier, but I am not sure that this is altogether an advantage.

These strictures on 'income' are not meant to imply anything but admiration for the concept of *marginal* user cost; that is obviously a most convenient portmanteau, which will save the lives of many old friends among static arguments.

There is, however, one qualification to this argument which only makes its appearance quite late in the book (p. 288), but well deserves to be considered here. So far as the initial 'export' is concerned, it is evident that it must come from stocks, for even consumption goods take some time to make. Thus far, the mechanism is not *via* increased 'saving', but *via* disinvestment in these stocks. And since the assumption of a high elasticity of supply of consumption goods in general is only made plausible by assuming considerable surplus stocks of raw material, it looks not impossible that the balancing may always take place to a certain extent by this sort of disinvestment, instead of only by the increase in production deduced by Mr Keynes.

Altogether, it is very important to observe the essential part played in Mr Keynes's argument – that is to say, in his theory of the way in which the consumption goods trades adjust themselves to a change in long-term expectations – by the assumption of a high elasticity of supply of consumption goods. So long as this assumption is justified, the argument is, on the whole, acceptable; and there is no doubt that it is often justified. But it is surely not true that it is justified whenever there is a large degree of unemployment – Mr Keynes's 'involuntary unemployment' – for the unemployment may be concentrated in the capital goods trades, and it is surely odd to assume away the difficulties of industrial transference. In these circumstances, an increased demand for consumption goods to be 'exported' from the consumption goods trades is most unlikely to produce an automatic margin. The natural result, one would think, would be a rise in the rate of interest, checking the boom.

This result, however, is combated (or apparently combated) by Mr Keynes's theory of the rate of interest, to which we must now turn.

It is a great strength of Mr Keynes's theory of interest that it conceives the rate of interest, from the outset, as a money rate. Interest arises out of the exchange of present money for future money, and the moneyness of the transaction does not cancel out,[5] any more than it cancels out in foreign exchange dealing. The determination of the rate of interest is thus a specifically monetary problem; through it 'the quantity of money enters the economic scheme'.

---

[5] It only cancels out if everyone expects all prices to remain strictly unchanged, expects them to remain unchanged with absolute certainty. This premise has lain unnoticed at the bottom of my classical economic arguments, but it confines their significance to a usually unimportant special case.

This monetary character of interest is, of course, no novelty; it has been generally recognised at least since the time of Wicksell. But the way of expressing it used by Wicksell and his followers has, of course, to be abandoned by Mr Keynes's – since a 'natural rate' of interest would be a concept foreign to the whole present trend of his ideas. Interest, for him, is simply the money rate; and, like Wicksell and his school, he regards that rate as primarily determined by monetary factors.

The particular way adopted by Mr Keynes to bring this out is his doctrine of 'liquidity preference'. The individual has a choice between holding money and lending it out – a choice that can be expressed by means of a demand curve, showing the amounts of money he will desire to hold at different rates of interest. The rate of interest will be determined at that level which makes the demand for money equal to the supply.

This looks a most revolutionary doctrine; but it is not, I think, as revolutionary as it seems. For over any short period, the difference between the value of the things an individual acquires (including money) and the value of the things he gives up (including money) must, apart from gifts, equal the change in his net debt – his borrowing and lending. The same will apply to a firm. If, therefore, the demand for every commodity and factor equals the supply, and if the demand for money equals the supply of money, it follows by mere arithmetic that the demand for loans must equal the supply of loans (when these latter are interpreted in a properly inclusive way). Similarly, if the equations of supply and demand hold for commodities, factors and loans, it will follow automatically that the demand for money equals the supply of money.

The ordinary method of economic theory would be to regard each price as determined by the demand and supply equation for the corresponding commodity or factor; the rate of interest as determined by the demand and supply for loans. If we work in this way, the equation for demand and supply of money is otiose – it follows from the rest, and fortunately, too, it is not wanted, because we have determined the whole price-system without it. But we could equally well work in another way. We could allot to each commodity or factor the demand and supply equation for that commodity or factor, as before; but we could allot to the rate of interest the equation for the demand and supply of money. If we do this, the equation for loans becomes otiose, automatically following from the rest. 'Savings' and 'Investment' are therefore automatically equal.[6]

[6] Cf. essay 6, pp. 76–7, above.

This latter method is the method of Mr Keynes. It is a perfectly legitimate method, but it does not prove other methods to be wrong. The choice between them is purely a question of convenience.

From the point of view of convenience, there are, no doubt, weighty arguments in favour of the 'liquidity preference' method. It is a mercy to be able to avoid the whole question of debt, with its holes and corners, its perils of double counting and non-counting. It is a great advantage, too, to have our attention clearly focused on the relation between money and interest; for the choice between holding money and investing it has a great many subtle points about it which needed to be made, as they are made here. On balance, I have therefore no doubt that this new way of tackling interest problems is a most valuable addition to our theoretical equipment.

It has, however, weak places. It is easy to slip into regarding the liquidity preference curve – the curve connecting interest with the demand for money – as a stable curve, so that we can concentrate our attention entirely upon this particular relation. But that is evidently not so, as Mr Keynes shows clearly. The demand for money does not only depend upon the rate of interest and the state of confidence (the desire for liquidity); it is influenced by other things as well, in particular by the level of money incomes. Now, the more important is the level of money incomes relatively to the rate of interest in determining the demand for money, the less does the comparative advantage of Mr Keynes's method become. In fact, whenever we find Mr Keynes coming to a problem where he has to emphasise the 'transactions motive' relatively to the 'speculative motive', we generally find him turning out conclusions which could easily have been reached by more familiar methods.

As an example of this sort of thing, let us revert to the question which we left in the air a page or two back – the results of an attempted expansion of the capital goods trades when the supply of consumption goods does not prove to be very elastic. Mr Keynes's analysis of this case would evidently lead to the conclusion that there would be an indefinite rise in the prices of consumption goods – producing a state of 'true inflation' at least in the consumption goods 'country'. But he would admit, on second thoughts, that this would lead to a more or less corresponding rise in the demand for money; and therefore that, unless the supply of money was indefinitely expanded, the rate of interest must rise, and the boom be checked. I do not think that this differs at all essentially from what has been said by earlier writers;[7] they would, however,

---

[7] Cf. F. A. Hayek, *Prices and Production.*

begin by assuming the supply of money not indefinitely expansible, and so proceed straight to a rise in the rate of interest. But they would admit, on their second thoughts, that if the supply of money were to be indefinitely expanded, the rate of interest could be kept down, and the inflation proceed without limit.[8]

This seems, then, a clear case where our choice of methods ought to depend upon our judgment of the relative importance of different factors; so that it will vary to some extent with the problem in hand. Contemporary problems are probably dominated to a great extent by the speculative motive. For them Mr Keynes's method will often be highly convenient. But we begin to understand why he lights upon such queer results, when, in an occasional light-hearted moment, he seems to take all time for his province.

One other difficulty about the 'liquidity preference' method needs comment. It is a much better method when we need concern ourselves only with one rate of interest, than for problems where we have to consider several rates, so that the loan market (which it leaves in the dark) is not homogeneous. Mr Keynes seems to mean by 'the' rate of interest, the long-term rate on gilt edged; he is, I think, precluded by his method from illuminating the relation between this rate and other rates as much as he could do, and has indeed done by other methods.[9]

III

Since Mr Keynes does not much believe in scarcity of any kind as a factor bringing about a trade crisis, and holds that booms usually come to an end while there is a considerable amount of 'involuntary unemployment' (apparently all round), he is obliged to find some other explanation of the collapse. While he is too wise to be dogmatic about any particular explanation, and admits that booms may come to an end for a variety of reasons, there is one cause which he

---

[8] The theory of unemployment and real wages could probably be partially rehabilitated on the same lines. But I have personally doubted for some time whether this was worth doing, and have been inclined to favour an approach to the problem of general wage-levels similar to that of Mr Keynes (cf. again essay 6, pp. 77–8). Mr Keynes's chapter XIX seems to me on the whole admirable.

[9] I think, too, that we have to trace back to this source the rather special difficulties most readers will feel about chapter XVII. It is not easy, on Mr Keynes's own method, to see why a liquidity preference for land will keep up the money rate of interest; or, indeed, why a liquidity preference for money will keep up the wheat rate of interest. One feels that these conclusions are right; but one would like a little more explanation.

distinguishes especially – one cause *par excellence*. It is essentially that which Mr Robertson has designated 'the gluttability of wants';[10] Mr Keynes focuses attention on it by means of his concept of the 'Marginal Efficiency of Capital'.

When we are first introduced to the marginal efficiency of capital, it has a singularly innocent appearance. It is, apparently, not in Marshall; but one is almost surprised to find that it is not. The marginal efficiency of any particular kind of capital good is defined as that rate of interest which would equate the present value of the net yields expected in future periods from an additional good of this kind with its supply price (p. 135). Then, if the marginal efficiency of any particular kind of capital good rises above the rate of interest, this implies that the demand price rises above the supply price, and the output of goods of this kind will expand, until equality is restored. In equilibrium,[11] output of each kind of capital good is determined so that its marginal efficiency equals the rate of interest (excepting when the output is nil). We may thus speak of the marginal efficiency of capital in general.

Thus it is changes in the marginal efficiency of capital relatively to the rate of interest which are responsible for changes in the activity of the investment industries, and ultimately for most changes in the activity of the whole system.

On what does the marginal efficiency of capital depend? After marking its dependence upon the expected trend of prices (for this is of course the way long-term expectations come in), and upon risk, Mr Keynes turns to concentrate attention mainly upon a third factor – the actual amount of capital goods already possessed by the community. *Other things being equal, the marginal efficiency of capital will be lower, the greater the amount of capital goods already possessed.*

This last proposition is of quite fundamental importance, for on it Mr Keynes bases, not only his theory of the trade crisis, but also a new theory of long-period unemployment which is even more novel and startling. Thus, before returning to examine the foundation, let us survey the superstructure.

The accumulation of physical capital during a trade boom, according to Mr Keynes, forces down the marginal efficiency of capital. For a while this may be offset by increasing optimism, but a time must come when it is only possible to maintain the

[10] A. C. Pigou and D. H. Robertson, *Economic Essays and Addresses*, pp. 122–5.
[11] It should be observed that in this sense the economic system is always in equilibrium. Positions of disequilibrium are purely conceptual *reductiones ad absurdum*.

activity of investment by reducing the rate of interest. Now, it is very difficult to reduce the long-term rate of interest beyond a certain point, because a very low rate of interest will not recompense the investor for the risk of capital losses due to changes in the rate of interest. Save under conditions of quite exceptional willingness to bear risks, the long-term rate is therefore most unlikely to fall below some such figure as 2 per cent;[12] and sooner or later a point will be reached when it is difficult to find new capital goods whose production will yield even such a low rate as this. The activity of the investment industries will then decline; and if the decline supervenes upon an expected expansion, it may be very sharp indeed, for expectations will be shifted suddenly to the worse.

Since the check takes place for reasons which are only remotely connected with the volume of employment, it may very well occur when employment is very far short of the maximum possible. And in a community where there is initially a very large stock of capital goods, the marginal efficiency of capital will generally be so low that the opportunities for employment in the investment industries will be severely restricted. Even optimism will stimulate only very moderate booms.

It would thus appear that in a wealthy community, cyclical unemployment is not the only danger. There is also a likelihood of secular unemployment, due to the limited possibilities of investment at a rate of interest reduced to its psychological minimum. And, as we have seen, it is the activity of the investment industries which determines (once the Propensity to Consume is given) the activity of the consumption goods industries. If employment is low in the one, it will be low in the other.

This does not mean that it would not be possible, under suitable conditions of the propensity to consume, for total unemployment to be very low, even while investment is low. But savings and investment must be equal; if investment is low, the consumption goods trades can only absorb the available labour if the desire to save is very low. Otherwise, there will have to be enough unemployment to cut down their saving.

I think we must admit that the danger here disclosed is a real one. It is a danger which has been concealed from the eyes of most economists by their assumption that people save for the same sorts of motives as entrepreneurs invest in real capital – that their object is

---

[12] Pp. 168–9, 201–2. In order that holding money should be a serious alternative to investing it, it is a necessary condition that the costs of holding money should be very small. This important point is brought out in chapter XVII.

to acquire a future return or income. This assumption is natural enough in a static, riskless world. But when we remember risk, it is surely evident that people save very largely for security; and their saving therefore gives no indication that in the future they will desire to consume. Risk, which makes entrepreneurs invest less, may make savers save more; it is consequently a potent engine of disequilibrium.

So far as Mr Keynes is emphasising risk-factors, his argument is wholly convincing; but he has more to say than this. For there is to be considered, too, his fundamental law of the Diminishing Marginal Efficiency of Capital. What are the grounds for this law? Why must we assume that the marginal efficiency of capital declines, as the quantity of physical capital possessed by a community increases? What are the sorts of *ceteris paribus* which have to be marked off in order that we should be sure of this result? Are they things which enable us to proceed directly to the conclusion, upon which so much of Mr Keynes's practical programme depends, that the marginal efficiency of capital is likely to be lower in the twentieth century than in the nineteenth?

As a result of Mr Keynes's work, these questions acquire a vast importance, and there can be scarcely any topics upon which it is more urgent for economists to make up their minds. For if we decide that they must be answered in the sort of way Mr Keynes implies they should be answered, there is only one choice before us. Either we must accept something like the policy he advocates, of stimulating investment and repressing saving by changes in social organisation; or our once benevolent science becomes a paean to destruction, whose heroes are earthquake, war, and conflagration, Attila and Genghis Khan, Great Raisers of the Marginal Efficiency of Capital and Creators of Employment.

It is an unfortunate thing that Mr Keynes's own investigations into the reasons for the diminishing marginal efficiency of capital are not nearly as thorough as one could desire. It is evident that he considers himself absolved from any detailed investigation, because he regards the principle as established from the fact that trade booms collapse. But this will not convince those who believe that booms usually (or often) collapse for other reasons, such as the imperfect elasticity of supply of consumption goods and the consequent hardening of interest rates. It would seem very desirable indeed that the theory of long-period unemployment should have some independent support.

The most helpful passage I have been able to find is that in which Mr Keynes lists the factors which kept up the marginal efficiency of capital in the nineteenth century. 'The growth of population and invention, the opening-up of new lands, the state of confidence and the frequency of war over the average of (say) each decade' (p. 307). It is evident that invention has much to do with the problem; for if the number of kinds of capital goods was fixed, then it would be very reasonable to suppose that the yields from each kind of good would diminish as the number of goods of that kind increased.[13] But if the number of kinds is not fixed, then it seems very possible that the invention of new kinds may be stimulated by the increase in productive power, and this might put off the decline almost indefinitely. Invention of new kinds of consumption goods will be as potent.[14] The whole question of invention thus needs very serious consideration; but I think it will tend to show that a theory which takes into account many dynamic considerations, and then assumes invention nil, should be handled carefully.

Population is, I think, Mr Keynes's strongest card. It does become very evident, when one thinks of it, that the expectation of a continually expanding market, made possible by increasing population, is a fine thing for keeping up the spirits of entrepreneurs. With increasing population, investment can go roaring ahead, even if invention is rather stupid; increasing population is therefore actually favourable to employment. It is actually easier to employ an expanding population than a contracting one, whatever arithmetic would suggest – at least this is so when the expansion or contraction is expected, as we may assume generally to be the case.

Consider the situation which is likely to arise when the population of this country is declining, and the populations of most of those countries with which she is in close trading connections are stationary or tending to decline. A time will come, so it already seems likely, when this tendency, and its probable future continuance, will not be the secret only of a few economists, but will be fully realised by the mass of the public. In these circumstances, the incentive to construct houses, ships, factories, all sorts of capital equipment will be depressed by the anticipation that capital is wearing out and population dying off at convergent rates. Investment will proceed only with great difficulty, and employment will be low, in spite of the fact that population may have already declined in the

---

[13] Conditions are, however, I think, conceivable where the increased supply of one type of capital goods would raise the marginal efficiency schedule for other types.

[14] It is possible, again, that the invention of new sorts of goods, though responsive to the increase in productive power, responds rather slowly. If this were so, Mr Robertson's 'temporary gluttability' would be acceptable, but not the long-period unemployment of Mr Keynes.

past. It is true that in a community with perfect confidence, the situation could be rationally met. With so little of a future to look forward to, most people would spend all, or even more than all, of their incomes, and a high degree of total employment could be reached, with nearly all labour in the consumption trades. But this will hardly be considered a likely state of affairs. For capital will still retain its value as a reserve against unforeseen emergencies, and this need for it will hardly decline.

Thus, whatever we decide in the end to think about the Diminishing Marginal Efficiency of Capital, this population point is enough in itself to establish the high significance of Mr Keynes's theory of long-period unemployment. Whether or not we are already engulfed in the dangers he diagnoses is a thing which can be disputed; but there is little doubt that we are heading for those dangers. They are, indeed, one aspect – perhaps the most important economic aspect – of that problem of adapting to less progressive conditions the institutions of a traditionally expansive civilisation, which already vexes us on many sides.

The technique of this work is, on the whole, conservative: more conservative than in the *Treatise*. It is the technique of Marshall, but it is applied to problems never tackled by Marshall and his contemporaries. In all this region they were content to take over the conclusions of the Ricardians, and never thoroughly tested these conclusions by means of their own technique. That testing has now been done, and the Ricardian conclusions found badly wanting. Thus we have to change, not so much our methods of analysis, as some important elements in the outlook which we have inherited from the classics. We have to realise that we can have too much, even of the economic virtues. It was indeed a happy age that could think the contrary; but the nineteenth century could only afford Ricardo because it sinned so luxuriantly against Malthus. Today we must find a new sin; if it can give us a century before the day of reckoning it will have done well.

8

Mr Keynes and the Classics

PREFATORY NOTE

Though this paper has already been reprinted in *Critical Essays in Monetary Theory* (1967), it is so well known that this collection would look absurd without it. It was written to be given at a meeting of the Econometric Society, held in Oxford in September 1936 and was published in *Econometrica* in April 1937. It bears the stamp of its origin. It was seeking to explain the Keynes theory to econometrists (and mathematical economists). In that attempt it succeeded, perhaps only too well. For it is no more than a part of what Keynes was saying, or implying, that can be represented in that manner, and it was easy to take it as the whole.

In the first place it should be noticed that (as was explicitly stated, but not sufficiently emphasised) the models being constructed are entirely concerned with that 'short period' during which the money wage can be taken as given. (Whether there is such a period is, of course, one of the issues; the assumption is nevertheless useful, indeed I think indispensable, as a first stage in exposition.) One of the consequences of making this assumption was the queer version of 'classical' theory which I found myself obliged to give. Of course, it is true that the majority of those whom Keynes would have called 'classics' would not have accepted that money wages could have remained constant when there was a change in money demand. There were nevertheless some who did admit that a rise in money demand could increase activity, without *for the time being* raising wages. Hume in his essay on 'Money', and Mill in his 'On the Influence of Consumption on Production' (*Essays on Unsettled Questions*, 1844), may be cited as examples. But it was misleading to call that minority view *the* 'classical' theory. (See 'The Classics Again' in *CEMT*.)

In the second place, it must be emphasised that the *LL* curve, exhibiting a relation between income and interest with a given supply of money, is also dependent upon the fixed money wage.

But it is not only in that respect that the *LL* curve is a weak element in the construction. It is now well known that in later developments of Keynesian theory, the long-term rate of interest (which does figure, excessively, in Keynes's own presentation and is presumably represented by the *r* of the diagram) has been taken down a peg from the position it appeared to occupy in Keynes. We now know that it is not enough to think of *the* rate of interest as the single link between the financial and industrial sectors of the economy; for that really implies that a borrower can borrow as much as he likes at the rate of interest charged, no attention being paid to the security offered. As soon as one attends to questions of security and to the financial intermediation that arises out of them, it becomes clear that the dichotomy between the two curves of the diagram must not be pressed too hard.[1]

The concluding section of the paper, in which income (or output) is introduced as a parameter in the marginal efficiency of capital schedule, is quite un-Keynesian. The introduction was so tempting mathematically; but the temptation would have been better avoided. Something of that kind may indeed have a place. The Accelerator (where the parameter is *rate of change* of output) is an improvement; something can be done with it, as I showed in my book on the Trade Cycle (1950); see also essay 15 below. A Capital Stock Adjustment principle (*Capital and Growth*, ch. 9) is a still better representation of what I had in mind. But whatever view one takes about this, it was never intended, in this or in any later versions, that investment changes should be entirely explicable in terms of output, or changes in output of whatever sort. There was always a residue that could vary independently.

Some of the deeper issues that are raised in this paper are considered at length in a quite recent paper (essay 23 below). I there use the lettering *IS–LM*, which has become conventional, not the *SI–LL* used here, which did not catch on.

I

It will be admitted by the least charitable reader that the entertainment value of Mr Keynes's *General Theory of Employment* is considerably enhanced by its satiric aspect. But it is also clear that many readers have been left very bewildered by this Dunciad. Even if

---

[1] See essay 19, part III, below.

they are convinced by Mr Keynes's arguments and humbly acknow-
ledge themselves to have been 'classical economists' in the past, they
find it hard to remember that they believed in their unregenerate
days the things Mr Keynes says they believed. And there are no
doubt others who find their historic doubts a stumbling block, which
prevents them from getting as much illumination from the positive
theory as they might otherwise have got.

One of the main reasons for this situation is undoubtedly to be
found in the fact that Mr Keynes takes as typical of 'Classical
economics' the later writings of Professor Pigou, particularly *The
Theory of Unemployment*. Now *The Theory of Unemployment* is
a fairly new book, and an exceedingly difficult book; so that it is
safe to say that it has not yet made much impression on the ordinary
teaching of economics. To most people its doctrines seem quite as
strange and novel as the doctrines of Mr Keynes himself; so that to
be told that he has believed these things himself leaves the ordinary
economist quite bewildered.

For example, Professor Pigou's theory runs, to a quite amazing
extent, in real terms. Not only is his theory a theory of real wages
and unemployment; but numbers of problems which anyone else
would have preferred to investigate in money terms are investigated
by Professor Pigou in terms of 'wage-goods'. The ordinary classical
economist has no part in this *tour de force*.

But if, on behalf of the ordinary classical economist, we declare
that he would have preferred to investigate many of those problems
in money terms, Mr Keynes will reply that there is no classical theory
of money wages and employment. It is quite true that such a theory
cannot easily be found in the textbooks. But this is only because
most of the textbooks were written at a time when general changes
in money wages in a closed system did not present an important
problem. There can be little doubt that most economists have thought
that they had a pretty fair idea of what the relation between money
wages and employment actually was.

In these circumstances, it seems worth while to try to construct a
typical 'classical' theory, built on an earlier and cruder model than
Professor Pigou's. If we can construct such a theory, and show that
it does give results which have in fact been commonly taken for
granted, but which do not agree with Mr Keynes's conclusions, then
we shall at last have a satisfactory basis of comparison. We may hope
to be able to isolate Mr Keynes's innovations, and so to discover
what are the real issues in dispute.

Since our purpose is comparison, I shall try to set out my typical classical theory in a form similar to that in which Mr Keynes sets out his own theory; and I shall leave out of account all secondary complications which do not bear closely upon this special question in hand. Thus I assume that I am dealing with a short period in which the quantity of physical equipment of all kinds available can be taken as fixed. I assume homogeneous labour. I assume further that depreciation can be neglected, so that the output of investment goods corresponds to new investment. This is a dangerous simplification, but the important issues raised by Mr Keynes in his chapter on user cost are irrelevant for our purposes.

Let us begin by assuming that w, the rate of money wages per head, can be taken as given.

Let x, y, be the outputs of investment goods and consumption goods respectively, and N_x, N_y, be the numbers of men employed in producing them. Since the amount of physical equipment specialised to each industry is given, $x = f_x(N_x)$ and $y = f_y(N_y)$, where f_x, f_y, are *given* functions.

Let M be the *given* quantity of money.

It is desired to determine N_x and N_y.

First, the price-level of investment goods = their marginal cost = $w(dN_x/dx)$. And the price-level of consumption goods = their marginal cost = $w(dN_y/dy)$.

Income earned in investment trades (value of investment, or simply Investment) = $wx(dN_x/dx)$. Call this I_x.

Income earned in consumption trades = $wy(dN_y/dy)$.

Total Income = $wx(dN_x/dx) + wy(dN_y/dy)$. Call this I.

I_x is therefore a given function of N_x, I of N_x and N_y. Once I and I_x are determined, N_x and N_y can be determined.

Now let us assume the 'Cambridge Quantity equation' – that there is some definite relation between Income and the demand for money. Then, approximately, and apart from the fact that the demand for money may depend not only upon total Income, but also upon its distribution between people with relatively large and relatively small demands for balances, we can write

$$M = kI.$$

As soon as k is given, total Income is therefore determined.

In order to determine I_x, we need two equations. One tells us that the amount of investment (looked at as demand for capital) depends upon the rate of interest:

$$I_x = C(i).$$

This is what becomes the marginal-efficiency-of-capital schedule in Mr Keynes's work.

Further, Investment = Saving. And saving depends upon the rate of interest and, if you like, Income. $\therefore I_x = S(i, I)$. (Since, however, Income is already determined, we do not need to bother about inserting Income here unless we choose.)

Taking them as a system, however, we have three fundamental equations,

$$M = kI, \quad I_x = C(i), \quad I_x = S(i, I),$$

to determine three unknowns, I, I_x, i. As we have found earlier, N_x and N_y can be determined from I and I_x. Total employment, $N_x + N_y$, is therefore determined.

Let us consider some properties of this system. It follows directly from the first equation that as soon as k and M are given, I is completely determined; that is to say, total income depends directly upon the quantity of money. Total employment, however, is not necessarily determined at once from income, since it will usually depend to some extent upon the proportion of income saved, and thus upon the way production is divided between investment and consumption-goods trades. (If it so happened that the elasticities of supply were the same in each of these trades, then a shifting of demand between them would produce compensating movements in N_x and N_y, and consequently no change in total employment.)

An increase in the inducement to invest (i.e. a rightward movement of the schedule of the marginal efficiency of capital, which we have written as $C(i)$), will tend to raise the rate of interest, and so to affect saving. If the amount of saving rises, the amount of investment will rise too; labour will be employed more in the investment trades, less in the consumption trades; this will increase total employment if the elasticity of supply in the investment trades is greater than that in the consumption-goods trades – diminish it if *vice versa*.

An increase in the supply of money will necessarily raise total income, for people will increase their spending and lending until incomes have risen sufficiently to restore k to its former level. The rise in income will tend to increase employment, both in making consumption goods and in making investment goods. The total effect on employment depends upon the ratio between the expansions of these industries; and that depends upon the proportion of their increased incomes which people desire to save, which also governs the rate of interest.

So far we have assumed the rate of money wages to be given; but so long as we assume that k is independent of the level of wages, there is no difficulty about this problem either. A rise in the rate of money wages will necessarily diminish employment and raise real wages. For an unchanged money income cannot continue to buy an unchanged quantity of goods at a higher price-level; and, unless the price-level rises, the prices of goods will not cover their marginal costs. There must therefore be a fall in employment; as employment falls, marginal costs in terms of labour will diminish and therefore real wages rise. (Since a change in money wages is always accompanied by a change in real wages in the same direction, if not in the same proportion, no harm will be done, and some advantage will perhaps be secured, if one prefers to work in terms of real wages. Naturally most 'classical economists' have taken this line.)

I think it will be agreed that we have here a quite reasonably consistent theory, and a theory which is also consistent with the pronouncements of a recognisable group of economists. Admittedly it follows from this theory that you may be able to increase employment by direct inflation; but whether or not you decide to favour that policy still depends upon your judgment about the probable reaction on wages, and also – in a national area – upon your views about the international standard.

Historically, this theory descends from Ricardo, though it is not actually Ricardian; it is probably more or less the theory that was held by Marshall. But with Marshall it was already beginning to be qualified in important ways; his successors have qualified it still further. What Mr Keynes has done is to lay enormous emphasis on the qualifications, so that they almost blot out the original theory. Let us follow out this process of development.

II

When a theory like the 'classical' theory we have just described is applied to the analysis of industrial fluctuations, it gets into difficulties in several ways. It is evident that total money income experiences great variations in the course of a trade cycle, and the classical theory can only explain these by variations in M or in k, or, as a third and last alternative, by changes in distribution.

1.   Variation in M is simplest and most obvious, and has been relied on to a large extent. But the variations in M that are traceable during a trade cycle are variations that take place through the banks – they are variations in bank loans; if we are to rely on them it is urgently necessary for us to explain the connection between the supply of

bank money and the rate of interest. This can be done roughly by thinking of banks as persons who are strongly inclined to pass on money by lending rather than spending it. Their action therefore tends at first to lower interest rates, and only afterwards, when the money passes into the hands of spenders, to raise prices and incomes. 'The new currency, or the increase of currency, goes, not to private persons, but to the banking centres; and therefore, it increases the willingness of lenders to lend in the first instance, and lowers the rate of discount. But it afterwards raises prices; and therefore it tends to increase discount.'[2] This is superficially satisfactory; but if we endeavoured to give a more precise account of this process we should soon get into difficulties. What determines the amount of money needed to produce a given fall in the rate of interest? What determines the length of time for which the low rate will last? These are not easy questions to answer.

2. In so far as we rely upon changes in k, we can also do well enough up to a point. Changes in k can be related to changes in confidence, and it is realistic to hold that the rising prices of a boom occur because optimism encourages a reduction in balances; the falling prices of a slump because pessimism and uncertainty dictate an increase. But as soon as we take this step it becomes natural to ask whether k has not abdicated its status as an independent variable, and has not become liable to be influenced by others among the variables in our fundamental equations.

3. This last consideration is powerfully supported by another, of more purely theoretical character. On grounds of pure value theory, it is evident that the direct sacrifice made by a person who holds a stock of money is a sacrifice of interest; and it is hard to believe that the marginal principle does not operate at all in this field. As Lavington put it: 'The quantity of resources which (an individual) holds in the form of money will be such that the unit of money which is just and only just worth while holding in this form yields him a return of convenience and security equal to the yield of satisfaction derived from the marginal unit spent on consumables, and equal also to the net rate of interest.'[3] The demand for money depends upon the rate of interest! The stage is set for Mr Keynes.

---

[2] A. Marshall, *Money, Credit, and Commerce*, p. 257.

[3] F. Lavington, *English Capital Market*, 1921, p. 30. See also A. C. Pigou, 'The Exchange-Value of Legal-Tender Money', in *Essays in Applied Economics*, 1922, pp. 179–81.

As against the three equations of the classical theory,

$$M = kI, \quad I_x = C(i), \quad I_x = S(i, I),$$

Mr Keynes begins with three equations,

$$M = L(i), \quad I_x = C(i), \quad I_x = S(I).$$

These differ from the classical equations in two ways. On the one hand, the demand for money is conceived as depending upon the rate of interest (Liquidity Preference). On the other hand, any possible influence of the rate of interest on the amount saved out of a given income is neglected. Although it means that the third equation becomes the multiplier equation, which performs such queer tricks, nevertheless this second amendment is a mere simplification, and ultimately insignificant.[4] It is the liquidity preference doctrine which is vital.

For it is now the rate of interest, not income, which is determined by the quantity of money. The rate of interest set against the schedule of the marginal efficiency of capital determines the value of investment; that determines income by the multiplier. Then the volume of employment (at given wage-rates) is determined by the value of investment and of income which is not saved but spent upon consumption goods.

It is this system of equations which yields the startling conclusion, that an increase in the inducement to invest, or in the propensity to consume, will not tend to raise the rate of interest, but only to increase employment. In spite of this, however, and in spite of the fact that quite a large part of the argument runs in terms of this system, and this system alone, *it is not the General Theory*. We may call it, if we like, Mr Keynes's *special theory*. The General Theory is something appreciably more orthodox.

Like Lavington and Professor Pigou, Mr Keynes does not in the end believe that the demand for money can be determined by one variable alone – not even the rate of interest. He lays more stress on

[4] This can be readily seen if we consider the equations

$$M = kI, \quad I_x = C(i), \quad I_x = S(I),$$

which embody Mr Keynes's second amendment without his first. The third equation is already the multiplier equation, but the multiplier is shorn of his wings. For since I still depends only on M, I_x now depends only on M, and it is impossible to increase investment without increasing the willingness to save or the quantity of money. The system thus generated is therefore identical with that which, a few years ago, used to be called the 'Treasury View'. But Liquidity Preference transports us from the 'Treasury View' to the 'General Theory of Employment'.

it than they did, but neither for him nor for them can it be the only variable to be considered. The dependence of the demand for money on interest does not, in the end, do more than qualify the old dependence on income. However much stress we lay upon the 'speculative motive', the 'transactions motive' must always come in as well.

Consequently we have for the General Theory

$$M = L(I, i), \quad I_x = C(i), \quad I_x = S(I).$$

With this revision, Mr Keynes takes a big step back to Marshallian orthodoxy, and his theory becomes hard to distinguish from the revised and qualified Marshallian theories, which, as we have seen, are not new. Is there really any difference between them, or is the whole thing a sham fight? Let us have recourse to a diagram (Fig. 8.1).

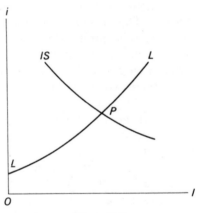

Figure 8.1

Against a given quantity of money, the first equation, $M = L(I, i)$ gives us a relation between Income (I) and the rate of interest (i). This can be drawn out as a curve (LL) which will slope upwards, since an increase in income tends to raise the demand for money, and an increase in the rate of interest tends to lower it. Further, the second two equations taken together give us another relation between Income and interest. (The marginal-efficiency-of-capital schedule determines the value of investment at any given rate of interest, and the multiplier tells us what level of income will be necessary to make savings equal to that value of investment.) The curve IS can therefore be drawn showing the relation between Income and interest which must be maintained in order to make saving equal to investment.

Income and the rate of interest are now determined together at *P*, the point of intersection of the curves *LL* and *IS*. They are determined together; just as price and output are determined together in the modern theory of demand and supply. Indeed, Mr Keynes's innovation is closely parallel, in this respect, to the innovation of the marginalists. The quantity theory tries to determine income without interest, just as the labour theory of value tried to determine price without output; each has to give place to a theory recognising a higher degree of interdependence.

III

But if this is the real 'General Theory', how does Mr Keynes come to make his remarks about an increase in the inducement to invest not raising the rate of interest? It would appear from our diagram that a rise in the marginal-efficiency-of-capital schedule must raise the curve *IS*; and, therefore, although it will raise Income and employment, it will also raise the rate of interest.

This brings us to what, from many points of view, is the most important thing in Mr Keynes's book. It is not only possible to show that a given supply of money determines a certain relation between Income and interest (which we have expressed by the curve *LL*); it is also possible to say something about the shape of the curve. It will probably tend to be nearly horizontal on the left, and nearly vertical on the right. This is because there is (1) some minimum below which the rate of interest is unlikely to go, and (though Mr Keynes does not stress this) there is (2) a maximum to the level of income which can possibly be financed with a given amount of money. If we like we can think of the curve as approaching these limits asymptotically (Fig. 8.2).

Therefore, if the curve *IS* lies well to the right (either because of a strong inducement to invest or a strong propensity to consume), *P* will lie upon that part of the curve which is decidedly upward sloping, and the classical theory will be a good approximation, needing no more than the qualification which it has in fact received at the hands of the later Marshallians. An increase in the inducement to invest will raise the rate of interest, as in the classical theory, but it will also have some subsidiary effect in raising income, and therefore employment as well. (Mr Keynes in 1936 is not the first Cambridge economist to have a temperate faith in Public Works.) But if the point *P* lies to the left of the *LL* curve, then the *special* form of Mr Keynes's theory

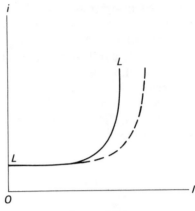

Figure 8.2

becomes valid. A rise in the schedule of the marginal efficiency of capital only increases employment, and does not raise the rate of interest at all. We are completely out of touch with the classical world.

The demonstration of this minimum is thus of central importance. It is so important that I shall venture to paraphrase the proof, setting it out in a rather different way from that adopted by Mr Keynes.[5]

If the costs of holding money can be neglected, it will always be profitable to hold money rather than lend it out, if the rate of interest is not greater than zero. Consequently the rate of interest must always be positive. In an extreme case, the shortest short-term rate may perhaps be nearly zero. But if so, the long-term rate must lie above it, for the long rate has to allow for the risk that the short rate may rise during the currency of the loan, and it should be observed that the short rate can only rise, it cannot fall.[6] This does not only mean that the long rate must be a sort of average of the probable short rates over its duration, and that this average must lie above the current short rate. There is also the more important risk to be considered, that the lender on long term may desire to have cash before the agreed date of repayment, and then, if the short rate

---

[5] *General Theory*, pp. 201–2.

[6] It is just conceivable that people might become so used to the idea of very low short rates that they would not be much impressed by this risk; but it is very unlikely. For the short rate may rise, either because trade improves, and income expands; or because trade gets worse, and the desire for liquidity increases. I doubt whether a monetary system so elastic as to rule out both of these possibilities is really thinkable.

has risen meanwhile, he may be involved in a substantial capital loss. It is this last risk which provides Mr Keynes's 'speculative motive' and which ensures that the rate for loans of indefinite duration (which he always has in mind as *the* rate of interest) cannot fall very near zero.[7]

It should be observed that this minimum to the rate of interest applies not only to one curve *LL* (drawn to correspond to a particular quantity of money) but to any such curve. If the supply of money is increased, the curve *LL* moves to the right (as the dotted curve in Fig. 8.2), but the horizontal parts of the curve are almost the same. Therefore, again, it is this doldrum to the left of the diagram which upsets the classical theory. If *IS* lies to the right, then we can indeed increase employment by increasing the quantity of money; but if *IS* lies to the left, we cannot do so; merely monetary means will not force down the rate of interest any further.

So the General Theory of Employment is the Economics of Depression.

IV

In order to elucidate the relation between Mr Keynes and the 'Classics', we have invented a little apparatus. It does not appear that we have exhausted the uses of that apparatus, so let us conclude by giving it a little run on its own.

With that apparatus at our disposal, we are no longer obliged to make certain simplifications which Mr Keynes makes in his exposition. We can reinsert the missing *i* in the third equation, and allow for any possible effect of the rate of interest upon saving; and, what is much more important, we can call in question the sole dependence of investment upon the rate of interest, which looks rather suspicious in the second equation. Mathematical elegance would suggest that we ought to have *I* and *i* in all three equations, if the theory is to be really General. Why not have them there like this:

$$M = L(I, i), \quad I_x = C(I, i), \quad I_x = S(I, i)?$$

[7] Nevertheless something more than the 'speculative motive' is needed to account for the system of interest rates. The shortest of all short rates must equal the relative valuation, at the margin, of money and such a bill; and the bill stands at a discount mainly because of the 'convenience and security' of holding money – the inconvenience which may possibly be caused by not having cash immediately available. It is the chance that you may want to discount the bill which matters, not the chance that you will then have to discount it on unfavourable terms. The 'precautionary motive', not the 'speculative motive', is here dominant. But the prospective terms of rediscounting are vital, when it comes to the *difference* between short and long rates.

Once we raise the question of Income in the second equation, it is clear that it has a very good claim to be inserted. Mr Keynes is in fact only enabled to leave it out at all plausibly by his device for measuring everything in 'wage-units', which means that he allows for changes in the marginal-efficiency-of-capital schedule when there is a change in the level of money wages, but that other changes in Income are deemed not to affect the curve, or at least not in the same immediate manner. But why draw this distinction? Surely there is every reason to suppose that an increase in the demand for consumers' goods, arising from an increase in employment, will often directly stimulate an increase in investment, at least as soon as an expectation develops that the increased demand will continue. If this is so, we ought to include I in the second equation, though it must be confessed that the effect of I on the marginal efficiency of capital will be fitful and irregular.

The Generalised General Theory can be set out in this way. Assume first of all a given total money Income. Draw a curve CC showing the marginal efficiency of capital (in money terms) at that given Income; a curve SS showing the supply curve of saving at that *given* Income (Fig. 8.3). Their intersection will determine the rate of interest which makes savings equal to investment at that level of income. This we may call the 'investment rate'.

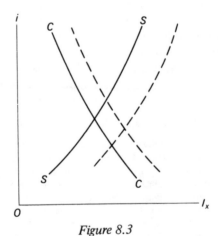

Figure 8.3

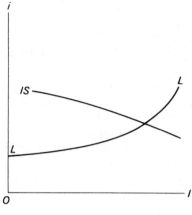

Figure 8.4

If Income rises, the curve *SS* will move to the right; probably *CC* will move to the right too. If *SS* moves more than *CC*, the investment rate of interest will fall; if *CC* more than *SS*, it will rise. (How much it rises and falls, however, depends upon the elasticities of the *CC* and *SS* curves.)

The *IS* curve (drawn on a separate diagram, Fig. 8.4) now shows the relation between Income and the corresponding investment rate of interest. It has to be confronted (as in our earlier constructions) with an *LL* curve showing the relation between Income and the 'money' rate of interest; only we can now generalise our *LL* curve a little. Instead of assuming, as before, that the supply of money is given, we can assume that there is a given monetary system – that up to a point, but only up to a point, monetary authorities will prefer to create new money rather than allow interest rates to rise. Such a generalised *LL* curve will then slope upwards only gradually – the elasticity of the curve depending on the elasticity of the monetary system (in the ordinary monetary sense).

As before, Income and interest are determined where the *IS* and *LL* curves intersect – where the investment rate of interest equals the money rate. Any change in the inducement to invest or the propensity to consume will shift the *IS* curve; any change in liquidity preference or monetary policy will shift the *LL* curve. If, as the result of such a change, the investment rate is raised above the money rate, Income will tend to rise; in the opposite case, Income will tend to fall; the extent to which Income rises or falls depends on the elasticities of the curves.[8]

When generalised in this way, Mr Keynes's theory begins to look very like Wicksell's; this is, of course, hardly surprising.[9] There is indeed one special case where it fits Wicksell's construction absolutely. If there is 'full employment' in the sense that any rise in Income immediately calls forth a rise in money wage rates; then it is *possible* that the CC and SS curves may be moved to the right to exactly the same extent, so that IS is horizontal. (I say possible, because it is not unlikely, in fact, that the rise in the wage level may create a presumption that wages will rise again later on; if so, CC will probably be shifted more than SS, so that IS will be upward sloping.) However that may be, if IS is horizontal, we do have a perfectly Wicksellian construction;[10] the investment rate becomes Wicksell's *natural rate*, for in this case it may be thought of as determined by real causes; if there is a perfectly elastic monetary system, and the money rate is fixed below the natural rate, there is cumulative inflation; cumulative deflation if it is fixed above.

This, however, is now seen to be only one special case; we can use our construction to harbour much wider possibilities. If there is a great deal of unemployment, it is very likely that $\partial C/\partial I$ will be quite small; in that case IS can be relied upon to slope downwards. This is the sort of Slump Economics with which Mr Keynes is large concerned. But one cannot escape the impression that there may be other conditions when expectations are tinder, when a slight inflationary tendency lights them up very easily. Then $\partial C/\partial I$ may be large and an increase in Income tend to *raise* the investment rate of interest. In these circumstances, the situation is unstable at *any* given money rate; it is only an imperfectly elastic monetary system – a rising LL curve – that can prevent the situation getting out of hand altogether.

---

[8] Since $C(I, i) = S(I, i)$,

$$\frac{dI}{di} = -\frac{\partial S/\partial i - \partial C/\partial i}{\partial S/\partial I - \partial C/\partial I}$$

The savings investment market will not be stable unless $\partial S/\partial i + (-\partial C/\partial i)$ is positive. I think we may assume that this condition is fulfilled.

If $\partial S/\partial i$ is positive, $\partial C/\partial i$ negative, $\partial S/\partial I$ and $\partial C/\partial I$ positive (the most probable state of affairs), we can say that the IS curve will be more elastic, the greater the elasticities of the CC and SS curves, and the larger is $\partial C/\partial I$ relatively to $\partial S/\partial I$. When $\partial C/\partial I > \partial S/\partial I$, the IS curve is upward sloping.

[9] Cf. *General Theory*, p. 242.

[10] Cf. G. Myrdal, *Monetary Equilibrium* (see above, p. 44).

These, then, are a few of the things we can get out of our skeleton apparatus. But even if it may claim to be a slight extension of Mr Keynes's similar skeleton, it remains a terribly rough and ready sort of affair. In particular, the concept of 'Income' is worked monstrously hard; most of our curves are not really determinate unless something is said about the distribution of Income as well as its magnitude. Indeed, what they express is something like a relation between the price-system and the system of interest rates; and you cannot get that into a curve. Further, all sorts of questions about depreciation have been neglected; and all sorts of questions about the timing of the processes under consideration.

The *General Theory of Employment* is a useful book; but it is neither the beginning nor the end of Dynamic Economics.

9

Hawtrey on Bank Rate

This was a review of R. G. Hawtrey's *Century of Bank Rate* (1938), which appeared in the *Manchester School*, April 1939. My own *Value and Capital* had lately been published, so I seized upon the opportunity, given to me by Hawtrey, to test out, empirically, some of my own ideas. It is a pretty crude piece of empirical testing; I am not at all proud of it. (I did what is largely the same job a good deal better in a much later paper, 'The Yield on Consols', which appeared in *Critical Essays in Monetary Theory*.) I have, however, thought it proper to include it in this collection, since it shows, already at near the date of *Value and Capital*, that I was seeking to apply a theory of the structure of interest rates which (whether it is Hawtreyan or Keynesian or neither) should go a bit deeper than anything which could be represented on an *IS–LM* diagram. There is not much more to it than that.

Hawtrey wrote a reply to my review (published in the October issue of the same journal). Apart from making some very pertinent criticisms of my 'econometrics', he was mainly concerned with maintaining that what he had said about what he called 'psychological reactions' was not new, but had always been an integral part of his theory. As I have said in a later paper on Hawtrey (included in *Economic Perspectives*) 'it is indeed true that there are references to them in his earlier works, but I do not feel that he had previously given them the same emphasis. They had not got over to me, and in that I am sure that I had plenty of company; it is clear, to take the leading example, that they had not got over to Keynes himself'. This later paper gives a more rounded expression of my view on Hawtrey than is given by this review.

The main differences between Mr Hawtrey's theory of monetary control and Mr Keynes's theory may perhaps be summed up under the following heads.

1. Mr Hawtrey believes that changes in business activity are primarily induced by changes in the willingness of traders to hold stocks of commodities. An increase in this willingness raises prices, that increases incomes, that raises the demand for consumption goods, and then (by the 'acceleration Principle') that raises, much more than proportionately, the demand for durable capital to make new consumption goods. Similarly a decrease in the willingness to hold stocks lowers activity in the consumption goods trades, and then (the Acceleration Principle working in reverse) that diminishes activity in the constructional trades, so long as there is any activity to diminish.

Mr Keynes, on the other hand, believes that it is the demand for durable capital goods which is the prime mover. Changes in that demand affect incomes directly (the 'Multiplier'), and the change in incomes affects the demand for consumption goods at a second remove. Changes in stocks are mainly incidental to the general changes in business activity, in whose causation they play only a secondary role.

2. Mr Hawtrey believes, at least as a matter of historical fact (and historical fact tends to merge into theoretical necessity), that the control of business activity by the monetary authority takes place mainly through the direct pressure of Bank Rate (and the other short-term rates which are associated with it). Bank Rate affects the willingness of traders to hold stocks, and a change in that sets going the chain of repercussions noted above. He does not believe in any important direct repercussion of monetary policy on the long-term rate of interest.

Mr Keynes believes that monetary control operates mainly through the long-term rate. Changes in the long-term rate affect the demand for capital goods, and thus set going *his* chain of repercussions.

These being the main differences between the rival points of view, let us consider how far the discussion is advanced by the new evidence which Mr Hawtrey presents.

I

Probably the most interesting part of the new evidence is that which concerns the influence of Bank Rate on the long-term rate of interest. This is a matter which can be probed very far by the careful use of financial statistics, and here Mr Hawtrey does seem to be on strong ground. In his *Treatise on Money*[1] Mr Keynes made an examination of some of the figures, and they seemed to show a close agreement between the movement of the yield on consols and the movement of Bank Rate, when fluctuations in Bank Rate were damped down to one-quarter of their true amplitude. On this apparent correlation he based his view that while monetary control affects short rates much more than long rates, nevertheless it operates mainly through long rates. Mr Hawtrey makes it clear that this correlation is only valid for the particular years which were being considered – and that, even within these years, it is mainly a matter of the short period 1919–24. The far wider sample taken by Mr Hawtrey (*A Century of Bank Rate*) does not show much trace of the correlation. Changes in Bank Rate have indeed affected the price of consols a little, it is true; but the effect has generally been limited to one or two points, mere ripples that leave the long-term rate substantially unaffected. It is very hard to believe, in the face of Mr Hawtrey's evidence, that monetary policy has in fact generally operated on business through the medium of the long-term rate, since its immediate effects on the long-term rate have nearly always been negligible.

There have, however, been certain important movements of the long-term rate during the century; how does Mr Hawtrey explain these movements? Here I am afraid I find his explanation unsatisfactory. He holds that changes in the long rate are simply reflections of changes in the activity of business; more active business, and the expectation of rising prices, stimulates the demand for capital; less active business depresses the demand, and the liquidation of stocks, which takes place when business is declining, provides a new source of funds, which may find their way into the bond market, and force down the long-term rate of interest from the supply side. Now these things may happen, there are some movements in long-term rates which may possibly be explained in these lines; but I find it very hard to believe that they are of such dominating importance as Mr Hawtrey suggests.

There is, however, another possible explanation. It is not alluded to by Mr Hawtrey, but since it is very much the most probable explanation from the theoretical end, I have been tempted to see whether the facts he provides bear it out. I have therefore to ask the reader's pardon for intruding a little investigation of my own, whose inclusion has swollen the present review into an article. Still it is a matter strictly pertinent to the issue on which this book turns.

[1] Vol. II, pp. 352ff.

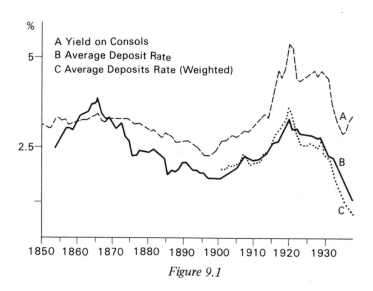

%

A Yield on Consols
B Average Deposit Rate
C Average Deposits Rate (Weighted)

5—

2.5—

A

B

C

1850 1860 1870 1880 1890 1900 1910 1920 1930

Figure 9.1

If one draws out into a chart (see Fig. 9.1) the statistics of the yield on consols since 1850 (subject to a correction, which is suggested by Mr Hawtrey, and which I have incorporated in the figure, this seems to be the best representative of the long-term rate of interest), one thing at least is immediately apparent.[2] The long-term interest rate is not one of those things (like the wholesale price index, or the output of pig-iron, or even Bank Rate itself) which swing about violently in the course of a Trade Cycle. It is quite extraordinarily insensitive to the Cycle – so much so, that if anyone were to remove from the curve A those oscillations about the trend which do seem to be correlated with cyclical fluctuations, he would rarely have to adjust the annual figure by more than $\frac{1}{10}$ of 1 per cent, so that the shape of the curve would be left substantially unaltered. The oscillations are so small that it is very hard to believe that they have any substantial economic importance. Consequently, one is driven to the conclusion that the important movements in the long-term rate have nothing to do with the Trade Cycle at all.

If this is so, it not only rules out Mr Keynes's theory of the dependence of the long-term rate on immediate monetary policy (at

[2] From 1880 to 1888 the yield on consols was prevented from falling below 3 per cent by the approaching conversion. Mr Hawtrey therefore gives figures of the prices of $2\frac{1}{2}$ per cent annuities for this period, and I have made a rough adjustment of the curve with their aid. (The uncorrected figures I have taken from J. Stafford, 'The Future of the Rate of Interest', *Manchester School*, 1937, p. 137.)

least as a historical generalisation), it also rules out Mr Hawtrey's theory of its dependence on current trade activity. Both of these are short-period theories, and the long-term rate turns out to be extremely insensitive in the short period. The only forces which do seem to move it are long-period forces.

Leaving out of account the little oscillations, the important things about the movement of the long-term rate can be summarised very briefly. (1) From 1850 to 1875 it was practically steady at about $3\frac{1}{4}$ per cent. (2) Between 1875 and 1897 it fell steadily from that level to about $2\frac{1}{4}$ per cent. (3) From 1897 to 1914 it rose steadily back to $3\frac{1}{4}$ per cent again. (4) Between 1914 and 1922 it rose from $3\frac{1}{4}$ to $5\frac{1}{4}$ per cent in 1920, and then relapsed to about $4\frac{1}{2}$ per cent. (5) It remained at about $4\frac{1}{2}$ per cent from 1922 to 1931. (6) After 1931 it fell to about 3 per cent in 1935, since which time it has been rising – a good deal more steeply than it used to do in its minor fluctuations of the nineteenth century – towards $3\frac{1}{4}$ per cent.

A curve drawn out on these instructions, with no more information than I have given in the preceding paragraph, would not diverge from the actual curve to any obviously important extent. Thus a valid theory of the long-term rate has got to explain these movements, and also to explain why these are the only significant movements to be found.

The reason why most movements of Bank Rate have had so little influence on the price of consols is clearly because they are expected to be short-lived. To quote Mr Hawtrey:

Suppose that at a centre where the normal short-term rate is 3 per cent, the short-term rate rises to 7 per cent. If it could be foreseen that the rate would remain at 7 per cent for three months and then drop to 3 per cent again, the extra cost of holding a long-dated security with borrowed money would be offset by a fall in price equal to 1 per cent (the equivalent of 4 per cent per annum for a quarter of a year). A trader who had intended to raise a bank advance to cover some expenditure might be led by a rise of the interest on the advance from 3 per cent to 7 per cent to sell Government securities instead. But if the price of the Government securities fell from 100 to 99, he would not gain by doing so. A similar calculation would apply to anyone who has to choose either between long-term and short-term borrowing or between long-term and short-term lending (pp. 147–8). [At 99 the yield to perpetuity of a 3 per cent stock is only 3.03 per cent.]

If the long-term rate is to be affected by more than this sort of amount, there must either be a change in people's expectations about the *normal* future level of the price of consols, or a change in the degree of certainty with which they hold such expectations, or a change in their relative willingness to bear the sorts of risks involved in short and long lending respectively. Of these possibilities the first is the only one which it is at all easy to test statistically; I propose to show that it probably does cover a large part of the explanation.

Just as the current price of consols is influenced a little by current short rates, so the price expected to rule at any future date may be thought of as determined in part by the short rates expected to rule at that date. If short rates are expected to have returned to 'normal' after three months, the price of consols may also be expected to have returned to 'normal'; but if high or low money rates are expected to continue for a long period, the price of consols expected to rule in the future will be affected by the continuance – and the present price of consols will be affected much more than it could have been affected by a change in short rates which was not expected to continue for long.

What seems to happen is not of course that people think they can foresee the course of short rates very far into the future; but that prolonged experience of high or low rates gradually alters their ideas of what rates can be considered 'normal'. This is the clue by which we can hope to get a statistical measure of the 'normal' rate.

Curve B in Fig. 9.1 has been drawn up in the following way. For each of the years 1854 to 1938 I have calculated the average of Bank Rate for the ten years ending in the year in question. (The number ten was taken very arbitrarily; it seemed necessary to take a period long enough to even out ordinary ups and downs of definitely cyclical character, and beyond that, not to take a period so long as to include too much 'ancient history'.) This average I have taken to represent, as well as any mechanically calculated figure can represent it, what it would have been reasonable for anyone to have regarded as the normal level of Bank Rate at each particular time. But then, remembering that the choice before most investors is not between investing long and investing short at Bank Rate, but between investing long and holding their money on deposit in a bank,[3] I have subtracted from this *normal Bank Rate* the amount by which the deposit allowances of London banks fell below Bank Rate at each

---

[3] Of course, other investors have other short-term markets at their disposal, so that consideration of the bank-deposit alternative alone cannot give the whole picture. Nevertheless, for the purposes of our present enquiry, we have only to pick out the most sensitive margin of choice; it seemed very likely that this would prove to be the margin between government securities and bank deposits; and the results of assuming it to be so seem sufficiently good to afford some verification of the hypothesis.

date. (That is to say, I have deducted 1 per cent before 1886, 1½ per cent between 1886 and 1920, 2 per cent after 1920. It should be emphasised that these deductions were made after calculating the retrospective averages, since it seemed reasonable to assume that the changes in the deductions would be regarded as permanent, as soon as they had taken place). Curve B may then perhaps be taken – in its general trend, though not of course in the rather meaningless fluctuations about the trend which is exhibits – as representing what could reasonably have been regarded as the normal level of interest on bank deposits over the period.[4]

As soon as one compares the curve B (the normal short rate) with A (the long-term rate of interest), the close consilience of the two curves in the middle period (1975–1914) becomes very striking. While A declines from 3¼ to 2¼ per cent, B declines with it from 2½ to 1¾ per cent, while A rises back to 3¼ per cent, B rises back to 2¼ per cent. During these years, there is an agreement between the trends of the curves which is too close to be accidental. The long rate equalled the normal short rate *plus* a risk-premium, and the risk-premium was very steady throughout the period, although one can notice a tendency for it to increase a little after 1900.

But although the fit is so good in the middle period, it is less good after 1914, and almost wholly absent before 1875. During the first twenty-five years covered by our chart, while the long-term rate was remaining so remarkably steady at about 3¼ per cent, the normal short rate (as we have calculated it) rose from 2½ per cent in 1854 to 3¾ per cent in 1866, falling back to 2½ per cent in 1875. That is to say, the very high money rates which marked so many of the years 1854–66 had scarcely any effect on the long rate of interest. For more than half of these thirteen years the rate on bank deposits exceeded the yield to perpetuity on consols, and yet it is evident that consols were not sold out sufficiently to make much impression on their price. How are we to explain the discrepancy?

---

[4] In the actual calculation of curve B, I have also had to make some allowance for the fact that deposit allowances have not always followed the extremer movements of Bank Rate. According to King (*History of the Discount Market*, p. 299), they did follow mechanically on almost all occasions, prior to 1886, so I have made no correction up to that date. Between 1886 and 1920, when the normal deduction was 1½ per cent, it became only 1 per cent when Bank Rate was 2 per cent, and rose to 2 per cent when Bank Rate was over 5 per cent. I have allowed for this by neglecting reductions of Bank Rate to 2 per cent, and treating 6 per cent Bank Rate as 5½ per cent, and so on. Similarly, when after 1932, the deduction became (temporarily, as has been understood) 1½ per cent from a 2 per cent Bank Rate, I have replaced the 2 per cent Bank Rate by 2½ per cent when calculating the average, and then deducting the full *normal* 2 per cent.

It can, I think, be explained on two grounds. For one thing, the attractive force of the high money rates may have been considerably less at that time than later on. In those days consols were the safe investment *par excellence*. Treasury Bills did not exist, so that short Government obligations were negligible. The banks had not yet acquired their later reputation of solidity, so that the high rates they offered on deposit alarmed the investor as much as they attracted him. Consols were definitely the safest income-yielding asset which there was. They might fluctuate a little in capital value, but the chance of a large loss was quite negligible – and that was more than could be said of any other security whatever. Had not England passed through a major European struggle – the Crimean War – with only a négligible addition to the National Debt, and with her credit entirely unscathed? No wonder it was hard to attract the investor out of consols.

It is true that the high deposit allowances led to a rapid growth of the London banks,[5] but even so, the volume of their deposits was only a fraction of the size of the National Debt. Under the circumstances, the London banks must have expanded much further, if risk-factors had not been operating against bank deposits and in favour of consols.

If the effect on consols was damped down for this reason, it becomes intelligible why they never moved sufficiently for people's expectations about their future value to be disturbed to any appreciable extent. In this connection it is important to remember that the possibility of conversion was always only just round the corner. Though Goschen did not actually convert till 1888, Gladstone had attempted a conversion in 1853. Consols fell in the meantime, but they never fell sufficiently to rule out the probability that conversion would be attempted again some time or other, and to prevent people from regarding a price not too far below par as the natural level at which consols should stand.

These are, of course, conjectures; yet they do perhaps permit us to conclude that the discrepancy between 1850 and 1875 must be explicable on some such lines. They are at least quite consistent with what happened in the next phase.

Dear money had failed to drive people out of consols, so that the long-term rate of interest continued immovable until (about 1875) money rates had remained low for such a long time that funds began to move *into* consols on an important scale. There were of

---

[5] King, *op. cit.*, p. 174.

course no obstacles to a movement in this direction. As the normal level of deposit rates dropped lower and lower, the long-term rate followed it down, until by 1897 the yield on consols was no more than $2\frac{1}{4}$ per cent.

The rise in the long-term rate which ensued after that was clearly encouraged by borrowing for the South African War, and by the Colonial Stock Act of 1900. The early stages of the rise seem to have been directly induced by these factors, and their effect remains noticeable in a perceptible widening of the gap between our curves – it had been hardly more than $\frac{1}{2}$ per cent before 1900, and it rises to about 1 per cent after 1900. Nevertheless, after 1902 the curves keep very well in step; the further rise in the long-term rate between then and 1914 is matched by a corresponding rise in the normal short rate.

After 1914 the fit of the curves is distinctly less good, though there remains a very distinct resemblance. I do not think that this diminution of correlation is at all surprising, in view of the extremely disturbed conditions throughout this later period. First the War, then the episode of the restored Gold Standard in the twenties, then the deterioration of political relations in the thirties – it would not be surprising if in these conditions people's ideas about the normal level of interest rates came to be governed less by the mere average of past experience, and more by the fluctuations of current economic and political conditions. This is so much the most probable explanation of an increased divergence between the series that I have thought it worth while to calculate a revised index of the normal short rate, in which I give current and very recent experience a heavier weighting. I have therefore taken, not the unweighted average of Bank Rate for the previous ten years, but a weighted average, in which the current year is given a weight of 15, last year 9, the year before 8, the year before 7, and so on. Making deductions to deposit rate as before, we get the curve C, which I have drawn on the chart for the years after 1900. Up to 1914 it gives a less good fit than Curve B, but after 1914 its fit is very appreciably better, being, I think, really very good indeed.[6]

---

[6] The weights were chosen on the following principle. I first of all decided to weight past years according to a descending series, in order to diminish the importance of the remoter past, as compared with the recent past. This suggested weights 10, 9, 8, 7. I then decided to mark up the actual current rate a little, since the part it plays is of a different character to that of a past rate, however recent. A mark of 15 gave the best fit – as is not surprising, since it gives the current rate the same weight of one-quarter as it was given in Mr Keynes's calculation.

Thus the correlation found by Mr Keynes between current Bank Rate and the current long-term rate seems to be accounted for; it is a consequence of post-war disturbance. But in addition to the greater influence of current rates in determining the normal level, there is another characteristic of the situation after 1920 which emerges strongly from our chart, and which has perhaps even greater significance. It is the startling increase in the gap between the long rate and the normal short rate. As we have seen, this gap had already increased to 1 per cent before the war; during the war it rose to nearly 2 per cent, and *it has failed to come down below that level at any later time.*

How is one to explain this widening of the gap? I can only suggest a number of reasons which may have contributed. One is purely technical – the 1920 reduction of London deposit allowances from $1\frac{1}{2}$ per cent below to 2 per cent below Bank Rate. I have allowed for this fully in my B and C curves, since it is operative for those individuals and concerns who are confronted with the alternative – either to buy Government stock, or leave their money on deposit in a London bank. However, there are other investors (such, for instance, as the banks themselves[7]) for whom the choice is different, since the short market which confronts them is different. It is therefore possible that my B and C curves have been brought down rather too low.

I do not think one ought to give very much weight to this;[8] and in any case it only accounts for part of the widening. Other factors must have been at work. One of these may have been a greater sense of the risk involved in holding consols, due to the heavy fall between 1914 and 1920. Consols were becoming a more speculative security. This can be checked up to some extent by using the earlier experience of the South African War. The fall in consols during the Great War was not actually of a very different order from that which took place on the earlier occasion. Anyone who bought consols early in 1899, and sold early in 1902 would have lost £19 in capital against interest earnings of £8 5s 0d; anyone who bought in 1914 and sold in 1920 would have lost £30 against interest earnings of £15. The widening of the gap which followed in the two cases was more or less in relation to the severity of the shock. Nevertheless, in the South African War case, the great widening took place *before* there had been any appreciable hardening of normal short rates – so that

---

[7] Or, at the other extreme, investors in savings banks and building societies.

[8] The earlier reduction of deposit allowances (in 1886) only had a transitory effect on the gap.

this factor cannot explain the initial widening; and further, if this were really the main cause, one would expect the gap to narrow as memory of the fall became more distant, and in neither case can any such narrowing be traced.

It seems much more plausible to attribute the widening mainly to the sheer weight of the Debt: South African War debts plus new trustee securities in the first case, War Debt in the second. It seems hardly possible to doubt that the size of the debt created in the War of 1914 must have had a great effect on the gap. Not only were Government securities more speculative; they had enormously increased in volume. Before 1914 the internal Debt of the central government was only about one-third of the National Income; from 1922 onwards it exceeded the National Income by about 50 per cent.[9] This vast mass of debt has had to be held somehow; and it could not possibly be held unless investors, on the average, were prepared to hold a larger proportion of their assets in the form of long-term Government stock than they had been used to do. Now it is reasonable to suppose that investors will be prepared to hold a certain proportion of their wealth in the form of Government stock, even if the yield on such stock is very low; its relative security and ready marketability make it an attractive second line of liquid reserves. But if they are required to increase their holding beyond a certain point, they will require a better return; they do not need any more of it as a liquid asset, it has to compete more and more with other property as a source of income.

This explanation of course also holds for the renewed widening of the gap which has occurred owing to the fall in Government stock since 1935. We should expect the gap to widen as soon as there is an expectation of a further extensive bout of public borrowing.

[9] Alternatively, we may observe that holdings of British and Foreign Government securities have increased from about 10 per cent of the total private property of Great Britain to about one-quarter – according to the estimates of H. Campion (*Public and Private Property in Great Britain*, p. 65). Total Trustee securities would presumably have increased in something like the same proportion.

10

A Note on Robertson

There was a review of Dennis Robertson's *Essays in Monetary Theory* (1940) which I published in *Economica* in 1942. I am not including it in this collection, but it is rather well known, so must be represented in some way or other. I shall confine myself to giving some extracts, to which I shall add some explanations.

The first thing which has to be said is that by that time I was feeling myself to be much closer to Robertson than to any other economist who was my senior. Most of the papers which have gone before in this collection had been criticised by him, before or after their publication; I owed him quite a debt. I felt myself to be temperamentally much closer to him than I was to the Keynesians, from whom he had separated himself so sharply after 1936, or a bit earlier. But my position was on the Keynes side of his. I regretted the feud, for such indeed it had become.[1] I really wrote the review for him, to persuade him to turn away from the polemics which I felt had become sterile, and to turn to more constructive work, on the basis of what I felt he had already achieved.[2]

I picked out three *positive* doctrines, which I associated (I still think quite rightly) with him. They were (1) his theory of Saving and Investment, (2) his theory of the Rate of Interest, and (3) his Doubled theory of Trade Crises. I quote some parts of what I said about them.

[1] See my description of it, from Robertson's point of view, in the Memoir I wrote of him, which is printed as an introduction to the paperback version of his *Essays on Money and Interest* (1966).

[2] That is what I meant by the 'Seurat' simile, for which I have been quite properly rebuked by A. Coddington (*JEL*, September 1979). I thought it might be more persuasive if I went against that kind of criticism in general, that if I said straight out that Robertson's own version was missing the mark.

(1) Disputes about the meanings of Savings and Investment may appear to be arid, but they are in reality of immense importance, because they involve decisions about definition which determine the whole course on which theory will subsequently proceed. Robertson's name is particularly associated with a set of definitions which seem to have pleased hardly anyone but himself, and which seem to have satisfied even him in diminishing degree as time has gone on, for in the later essays he sets less store by them. This does not look a very promising beginning. But when one looks, not at the precise form of the definitions, but at the class to which they belong, the picture is very different. 'On my definition, Saving and Investment are not necessarily equal, and it is on the difference between them that the *movement* of the price-level (not, as in Mr Keynes's scheme, the *state* of the price-level as compared with some normal state) depends.' That protest was made against the Keynes of the *Treatise*; it stands, with changed emphasis, against the *General Theory*; but since the time of the *General Theory* the need for definitions of the Robertson sort has been increasingly felt.... I still do not feel that his definitions will quite do; they were concerned too much with constancy of the price-level, too little with employment, income and 'business activity' which have come to seem more important. It is even uncertain whether we want equilibrium between Saving and Investment to mean *constancy* of anything – at least in any stricter sense than is implied in Marshall's short-period equilibrium; a situation of which we can say that it would go on indefinitely if other things remained equal, although in fact we know that mere lapse of time is bound to alter some of the things we have put into the pound....

(2) My own feeling still is that what he has to say about the Rate of Interest is less important than what he says about Saving and Investment; but I say it without much confidence, though I notice that in some moods he has a 'private heresy' in that direction himself. He has no difficulty in showing that the theory of Liquidity Preference is a very rough and ready description of the way the forces governing interest work; he emphasises (as I should readily agree) that there are three margins at work, not two; he shows very conclusively that whereas a change in the supply of money due to the creation or destruction of bank credit operates first on interest and thence on prices, a change in the velocity of circulation operates directly on prices and thence on interest. It is clear that the Liquidity Preference technique is not very well adapted for dealing with this latter case, since it can only treat dishoarding into commodities as if it were dishoarding into securities combined with dissaving. There is a disturbance of the Saving–Investment relation as well as a disturbance of the Liquidity Preference relation; both 'curves' have shifted, so you cannot tell where you are....

(3) The doctrine that a trade boom can come to an end in two main ways – on the one hand through rises in costs, ultimately traceable to the inelasticity of the credit system (not an unnatural inelasticity, but a natural and desirable inelasticity, which fulfils a useful function in preventing the boom from degenerating into true inflation); on the other hand through the depressing effects of successful capital accumulation, operating in a world where the appearance

of innovations is discontinuous – this doctrine, firmly held through good and evil days, is the very core of Robertson's teaching. It was first foreshadowed in his *Study of Industrial Fluctuations*, more than twenty-five years ago; at that time it was grounded more in inductive research than in high-flown theory. That it should have been possible, at that time, to distil such a conclusion out of the welter of facts seems to me proof of almost miraculous insight. Nowadays, but not then, it has become easy to reach it along the theoretical route; though perhaps even now the majority of economists are too pre-occupied with one sort of danger (whichever it is they fancy) to keep the other clearly in mind at the same time. . . .

I am not at all proud of these passages, but it would have been wrong to suppress them. It will be important to show, for what follows, that in 1942 – after 'IS–LM' (essay 8 above) and after *Value and Capital* – I was still in quite a muddle. How I extricated myself from it, bit by bit, will appear in following essays. The first bit of clarification came while I was writing the Rist review (essay 11) which immediately follows.

Where I had been quite right was in emphasising the importance, in Robertson's thinking, of the fact that he began from fluctuations – the subject of his first book, published in 1915. Fluctuations which he looked at as *temporary* divergences from an 'equilibrium'. Fluctuations not only of output and employment, but also of prices. The classical, or Victorian, trade cycle, with these fluctuations going together, could then be taken for granted. Moderation, or damping, of these fluctuations, was the central (relevant) objective of policy.

In their work in the twenties, both Robertson and Keynes had shared this outlook. It is apparent in Robertson's *Banking Policy and the Price-Level* (1926) and in Keynes's *Treatise* (1930). They had also shared a view of price-formation, inherited from Marshall, according to which all markets were what I would now call flexprice markets. Prices responded immediately (or as nearly immediately as matters) to fluctuations in demand and supply. This had indeed made it quite hard to see how output and employment *could* fluctuate, when prices were so flexible – a point which in his early books caused Robertson quite a lot of trouble.

It caused both of them a lot of trouble when they came to appreciate the importance of saving and investment. For if, in any period in which there were changes in outputs, prices must also be changing, the income of the period will be different according as it is valued at opening or at closing prices; and what does one do about that when one is comparing what actually happened with what would have happened under different assumptions? Robertson got quite tied up with this in 1926 and Keynes did not fully extricate himself from it in the *Treatise*.

In the *General Theory* Keynes formally cut the knot by assuming (when he needed to) that prices, and, of course, wages, remained constant during the period, so that the money value of saving and investment could stand for the value in real terms. Robertson would not accept that, he would ask (as many have done since) how is it possible that prices should stay constant when demands and supplies are varying. In order that that question should be answered, it was necessary that there should be a proper theory of the working of a fixprice market. That did not exist in 1942; it lay a long way ahead.[3]

But this was no more than a part of his trouble. The *General Theory* was certainly taken by Robertson to imply an abandonment of the whole 'cyclical' approach to which he remained committed. He still wanted to think of the problem of employment as a problem of fluctuations about an 'equilibrium' – which was not only to be such that in it activity was to be *normal*, but also such that prices were stable at a *normal* level. He felt that to abandon that equilibrium was to abandon all concern with price stability.

I don't personally think that Keynes himself had abandoned all concern for price stability, but in feeling that his work, in the hands of others, would tend in that direction, Robertson was surely right. And I still think that he was right in judging that tendency to be very dangerous. But he never quite explained, even to himself, just why it was dangerous.[4] Perhaps that is why the campaign which he waged, over the rest of his life, on behalf of monetary stability, did not make more impression. It won him many friends in banking circles, among people who had the same feeling as he had; but it left him, among economists, rather isolated.

It should be emphasised that it was *normal* stability of prices that he stood for – not absence of fluctuation, but absence, or near-absence, of trend. Though fluctuation should be moderated, it could not be avoided. This was a condition which (he held) had existed, at least approximately, before 1914; and he believed that it had continued to exist between the wars, in Britain and in America, after the immediate post-war flurry. In spite of the violence of the depression of 1930, the price-level in the late thirties had come back

[3] My own version of what I think to be that proper theory is in *CG* (1965), chs. 7–9; and see below pp. 231–5.

[4] I now believe that it was precisely Robertson's preoccupation with flexprice markets which prevented him from giving a clear explanation why inflation is dangerous. See below, p. 279.

to be not so far from what it had been in the more stable of the years before 1929. He clearly thought that after 1945 the same phenomenon would be repeated, if the holy cords were not cut by those who were gnawing at them! Of course, he lived long enough (he died in 1963) to know that that was not to be. But it was not, in the first post-war years, an unreasonable expectation; as will be seen,[5] I shared in it myself.

[5] See below, essay 14.

11

A French View of Money

This was a review article on the book by Charles Rist, *History of Monetary and Credit Theory*, which had appeared in 1940 in an English translation. My review appeared in the *Economic History Review*, in a number that is dated 1943, but cannot have appeared until the end of that year or even afterwards. I was writing, as will be seen, for historians; but that does not make this paper unsuitable for inclusion in this collection, since my contention that monetary theory is 'in history' is a theme which I have maintained throughout.

The 'cyclical' bias which, following Rist, I have here attributed to British economists, is that which, in my comments on the preceding essay (10) I have particularly associated with Robertson. As will appear in that which follows (essay 12) it might equally have been associated with Pigou. Rist would have found it in Hawtrey and in the Keynes of the *Treatise*; it may be that he was right there also. The later Keynes, and his followers, were deviating from it in one direction; Rist would diverge in the other. For him it was not hard enough. One must remember his experience, so like ours in the days of slipping standards after 1970. 'Pauvre franc' I remember hearing a countryman say in 1937 as he spun a coin on a table, 'tu es devenu bien cher!'

I had not met Rist when I wrote this review. But I did see him in Paris at the end of the war, and I know that he appreciated my endeavour to understand his position.

The history of economic theory is a subject which can be approached from several different angles. In the first place, it can be studied, as the normal historian would study it, as one element in the general *Weltanschauung* of those periods (such as the early nineteenth and perhaps the middle twentieth centuries) when economists have played a significant part in the formation of public opinion. In the second place, it can be studied for its own sake as the evolution of a technique, in the spirit of the historian of Greek mathematics or Renaissance painting. These two approaches are very different, but they have this in common, that they can be perfectly objective. There is, however, a third approach which, in the field of monetary theory, is still perhaps the most common. The author, having himself developed strong views on the problem, turns to the work of his predecessors partly to fortify himself in his own views, partly to explain to himself how it has been possible for other people to come to hold views different from his. In this case the past is studied not for its own sake, but directly for the light it may be expected to throw upon present controversy.

Professor Rist's *History of Monetary Theory* is an extremely interesting and important book, but it is definitely a history of the third type, so that to the pure historian it may perhaps be found a little disappointing. Professor Rist holds views on monetary theory, and perhaps still more on monetary policy, which are very different from those of what may now be regarded as the dominant school of English opinion. To a very large extent this book is a defence of his views. The great figures of the past are invoked, not for their own sakes, but because some of them (Thornton and Tooke in particular) can be enlisted under the banner borne by Professor Rist, and because others (Ricardo, Marshall and the early Wicksell) can be called upon to explain those strange aberrations of opinion which have culminated in what are considered by Professor Rist to be the dangerous fantasies of Hawtrey and Keynes.[1]

So much must be said by way of criticism; yet it has to be admitted that the particular points at issue in this theoretical controversy are such that real light is thrown upon them by this historical approach. Monetary economics, try as economists will to reduce it to a 'pure theory', is in fact the study of a particular social institution, and an institution which has inevitably developed in different ways in different social *milieux*. English theories of money, however 'general' they may claim to be, do not in fact escape the influence of English monetary experience; though it is true that they are made a little less insular than might be expected from that background by the peculiar intimacy of English financial relations with another country of exceedingly different institutions, the United States. It is in practice exceedingly easy for the English economist to forget these

[1 It was Keynes of the *Treatise* that Rist has in mind. He had had no opportunity, when he wrote his book, to study the *General Theory*.]

limitations; and, therefore, whatever one may think of Professor Rist's conclusions as 'general' principles, there can be no doubt that the book in which he advances them is very salutary reading. For in spite of the learning which he displays in the field of English monetary literature, the experience out of which his views have been distilled is evidently French experience. It is highly salutary to discover how very different the monetary problem appears when it is seen against the French background, especially when it is seen by one whose insight into these matters, taken on its own ground, is not markedly less than that of his great English antagonists.

Perhaps the most striking way in which the French background affects the whole approach to the monetary problem is in the type of monetary disorder which is the centre of interest. To the modern English economist, the prime object of monetary policy is to abate the violence of trade fluctuations; the same would have been true for the most part even in the nineteenth century, though in those days the objective would have taken the more specialised form of diminishing financial crises. Obviously this concentration of interest springs from English experience. Trade fluctuation has been the main English form of monetary disturbance, even the disturbances of 1919–22 could be explained in large measure along the usual cyclical lines. With the French economist, the concentration of interest is entirely different. Although France experienced many of the classical fluctuations of the nineteenth century, they were for the most part less intense than in England (and *a fortiori* America). To the modern mind their impress has been almost entirely effaced by that of the currency disorders of 1914 onwards, which obviously belong to the same pattern as those under Louis XV and as the Assignats, and have no relation at all to the cyclical scheme. It is thus most interesting to find that while English and American economists unanimously envisage the events of 1930–1 as a peculiarly violent cyclical crisis, to Professor Rist they appear as nothing else at all but a logical consequence of the currency disorders after 1914.

This difference of approach reflects itself (as such differences will) in a difference of definition. Since the English economist is mainly interested in fluctuations of credit, he has steadily widened his definition of money, first (with Ricardo) to include bank notes, and later on to include bank deposits as well. He can do this with impunity because he is forgetting the possibility that deposits may not be convertible into notes, while if notes are not convertible into gold, then so much the worse for gold! All that matters to him are changes in the price-level, in the value of paper money and paper credit in terms of goods; and he can concentrate attention on the short-term fluctuations in this value, because he takes for granted a situation in which confidence in some measure of long-term stability is never lost.

Professor Rist's problem, on the other hand, is one of a situation in which that fundamental confidence cannot be taken for granted. It is only with an effort that he can bring himself to realise that there does exist across the Channel a Planners' Paradise which has demonstrated, in 1797 and again in 1931, that the suspension of convertibility need not imply a failure of confidence in the solidity of paper money. Things are not like that in France. The Bank of France, he reminds us, has never been able to develop an Open Market Policy like that of the Bank of England; and the reason is that it has never believed in its heart that its government's promise to pay made a reliable asset. The central problem for him is the relation between solid money (gold) and *ersatz* money (paper), the paper which needy governments compel their people to use instead of gold, in spite of the fact that (excepting in England) it is deficient in one of the basic requisites of a sound money, the capacity to act as a store of value. The Englishman may widen his definition, but the Frenchman must narrow his, in order to emphasise distinctions which seem to him vital.

In other places than this, one would be tempted to expatiate upon the significance of this analysis of Professor Rist's for the organisation of international monetary arrangements. It does not appear that Professor Rist has yet been in a position to make any pronouncement upon the Keynes and White plans of 1943; nevertheless, from this book (in spite of the fact that the original French version of it appeared in 1938) it is possible to deduce very clearly what his criticisms of those plans would be. They would constitute a more damaging attack than any which has appeared up to the present. In the first place, he would question whether it would be possible for any government to regard its holding of 'bancor' (or whatever it was called) as being really as good as gold. Gold can always be exchanged for any other asset if a particular seller can be found who is willing to sell, and that is usually easy enough; 'bancor' could only be so exchanged if the transaction was one which met with the approval of the international 'bank'. However thoroughgoing the assurances offered that such approval would always be forthcoming for all ordinary transactions, one could not be sure that there would not be a difference of opinion in some particular case. And so it would be preferable to have gold. He would, therefore, maintain that it would be impossible for any mechanism of international credit to assuage the gold hunger which must be expected to arise after the war, both because of the rise in gold incomes in many countries and because of general unsettlement making for liquidity preference. It is also quite evident what would be the nature of Professor Rist's alternative plan. He would recommend a devaluation of all currencies in terms of gold (and he would not mind very much if the devaluation could only be secured along the route of competitive depreciation), devaluation which would have to be carried to such a point as would make the additional value of gold in terms of commodities sufficient to provide all the 'liquidity' which anyone needed.

These, however, are matters for the future; and although, as Professor Rist rightly says, economic man lives in the future, it is the past which is the field of the economic historian. There are several matters in the interpretation of the past on which considerable light is thrown by his book; on one of them I should like to make a few comments.

With his historical approach and his 'gold' bias, it is natural that Professor Rist should be attracted by the still imperfectly solved problem of the mechanism by which the nineteenth-century gold discoveries exercised their economic effects. From his point of view, gold mines are the perfect form of international public works; in the booms of the eighteen-fifties and sixties, and again in the nineteen-hundreds, we have superb examples of their effectiveness. They are the perfect public works, because while like other public works they generate income which expands effective demand, they avoid the disadvantage of productive investment (that sooner or later it will increase the effective supply of finished goods, and will then diminish the incentive to further investment) and they also avoid the disadvantage of ordinary unproductive investment (that it diminishes the creditworthiness of the financing authority). Now this line of argument seems to me essentially right; it can hardly be doubted that the exceptionally prolonged activity of these two boom periods was due to the steady stimulus provided by the goldfields. Further, the view that the gold acted mainly by increasing effective demand, and only to a very secondary extent by lowering interest rates (more correctly, by retarding the rise in interest rates), seems wholly borne out by the fact.

Up to this point I feel myself in agreement with Professor Rist; but there are several ways in which he seems to carry his argument too far. Most of these are due to what appears to be an excessive emphasis on these monetary factors in the economic development of the time. One may grant the importance of the effect of the gold

discoveries on business activity and on employment, without necessarily rejecting the classical contention of Cairnes and Marshall that
such sterile activity as goldmining would not have any beneficial
effect on the average real wages (in communities other than those
in which the gold mines were situated) of such persons as remained
in employment throughout. Marshall is mocked by Professor Rist for
his statement to the Gold and Silver Commission that the prosperity
of Great Britain in the fifities and sixties was due to Free Trade. If,
however, we reflect that to Marshall 'prosperity' is much more likely
to have meant high real wages than high employment, it does not
seem clear that Marshall was wrong. As far as one can tell from the
fragmentary statistics which are all that seem to be available for that
period even in Clapham and Bowley,[2] the notable rise in real wages
after the Hungry Forties took place in the years 1847–50, *before the
gold influx started*, and most evidently must have been due to the
repeal of the Corn Laws. From 1850–60 no distinctive rise in real
wages seems to be traceable. Real wages certainly rose a little in the
export trades (and this is interesting verification of Professor Rist's
account of the mechanism), but in other trades there may well have
been a fall.

Again, it has been shown by Dr Rostow in his important articles
in this *Review*,[3] that the 'shortage' of gold in the seventies and
eighties provides a very unconvincing explanation of the 'Great
Depression' of those decades. Professor Rist is himself inclined to
adduce the low interest rates of that period as a proof that gold
production exercises its effect on the side of effective demand, not
through the money market; but in this case it is not clear that the
evidence is in favour of his exact thesis. The traditional 'gold'
explanation of the Great Depression has been based, not on the very
moderate check to gold production, but on the increased demand for
gold from the new gold standard countries of Germany and the
United States; now it is not clear how this demand, being a change in
liquidity preference, could operate on effective demand except by
raising interest rates. If it did not do so, but instead of that interest
rates remained abnormally low,[4] then there must have been some

---

[2] J. H. Clapham, *Economic History of Great Britain*, vol. II (1932), ch. 1; A. L. Bowley, *Wages in the United Kingdom in the Nineteenth Century* (1900).

[3] 'Investment and the Great Depression', *EHR*, VIII; 'Investment and Real Wages', IX.

[4] It has been claimed by Mr Hawtrey (*A Century of Bank Rate*, 1938, pp. 100–5) that the shortage of gold at this period did produce financial stringency, indicated, not by persistently high interest rates, but by a rise at an unduly early stage of each attempted recovery, so that the recovery was nipped in the bud. This is theoretically possible; but it is

powerful force diminishing the demand for capital; the check to gold production hardly looks sufficient.

Now it is on such a matter as this that Professor Rist's determined refusal to mix up the problems of money and credit (instructive though it is in some ways) seems to play him false. It is true, as we have seen, that an increase in effective demand due to an expansion of productive investment will be followed, sooner or later, by an expansion of the supply of commodities; while an increase in effective demand due to gold discoveries will not be so followed. But it is not true that in consequence the first can be dismissed as a 'short-period phenomenon' in comparison with the second. When the investment consists in the construction of durable goods which take a long time to complete, the increase in the supply of finished goods, which follows on a particular wave of investment, may be considerably delayed and only come forward gradually. When the investment consists in the opening-up of new lands, the reflux may be delayed so long that it is quite as 'long-period' a phenomenon as the exhaustion of the impulse of gold discoveries. The distinction between the two sorts of stimulus is important but it is not a temporal distinction, as Professor Rist is inclined to make it.

In the particular case of the seventies and eighties, the most plausible explanation of the 'depression' seems to be nearer to Dr Rostow's than to Professor Rist's or to Mr Hawtrey's. The railway-and steamship-building of 1840–70 had been, in the end, a vastly more productive form of investment than any of those which had led the way in the earlier phases of industrialism. But they were slow to develop their full potentialities. When at length they did so, it became possible, for a couple of decades, to reap the harvest of the earlier investment in the form of a greatly increased output of consumption goods which needed a minimum of further investment to bring them to fruition. Whence there followed the two phenomena whose conjunction impressed Marshall: a low level of activity and rapidly rising real wages; though it may be that he was inclined to overstress the necessity of the conjunction.

It so happened that at the same time there was a potential shortage of gold. But the potential shortage never became an actual shortage because the activity of industry never rose to such a point as to

---

questionable whether Mr Hawtrey has not been too much influenced by the movements of *bank rate*. This was a period in which the Bank's control over the market was notoriously ineffective. The movements adduced by Mr Hawtrey look suspiciously like vain jabs at a brake that won't act.

impose a real strain upon the gold supply. We may agree with Professor Rist that the slackening in effective demand from the gold-getters was one cause of this; but there was another, probably more important, cause to which he gives too little attention.

This review has been largely concerned with differences of opinion: differences about theory and about policy, differences which ulti-mately spring from the different national backgrounds. But these are differences which needed to be brought to the surface; their ventila-tion is a necessary preliminary to understanding. The publication of this book is in fact a notable step towards better understanding between English and French economists. It makes one hope that when the Channel is open again we shall see a renewal of that intellectual co-operation which did exist in the nineteenth century but has been so lamentably lacking, thus far, in the twentieth.

12

A Review of Pigou

This review of A. C. Pigou's little book, *Lapses from Full Employment* (1945), appeared in the *Economic Journal* in December 1945. I do not claim much for it; but I have included it because Pigou's book is such a particularly clear example of the 'cyclical' approach, which, as has been shown in essay 10 and the prefatory note to essay 11, needs to be identified if the writings of that period are to be understood.

'Some parts of the argument,' says Professor Pigou in his preface to this book, 'unpractised readers – and maybe others also – will almost certainly find difficult.' The present reviewer must candidly admit that he, for his part, found the argument very difficult; not so much in matters of detail, but for the difficulty which one has at a first reading in seeing where the argument is tending. When at least one has puzzled it out, one sees that various clues are provided in the preface; but in view of the oblique approach to the subject which is adopted in the text, a more direct statement of objectives in the preface would have been exceedingly helpful.

The obstacle which stands in the way of one's understanding is that a large part of the argument (indeed, all the first half of the essay) runs in terms of the relation between wages (money wages) and employment, itself a highly controversial matter, on which more than one book of this size could easily be written. But the book is not really *about* the relation between wages and employment; the discussion of that subject is ultimately needed only as background. What the argument ultimately leads up to is an even more topical question – the opposition between the 'Beveridge' policy of diminishing unemployment by expanding demand and the 'White Paper' policy of stabilising demand. It is true that we are given a hint about this in the preface, for Professor Pigou expresses himself to be broadly sympathetic with the White Paper policy; but he does not explain that the arguments which follow are directed to showing that a policy which stabilises demand will not merely stabilise employment, but will also increase employment on the average. If this can be shown, it presumably reinforces the 'White Paper' as against the 'Beveridge' prescription; but Professor Pigou has left his readers to draw such practical deductions for themselves.

The view about the relation between wages and employment which is needed as background looks at first sight very different from the Keynesian view, which has almost been taken for granted in much recent discussion. But the difference between Professor Pigou and the Keynesians is nowadays not one of analysis, it concerns the estimation of social probabilities, which mountains are regarded as inflexible, which it is possible by taking thought to move. Sir William Beveridge has admitted that 'there is a real danger that sectional wage bargaining, pursued without regard to its effects on prices, may lead to a vicious spiral of inflation.' In Professor Pigou's world such sectional bargaining is taken for granted. Because trade unions and other labour organisations will push up wages when they see an opportunity, the full employment equilibrium (which Sir William Beveridge sets as his ideal) is not an equilibrium at all. It is bound to be upset by pressure on the wage level. If the monetary system were to be elastic (as Sir William Beveridge would like to make it) the vicious spiral would be unavoidable. But in fact the monetary system is not perfectly elastic. Equilibrium is therefore found at a point where there is enough unemployment to stop the pressure for higher wages. Analytically it is true to say that the unemployment is caused (via the interest mechanism) by the strain which is put upon the monetary system by the high wages. But this strain cannot be prevented by doctoring the monetary system except at the price of an inflationary breakdown. The *amount* of unemployment is therefore more a consequence of the wage-policy pursued than of the characteristics of the monetary system.

If trade unions and wage boards were less insistent in their demands, then (according to this construction) unemployment would be diminished; if there were 'thoroughgoing competition in the labour market', unemployment would be absent altogether. These consequences follow from Professor Pigou's construction, and they are emphasised by the title which he has chosen for his book; it seeks to underline the thesis that there is a *tendency* to full employment in a free market, so that unemployment is a 'lapse' from this ideal equilibrium. But though these consequences are emphasised in the title, they do not seem to embody the practical moral which is to be drawn. In the greater part of the analysis, wage policy of the sort described is a datum; the question under discussion concerns the means which remain over for minimising unemployment if it has to be taken for granted that labour organisations will behave in this way.

It might appear at first sight as if no such means could exist. If wage-rates are only kept from rising by the existence of unemployment, anything which diminishes unemployment will result in a rise in wages, and the rise in wages will continue until the equilibrium amount of unemployment is restored. Looked at in this way, the approach would seem to result in pure fatalism. Actually, Professor Pigou's position is not so fatalistic. This is because he assumes a certain amount of rigidity in wage-rates; wages are fixed, not altogether with respect to the amount of unemployment existing at the moment, but more with respect to the amount of unemployment to be expected over a longer period. The amount of unemployment is therefore not entirely a matter of wage-policy; it can also be affected by fluctuations in the demand for labour about the normal level, even though it cannot be affected by long-run changes in the demand for labour as a whole.

On these assumptions, the existence of fluctuations is likely to increase the amount of unemployment (that is to say, it will raise the average amount of unemployment over the whole fluctuation above what it would have been if the demand for labour had been constant at its average level) in three distinct ways. In the first place, if the fluctuation is large enough to cause the demand for labour in certain occupations to be greater at the top of the boom than the supply of labour to those occupations, some of the demand at the crest of the wave will go to waste; the extra employment at the top will therefore fail to offset the lost employment at the bottom. (On this point, an obvious objection – that shortage of labour at the top may cause demand to be postponed rather than lost altogether – does not seem to have been answered. The connection, which Professor Pigou would presumably admit, between fluctuations in trade as a whole, and fluctuations in the demand for durable goods, would seem to make this possibility a real one.) Secondly, since in practice the demand for labour is likely to fluctuate more in some occupations than others, the high liability to unemployment will reduce the numbers of workers who will be attached to the more fluctuating occupations, so that a particularly large amount of their boom demand will go to waste. Thirdly, since wages move up more easily than they move downwards, the average level of wage-rates will probably be higher in a fluctuating economy than in one with a steadier demand. For this reason also average unemployment would be higher.

These principles hold without qualification in conditions where wage-rates are inflexible in the course of a fluctuation, and where the distribution of labour among occupations does not respond to the changes in demand in the course of a fluctuation. The greater the responsiveness to the fluctuations on the part of wage-rates and of the distribution of labour among occupations, the less extra unemployment the fluctuations will cause. The damping effect of these adjustments is, however, subject to an important proviso. The responsiveness of wage-rates and labour movements must be properly timed; if the response is lagged, so that wages rise when they ought to be falling, or labour moves in when it ought to be moving out, naturally that makes matters worse.

'The Theory of Economics does not furnish a body of settled conclusions immediately applicable to policy. It is a method rather than a doctrine....' The familiar words come back to one's mind when one finds Professor Pigou wearing the Keynesian hat and producing from it such a very un-Keynesian (or un-Beveridgian) rabbit. Is it a convincing rabbit? It is a bit sour in the face, but for my part I do not find it altogether unconvincing, save on one point. The arguments adduced on pp. 22–5 to show that in the long period there must be some significant elasticity to the demand curve for labour, even if the interest mechanism will not work, are probably acceptable in themselves; but is it legitimate to carry them over to the study of fluctuations? Is it not probable that at the bottom of a slump the relevant demand curve will be nearly, if not quite, inelastic over the relevant range? This could be admitted by Professor Pigou without substantial damage to his main theses; but he could not then maintain the paradox that even in a slump there is a 'tendency to full employment'.

Part III
Preparations

13

World Recovery after War –
a Theoretical Analysis

PREFATORY NOTE
This was originally written to be presented to the Economic Society of Copenhagen, Denmark, in March 1947. But it was not delivered on that occasion, since my plane was delayed for three days at London on account of weather (!) and I was unable to get to the meeting at the date which had been fixed. I had already agreed to publish the paper in the *Economic Journal*, where it appeared in the June number. So when I did get to Copenhagen (by sea) in the December following, I had to provide a new paper, which is in substance that which follows (essay 14). I would like that essay to be regarded as an appendix to this.

In spite of its being written in terms of a particular situation, which has happily proved to be transitory, there is much that this essay contains which I still feel to be of permanent value. It has not only been in those immediate post-war conditions that inelasticity in the supply of consumption goods (or at least of a major component of the consumption goods basket) has been of importance; nor is it only in such conditions that the influence of consumption goods prices on wage-settlements has been important. The changes that have to be made in the Keynesian system when these things are allowed for are worked out in this essay. This is the first place where I worked them out properly, but I have often been obliged to return to them since.[1] Whether, when one has made these amendments, one is still a Keynesian, is a matter of definition.

There is, however, no doubt that, having made them, I had come much nearer to Robertson. He recognised this himself, in a paper which he published the following year.[2] He there quoted with delight

---

[1] See, for instance, below pp. 309ff.

[2] 'What has Happened to the Rate of Interest?', reprinted in *Utility and All That* (1951), pp. 80–94.

the last sentence of my paper, 'The rate of interest is the price of time'; but it was not only that bit of rhetoric which showed that we had come much closer together. When I had said that 'it is not obvious that a condition of immediate full employment is a sensible objective in the conditions we are studying,'[3] I had given him the main thing he had been striving for, all those years.

It should, however, be noticed that the main reason why I had come so close to him was that I could then share his view that there was a fair chance that, after reconstruction, some sort of monetary stability would be restored. That was why I could take a view of interest rate policy which was similar to his. The way in which my thinking developed when I lost confidence in that restoration will appear in essays 19 and 24.

I

I propose in this paper to try to construct a theoretical framework which may help us in our thinking about the condition of the world at the present time. This may seem an odd thing to do, but in fact it is the kind of thing economists always have to do, either in their private thoughts or in face of the world, in order to make up their minds what they think ought to be done, what policies ought to be supported and which rejected. Ricardo's *Principles* is a piece of model building of this sort in face of the Corn Law crisis in England; Keynes's *General Theory* a piece of model-building in face of the Great Depression. Keynes did in fact give us another model even more exactly parallel to the kind of thing I want to attempt in this paper – the theory of a war economy which he used as a foundation for his 'How to pay for the War'. I cannot indeed hope in this paper to get as far as Keynes could be relied upon to do; I shall try to diagnose, but I shall not venture far into the field of prescription. Perhaps I shall tempt you to do some prescribing on the basis of my diagnosis; or perhaps the diagnoses themselves will give you enough to discuss.

There are several ways in which the present economic problem is especially refractory to the kind of analysis I want to give it – reasons which I will mention at the start, so as to show you that I am not unaware of the inevitable shortcomings of my treatment. These difficulties become especially apparent when the present problem is contrasted with the war mobilisation problem with which

[3] In note 6 (p. 156) below.

Keynes was concerned in 1939–40. That was a national problem; this is fundamentally international, for what we have to do now is to recreate the international economy, and the processes of doing that cannot be understood on national lines. Yet today it is particularly difficult to think internationally, not only because of the ordinary political and psychological reasons, but because of another reason which specially concerns the economist. On the national level it is fairly easy for the economist to think realistically, because he has excellent statistical material against which to check up his ideas. On the international level it is always more difficult, and at present it is peculiarly difficult, because of the abnormal lack of international statistics. One's thinking is therefore bound to be more abstract than one would desire.

Once again, in 1939–40 one was proceeding from a relatively free market economy, whose principles of action were fairly well understood. Economic incentives were then fairly well usable, even if one preferred not to use them. The normal stimuli were always just round the corner. Today the whole world is caught up in a maze of more or less effective regulations; to predict the consequences of any step is therefore abnormally difficult. It may well be maintained that to make any sort of an economic model of a world in this situation is an absurdity. Doubtless there is much in this; but it may nevertheless be claimed that this difficulty is to some extent offset by the other one. The world as a whole is likely to work in a way which is more predictable economically than any one country may do. This is partly because a relatively free market economy has already been restored in some important countries, notably the United States; and partly because the world is still a world of separate national units, who are likely to pursue self-interest in their dealings with one another, whatever the principles on which affairs are conducted within the national frontiers.

With these qualifications and warnings duly set out, I will proceed to construct my model. It will be obvious that it owes a great deal to Keynes – as anything written by an English economist on matters of this sort is bound to do – but in developing it I shall have to emphasize some points of theory which Keynes did not emphasize, maybe because they were not relevant to the conditions he had in view. But it seems to me that they decidedly are relevant now; and perhaps they ought always to have had more attention than Keynes gave them, if the *General Theory* was to have the generality it claimed.

When the problem of reconstruction is reduced into terms of the basic categories of economic theory, it seems to come out as follows. During the war a large proportion of the productive resources of the world were withdrawn from what we may call the 'normal productive process' – production with the aim of satisfying the present or future wants of individual consumers – and were used for the special purposes of war. During the war, it was proper to reckon that war use as an economic use, to consider waging war as a part of the process of production, and to reckon the national product of a particular nation as including its war output as well as its output of 'peace-time' goods and services. But as soon as war is over – at least as soon as it is really over – that ceases to be correct. It becomes far more useful and far more conductive to clear thinking, if we cease to regard 'war output' or what remains of it as production. It is no longer an end of the productive process; it is a mere cost, like the expenditure of a business on fire extinguishers. It might be a good thing if we marked the change by shaping our definitions of national income accordingly.

What is the state of the 'normal productive process' at the moment when it again becomes *the* productive process, so that it can again take the centre of the stage? After a prolonged war, it will be a very sorry one. Its capital equipment will have suffered from war destruction, both directly and because it will have been raided for war purposes; even more important, maybe, is the fact that for years it has been starved of labour so that it has gradually run down. For years consumption has run ahead of production, in the relevant sense; and after prolonged consumption of capital we must expect not only that its current productivity will be low, but that to start it up again in full production will be no easy matter.

The one thing that does happen, when hostilities cease, is that the labour which had been withdrawn, now becomes again available. Thus the typical situation, at the beginning of a period of post-war reconstruction, is that a labour supply, itself not much below normal, is being applied to a capital supply much below normal. Static analysis would suggest to us that in these conditions both the average and the marginal product of labour would be abnormally low. Doubtless there is much truth in this view, as we see by all the current outcry about low productivity; but this is not a case in which static analysis is sufficient – we are dealing with a situation which is the reverse of static. In the short period labour co-operates with capital, and a shortage of capital diminishes the productivity of labour; in the longer period, on the other hand, labour produces capital goods, and the shortage of capital equipment means that there is an abnormal amount of opportunity for labour to produce things which will be highly useful in the long run; it is the short-run productivity of labour which is so low, the long-run marginal productivity is abnormally high.

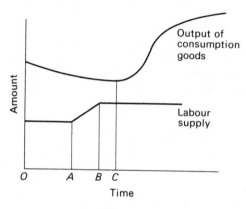

Figure 13.1

Let us try to put this position into schematic form. In Fig. 13.1 we measure time horizontally, beginning at a point a little earlier than the cessation of hostilities. The lower line measures amount of labour available for the 'normal productive process'. It begins at a low level while the war is still on, then rises sharply during *AB*, the phase of demobilisation, and finally settles down to its higher 'normal level'. The higher line represents the output of consumption goods, as we may expect it to develop if the process of reconstruction is carried through efficiently. It is initially at a low level, corresponding to the low supply of labour during the war. It may be constant at that low level, or may actually be falling; it will almost certainly have been falling at some stage during the war, and the fall may be continuing during the last stages of hostilities.[4] This then, is the course of the upper curve during the phase *OA*, and we must expect the same trend to continue after the point *A* is reached, for

---

[4] It is, of course, true that during the late war some of the belligerents, notably the United States, showed at least an apparent increase in real consumption. It should, however, be remembered that the usual index-numbers have a persistent tendency to exaggerate real consumption in times of shortages. We are becoming familiar with this phenomenon in Britain, and it is at least equally important in America. That there has been a fall in consumption, for the belligerents as a whole, will not I think be questioned.

the additional supplies of labour cannot produce a significant addition to the supply of consumption goods at once; it will take time before they can make themselves felt. It is only at a point C, which may be before or after B, according as the demobilisation is slow or rapid, that the additional supplies of labour will change the trend of the output curve. From this point C onwards the output curve will turn upwards, gradually at first, but later perhaps with increasing momentum. Finally, perhaps, when the process of reconstruction is complete, it will merge into a normal upward trend, corresponding to normal economic progress and capital accumulation.

Let us now consider in more detail the economic situation at an early stage of this process – to fix the ideas, let us say at point B. At this stage the output of consumption goods is still mainly determined by the low input of labour during the war; the present high input of labour is contributing (perhaps very powerfully contributing) to a future high output, but it can do little for present output. In Keynesian language, we may say that it is technically necessary to employ the increased labour force, now available, in making investment goods rather than consumption goods. Thus in spite of the fact that the labour force, previously used for war purposes, has been returned to the 'normal productive process' it does not as yet produce additional consumption goods. Thus in terms of incomes and prices, the war situation still persists, consumption still has to be kept down to an abnormally low proportion of income, if inflation is not to develop.

There are, of course, several ways in which the necessary restriction of consumption spending can be brought about. In the first place, the direct war-time restrictions on consumption can be maintained; people can be obliged to save a large proportion of their incomes from sheer inability to find anything on which they are allowed to spend their money. In the second place, consumption may be restricted by the pressure of taxation, the war-time taxes being maintained, not to finance war expenditure, but to finance this abnormal reconstruction investment. Even if the investment is itself carried out by private entrepreneurs, the taxation method can still be used; for if the taxes provide a budget surplus, used to repay a part of the war debt, the Government does in fact put the corresponding part of the funds it collects at the disposal of entrepreneurs. Finally (or in the third place), it is possible that the requisite saving may be induced by a rise in the prices of consumption goods relatively to the wage-level. For the abnormal profits so induced are very likely to be saved – even if only in the form of reinvestment – so that the requisite proportion of saving to income can be induced in this way. But of course it will often happen that this simple use of the price-mechanism will unsettle the wage-level, so that the use of this method becomes an incident in an inflationary process, and in no way a cure.

Among these various techniques which may be used to maintain monetary stability (or lessen instability) during the early stages of reconstruction I have not listed the rate of interest; and I have done this deliberately, because I do not believe that for the problem we are at present discussing it can be of any help. It is extremely difficult to believe that when consumption has to be kept at a level which is much below what people feel they can afford with the incomes they are earning, and which is also much below the level to which they were accustomed in the past, and to what they feel themselves to be entitled, that in these conditions they can possibly be persuaded to save adequately by a financial inducement of any reasonable size. It is true that a high rate of interest would check investment, but in the conditions postulated, this is an extremely bad way of maintaining monetary stability. Suppose, for instance, that at prices which are low enough not to set off a wage–price spiral, the value of the consumption goods which can be produced is only 70 per cent of the social income at full employment, while the proportion of their incomes which people are prepared to save, at the greatest possible interest inducement, is only 15 per cent. It would then be possible to maintain equilibrium between saving and investment by using the rate of interest to cut down investment; but the results of doing so would be very serious. For the social income would have to be cut so that consumption came to 85 per cent of it; now if 70 per cent of full employment income is 85 per cent of actual income, actual income must be about 82 per cent of full employment income, and therefore investment must be cut down from 30 per cent of full employment income to about 12 per cent, the remaining 18 per cent being lost in unemployment. Not only would a serious unemployment problem be likely to result from such a policy as this, but the whole process of recovery would be by so much slowed up.[5]

[5] The effects on the Keynesian system of introducing the assumptions (1) that the supply of consumption goods, in terms of wage-units, is inelastic; (2) that the level of money wages does not depend only on employment, but also on the prices of consumption goods – both of which assumptions seem to be appropriate to post-war conditions – are very far-reaching. If the prices of consumption goods cannot rise beyond a certain point in relation to wages without setting off a wage–price spiral, this implies that the price-level

This is no doubt the consideration which has been present in the minds of those economists who have urged the maintenance of a cheap money policy even in potentially inflationary conditions; and it would be impossible to deny that it is a very weighty consideration indeed. But there is another aspect of the matter which has received far too little attention, and which tells in the other direction. This neglect is not surprising, because it corresponds to one of the most serious gaps in Keynes's *General Theory*; in consequence people who think in terms of that theory just do not have it brought to their attention. Other economists, such as Mr Hawtrey and Professor Hayek, have taken the point into account; for myself I am not convinced that it is of much importance for the under-employed economy which Keynes was studying, but in conditions of full employment and shortage, such as those we are now living in, the case seems to be quite different.

Let us go back to our diagram (Fig. 13.1). At position *B*, as we have been saying, current consumption cannot be increased very much by employing extra labour in the production of consumption goods; the additional labour now available must be used for what, from the point of view of the current period, is investment. But having decided that it must be used for investment, we have not made the only decision which needs to be made about its use; there is still the question of the sort of investment for which it is to be used. And there is one question of this character which is directly relevant even to the elementary matters which were all we could represent in our diagram. The labour which is being used for investment can be used for investment of longer or shorter period, that is to say, the additional consumption goods, whose production is made

---

of consumption goods, measured in terms of wage-units, cannot rise above a determinate maximum. It then follows, if the supply of consumption goods is inelastic, that the value of consumption, in terms of wage-units, cannot pass a determinate maximum. The value of the social income in terms of wage-units, which governs the level of employment, then depends on the multiplier in the opposite way to Keynes's. The larger the proportion of income which is saved (in the sense of not spent on consumption), the larger will be the size of the social income corresponding to this fixed maximum level of consumption, and the larger in consequence will be the maximum level of employment.

It is true that this maximum potential volume of employment may fail to be actual, since investment may be restricted below the level at which consumption spending would reach its maximum in terms of wage units. And it is also true that as recovery progresses, the consumption maximum will increase so that after a certain stage in recovery the maximum level of employment, based on these considerations, will pass the available labour supply, even if saving is not deliberately stimulated; and when that happens, we are back in a Keynesian world.

possible by the new input of labour, may come in early or come in late. And surely it is a matter of tremendous importance which way this decision is made. Of course, it is bound to be made with an eye on all sorts of technical rigidities which cramp the choice very seriously; some things which are badly wanted cannot be produced except after an exceptionally long time; the possibilities of 'hurrying-up' are therefore distinctly limited. But it can hardly be denied that some such possibilities do exist, and that it is a matter of first-rate importance that any such opportunities should be taken.

This for two reasons in particular. On the one hand, the period before the output curve turns decidedly upward is in any case a period of strain, with inflationary tendencies which can only be suppressed, if at all, with difficulty. The longer this strain persists the harder will it be to maintain control of the explosive forces. On the other hand, even if we are not concerned with a case in which the output curve, in its initial phase, is actually trending downward, some important constituents are likely to be trending downward, so that there is a danger of breakdown (through adverse effects of the level of consumption on the efficiency of labour, if for no other cause) until the relieving force comes into action to reverse the trend. A policy which concentrates investment on long-period investment thus tends to prolong the strain in what may be a very dangerous way. It may be compared to a military policy which, if adopted by the Allies in 1942, would have concentrated resources on preparation for the invasion of Normandy, and left Rommel in Africa to look after himself. Yet in view of the 'greater productivity of more roundabout methods' as Böhm-Bawerk called it, such concentration on long-period investment will be very tempting. If more time is taken, it is possible to do a better job. New buildings are so much more attractive than patched-up old buildings; labour employed in making new fixed capital goods is ultimately so much more productive than labour used for infusing working capital into old processes. The trouble is, however, that these more attractive forms of investment take so much longer to yield final output.

It is in this direction, then, that the rate of interest does seem to have a real function in the regulation of the reconstruction process. In so far as a high rate of interest diminishes the total volume of investment below that which is attainable with available resources, it does harm; but in so far as it diverts labour from longer to shorter processes, from processes which will take a long time to produce final output to processes which will yield consumption goods more quickly, it may ease the difficulties of transition very

considerably. The ideal economic system for the conditions we are
studying thus appears to be one in which the volume of saving is
controlled otherwise than through the rate of interest – by direct
controls on consumption, or through budget surpluses – but in which
the rate of interest is left some part to play in the allocation of the
funds devoted to investment, assuming (that is) that the demand for
labour for investment purposes exceeds the supply, as will probably
be the case in the conditions we are examining.[6]

The task of monetary control in these conditions is bound to be
a very difficult one. The contractionary pressure must not be so great
as to endanger the maintenance of a high level of employment, but
at the same time some pressure must be exercised. In practice, a mere
change of policy in the direction of dearer money may involve so
great a shock as to endanger the maintenance of employment. We
seem to be between the Devil and the Deep Sea.

---

[6] The effect of a rise in the rate of interest is (1) to diminish the total investment
demand for labour; (2) to transfer labour and other resources from longer to shorter
processes. This comes about in the following way. The demand curve for far future output
(F) is moved to the left so that the demand for labour and other resources to be used in the
production of F is thereby reduced. On the other hand, the demand for near future output
(N) is affected to a negligible extent. The primary effect on the demand for labour
(assuming the supply price of labour to be fixed) is thus that less labour is demanded for
the production of F and no more labour for the production of N. In the case of other
resources, however, the corresponding reduction in demand for them from F production
may be expected to cause them to be transferred to N production – either because their
prices are more flexible or because the reduction in demand from F allows more of
them to be allocated to N. As a result of this transference, the demand for labour in N
production may be expected to undergo some expansion – though not enough to offset the
initial decline in demand from F.

If the economy would be in a state of over-employment at the lower rate of interest,
then both the transference of resources and the reduction in the demand for labour may be
desirable. If the economy is not over-employed at the lower rate of interest, the transference of resources may still be desirable, even though the decline in the demand for labour
would be *prima facie* undesirable. It is, however, not obvious that a condition of immediate
full employment is an economically sensible objective in the conditions which we are
studying. It will be remembered that in the early stages of mobilisation for war it was
accepted that it would have been foolish for the armed forces and the munition industries
to absorb at once labour which they were not yet in a position to use. One cannot help
suspecting that the same thing is true of the 'normal' peace-time industries when their turn
comes for re-expansion. The point is less important than it was in the case of the war
industries, since the peace-time industries do not have to expand their output to the same
relative extent; nevertheless it has some weight. Of course, those who are unemployed for
this cause have a claim to their share of the output of consumption goods; but it is not
equally clear that they have a claim to a share in the use of scarce materials and plant, if
they would use these capital goods for purposes which are less essential and less urgent than
the purposes for which these goods might otherwise have been used.

It is therefore important to notice that there is another possible way by which the necessary 'hurrying-up' can be induced without using the interest weapon. If people can be brought to expect a future fall in prices this will have the same effect as a rise in interest-rates, since it will make longer processes of production appear less profitable than shorter processes This then is a further argument in favour of maintaining equilibrium by high prices of consumption goods, if this method can be used without setting off a wage–price spiral. If wages can be held steady, and confidence in their steadiness can be maintained, it will be obvious that as productivity improves, prices must fall. And this expectation will check excessive investment in the longer processes. If, however, people are given ground to expect that improvements in productivity will result in higher wages rather than lower prices, the case for control by the rate of interest is by so much reinforced.

II

I now proceed to the second part of my paper. So far I have been discussing the problem of reconstruction as if one were dealing with a closed economy – very much as if the war had ended with the creation of a world state, and we were discussing what would be the right economic policy for such a state to adopt. Actually we are dealing with an international system, comprising many governments and many states, whose national economies have been damaged to many different degrees. In order to make our model useful, we ought to rethink it in terms of these national economies. How far can that be done?

When our diagram of the productive process is applied to a single country, which is not a closed economy, it requires to be modified to take account of imports and exports. But it is not sufficient to take all imports together, and all exports together, as if they were single categories (in the way that consumption goods are a single category for our purposes). It is necessary to classify internationally traded goods according as they are consumption goods or invest-ment goods. Further, in view of our distinction between short and long processes, it seems likely that investment goods will need to be further subdivided. We shall need to distinguish those investment goods which need longer processes in order to be turned into con-sumption goods from those which need shorter processes – Slow Investment goods and Quick Investment goods, we may call them.

Since the distinction between shorter and longer processes is closely related to the distinction between working capital and fixed capital, we shall not go far wrong if we think of the typical Quick Investment goods as raw materials, and the typical Slow Investment goods as machines. But it will be evident that this identification must not be pressed too far.

One of the principal differences which we have to take into account when we turn to consider the open national economy instead of the closed world economy, is that the relative inelasticity of the supply of consumption goods in the early stages of recovery (a point which has been fundamental to our argument up to the present) no longer holds. It is possible for a particular country to ease its position in this respect by importing consumption goods – though since they must be imported from some other country, and the inelasticity of supply still holds for the world economy, the position of the importing country can only be eased in this way by making that of the exporting country more difficult.

The export of consumption goods from a country which is still at an early stage of recovery simply reduces the supply available on the home market and therefore aggravates the inflationary pressure which we have been analysing. Import, on the other hand, diminishes the inflationary pressure. To revert to the numerical example I used earlier: suppose that the home supply of consumption goods, sold at prices low enough to prevent a wage–price spiral, is 70 per cent of full employment earnings, while people are only prepared to save 15 per cent of their incomes without special restrictions. In this case the importation of consumption goods will narrow the gap; if it were possible to import an amount which (valued at the same price-level) would reach 15 per cent of full employment earnings, then the gap would be closed and special restrictions on consumption would no longer be necessary.

The export and import of investment goods has no such necessary effect on the immediate situation, so far as the inflationary danger is concerned. It is true that an ultra-cheap money policy may have the result of making investment expenditure contribute actively to the inflationary pressure, but one would guess that this is a less serious danger than the one we are considering. If it were to happen, then it would be true that exports of investment goods would be inflationary, imports deflationary – just as with consumption goods. It seems to me, however, that we should pay more attention to the effect of the export and import of investment goods on the rate at which the output of consumption goods can be expected to return to a normal level. And here the distinction between Quick and Slow Investment goods is of fundamental importance. Export of Quick Investment goods has a quick effect in delaying the expansion of the output of consumption goods; thus if it takes place from a country which is still in serious difficulties, it prolongs the period of intense strain. On the other hand, the import of Quick Investment goods reduces the length of time for which intense strain may be expected to continue – it is a source of relief only one degree less immediate than the import of consumption goods. Exports and imports of Slow Investment goods are, from the point of view of the immediate situation, matters of altogether less importance.

International trade is in principle a two-way affair; exports and imports must balance. We know that in the short run such a balance is not necessary, because of borrowing and lending. But from our present point of view there is a possible lack of symmetry which goes even deeper than that. We should all recognise that if America supplies consumption goods to Britain on loan, demanding no immediate payment, that eases the inflationary pressure in England, but adds to the pressure in the United States. It is my present contention that something of the same sort occurs when Britain imports consumption goods, and pays for them by *slow* investment goods. In both cases she is absorbing scarce goods of present utility and paying for them with what is wholly, or at least in part, a draft on the future.

It will be evident from this analysis that there are two sorts of countries which are likely to be relatively well placed in a period of strain such as we are discussing. They are (1) countries which have been relatively little damaged by the war, (2) countries which normally export the more necessary consumption goods. A country which still retains some capacity for exporting consumption goods can always prevent its internal situation from becoming too explosive by restricting exports; if it has to import less investment goods in consequence, this merely retards its full recovery without involving a danger of breakdown. But a country which normally exports investment goods (especially if they are slow investment goods) is much more at the mercy of other countries, unless it has sufficient internationally acceptable monetary reserves to be able to run a deficit on its current trade.

You will not expect me, at the end of this paper, to go round the world, using my very imperfect knowledge of present economic conditions to try to fill the 'economic boxes' I have been constructing: guessing what is the position of this or that country at the moment with respect to my diagram. I think it will be more useful if I conclude with some suggestions as to the bearing of my analysis on one fundamental question – what is the significance of post-war trade crises? Are we to expect a crisis and depression, such as has usually occurred after previous wars, in the conditions of today? You will not expect me to be so bold as to say a definite yes or no to this last question; all I shall presume to do will be to suggest some relevant considerations.

I think that we are now in a position to understand quite clearly why it is that after previous wars a cycle of crisis and depression has often supervened, even at a fairly early stage of recovery. If interest rates are kept low – not necessarily low in absolute terms, but low enough to maintain fairly full employment – then, as we have seen, there will be a shortage of consumption goods, and we must expect that (in the absence of special measures to restrict consumer spending) an inflationary situation will develop. Even in 1919–20, governments were fairly helpless in the face of such an inflationary situation; the only way in which they could meet it was by a re-striction of credit. And, as we have seen, it was to be expected that such a restriction of credit would lead to very severe unemployment; but on the other side it would *hurry up* the real process of recovery, by ensuring that those people who remained employed turned their energies in the direction of producing the things most urgently needed. The result of a restrictive policy may therefore in the end have been to accelerate recovery. The slump which ensued upon restriction was definitely not of the type which threatens to have 'no bottom'. The people thrown out of work were due to be re-employed after a certain lapse of time; and when they were re-employed they would be re-employed much more productively than during the first hectic boom.

Although the policy of 1920 thus appears to have been more justifiable in the conditions of 1920 than it is usually admitted to have been, it does not, of course, follow that a similar policy would be justifiable today. The present position (perhaps merely because we are nearer to it) appears to be distinctly more complex. In some European countries (particularly my own) there would appear to be a case for similar restriction; though with the present control apparatus (itself getting a little soiled through long wear, but re-maining fairly effective) it would not be necessary to restrict so violently as in 1920 in order to attain the beneficial results. In spite of these advantages, I cannot think that we in Britain are likely to adopt such a policy. If we continue on our present lines, we are likely to have a very slow recovery, which will be much dependent on conditions in other countries; if external conditions turn unfavourable, we shall be lucky if we make any progress at all.

In the United States there appears to be a situation of greater theoretical interest, about which it is harder to prophesy, but on the course of which almost all else depends. The relaxation of controls in the United States means that it is possible for that country to go the way she went in 1920, but though possible, this does not seem at all likely. The evidence suggests that America is well ahead in the process of recovery so that any further rise in prices which may occur ought not to be very serious. If America really is round the corner, then I see no reason why she should not continue with a fairly orderly expansion, which may last a long time before she encounters a glutted market. The consequences for Europe of a development of this kind would be on the whole favourable; America might be expected to continue as a lender, to a sufficient extent to prevent extreme crisis in Europe, even if Europe's own efforts at recovery remain for long relatively ineffective. If, on the other hand, renewed inflationary tendencies appear in the United States (if her consumers are unwilling to wait for the increased supplies of consumption goods which are undoubtedly on the way), then I should judge that America would be more likely to seek relief by restricting her exports (restricting lending in order to restrict exports) than by credit restriction. If this were to occur, it would be a bad look-out for Europe.

In any case, European countries would be wise to do what they can to accelerate their own and each other's recovery. There are other instruments of economic policy which can attain the same objective as a rise in interest-rates; and some of these may well be less destructive instruments. But we should not forget that in these days of scarcity time is short; and the rate of interest is the price of time.

14

'Full Employment' in a
Period of Reconstruction

How this paper (which was published in the Danish *Nationaløkono-misk Tidsskrift* in 1947) came to be written is explained in the prefatory note to essay 13 above, where I have also said that I wish it to be regarded as an appendix to that essay. It is really a very formal appendix, translating some, but by no means all, of the analysis that had there been given into rather conventional textbook, or 'macro-economic' terms. Modern readers, of whatever 'school' would find no difficulty in doing this for themselves. I have neverthe-less felt that it should be included here, for two reasons. One is to show (for the record) that I was already capable, in 1947, of formu-lating the regular objections which have been raised by the economic establishment in England against such things as the budgetary policy of Sir Geoffrey Howe, since 1979. The other is to bring out, by contrast, the difference between the formal approach of this essay and the deeper analysis of essay 13. Where, for instance, in this version, is the distinction between Quick and Slow Investment goods, of which in essay 13 I made so much? These are some of the things, and they may be most important things, which get left out if one allows oneself to be *too* macro-economic.

---

1. The purpose of this paper is to examine certain qualifications to the doctrine of 'Full Employment', as presented by Keynes in the *General Theory*. These qualifications have, I think, a fairly wide application; but they are particularly important when we are con-cerned, as we still are at present, with war-damaged and therefore underequipped economies, instead of the economies with surplus capacity which were in Keynes's mind when he was writing. Thus they are qualifications which it is especially important for us to have in mind when we are discussing the economic problems of today. Nevertheless, what I am going to offer is not a theory of the present-

day economy, which is so characteristically a controlled economy. I am concerned with more underlying forces.

According to the assumptions on which Keynes proceeded in the *General Theory*, an increase in effective demand will always lead to an increase in employment, until a certain critical level of employment, called Full Employment, is reached. At this point a shortage of labour develops and wages tend to rise; so that if effective demand increases beyond this point it spends itself in an inflationary rise in wages, not in a further increase of employment. It is, of course, admitted that Full Employment in this sense does not necessarily mean the absence of unemployment; various factors are listed which may cause the shortage of labour to develop before the unemployment index has fallen to a negligible figure. It is even possible that the shortage in question may be an artificial shortage rather than a true shortage; trade unions may take advantage of a relative tightness of the labour market to secure wage-advances before the unemployed have been anything like fully absorbed. Thus even in Keynes Full Employment is at bottom nothing more than the maximum level of employment which can be reached by an expansionary policy – a policy, that is, which relies upon a general expansion of demand, its direct effects and indirect repercussions. It is admitted that this level may fall short, perhaps far short, of the level of employment which we should regard as socially desirable.

Nevertheless, in spite of these qualifications, it should be noticed that in Keynes the level of money wages is fundamentally always a function of the volume of employment. So long as *employment* remains below the critical mark, wage-rates can be trusted not to rise in an inflationary manner. It is only when the demand for labour approaches the supply to within a certain limit that labour becomes scarce, and it is when labour becomes scarce that money wages tend to rise.

This particular assumption was indeed questioned by several of Keynes's critics, who were puzzled by the queer psychology on the part of labour which appeared to be implied in it. Is it really conceivable, they asked, that wage policy runs in terms of money wages alone, not (as we have been brought up to suppose) in terms of real wages? Is the worker really so insensitive to the buying-power of his wages? The existence of cost-of-living sliding scales is a powerful argument to the contrary. It is indeed so powerful an argument that on this issue the critics have never confessed themselves beaten; nevertheless, even on this issue the Keynesian Juggernaut bore down opposition. The assumption of money wages depending on employment became a part of the Keynesian orthodoxy, even though it had to be modified in practice, even by Keynes himself, when he came to deal with the economics of war-time. The theoretical consequences of making an amendment on this point seem, however, never to have been worked out.

I would now begin by granting that the position adopted in the *General Theory* was quite a strong one in the situation of the 1930s. For the purposes of analysing depression, when prices fall, but there remains a considerable resistance to wage-cuts, it is a liberation of the mind when one starts to think (in Keynes's manner) in terms of money wages; so that one can discard the awkward implication that the worker's 'supply-price' rises as the demand for his services falls off, which is unavoidable if one persists in thinking of the demand and supply of labour in real terms. Further (and even more to the point) when it comes to analysing recovery – whether natural or induced by public policy – Keynes has on his side the volume of experience which tends to show that employment can often increase a long way from the depths of depression without there being any very important pressure on the price-level of consumption goods; changes in real wages are then not large enough to be relevant. It will be remembered that on this point researches subsequent to the publication of the *General Theory* suggested that even those qualifications which Keynes did introduce in his text were un-necessary; thus the original doctrine could have been made even more absolute than it was. This is how the position appeared up to 1939. It is only in the light of war-time and post-war experience that it has finally become evident that amendment is in fact needed.

In the light of this new experience, it is now fairly safe to say: (1) that the level of money wages *is* affected by the level of con-sumption good prices, so that real wages *are* relevant; (2) that the supply of consumption goods cannot be relied upon in all circum-stances to be highly elastic, or even elastic at all. What gave the supply of consumption goods its apparent elasticity in the short period, in the conditions when Keynes was writing, was the excess capacity of the consumption goods industries, which was an in-heritance from the years of acute depression which immediately preceded. With surplus plant and surplus materials, nothing was wanting but an expansion in demand to produce an expansion in output with the minimum of delay. These conditions were present in 1934–5, but in 1947–8 they are wholly lacking. For the analysis of post-war economics, the assumptions that prices vary only slightly with demand, and that the money wage-level is little affected by prices, simply will not do.

2.   Let us then assume that we are in a position in which (1) an increased demand for consumption goods will lead to a significant increase in their prices in terms of money wages; and in which also (2) the prices of consumption goods cannot rise beyond a certain point, relatively to the wage-level, without unsettling the level of money wages. It follows that in the absence of controls, inflation may set in at a point well short of Keynes's full employment point, if that is understood to mean a point at which there is a general shortage of labour. We have to recognise that there are in principle not one but two 'explosion points', one of them being Keynes's full employment point, where there is a scarcity of labour, and the other being that at which the fall in real wages, resulting from expansion, leads to pressure on the money wage level. Of these two points, it is of course that one which is reached first, in a process of expansion, which will be the effective check. Keynes's theory is the economics of a system in which the full employment point is reached first. It is, however, not necessary that it should be reached first. It seems probable that in present conditions it is the 'cost-of-living' point, as we may call it, which provides the effective check; and, as we shall see, the economics of a system in which the 'cost-of-living' check is the effective one, is appreciably different from the Keynesian structure.

It must, of course, be admitted that the cost-of-living check cannot operate effectively at a very low level of employment. If there is a great deal of employment, trade unions may desire to press for higher wages, but their desire is not very likely to have effective results. Thus it is not surprising to find that the world has been able to pass from a situation in which the full employment check was operating into one in which the cost of living check is operative – and public policy has been quite largely adjusted to the new state of affairs – without there being any general realisation among economists of how considerable a change has taken place. It is, however, quite time for economists to become conscious of the change, if their thinking is to be properly appropriate to the new state of affairs.

Figure 14.1 shows a supply curve of consumption goods, on the assumption of a given level of money wage-rates. If the demand for consumption goods expands, the point of equilibrium will move to the right along this curve. Since we are assuming that the capital equipment (fixed or working capital) needed to make consumption goods is in limited supply, as far as the current period is concerned, it must be expected that the supply curve will be steeply upward sloping, over the range at which a shortage of capital equipment

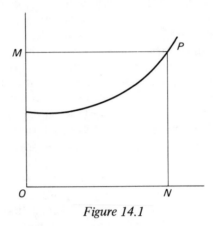

Figure 14.1

begins to be felt. Thus if the demand for consumption goods reaches a point where this steep upward slope is encountered, the prices of consumption goods – in the absence of controls – will rise steeply. It is assumed that this rise cannot be beyond a certain point (marked OM) without resulting in a rise in wage-rates. The result of such a rise in wage-rates proceeds according to the usual Keynesian mechanism, the whole system merely repeating itself at a higher (money) wage and price level. Thus if the price level of consumption goods reaches OM, it touches off an inflationary process, just as (according to Keynes) an increase in effective demand will do if labour in general is 'fully employed'.

The maximum output of consumption goods which can be achieved without inflation and without controls is thus indicated by P the point at which the horizontal line through M intersects the supply curve. In this position the output of consumption goods is measured by ON, and the value (C) of this output (which equals consumers' expenditure, and also equals the gross earnings of capital and labour in the production of consumption goods) is measured by the rectangle $OMPN$.

Total gross income $Y = C + I$, where I is the gross earnings of the factors of production in the production of other than consumption goods. Adopting the usual Keynesian assumption that C is an increasing function of Y, it follows that Y is an increasing function of C. If the maximum value of C which is consistent with the avoidance of inflation is that shown by the rectangle $OMPN$, the maximum value of Y which is consistent with the avoidance of inflation can be deduced from it by the use of this (inverse) consumption function. The maximum expenditure on other than consumption goods which is consistent with the avoidance of inflation is then given by $Y - C$. The maximum employment in other than consumption goods industries depends upon the number of workers whose labour can be absorbed into these industries with the demand for their products at this level.

Suppose, for instance, that the consumption function takes the simple form $C = aY + b$, (a being supposed, as usual, to be less than 1). Then if the maximum value of C (indicated by the rectangle *OMPN*) is C', the maximum value of Y will be

$$Y' = \frac{C' - b}{a}$$

and the maximum value of $Y - C$ will be

$$\frac{C' - b}{a} - C' = C' \left(\frac{1 - a}{a}\right) - \frac{b}{a}$$

This measures the maximum demand for the products of investment and other non-consumption industries, which is consistent with the avoidance of inflation. Let n_2 be the number of workers who can be employed in these industries with the demand for their products at this level; and let n_1 be the number of workers who will be employed in the consumption goods industries to produce the product *ON*. Then $n_1 + n_2$ is the maximum employment consistent with the avoidance of inflation for 'cost-of-living' reasons.

If $n_1 + n_2$ is greater than 'Full Employment' in Keynes's sense, then we are in a Keynesian world. But if it is less – and it is my contention here that there is no reason why it should not be less – then we are in a world with quite different properties.

3. Before saying anything about the effects of controls (in the war-time and post-war sense) it will be well to begin by working out the economics of our system under essentially *laisser faire* conditions, or with no greater intervention by the State than was contemplated in the original model of the *General Theory*. This analysis, though it stops some way short of being realistic, will be useful as a step towards understanding of the new mechanism; and it will also be useful as a basis for comparison with the familiar Keynesian structure.

Let us assume, then, that we are in a situation where $n_1 + n_2$ (as defined in the previous paragraph) amount to a total which is less than Full Employment, in the sense of an overall shortage of labour. Although, as explained, this implies that there is a shortage of capital equipment in the consumption goods industries, it is nevertheless possible (though perhaps unlikely) that the incentive to invest will be low – either because of pessimistic anticipations and uncertainty impeding investment directly, or because of high liquidity preference and high rates of interest. If the incentive to invest is low, then actual employment will be less than $n_1 + n_2$, and the Keynesian theory will hold precisely; any method which encourages investment will stimulate employment.

If, on the other hand, the incentive to invest is greater than that which would induce an employment level of $n_1 + n_2$, then it would be the mechanism which we have been discussing which would operate, so that it would be cost-of-living inflation which would set in. This inflation, however, would be checked if the monetary supply is not perfectly elastic; for the increasing demand for money which would follow upon the rising wages and prices must then lead to a rise in interest rates. Further inflation would thus be prevented by a rise in interest, which would cut down the amount of investment to an amount which the system could tolerate.

We have thus to envisage the possibility of an equilibrium situation, in which investment is checked by high (or relatively high) interest rates, and in which there is an appreciable amount of un-employment. But it is not an underemployment equilibrium in Keynes's sense. For the result of monetary expansion, directed towards lowering interest rates and expanding investment, would be to increase the effective demand for consumption goods (according to the multiplier); but this would raise the prices of consumption goods, and this would lead to a rise in money wages. It follows that any increase in employment which resulted from an increase in the money supply could only be temporary; the main effect of increasing the money supply would be to increase money wages and prices – exactly as if the quantity theory were in operation!

Thus, in the position we are analysing, and expansionary policy of the usual Keynesian sort would be futile; but what means would be available for increasing employment? The most obvious, and most important, means would be to find some way of increasing saving: to diminish, that is, the amount spent upon consumption goods out of a given money income. It follows from the formulae of the preceding section that if a or b can be diminished, $Y' - C'$ will be increased and thus n_2 will be increased. The cost-of-living explosion point will correspond to a larger amount of employment; employment will thus be expanded beyond what would have been possible with a lower propensity to save.

Monetary expansion is futile, but saving is effective as a means of expansion – our system certainly looks as if it is in a very 'classical' condition. In many ways this is so; but it should be noticed that not many 'classical' economists (in Keynes's sense) thought of saving as increasing *employment*. Also (and this is more important) an increase in the propensity to save would not, in our system, increase employment automatically. An increase in saving might still leave interest rates unaffected; if this happened, investment expenditure might not be increased, while consumption expenditure would be diminished, so that employment would be diminished. Employment would in fact be reduced below the 'cost-of-living explosion point' so that there would unquestionably be a state of underemployment in Keynes's sense, which would need to be counteracted by expansionary measures of Keynes's type. It is only true that an increase in saving would increase employment if the increase was accompanied by expansionary measures, such as a reduction of interest rates through monetary expansion, or any other measure which stimulated the employment of labour in the non-consumption-goods industries.[1]

4. The most efficient way of stimulating saving (in the relevant sense) is, of course, by taxation. If we assume, as seems reasonable for a first approximation, that the consumption function indicates a relation between consumption expenditure and income after direct taxation, then we can deduce that direct taxation increases employment, or potential employment, by precisely the number of workers who can be employed by an additional non-consumption expenditure equal to the revenue of the tax. For if T is tax revenue, and the consumption function is $C = a(Y - T) + b$, we can invert it in the form

$$Y' = \frac{C' - b}{a} + T$$

[1] It may be admitted, however, that if the diminution in demand for consumption goods led to a fall in money wage-rates, thus diminishing the demand for money at a given level of employment, it is then possible that interest rates (with a given supply of money) would fall automatically, so that the needed stimulus to investment would come about automatically. This may serve as a rationalisation of a full 'classical' position; but I do not regard it as consistent with the assumptions on which I am working here. It is essential to my argument that there is only a limited degree, and a particular sort, of flexibility in wage-rates.

so that the extent to which the social income (in wage-units) can be expanded by direct taxation is exactly equal to the amount of tax revenue.

Substantially the same thing holds for indirect taxation, so long as the indirect taxes do not upset the prices of those consumption goods which are relevant for wage policy. But if the prices of consumption goods, in our sense, are affected, the situation is more complicated.

The situation in the consumption goods industries, following upon the imposition of a tax on consumption goods, is shown in Fig. 14.2. Since it will be the price-level of consumption goods including tax which will now be unable to exceed *OM* (measured in wage units), the price-level excluding tax will have the lower maximum *Om* (*Mm* measuring the average rate of tax). The amount which can be produced at this lower price will be *On*; thus output of consumption goods will have to be reduced by an amount *Nn*, and there will be a corresponding fall in employment in the consumption goods industries.

Consumers' expenditure on consumption goods includes tax and is thus reduced from *OMPN* to *OMQn* only. Nevertheless this is a reduction and the total social income must therefore be reduced (according to our formula $Y = (C - b)/a$) by an amount equal to $\Delta C/a$ where ΔC is the difference between these two rectangles. On the other hand, earnings in the consumption goods industries are only *Ompn*, so that the amount available for expenditure on invest-

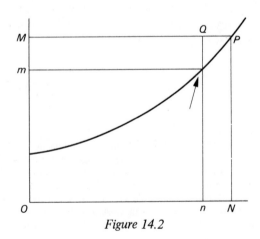

Figure 14.2

ment (or non-consumption) is increased by the tax revenue (as in the case of direct taxation), though it is reduced by the reduction in output of the consumption goods industries, the latter being subject to a multiplier effect. In order to get the total effect on employment, we have thus to take into account: (1) the direct effect on employment in the consumption goods industries, which will certainly be a diminution of employment; (2) the indirect effect on the investment goods industries, which may go in either direction, according to the multiplier effect of contraction in the consumption goods industries is or is not offset by the additional 'saving' due to the tax revenue.

To put this in another way. If the government balances its budget, the receipt of additional revenue will allow it to increase its expenditure, and this will ordinarily increase employment directly. But if this is done and nothing else is done, when the revenue is raised by indirect taxes and the economy was initially on the edge of a cost-of-living inflation, then the rise in the prices of consumption goods will set off the inflation. Restrictive measures to counteract this will have to be taken; and the question is whether the adverse effect on employment of these restrictive measures will offset the favourable effect due to the spending of the additional revenue, or will not.

It appears, however, that from our analysis something can be said which gives a clue to the probable answer to this question. If the supply of consumption goods is very inelastic, the necessary reduction in the output of consumption goods will be small, so that the rectangle $QPNn$ will be small, and even when the multiplier effects is applied to it the result will still be small. Thus the favourable effect on employment of the additional expenditure possible with a still balanced budget (or a not more than before unbalanced budget) will, in all probability, be greater than the adverse effects of the necessary restriction in consumers' demand, and the reduction in the social income as a whole needed to induce that restriction in demand. But if, on the other hand, the supply of consumption goods is elastic, the reverse will hold.

It is obvious that the whole of this argument can be applied, in reverse, to the case of subsidies, which are nothing but negative indirect taxes. In cases where the supply of consumption goods is elastic, the effect of indirect taxation would be likely to be unfavourable, so that the effect of subsidies would be favourable. In cases where the supply of consumption goods is inelastic, the effect of subsidies is likely to be unfavourable. The case for withdrawing subsidies is the same as that for imposing indirect taxes.

5. All the above analysis, because it has implied a *laisser faire* economy, with no more control than can be exercised through budgetary policy and monetary policy, is today unrealistic, if applied to most European countries. But it still has an indirect relevance, because it does illustrate the situation which would arise if controls were relaxed. And the case for relaxing controls is becoming on other grounds a very strong one.

It is becoming widely recognised in Britain (I have at this point to speak of my own country) that controls, carried to the length which we have carried them, have a very deleterious effect on productivity. But if we relaxed our controls and did nothing else, we should merely precipitate inflation; and it is therefore becoming agreed that controls could only be relaxed as part of a deflationary policy, directed towards reducing the level of demand to what the economy, in a less highly controlled condition, could bear. My general analysis is sympathetic to this point of view; but it leads me to emphasise the danger of excessive contraction – if the controls were swept away wholesale, and the main reliance for the avoidance of inflation were put upon cuts in governmental and industrial expenditure. For it seems to follow that from what has been said that such a policy would be liable to lead to large-scale unemployment; though it is indeed possible that in spite of that unemployment, real recovery might be more rapid under such a contractionary policy than it is likely to be on present methods. Nevertheless, a contractionary policy of this type is definitely not the best alternative which ought to be open.

The best alternative, I would suggest, would be something of the following type. Controls over production should be relaxed as far as possible, but controls over consumption (especially in the form of high taxation and a budget surplus) should be retained until supplies are more abundant. Such a policy would be made more tolerable if people could be made to see that the high taxes are necessary in the interest of employment. It is true that the maintenance of consumption restrictions itself involves a drag on productivity, owing to the lack of incentive which would persist; but the lack of incentive is far from being the only thing which is restricting production at present. From the point of view of incentive, it would be far better if controls over consumption could be relaxed with the rest; but the time for that is definitely not yet. It should only come as a 'reward' for the successful completion of the first stages of recovery. The fact that it will be not merely a reward but a positive help to the achievement of the later stages does not mean that we do not have to do without it in the earlier stages. It is of the nature of a process of recovery that it gets easier as it goes on.

15

Harrod's Dynamic Theory

PREFATORY NOTE

This essay, which began as a review of R. F. Harrod's *Towards a Dynamic Economics* (1948), was published in *Economica* in May 1949. As I wrote it, it turned into something else, into nothing less than a first sketch for my *Contribution to the Theory of the Trade Cycle* (1950). The main features of the latter work (*TC*) are already present in it, but I do not think that it is altogether superseded by *TC*. Though I did there make an acknowledgement to Harrod, the precise way in which my model grew out of Harrod's is not made as clear as it is here. The steps by which I modified the Harrod model (and the reasons for which I felt myself obliged to take them) are here set out in order.

My equilibrium path is the same as Harrod's warranted path, and (for the same reasons as his) it is unstable. But (as I say) 'mathematical instability does not itself elucidate fluctuations. A mathematically unstable system does not fluctuate; it just breaks down'. A fluctuating model, even if it is unstable in the large, must be stable in the small, in order that the path which it actually follows should be determinate. In order to get that *local* stability, I had to introduce lags.

The lags that I introduce in the paper are of the simplest sort; they are nevertheless sufficient to bring out my main results. The more complicated lags that appear in *TC*, though they are amusing mathematically, do not really add much that is of economic importance. Anyone who was worked through the paper (it does need a bit of working through) will have got, with one exception, nearly everything that is of importance in the book. For I do not now regard the later chapters of the book, on the duration of the cycle, and on the monetary factor, as being of much importance.

The important exception is chapter 4 of the book, on 'Induced Investment', a chapter which really is economic, not mathematical. That chapter was largely written under the influence of Robertson, who had submitted the present (Harrod) article to searching criticism. The Accelerator (of which, following Harrod, I made such important use) had long been a basic element in his own thinking.[1] But he had passed the point where the very formal version I gave of it in the article was tolerable. He made me insist upon the distinction between actual output (which may be taken to respond to demand for output) and the output for which existing plant is optimum. When that distinction is developed, as I did develop it in chapter 4 of *TC*, the difference between the Acceleration Principle and the Capital Stock Adjustment Principle, which has later been thought to have superseded it, is considerably diminished. (My own version of the latter principle is developed in *Capital and Growth*, chapters 6–11.)

I

Mr Harrod's book may be regarded as falling into two parts. One of them (chapters 1, 3 and 4) outlines a new 'dynamic' theory of economic progress and of the trade cycle; the other (chapters 2 and 5) is specially concerned with interest. There is, of course, some overlapping; but the two parts are fairly well separated. One could, I think, say a good deal about the part on interest without much reference to the other part and one can certainly say a good deal about the dynamic theory without any reference to the part on interest. Personally, I find the dynamic theory a good deal more interesting. I can find quite enough to say about it to fill the space which could conveniently be allotted to me on this occasion; I propose, therefore, to take the drastic step of leaving the part on interest altogether on one side.

Dynamics, according to Mr Harrod, is a study of 'an economy in which rates of output are changing'. This definition is contrasted with that given in my own *Value and Capital* – 'that part of economic theory in which all quantities must be dated' – and also with that used by the econometricians, such as Frisch and Kalecki, which Mr Harrod takes to be particularly concerned with the effects of lags. Certainly there is no need to fight over definitions; I have myself no desire to defend the *Value and Capital* definition for purposes outside its immediate context. It had convenience as a means of organising a particular discussion; I would claim no more for it. But I think that both the econometricians and myself have the right to enquire whether Mr Harrod has paid sufficient regard to the aspects of a dynamic progress to which we have drawn attention. In fact, he seems to be open to some criticism on both grounds. It is very

[1] See above, pp. 128–9.

awkward to analyse a dynamic process (in his sense) without paying more regard than he does to the question of dating; and once one begins to date, it is hardly possible to slide over the question of lags. But instead of arguing this matter in general terms, let us look at it in terms of the details of Mr Harrod's theory.

The central feature of that theory is a certain equation[2] which (modifying Mr Harrod's notation a little[3]) I will write in the form $gc = s$. s is saving, expressed as a proportion of income (or output); g is the rate of growth of output (increment of output expressed as a proportion of output); c is the ratio of investment to the increment of output. Those whose minds (like my own) find it difficult to think in terms of these ratios will prefer to multiply up by income or output (Y). gY is then identifiable as the increment of output during the period, which could be written dY/dt. The equation thus becomes

$$c \frac{dY}{dt} = sY.$$

This is recognisable as our old friend, the equation of Saving and Investment. (Y, it should be understood, is measured in terms of goods, not in terms of money or of 'wage-units'.)

The reason why Mr Harrod prefers to write a familiar equation in this unfamiliar form is that he is anxious to stress the dependence of investment on the rate of change of output – the 'Relation' which other economists have called the 'acceleration principle'. In given conditions of technique, and with a given rate of interest, the ratio (c) between *ex-ante* investment and the change in income may perhaps be properly regarded as more or less constant. If this is so, and if the saving ratio s may also be regarded as constant, then the fundamental equation

$$c \frac{dY}{dt} = sY$$

can be treated as a differential equation, and solved as such. The solution is $Y = Y_0 e^{gt}$, where Y_0 is the level of income at time zero, which must be supposed to be given, and g is now *defined* as s/c, where both s and c are now to be taken as given constants. The

---

[2] This equation first appeared in his 'Essay in Dynamic Theory' (*EJ*, 1939).

[3] Mr Harrod writes the equation $GC = s$. I have replaced his big letters by small ones because I prefer to keep big letters for the main economic quantities, such as Y, using small letters for their ratios.

economic meaning of this solution is, of course, that the economy expands at a constant rate *g*.

The solution is got by assuming that the economy is all the time in a state of Keynesian equilibrium, with *ex-ante* investment equal to *ex-ante* saving. The path defined by the solution is therefore not the path which will actually be followed; it is the path which would be followed if the system remained continually in this sort of equilibrium. (Mr Harrod calls it the 'warranted' rate of growth.) And that means, as we shall see, very little more than that it is *a possible* path of development.

The use of the concept of equilibrium in such matters as this is very tricky. In the Keynesian system, we were first told that the savings-investment equation determined the level of output; then it became clear that it only determined the equilibrium level of output; the actual level, at any particular time, might depart from the equilibrium level. This was an important qualification, with many consequences not yet all of them fully appreciated; but it did not in itself seriously affect the usefulness of the Keynesian construction, because the Keynesian equilibrium is *stable*. If *ex-ante* saving exceeds *ex-ante* investment (under Keynesian or near-Keynesian assumptions) output will tend to fall, thus tending to restore equilibrium. And *vice versa*. Because there are these stabilising forces tending to hold the system to an equilibrium position (or, as we might say, more dynamically, to hold it on an equilibrium path), it is probable that divergences from a Keynesian equilibrium would be limited. Great divergences must be short-lived. Thus, in so far as the Keynesian system is valid, it does not only explain 'tendencies'; it does, at least in a rough sort of way, explain the facts. If it is valid, then it is a first approximation to what does actually happen. It has this property in virtue of its mathematical *stability*. The ordinary supply and demand theory for a single commodity has the same property for the same reason.

Mr Harrod's equilibrium path – his 'warranted rate of growth' – does not have this property. His system is mathematically unstable. A rise in the rate of saving (*s*) raises the warranted rate of growth (*g*), thus causing the equilibrium path to slope more steeply upwards. There is sense in this. With the demand for the use of savings coming from the increase in output, an increased supply of savings can only be absorbed if output increases more rapidly than before. But an increase in *s* will not cause the economy to move on to this new path. Just as in the Keynesian case a rise in *s* causes *ex-ante* saving to exceed *ex-ante* investment, and therefore tends to diminish output. But this means (under Mr Harrod's assumptions) that the system tends at once to move away from its equilibrium rate of advance. Instead of expanding as it 'ought' to do, it starts to contract.

Mr Harrod is, of course, well aware of this instability; he draws a number of interesting conclusions from it, some of them, I think very important conclusions. In a sense he welcomes the instability of his system, because he believes it to be an explanation of the tendency to fluctuation which exists in the real world. I think, as I shall proceed to show, that something of this sort may well have much to do with the tendency to fluctuation. But mathematical instability does not in itself elucidate fluctuation. A mathematically unstable system does not fluctuate; it just breaks down. The unstable position is one in which it will *not* tend to remain. That is all that the condition of mathematical instability tells us. But, on being barred from that position, what will it do? What path will it follow? Mere knowledge of the unstable position does not tell us.

Perhaps I may put my difficulty graphically. In Fig. 15.1 time is measured on the horizontal axis, and output on the vertical (the latter, as seems appropriate for these 'growth' problems, being reckoned on a logarithmic scale). We begin with output OA at time zero. s and c being given, AA' is an equilibrium path. Suppose that this path is followed from A to B, but that at B the rate of saving (s) rises. The new equilibrium path will be such as BB'. But the rise in the rate of saving does not cause the economy to move along BB',

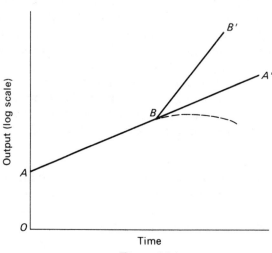

Figure 15.1

or along anything like it. It has the opposite effect, causing a divergence to the other side of BA'. But about the course of that divergence and about its direction we learn practically nothing. In practice, with these strong centrifugal forces at work, we must suppose that we shall almost always be dealing with an economy which is somewhere or other on some such divergent path. So long as the actual course of events on such a path is left undetermined, little use can be made of the theory. It is extraordinarily hard to use it either for the explanation of events, or for the prediction of what is likely to result from changes introduced by policy.

II

Faced with this difficulty, I have been tempted to go beyond the ordinary functions of a reviewer, and to enquire whether it is not possible, by some modification of Mr Harrod's assumptions, to overcome the deficiency. The prize is a great one, for no one can study Mr Harrod's work at all deeply without feeling that results of really great significance are just round the corner. What we have to do is to introduce just sufficient frictions to give the model mathematical stability, while not sacrificing the economic instability on which the substance of the argument depends. Can this be done?

It can be done as soon as we are allowed to make some use of lags. It is not generally realised (Mr Harrod has certainly failed to realise it) that the great function of lags in this sort of dynamic theory is to impart just that measure of stability in the small – day-to-day stability we might call it – as is required in order to make the movement of the system economically determinate. The lags are needed to hold the system to a given path. Mr Harrod's theory, in the form he has given it, may be regarded as an indirect proof of this; because he will have no lags, his system explodes out of the time dimension. A dynamic system which is economically unstable, having a high propensity to fluctuate, cannot be efficiently studied unless some of the variables are lagged.

The easiest way to introduce lags is to work in terms of period analysis. Instead of treating time as continuous, we break it up into successive periods. The increment of output, which formerly appeared as dY/dt, will now appear as $Y_n - Y_{n-1}$. If there are no lags, the basic equation will then have to be written

$$c(Y_n - Y_{n-1}) = sY_n, \qquad (1)$$

the properties of which are substantially the same as those of Mr Harrod's equation.[4]

But as soon as the equation is written in this form, it does at once look decidedly queer. It is not really reasonable to assume that current investment should depend upon the increment of output *in the same period* (especially if periods are fairly short), and still less is it reasonable to assume that saving depends wholly upon the income of the same period. If we make the simplest possible lagging assumptions, we shall make investment depend upon the increment of income in the preceding period, and *consumption* upon the income of the preceding period. Current saving would then equal $Y_n - (1 - s) Y_{n-1}$, so that the basic difference equation becomes

$$c(Y_{n-1} - Y_{n-2}) = Y_n - (1 - s) Y_{n-1}$$

or

$$Y_n = (1 - s + c) Y_{n-1} - c Y_{n-2}. \qquad (2)$$

An equation of this kind is completely stable in the short run, for an increase in s reduces Y_n as it should. It can therefore be used to trace out a path which is such that an economy might possibly follow it.

The properties of such paths have been widely studied by mathematical economists.[5] Without going into detail, the following general conclusions may be mentioned. s and c being given, the path is completely determined when *two* initial positions (say Y_0 and Y_1) are given. Associated with any particular difference equation, there will be a 'full equilibrium' position, which is such that it can be maintained indefinitely if it is once fully established. For very low values of c, the system approximates to the Keynesian type, and therefore moves steadily towards its full equilibrium. For very large values of c, the system tends away from full equilibrium. For intermediate values, it oscillates about the equilibrium position, the oscillations having a diminishing amplitude if c is less than 1, and an increasing amplitude if c is greater than 1. These are the results for the 'second-order' equation, in which Y_n depends upon its *two* previous values.

---

[4] For its solution gives g (the proportional increment of output) equal to $s/(c - s)$. When s is small relatively to c, this is approximately the same as s/c.

[5] The best general description of this work, in non-mathematical language, is that by A. H. Hansen and P. A. Samuelson, in *Fiscal Policy and Business Cycles*, ch. 12. The best account in terms of fairly elementary mathematics is in A. Smithies, 'Equilibrium Analysis and Process Analysis' (*Econometrica*, 1942).

Similar, but mathematically much more complex, results appear to hold for difference equations of higher orders.

These results have attracted much attention because they seem to show that on quite simple assumptions a system may be constructed which has an automatic tendency to develop fluctuations. But the more one works with this structure, interesting as it is, the more one feels that its fluctuations are really too simple. They do not take account of some of the most elementary features of the real problem, which must surely find a place, and a central place, in a realistic theory. The mathematical economists do seem to have got hold of a part of the mechanism, but there are other things which they have left out which need to be brought in.

Now Mr Harrod has got some of these other things. Although his system will not do in the small, it is better than theirs in the large. Is it impossible to build up a construction which will combine the merits of each?

III

The reader may have noticed that the lagged Harrod equation (2) would, in itself, be unsatisfactory for the purposes of the mathematical theory which we have just described. For if we seek to determine its full equilibrium level of output (which can always be determined from a difference equation by putting its various Ys equal to one another) the answer must clearly come out as $Y = 0$. This would not perhaps worry Mr Harrod very much, because he is seeking to analyse a dynamic process, not an equilibrium situation. He does not want his system to settle down to 'equilibrium'.

But this means that the only solution of the difference equation in which he will be interested is that which occurs when c is relatively large, so that the system becomes 'explosive'. He is quite ready for his system to explode, provided that it does not explode too fast!

Nevertheless, since the system is to fluctuate, having down-tracks as well as up-tracks, it is important that the down-tracks should be checked somewhere. After all, slumps do have bottoms; something has to be introduced to stop the slump tending to an 'equilibrium' with no output at all.

The only provision which Mr Harrod makes to meet this need is the suggestion that some part of the investment of a period may be 'long-range' – so that its 'worthwhileness is not deemed to have any relation to current requirements'. I believe that this is the solution;

but by treating this long-range investment as a fraction (presumably in principle a constant fraction) of current income, Mr Harrod makes it impossible for it to give him any really substantial help. For whether the long-range investment depends upon Y_n, Y_{n-1} or Y_{n-2}, its introduction in this guide only affects the coefficients in the difference equation; and no juggling with the coefficients will prevent an equation of the form

$$\alpha Y_n + \beta Y_{n-1} + \gamma Y_{n-2} = 0$$

from having its equilibrium solution at zero output.

I believe that the readiest way out is to make the long-range investment depend, not upon current output, but upon the trend value of output. Evidently we must not treat long-range investment as a constant; for if we did so, though we should get a bottom to our slumps, we should lose the possibility of the upward trend, on the introduction of which into the model Mr Harrod sets so much store. If, however, we make the assumption that the long-range investment depends, other things being equal, upon the natural growth of the economy (in productivity and perhaps population), we can get a bottom to our slumps and still retain the general progressive movement.

I would therefore suggest that we introduce a term $H(1+g)^n$ for the long-range investment, where H is a constant, and g (also a constant) is now Mr Harrod's *natural* rate of growth. The introduction of this term certainly seems to be worth trying, and it proves to have the most interesting effects.

IV

On introducing this term, the difference equation (2) is transformed into

$$H(1+g)^n + c(Y_{n-1} - Y_{n-2}) = Y_n - (1-s)Y_{n-1}. \qquad (3)$$

This equation is just a shade harder to handle than (2), but in fact by a simple device we can reduce it to an equivalent form.

The nearest thing to an equilibrium solution which is possible for this new equation is that which gives a steady advance at the *natural* rate. At such a steady advance, we should have $Y_n = E(1+g)^n$, where E is a constant. Substituting this trial solution in (3), we find

$$H(1+g)^n = E(1+g)^n - (1-s+c)E(1+g)^{n-1} + cE(1+g)^{n-2}$$

whence

$$E = \frac{H(1+g)^2}{(1+g)(s+g) - cg}. \tag{4}$$

If, as we may properly assume, there is enough saving to look after the investment engendered in the steady advance, E will be positive.

Now write $Y_n = E(1+g)^n (1+y_n)$, so that y_n is the proportion by which actual income in the nth period exceeds (or, if y_n is negative, falls short of) its *moving* equilibrium value. Substituting this value in (3) and using (4), we get

$$y_n - \frac{1-s+c}{1+g} y_{n-1} + \frac{c}{(1+g)^2} y_{n-2} = 0, \tag{5}$$

which is a simple difference equation of exactly the same type as (2). Its full equilibrium solution is at $y_n = 0$; but this no longer corresponds to zero output, but to the output which gives a steady advance.

What we have now found is that in our revised model, the proportional divergences from the moving equilibrium output will obey the same laws as were obeyed by the level of output itself in the simple model (2). Thus if $c/(1+g)^2$ is small, any displacement from the moving equilibrium will be followed by a steady movement back to the equilibrium. The moving equilibrium can then be regarded as stable. For larger values of c, we should get fluctuations about the moving equilibrium, which (as c increased) would first be damped, and would then become 'explosive'. Finally, for very large values of c, we should get a steady divergence from equilibrium as the result of any chance displacement.

Now it is, I think, these latter possibilities (relatively neglected by the econometrists) to which Mr Harrod seeks to draw our attention. In order to study them conveniently, we may perhaps fix our attention upon one particular value of c, which makes the difference equation more than usually easy to handle. This is the minimum value which gives a steady divergence from equilibrium, without there being any fluctuations induced by the difference equation itself. It can be calculated to be $c = (1+\sqrt{s})^2$. Substituting this value of c in (5), we get

$$y_n - 2\lambda y_{n-1} + \lambda^2 y_{n-2} = 0, \tag{6}$$

where $\lambda = (1+\sqrt{s})/(1+g)$. It is obviously safe to assume that $\lambda > 1$.

The solution of equation (6) is $(nA + B)\lambda^n$, where A and B are constants, depending on the initial positions. Thus if we start from a position which is such that A is positive, y will steadily increase (at least after a limited number of initial periods), and if we start from a position in which A is negative, y will steadily diminish (subject to the same proviso). We have therefore verified that we are dealing with an 'explosive' equation; and we may be sure that for higher values of c we should get cases which would be still more explosive.

If we start from an equilibrium position, with $y_0 = 0$, we are bound to have $B = 0$, since by putting $n = 0$, we see that $y_0 = B$. A is determined by the value of y in period 1, being equal to y_1/λ when $B = 0$. Applying the general formula, we see that $y_n = n\lambda^{n-1}y_1$. Thus if we began with an upward displacement, so that y_1 was positive, y_n would increase from period to period in a ratio which at first exceeded λ, but gradually approached the limiting value λ as n became large.

V

Thus the difference equation tells us that if there chances to be an upward displacement from the equilibrium level, y will expand indefinitely. But y cannot expand indefinitely! For y, it will be remembered, is not the equilibrium level of output, which *can* expand indefinitely, given sufficient time; it is the proportion in which actual output exceeds the moving equilibrium output, and in that moving equilibrium the natural growth of the system has already been allowed for. It is therefore reasonable to assume that there is some maximum level which y cannot exceed – something which we may call the Full Employment level. Until that limit is reached, output can expand, both by natural growth and by a reduction in the percentage of unemployed resources. Once, however, the limit is reached, only natural growth is possible. And that means that y has reached its maximum value.

Let us write the full employment limit of y as f. Then if we have started, as before, from the moving equilibrium, and have encountered the full employment ceiling in the nth period after the initial divergence, we have the following situation. $y_{n-2} = (n-2)\lambda^{n-3}y_1; y_{n-1} = (n-1)\lambda^{n-2}y_1$; but y_n does not equal $n\lambda^{n-1}y_1$, but is kept down to the lower value f. What then happens to y_{n+1}? In order to discover this, we have to go back to the difference equation (6), for there is no reason why it should not continue to hold.

$$y_{n+1} = 2\lambda f - \lambda^2 y_{n-1}$$

This may be greater or less than f, but if it is greater than f, it will have to be replaced by f, since f is its greatest possible value. We pass on to y_{n+2}. Applying the difference equation to this, we see that its maximum possible value is $2\lambda f - \lambda^2 f = f[1 - (\lambda - 1)^2]$. This is definitely less than f; so that, *having reached its full employment limit, the system must begin to turn round again and output to go down, at least relatively to the trend.*

This conclusion is quite generally true. If we go back to the more general equation (5), we see that two successive ys which are equal and positive must be followed by a third which is lower than they are. This follows from the same inequality as gave us our fundamental condition that the (moving) equilibrium level of output should be positive.

What happens next? Effectively we are now starting from two successive ys which are both equal to the same positive magnitude f. We have to use the difference equation to work out the ensuing path. It is not difficult to show that successive ys will continue to fall, and that a point must be reached at which output does not merely fall relatively to its moving equilibrium, but falls absolutely.

When this happens, I think that we must reconsider our difference equation. If the system continued on the path determined by the same difference equation, output would ultimately fall to zero; our model, having agreed with experience quite well up to this point, would therefore at this point begin to diverge sharply. Can we see why? The induced investment, on which so much has depended, is investment induced by an *expansion* in output; if we maintained the same difference equation on the downswing as on the upswing, we should be letting it go into reverse and becoming negative when output began to fall. This does not look right. It is true that there are some sorts of investment (investment in working capital) for which a construction of this sort might be plausible. Increases in output induce investment in working capital, of the sort which we have so far taken into account; and it is reasonable to suppose that reductions in output will cause entrepreneurs to find their working capital excessive, so that they will take steps to reduce their excessive stocks. So far as fixed capital is concerned, however, this is not possible. There does therefore seem to be a changed situation in the downswing from what there was in the upswing, and it is reasonable to allow for this change by changing the form of the difference equation. Let us say, as a first approximation, that when output turns absolutely downwards, the induced investment term $c(Y_{n-1} - Y_{n-2})$ simply drops out. It becomes zero, but does not become negative. Suppose this occurs, what happens?

The difference equation now takes the form

$$H(1 + g)^n = Y_n - (1 - s) Y_{n-1} \qquad (7)$$

instead of the form expressed in equation (3). This is a much easier equation to handle than equation (3), but it will be convenient to set out its solution in a similar form. It will have a similar moving equilibrium, which we may write $L(1 + g)^n$, and the value of the constant L can be determined by a similar substitution. We get

$$H(1 + g)^n = L(1 + g)^n - (1 - s) L(1 + g)^{n-1}$$

or

$$L = \frac{1 + g}{s + g} H. \qquad (8)$$

Comparing this with the expression previously got for E [(4) above], we see that L will always be less than E, so that the new moving equilibrium will always be lower than the old.

Now write $Y_n = L(1 + g)^n (1 + z_n)$, so that z_n is the proportion in which actual income exceeds the new (lower) moving equilibrium level. Substituting this in (7) and using (8) we get

$$z_n = \frac{1 - s}{1 + g} z_{n-1}.$$

The coefficient $(1 - s)/(1 + g)$ is necessarily positive and less than unity. Starting, therefore, from a given value of z_0, the successive zs get smaller and smaller, in geometrical progression. By what is essentially the Kahn convergent series, the system tends towards its lower moving equilibrium $L(1 + g)^n$.

But it will not get there. For once z has fallen so far as to become less than a certain ratio (which, as can readily be verified, is the not particularly small ratio g/s), the fall in the proportion z by which actual output exceeds the lower moving equilibrium output becomes less than the rate at which that moving equilibrium is itself rising; and once this happens, actual output will begin to rise. The original difference equation should then come back into operation, and that will start a new expansion *relatively to the natural growth*.

The simplest way of proving that this must be so is the following. Suppose, for a moment, that there is no induced investment until the lower equilibrium has actually been reached. Then the system will start taking up successive positions which are actually on the lower equilibrium line. In these positions the ys (measured, as before, from the upper equilibrium) are negative and equal. Now if y_0 and y_1 are both equal to $-a$, we shall have [by (6)] $y_2 = -2\lambda a + \lambda^2 a$, so that $y_2 - y_1 = (\lambda - 1)^2 a$, which is certainly positive. It can further be shown, by the usual methods, that $y_n - y_{n-1} = (n - 1)\lambda^{n-2}(\lambda - 1)^2$, which will always be positive. The same result can be shown to hold for the more general case, in which we assume a larger value for c.

Thus, if the system actually hits its lower equilibrium, it will then be bound to start an upward expansion. If induced investment appears before it has hit the lower equilibrium, that is simply a further expansionary influence. The output so generated will then be greater, for each period, than that which we have just calculated. The expansion is therefore demonstrated *a fortiori*.

VI

Our model is now complete; and by our algebraic method, we have shown its internal consistency. For further discussion, it will be convenient to have a graphical representation.

Figure 15.2 represents the same variables as Fig. 15.1: time on the horizontal axis, and on the vertical the logarithm of output (or investment). Steady progress is therefore represented by a straight

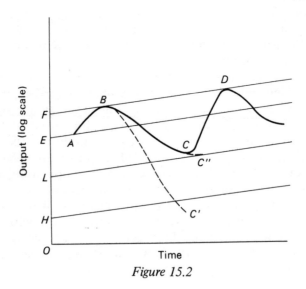

Figure 15.2

line which slopes upwards, and steady progress at the 'natural rate of growth' by a straight line of given slope. There are four such lines which play a part in our model. First, there is the Full Employment line F. Secondly, there is the 'upper equilibrium' line E; and thirdly there is the 'lower equilibrium' line L. Finally, there is the 'long-range investment' line H, the upward slope of which is responsible for the upward slopes of E and L. It should again be emphasised that output is being measured in real terms, so that F may slope upwards, on account of an upward trend in productivity, even if population is constant. H slopes upwards at the natural rate of growth, because, by assumption, it is geared to the trend. E and L slope upward because they depend on H.

We know that L must lie above H, because of the Keynesian multiplier argument. We know that E must lie above L, because E includes the multiplier effect of induced investment (at the natural rate of growth of output) as well as the multiplier effect of the long-range investment. We shall assume for the present that E lies below F, though it should be noticed that we have not proved that it must do so.

The E-line is such that the economy could possibly advance along it in a smooth manner without fluctuation. But it will do so only if it is held to it in some manner, for any chance divergence in either direction will set up a movement away from the equilibrium E. Suppose that there is a chance divergence in an upward direction. Output then begins to grow at more than its natural rate of growth, and though there may be some tendency for the actual rate of growth to slow up after some time has elapsed, the actual rate will always exceed the natural rate (at least according to the value which we have given to c). And that means that the actual path AB must hit the ceiling F sooner or later. But when it hits the ceiling, the rate of increase in output is slowed up, and therefore (in the next period) induced investment is cut down. But the induced investment, which corresponds to an increase in output at the natural rate (which is all that is allowed by the ceiling F) is only sufficient to engender a level of output which approximates to the E line, not one which goes along the F line. Output therefore tends to move back, on the course BC', towards the E line. But as output moves back, the rate of increase in output falls below the natural rate, and in consequence actual output tends to fall below the E line. The track which would be generated, on this principle, after the 'upper turning-point' B had been passed, would plunge downwards indefinitely, tending towards an output of zero. I show it on the diagram by the dotted line BC'.

It was, however, at this point that we felt it necessary to introduce our second complication. A downward movement in actual output, when it becomes an absolute fall, not merely a fall relatively to the natural rate of growth, should not be thought of as causing induced investment to become negative (or at least as only doing so to a minor extent). The path BC' is therefore too pessimistic. If zero is the lowest point to which induced investment can fall, then on the downtrack we have a situation in which the only investment occurring is that which is represented by H. And L is the equilibrium to which the system will tend when the only investment is that represented by H. The system will therefore move along a path BC'', which is determined by the familiar multiplier theory of Keynes (or Kahn). This path will merge into the L line at a point C''.

But since the L line is upward sloping, the path BC'' will have begun to turn upwards at a point C, which precedes C''. At this point the 'accelerator' comes back into gear. It must then bring about a positive induced investment, which will cause the actual path to diverge from CC'' in an upward direction. The rate of growth will then soon be in excess of the natural rate, and the path CD must therefore intersect the E line sooner or later. When it does so, it will still have a rate of growth in excess of the natural rate, and will therefore keep on rising. Finally, it must hit the F line, and when it does so, it is bound to turn down as before, for exactly the same reason as before.

There has thus been engendered a complete cycle, and a cycle which is completely self-perpetuating. It must turn down when it gets to the top, and when it approaches the bottom it must turn up. So long as the fundamental data remain unchanged, actual output must fluctuate between the limits L and F, and will do so indefinitely.

VII

Further, what has been accomplished is something more than the making of a special model, which happens to show a fluctuation, something like the observed sort, for certain values of its parameters. We have used special values for purposes of illustration, but the cycle which has been engendered does not depend on the special values chosen. All that is necessary is (1) that the relations between income and consumption, on the one hand, and between investment and changes in income, on the other, should be such as to impart a rather strong tendency to instability in the level of output; (2) that the system should have an upward trend, and that some investment should be geared to that upward trend; (3) that the supply of resources, at any given time, should not be inexhaustible; (4) that falls in output should not induce disinvestment, in the way that rises in output induce investment, except (possibly) to a minor extent. These conditions are certainly not at all restrictive; all of them (except possibly the first) are things which we should naturally expect to be true. And the first condition, though its validity is certainly far from self-evident, is not intrinsically unplausible. We do therefore seem to have shown that a cycle, which is strongly reminiscent of that which we experience, can be explained on the basis of a minimum number of hypotheses, each of which is very reasonable in itself. It is hardly possible for a *theory* of the Cycle to do more than that.

Besides, from this point we can again go forward. The next thing to do should be to reconsider the very simple difference equation on which our formal analysis (though not the real essence of our argument) has been based. It is, as a matter of fact, most unlikely that the two relations (between income and consumption, and between investment and change in income) are as simple in form as we have assumed them to be. We have taken a simple form, in order to keep our main difference equation down to the second order; but there can be little doubt that the equation we thereby got is over-simplified, though it should be noticed that the mathematical difficulties accumulate very rapidly when we introduce additional complications in this direction. There is, however, one generalisation which can be made without incurring these mathematical difficulties. We can allow for the probability that a part of consumption will depend upon current income as well as a part on previous income; an amendment in this direction makes the system *more* liable to fluctuate.[6] This has a bearing on the weakest of the four assumptions listed in the previous paragraph. It will probably have been noticed that in order to get our model to work, we did apparently need a rather large value for the capital coefficient c; it looked as if it had to be distinctly larger than unity.[7] So large a value for c is not altogether unplausible (Mr Harrod is evidently prepared to accept a value of this order of

---

[6] We can also allow for the possibility that a part of consumption may be geared to the trend of income without introducing additional difficulties. The effect of this amendment would be to diminish the amplitude of fluctuations, but not to diminish the probability of their occurrence.

[7] When $c = 1$, it means that an increase in real output by £100 millions (at given prices) causes an increase in investment by £100 millions (at prices which correspond).

magnitude); nevertheless when we remember that 'long-range' investment is being otherwise allowed for, a doubt must remain whether so large a value of c is realistic. It is therefore useful to notice that if only a part of consumption is lagged, we can manage to work our model with much smaller values of c. The value of c can be appreciably less than unity, and we can still get the required instability in the level of output.

Such things evidently need much further enquiry; but the way to that enquiry is now open. It will then be of great importance to study the changes in the model which may occur through changes in the sizes of some of the parameters, and to enquire whether they have any correspondence with observed changes in the behaviour of the actual economy through various cycles. If it could be shown that there is such correspondence, the theory would receive striking confirmation. I am in fact inclined to think that some of this confirmation can be sighted without looking very far. One thing which clearly could happen would be that the value of c was not large enough for the upward swing (AB or CD in Fig. 15.2) to hit the Full Employment ceiling. If this were to happen, the boom would turn down before it hit the ceiling; but the rest of the cycle could apparently go on as before. Does not this look very like the case of the boom which 'peters out'? Mr Harrod has done some useful work on the factors determining the size of c; by using his researches on this point, and concentrating on the effects of changes in his factors in this direction, it does look as if the theory we have been advancing should be capable of some indirect verification.

Again, it is clearly not realistic to assume that the 'height' of the H line (the long-range investment) will, as we have drawn it, be constant in all circumstances. Such things as wars and their aftermaths (and maybe other disturbances too) must be thought of as causing 'autonomous' fluctuations in long-range investment. The effects of such fluctuations could be analysed. A considerable upward hump in the H-line could, for instance, push the corresponding E *above* the Full Employment line. If this happened, there would be no tendency for output to turn down when it reached the Full Employment level. Let us consider the matter, for instance, in terms of equation (6). We saw that in a system which was 'driven' by that equation, two successive ys which were both equal to f would be succeeded by a third which was equal to $f - (\lambda - 1)^2 f$; if f is positive, this must be smaller than f. But if f is negative, as in the case we are considering, the third y will be *larger* than f; being above the Full Employment level, it will then have to be replaced by f. Thus the system can remain in Full Employment as long as the hump in the *H*-curve lasts.

This is itself a highly suggestive result; one further modification, which can be introduced into our structure, not only without damage but with benefit, makes it more suggestive still. It is not quite right to treat 'Full Employment', as we have done hitherto, as a rigid barrier; it is better to regard it as a zone which, if penetrated, calls forth rapidly increasing resistances to the expansion of output, but in which some increase of output can, up to a point, still be attained. This modification makes no real difference to the structure of our theory; the slowing-up of expansion, due to the resistances, will still cause output to turn downwards once the zone is fairly penetrated, so long as the equilibrium level *E* is lower than the level at which the resistances begin. But if we allow that the resistances begin (as I think they do) at a level of output which is short of that where there is a tendency to full inflation, we get another important result. We can see why it is that the ordinary commercial boom, carried by induced investment, is most unlikely to penetrate through the resisting medium so far as to cause any serious inflation; the resistances will cause it to turn downwards before it gets to that point. It is only when there is a big hump in the *H*-curve, pushing the equilibrium level well into the Full Employment zone, that the system can have enough 'steam' in it to carry it to the inflationary point. The ordinary commercial boom is unlikely to do that. Our theory therefore affords a ready explanation of another well-established practical generalisation, which was previously rather out of touch with theory; it shows why it is that inflation is so liable to occur in conditions of war and post-war reconstruction, but rarely (if ever) results from a purely commercial boom.

I should, however, not like it to be inferred from these arguments that a continued boosting of the *H*-curve, so as to keep *E* above *F*, is a desirable solution of the cycle problem. For what is bound to happen, in this 'over-employment' situation, is that induced investment is kept steadily below its normal relation to current output. And since, on the whole, the induced investment is *needed* in order to enable output to be produced efficiently, its repression (certainly its continued repression) is bound to have adverse effects on the efficiency of production. Thus even if the danger of open inflation can be somehow averted, this 'solution' can cure the cycle only at the price of a severe loss in efficiency. The true object of policy should be to keep the equilibrium line as near as possible to the Full Employment mark, but not to push beyond it. If this is done, it will also be

necessary to have measures at hand to correct the downward divergences from equilibrium, which are then liable to occur. This policy
is much harder than its alternative; but if it can be achieved, its
results will be infinitely preferable.

16

Inflation and the Wage-Structure

PREFATORY NOTE

This was my presidential address to the Economics section (Section F) of the British Association for the Advancement of Science, given at the Bristol meeting in September 1955. It was published that same month in the *Economic Journal*, under the title 'Economic Foundations of Wage Policy', and was reprinted in my *Essays in World Economics* (1959). I have given it a new title since the old – suggested by the title of a book by Barbara Wootton, *Social Foundations of Wage Policy*, which was then arousing a good deal of attention – would now seem to suggest that the issue was being treated as narrowly economic, instead of being a matter of the inter-play between social and economic factors, as I was in fact regarding it.

I like to look at this as following on from my essay on post-war recovery (13 above). By 1955 the phase of reconstruction was over, and Britain, as well as several other countries, was beginning on that period of remarkable prosperity which was to last another fifteen years. It was a period with an ever-present danger of cost-inflation, or wage-inflation, which was nevertheless sufficiently held in check. How? If I had been writing my paper at the end of that period, instead of at the beginning, I would still have given the answer which is here implied. It had nothing to do with monetary policy, or fiscal policy; it was simply that for all that time the *external* economic pressures, to which a wage-structure (any wage-structure) is always exposed, were never of such violence as to upset the stability of social relationships. The 'optimism' which I expressed at the end of the paper could be no more than an assertion of the possibility that this might happen; it was not a prophecy that it would happen, as in fact it did. Of course, I did not foresee that the British terms of trade would remain nearly constant, throughout the late fifties and over the whole of the sixties; but I did show that a violent movement, such as occurred in the early seventies, must upset the stability, as indeed it has.

This was the last of my papers which I discussed with Robertson. He did not share my 'optimism', so was shocked by my terminology, my 'Labour Standard'. But with my view that the 'social' wage-system was a fair-weather system, he had no disagreement.

In the year 1929, when the British Association was meeting at Cape Town, the President of Section F was Henry Clay, and he took as his subject 'The Public Regulation of Wages in Great Britain'.[1] I remember, from that time, how great a stimulus that paper was to my own thinking, and I have not changed my opinion of it. Of the problem of wages, as it then stood, Clay gave what I still believe to have been a substantially correct analysis. But a tide of events, which set in almost as he spoke, was to bring about a great transformation. The revolutions which have occurred in the realm of fact, quite as much as those which have occurred in the realm of ideas, have presented us with a wages question which looks very different from the wages question of 1929. Nevertheless, underlying the differences, some of them real differences, some of them seeming, there is a certain continuity. I propose, in this paper, to survey some aspects of the developments which have occurred, and to attempt an estimation of their significance. I believe that the time has come when it is desirable to make an effort to bring the whole matter back into focus.

The first thing on which Clay had to remark, from the standpoint of 1929, was the spread of collective bargaining (and other forms of *public regulation*) from the mere fraction of the wage-earning population (perhaps a quarter) which had been covered some twenty years previously, to a point where (as he said) 'we may safely conclude that there are few important gaps left in the provision for the settlement of wages by collective bargaining in Great Britain'. But then he went on:[2]

The precise nature of this change is worth some consideration. It was not the introduction for the first time of standardised rates of pay in time-work occupations. Even if we leave out of account the considerable part of the field covered by Trade Unionism at the beginning of the century, it is probable that in most districts, in which an occupation was followed by considerable numbers, there were customary rates commonly recognised, which the majority of employers observed. These rates were not so definite and secure as they became

[1] *EJ*, XXXIX, p. 323.
[2] *Ibid*., p. 324.

when they were embodied in a collective agreement; but outside the so-called 'sweated trades', they were a limitation on the freedom of the individual employer to vary rates. Immediately, wages were fixed for him rather than by him, although ultimately they had to conform to the demand for labour, of which he was the channel. Nor was the change a universal substitution of collective for individual bargaining about rates. In piece-work industries after the change, as before, the vast majority of rates were settled by an individual bargain between the workman and the employer's representative.... The significance and essential change was the change in procedure. Wage-rates in any case have to be adjusted to changes in the demands for different kinds of labour, changes in the purchasing power of money, changes in the general prosperity and activity of industry. Before the war, outside the organised industries, the adjustment was made by the individual action of the employers, who first felt the need; today the process of general wage-changes has, we may say, been constitutionalised.

I have quoted this passage from Clay's paper because it seems to me to describe, with considerable precision, just what it was that had happened. It has never been the general rule that wage-rates have been determined simply and solely by supply and demand. Even on pure grounds of efficiency, it is desirable that the wage which is offered should be acceptable, acceptable both to the worker himself and to those with whom he is to work. There has in consequence always been room for wages to be influenced by non-economic forces – whether by custom (which, economically speaking, means supply and demand of the day before yesterday), or by any other principle which affects what the parties to the wage-bargain think to be *just* or *right*. Economic forces do affect wages, but only when they are strong enough to overcome these *social* forces. Now what happened, as a result of the spread of public regulation, was that the social forces grew in strength. As Clay put it:

The mere fact of publicity, or organised discussion, invites appeal to social and ethical standards of 'fair' and 'living' wages, to pseudo-principles such as the sanctity of pre-war *real* wages, to the unpopularity of reducing the rates of wages of the lower paid workers, none of which have any bearing on the capacity of industry to pay wages and provide employment.

The main thing is that the new procedure insulated the wage structure from its old exposure to economic pressures, so that it could move – to a considerable extent – on a course of its own.

But the economic forces were not abolished by the increased resistance which could be offered to them; if they were not allowed to influence the determination of wages, they would express themselves in other ways. If the actual wage-level drew too far away from the 'equilibrium' wage-level, being (as in fact it would be) above the equilibrium wage-level, the discrepancy would express itself in a growth of unemployment. And though the 'social' wage-structure could stand up to a certain amount of unemployment, there must (so Clay thought) be a limit beyond which it must give. Then, after much pain and grief, there would be a return to something nearer to an 'equilibrium wage'.

This is what Clay expected to happen; but, as we know, it is not what did happen. Unemployment did increase, as he expected; but though the wage-structure yielded a little, on the whole it did not give way. What did give was another link in the chain – the Gold Standard.

In the new world which began after 1931 the problem of wages is bound to have a distinctly different character from that which it had in the older time. Since 1931, wages questions have been closely associated with monetary questions, it is even true that the *general* level of wages has become a monetary question. So long as wages were being determined within a *given* monetary framework, there was some sense in saying that there was an 'equilibrium wage', a wage that was in line with the monetary conditions that were laid down from outside. But the world we now live in is one in which the monetary system has become relatively elastic, so that it can accommodate itself to changes in wages, rather than the other way about. Instead of actual wages having to adjust themselves to an equilibrium level, monetary policy adjusts the equilibrium level of money wages so as to make it conform to the actual level.[3] It is hardly an exaggeration to say that instead of being on a Gold Standard, we are on a Labour Standard.

I should like to make it quite clear, before going further, that I myself regard the Labour Standard as an unquestionable benefit. So long as we retain it, we are protected against the unemployment that arises from a discrepancy between the actual wage-level and the 'equilibrium wage-level'; and though there are other causes of unemployment than this, it has been one of the main causes of unemployment in the past, and it is a great gain that this cause of unemployment has been removed. It is not a gain which anyone should desire to give up; it is nevertheless not a simple matter to find ways by which we can be sure of preserving it.

---

[3] I do not want to suggest that it does this perfectly; but this is what it is trying to do. The problems which arise when demand is extended too far, or not far enough, to maintain the desired general level of employment, are of major importance; but they lie outside the scope of this paper.

For the Labour Standard, in our twenty years' experience of it, has been shown to possess a number of defects, of which some are decidedly dangerous. The first set of defects, which merit attention, though they fall rather outside my present subject, relate to the international consequences of the new arrangements. If the value of the pound is fixed in terms of British labour, and the value of the mark is fixed in terms of German labour, the pound–mark exchange will not remain steady unless the value of British labour in terms of German labour remains steady. But this last is a matter of the real economic progress and economic policies of the two countries; it requires something more than a monetary arrangement to control it. While the Gold Standard was an international standard, the Labour Standard is a national standard; even at its best, it is bound to be a source of difficulty in the sphere of international currency relations. But these difficulties are very familiar; I need do no more than allude to them in this place.

Already, in the first years of the Labour Standard, these international repercussions were a grave preoccupation; indeed, at that time they were the only consequence of the change which aroused much anxiety. But as time has gone on another weakness has been revealed, which (at least for the time being) has pushed the international weakness into the background. Whereas, under the Gold Standard, the value of the national money in terms of the Standard was fixed by the State (and the maintenance, or in a few cases the regulation, of this gold value was recognised as a major responsibility of the State), under the Labour Standard the value of money in terms of labour undergoes no deliberate determination. It is a mere by-product of the process of wage-fixing; wage-fixing being sectional, the value of money in terms of the standard comes to be determined by impersonal forces, and those forces seem to have a strong tendency to pull it one way.

It is not surprising that this danger took some time to declare itself. In the last days of the old system, when the new (fortified) wage-structure was resisting the monetary pressures that were being exerted upon it, successful resistance expressed itself in the form of rigidity. Economic forces were pressing wages downwards; social forces held them up. The net effect was that the level of money wages held firm. It was very natural for Clay, in 1929, to think in terms of rigid wages. Over the years 1924–8 (the only 'normal' years which were available to him as a basis for generalisation) the Bowley index of weekly wage-rates in Great Britain had been rock-like – it has never moved by as much as a point. Under the impact of the Depression, there was indeed a marked *fall* in wages (though much less than the fall in the cost of living); but it was some time before the relief of that pressure led to a rise which went beyond the previous level. As late as 1937, the wage-index was within 1 per cent of its 1924-8 figure. Thus the Labour Standard started operations with the very natural assumption that the level of wages (or the value of money in terms of labour) could, at least in Britain, be taken as given. With rigid wages, the problem of the new standard was one of external stability; internal stability did not seem to be a problem.

During the war years the position was, of course, very different; but war inflation is no new experience, and the significance of war inflation for the future of the Labour Standard did not reveal itself at once. It is only in the years since 1945, which have been marked by a continual rise in the wage-index, rarely falling short of 4 per cent per annum, that the existence of a special problem of the Labour Standard has become apparent. Must we conclude, from the experience of the last ten years, that the Labour Standard has an inherent inflationary bias? If so, is it much more dangerous than the similar biases which have been detected in other monetary systems? These are the main questions which I want to discuss in the rest of this paper.

One further point must be cleared out of the way before I can begin. It is possible to argue that the main evil of monetary instability, as it was known in past times, was the unemployment which periodically accompanied it; if we have to expect an age of monetary instability, but are guaranteed against the accompanying unemployment, the expectation can be borne with equanimity. There is something in this argument, but the optimism which it engenders can be carried too far. A rapid rate of wage-inflation must surely be an evil, if only because of the diversion of effort into fixing and refixing of wages and hitherto stable prices, effort which might otherwise be used for more productive purposes. A very rapid rate of wage-inflation could threaten the continuance of the Labour Standard altogether. I would, however, admit that there is some rate of wage-inflation which, if it can be prevented from accelerating, is by no means intolerable; the question is what means exist for keeping it within tolerable limits.

Let us, then, go back to the labour market, and look at it more closely. Granted the Labour Standard, can we lay down any general principles about the ways in which wages are likely to be determined? What are the factors making for inflation, and what (if any) are those by which the inflation may be held in check? These are questions which can, I believe, be answered if we tackle them in the spirit of Clay's analysis, though we get no sensible answers to them if we persist in treating them as pure problems of economics, in a narrow sense.

The purely economic analysis of collective bargaining, in terms of the theory of bilateral monopoly, used to conceive of wage-rates being fixed, on a balance of bargaining advantage, between a trade union which sought to push wages as high as possible without causing intolerable unemployment, and an employers' association which sought to press wages as low as possible without causing a shortage of labour. If one thinks in those terms the prospects of anything like stable wages, under a Labour Standard, do indeed look bleak. For the labour market then becomes a pure case of unstable equilibrium. It is not necessary to suppose that each trade union is completely safeguarded against the danger of unemployment in its own trade. If it is laid down that a rise in wages in the A-industry is not to produce any general increase in unemployment, that is enough. For effective demand (for goods in general) will then have to be expanded somewhat when A-wages rise.[4] But that will increase the bargaining power of the workers in other industries, so that if wages in these other industries are determined on the same bilateral monopoly principle, they will rise too. But that, under the assumptions we are making, will call forth a further increase in effective demand, which provides an opportunity for a further rise in the A-industry. The only thing which would slow down the general rise in wages would be the time taken to negotiate wage-changes, and that, if it was to people's interest to speed it up, could presumably be speeded up.

Now I would quite admit that there are some occasions on which the actual process of wage-fixing takes a form which is not far away from that implied in this model; but I find it hard to believe that it has any general validity. We are now learning that the pure theory of monopoly has a very limited application to the behaviour of business-men on the markets on which they sell their products; it is even less likely that it has much application to the labour market – on either side. We get a better clue to actual behaviour if we think of wages as being determined by an interplay between social and

[4] How far this rise in demand comes about *naturally* (if monetary and fiscal policy does not prevent it), or how far deliberate intervention is needed to procure it, is a question that I do not have to raise in this paper. It will be simpler to talk as if 'steps have to be taken' to procure the increase in demand; but by using such expressions I do not mean to prejudge the question whether these steps are of a positive or negative character.

economic factors, instead of being based on economic factors – and crude economic factors at that – alone. As we have seen, this was true to a considerable extent under the old conditions. It is still more likely to be true under the Labour Standard, when everyone is bound to have some realisation that the number of shillings in the pay packet are not the thing that really matters. Money wages are not demanded for their own sake, but as a means towards something else.

The only exception to this rule which I can think of, and it is a very partial exception, is that a wage claim may sometimes be made on the basis of comparison with what the wage of that class of labour has been in the past. It certainly was true, in the old days, that a wage-cut would be followed, at the first opportunity, by a demand for a restoration of the wage to its former level. But with the increased strength of the unions, under the Labour Standard, all that is left of this point is the general resistance to any cuts in previously agreed wage-rates, which is one of the principles on which the new wage-system seems to proceed. It is true that if wages can go up, but cannot go down, that is enough in itself to give the system an inflationary bias; it does not, however, follow that the bias will be so strong as to be unmanageable.

Otherwise, if we think of the grounds on which cases are made for a rise in the wages of any section of labour, the mere money value of the wages received has nothing to do with them. Wage disputes are not concerned with money wages; they are concerned with the relations of money wages to the money values of other things. But the things with which comparison is made differ from one wage-dispute to another; it will be useful to classify them under three heads. Of course, it may often happen that more than one sort of comparison is playing a part in some particular claim; nevertheless, the distinction between them is readily recognisable in practice. And the economic significance of claims on one ground or another is decidedly different.[5]

The three things with which comparison is most naturally made are: (1) the prices of the things labour buys – the cost of living; (2) the wages of other workers – differentials; (3) the profits earned

---

[5] I should like to emphasise that the classification I am making does not merely refer to the grounds on which claims are put forward by the Unions; the same motives play a part in determining the attitude taken by employers to the claims which the Unions make. Doubtless it is true that supply-and-demand considerations have more influence on employers than they have on the Unions; but it is impossible to make sense of what happens unless one admits that the same general principles of equity in wage-determination are accepted, in a large measure, by both sides.

by the employer. I propose to discuss these three comparisons rather separately, but in each case from a double point of view. On the one hand, I want to ask about the conditions in which wage-claims on the basis of each comparison are most likely to be pressed – a question which, if we can answer it, may throw some light upon the probable extent of wage-inflation in the future; on the other hand, I want to say something about the attitude which other members of society should take towards wage-claims made on one basis or another, with special reference to the economic arguments by which that attitude may be (or perhaps I may dare to say should be) affected.

The first of my three heads is the cost of living. The ratio of wages to the cost of living is what the economist calls real wages; the desirability of having real wages as high as possible, consistently with high employment, is a social objective which he is inclined to take for granted. Nevertheless, it is clear that wage-claims are not ordinarily made on the mere ground that the workers would like to have higher real wages; rises in real wages do for the most part come about in fact as a consequence of rises in productivity (either at home or abroad) without wage policy playing, at bottom, any more than a passive part in the process. When the cost-of-living motive does become important, in relation to wage-claims, is when extraneous factors are tending to produce a rise in the cost of living relatively to wages – or what comes to the same thing, a fall in real wages. It is in such circumstances that the cost-of-living motive takes the lead, and becomes, under the Labour Standard, an independent force making for inflation.

But in a modern economy, what has normally to be expected is rising productivity; and rising productivity, combined with constant money wages, means falling prices. So long as this tendency remains dominant, there is no need for there to be any pressure for rising money wages on account of the cost of living. The cost of living appears as an independent cause of wage inflation only at times when the normal course of economic progress is interrupted; its appearance is a symptom that something more fundamental is going, or has gone, wrong. Thus it is, of course, a major issue in war-time; it is also important whenever the march of rising real wages suffers a setback, due (for instance) to some change, adverse to this country, in our economic relations with the world outside. The novelty of the Labour Standard is that in the latter case, as well as the former, the cost-of-living motive becomes a source of inflationary pressure. In this respect the lessons of the Korean episode were perhaps more significant than those of the war with Hitler.

The only anti-inflationary measures which are available, under the Labour Standard, to deal with such situations are price-control and, if necessary, rationing; it is one of the costs of the Labour Standard that these measures require to be introduced in order to deal with slighter and more temporary falls in real wages than would previously have required such drastic treatment. Further, though this is the only way out, it is difficult to make it wholly effective; if it is not wholly effective, it brings other troubles with it.

Suppose, for instance, that some external event (say an adverse movement of the terms of trade) makes it necessary to reduce consumption by a small percentage. If the reduction could take place by a rise in prices, without wages rising, prices would fall again when the shortage was over, and consumption would recover without further action. Alternatively, if the rise in wages could be wholly prevented by control over prices, the reduction in consumption (which cannot be avoided) would be brought about by an excess of demand over supply; supplies would recover when the shortage was over, and the controls could be lifted forthwith. But if the controls do not wholly prevent the rise in wages, or are introduced too late to have that effect, there may be an *apparent* rise in real wages amid the shortage; though consumption has to be diminished, the ratio of the money wage to the controlled price-level rises. In this case a mere recovery of supplies to their old level will not immediately enable the controls to be lifted without a renewal of inflation. For though the old real wage could be re-established, the apparent real wage (in the sense of the ratio of wages to prices) cannot be made effective on a free market until productivity has risen further. I think one can detect an element of this story in our own recent experience. It is one of the drawbacks of using controls to meet a temporary emergency that a 'phoney' relation of wages to prices can be established under the shelter of the controls, a relation which does not truly measure the real gain of labour; yet it is this 'phoney' relation which is sought to be maintained, in place of a maintenance of the real standard of living, when the controls are removed.

I turn to my second heading – relative wages in the narrower sense, the relation of one wage to another. If we have to take it for granted that it is hardly possible, under the Labour Standard, for the money wages of any group of workers to be *reduced*, it follows that troubles about wage differentials can themselves be a cause of inflation. In the simplest possible terms, if *A*-workers think that their wages should be 10 per cent higher than those of *B*-workers, while *B*-workers think that their wages should be equal to those of A-workers, the satisfaction of the claims of one party must necessarily give rise to claims by the other. If both sets of workers are employed in the same industry, a series of concessions to such claims may push the costs of this industry right out of line with those of other industries; then, even under a Labour Standard, the industry will find itself in difficulties. But if troubles about differentials become widespread, this brake on the wage-rise may disappear. The increase in effective demand, which has to be induced in order to prevent the first wage-rise from causing unemployment, facilitates wage-increases elsewhere. The industries which have been left behind in the advance then become sensitive in their turn, but because of the inter-industry differentials which have come into existence through the sectional advance and because of the rising cost of living. It accordingly appears, without going farther, that though wage-differentials can give rise to a certain amount of soreness without causing more than localised trouble, they must, on the whole, be moderately acceptable if they are not, under a Labour Standard, to be themselves a source of inflation.

But how can wage-differentials be acceptable? To those who feel the ethical urge to equality as a guiding impulse, the clearest thing about wage-differentials is that they ought always if possible to be reduced. Such sentiments have lately been expressed with cogency by Mrs Wootton, the title of whose book[6] I have deliberately echoed in the title of this paper. Nevertheless, one can appeal to Mrs Wootton herself for a demonstration that these sentiments, though they are without doubt *one* of the 'social' forces at work on the wage-structure, are in practice overlaid by other 'social' forces which work in the opposite direction. In practice, differentials do tend to be acceptable if they have custom behind them – if they are in accordance with what the people who suffer from them, as well as those who gain from them, have come to expect. Thus in conditions when the level of money wages is, broadly speaking, stationary, the purely egalitarian urge to raise the wages of the lower-paid workers relatively to others is not often in practice very strong. It is true that egalitarian sentiments have more power when wages are changing. Especially if the impetus to a wage-rise is derived from the cost-of-living motive, it is recognised that a fall in real wages is a more serious matter for the lower-wage than for the higher-wage groups; the former have a stronger case for a cost-of-living bonus than the

[6] Barbara Wootton [now Lady Wootton], *The Social Foundations of Wage Policy* (1955).

latter. In such circumstances wage-differentials do tend to narrow: sometimes actually in money terms, but more often by giving both groups the *same* rise in money terms, in spite of the difference in the wages from which they began. This has in fact the effect of diminishing the real advantage of the better paid, in view of the higher price-level.

Thus, if one looks entirely at these 'social' forces, custom is the static and equality the dynamic element; time, especially when aided by inflation, might be expected to iron all differentials flat. Certainly there is a tendency in that direction; but how far it can go depends upon the economic obstacles which may lie in its path. There are economic factors to be taken into account, though the precise way in which they can operate under a Labour Standard needs some consideration.

Let us begin from a state of all-round full employment of labour, in which there is yet no 'over-employment'; the demand for labour equals the supply in all trades. Now suppose that wage-rates, in some particular trade, are raised to such an extent as would cause a substantial reduction in employment in that trade, if there were no expansion of demand in general. If, however, demand is expanded, the appearance of unemployment may be prevented. But the expansion of demand will have to take a particular form (involving special protection for the high-wage industry) if its difficulties are therby to be overcome. Otherwise, though the demand for its products will indeed be expanded (so that employment of the high-wage labour will fall less than it would have fallen if the expansion had not occurred), the demand for other products will be expanded at the same time. Among the labour producing these products we have assumed that there is no unemployment. A moderate increase in demand will accordingly produce a situation in which there is some fall in employment in the A-trade (as we may call it) combined with an excess of demand over supply (involving unfilled vacancies) in other (B) trades. There are now two cases, according as the workers who are unable to get employment in the A-trade can, or cannot, step into the vacancies which have appeared elsewhere. If they can, there will be no net unemployment as a result of the change in relative wages; all that will have happened is a transfer of labour from A to B. But if there are difficulties in the way of the transfer, it may be necessary to create a severe shortage of labour in the B-trades before the labour displaced from the A-trade can be absorbed. The maintenance of full employment then implies the creation of severe labour shortages.

But let us take the milder case first. It is highly probable that the situation implied in this case is no novelty. If the workers in skilled trades, by the use of bargaining power, push their wages to an unnecessarily high level, they limit the scope for employment in those trades, but they do not necessarily cause any labour to be unemployed; all that happens is that some people, who might have got employment in those trades, have to seek it elsewhere. This sort of thing could occur under the old conditions, and it can still occur under a Labour Standard. Differentials which owe their origin to no better cause than this can last a long time, and become hallowed by custom. And differentials which did once have an economic function, but are maintained by custom after they have lost it, fall from the economic point of view into a similar category.

It is obviously probable that the wage-structure, at any particular time, will contain many 'unnecessary' or 'uneconomic' differentials of this type; but their identification can never be a simple matter. The test which the economist would be inclined to use, whether or not a reduction in wages would increase employment and output in the trade affected, is not easy to use, nor is it in all cases quite conclusive. It is true, if this test is satisfied, that the additional employment is a clear gain to the workers who move (for they need not move unless they think it is to their advantage to do so); while the consequential increase in output is a clear gain to the consumers who take the additional units (for they need not take them unless they conceive themselves to gain by so doing). It is true that these shifts are clear gains, while the loss to the workers who were previously employed (and whose wages are reduced) is in some sense 'balanced' by a reduction in cost which is a gain to other parties. But though these principles may be accepted, some weight can neverthe-less be given to the counter-contention that the lowering of (relative) wages may lower standards of skill and craftsmanship, in such a way as to wipe out in the longer run much or all of the short-run gain. Those concerned have a strong interest to make as much as they can of this counter-argument; we can recognise that, and still admit that there are cases in which it does have a certain validity.

It does nevertheless seem clear, in the light of this analysis, that actual differentials are always, to a considerable extent, historically determined; their correspondence with those which would ensure maximum efficiency in the distribution of labour cannot be expected to be very close. It follows that the 'squeezing' of differentials (which we have seen to be a feature of cost-of-living inflation) has some economic as well as social function. It squeezes out differentials which have become fossilised; in doing so, it serves the cause of efficiency as well as that of distributive justice.

All the same, the fact that it does so is really no more than an accident. Since it is not itself impelled by any motive of economic efficiency, it can easily go too far. If it overshoots the mark, and reduces differentials below the amounts which are economically justified, we get a new problem, which is in fact a problem of the second case which I left over a little while back, and to which I must now turn.

If the differential between skilled and less skilled is fixed too low, so that it is the relatively low-wage labour which is overvalued, an intensity of demand which is sufficient to maintain full employment among skilled workers will be insufficient for the full employment of the less skilled; an intensity which is sufficient to employ the less skilled will cause a shortage of labour in the skilled trades. An intensity which is between these two limits will leave some unemployment among the less skilled, and some unfilled vacancies among the skilled; but the less skilled will *not* be able to move over to fill these vacancies. Those who are unemployed are unlikely to be suitable to fill the vacancies, even if they are trained; while those who would be suitable will not move, because the incentive is insufficient. It is accordingly impossible, if differentials are too narrow, to maintain full employment without creating a scarcity of skilled labour.

Such a scarcity need not be inflationary, but it is only too likely to work out in such a way that it will be. For it is necessary, at this point, to distinguish between those trades in which the collectively agreed rates have a close correspondence with actual earnings, and those in which the agreed rates are minima, so that actual earnings can easily move out of line with what has been collectively fixed.[7] If the skilled trades, whose wages had become relatively depressed, were all of the first class, then (so far as I can see) the shortage of skilled labour would create inefficiencies, but would not lead to any general movement in wages. If, at the other extreme, they were all of the second class, it would be impossible to reduce *earnings* differentials below the amount which was economically justified.

[7] The importance of this point was brought home to me by the studies of Mr Kenneth Knowles, which have appeared in the *Bulletin* of the Oxford Institute of Statistics from 1951 onwards. (See in particular his 'Structure of Engineering Earnings', *Bulletin*, September 1954.) But this is not the only place in which my reflections have been stimulated by a consideration of the facts which Mr Knowles has so ably brought together.

Any attempt to do so would merely cause the earnings of the higher-wage group to rise above their minima; the market for their labour, under the conditions of scarcity, would become a competitive market. In fact, however, we have neither of these extreme cases; the actual situation is a mixture of the two, some skilled trades belonging to one type, some to the other. The effect of labour scarcity must then be a rise in earnings in the 'free-wage' trades; but this creates a disparity (which is felt to be a disparity) between them and the other skilled trades in which wages are 'fixed'. Conditions thus become favourable for a rise in wages in the 'fixed-wage' skilled trades; and such a rise, in the circumstances supposed, is not without economic justification. But these 'fixed' wages are a part of the regular structure of agreed wages; a rise in any part of it tends to produce a general tendency to an upward movement, working through the 'social' links which tie the various parts of the structure together. This is the way in which an attachment to 'wrong' relative wages can be an inflationary element; its inflationary influence cannot be removed (consistently with full employment) until people become prepared to accept economically reasonable differentials – differentials which are sufficient, that is, to ensure that lasting shortages of important classes of skilled labour are avoided.

I would emphasise the word 'lasting'. It does not follow from my analysis that a temporary scarcity of some particular kind of skilled labour, even if it leads to a sharp increase in the earnings of that trade, out of line with those of other comparable trades, need have very far-reaching effects on the wage-structure in general. Since it takes time, often a considerable time, to select and train additional workers for any specialised trade or occupation, it must be expected that the wage (or earnings) which will equate supply and demand in the short run, after a rise in demand has taken place, will be higher than that which would induce a sufficient supply in the long period. This is indeed one of the common ways in which unnecessarily high differentials come into existence; wages are pushed up at a time of initial scarcity, and they fail to come down at the later stage when there has been time for the supply of labour to become more ample. Ideally, what should happen in such cases is that the agreed minimum should be kept in relation with the long-run supply-price of labour, while the incentive to move (only temporarily required) should be given, by a temporary rise in wages above the minimum. For sufficiently temporary scarcities, one can perhaps detect a tendency for the wage-system to be operated in something like this manner. It is indeed more in accordance with trade-union principles that negotiated wages should reflect what can be maintained as a regular thing over a period than that they should fluctuate up (and, at least relatively, down) with every fluctuation of demand and supply on the labour market.

This brings me to my last heading, profits – on which I shall have to be brief, and must therefore do much less than justice to the subject. It is obvious that when businesses are earning high profits they can be more easily brought to concede claims for higher wages; it follows for this reason alone that it is in conditions of high profits that claims for higher wages are most likely to be made. But under the Labour Standard we have the complication that profits in general are not compressed by a rise in wages in general; thus if it should be the case that the level of profits necessary to induce full employment was itself so high as to call forth wage claims automatically, indefinite wage-inflation would be inevitable from this cause alone. But though it is easy to make our flesh creep with this argument, the assumptions on which it is based are not really very convincing. If wages were centrally negotiated, between a Grand National Trade Union and a National Employers' Association, inflation might indeed proceed in this manner for a time; but the futility of the proceeding would rapidly become apparent, so that the wage-bargain would have to be merged in a treaty which would cover far more than the determination of wages. But as things are, both the structure of the trade-union movement and the variety of the systems of wage-payment that are practised (on the whole for good reasons) in different trades make such centralisation exceedingly unlikely. So long as wage-bargaining remains sectional, the profit comparison, though it must always be an element in the determination of wages, can hardly become so dominant as it has been assumed to be in the argument to which I have just been alluding.

Though wage-claims on other grounds are more likely to be pressed in conditions of high profits, a direct claim for higher wages on the grounds of the profits that are being made by employers is a dangerous claim to make. It can so easily be turned the other way up. If it is laid down as a rule that wages should go up when profits are high, the consequence, that they should not go up (or should even go down) when profits are low, cannot easily be resisted. This is a lesson which trade unions have had much opportunity to learn in the past; and on the whole their history would suggest that it is a lesson which they have learned. Even in conditions of full employment, there remain enough industries with relatively low profits to ensure that the lesson will not quickly be forgotten. The principle that it is wiser to put forward wage-claims on other bases than the profits of the employer is one which may be reckoned, for British trade unions are least, as a permanent acquisition. It is an acquisition for which (I believe) the economist has every reason to be thankful. Not only does it diminish the danger of inflation; it has also some effect in diminishing the danger of business monopolies defending themselves by a *de facto* collaboration with labour monopolies – handing over to their employees a share in their monopoly profits, in order to have the help of their employees in defending themselves against potential competition.

In its relation to the present situation of this country, the argument of this paper has been intended to be rather optimistic. For it is implied in what has been said that the continual rise in money wages since 1945 is not a necessary consequence of Full Employment (or of the Labour Standard); it is sufficiently explicable in terms of factors that are peculiar to the time through which we have been passing. Especially over the last four years, the main factors pushing up wages have been: (1) the dismantling of the controls, with its somewhat 'phoney' effect on the cost of living, and (2) the difficulty that has been experienced in the establishment of a new pattern of relative rates after the war-time disturbance. But these are difficulties which, in the absence of external shocks, we can expect to overcome. A condition in which the wage-level has again become relatively stable, so that movements in basic rates are exceptional rather than normal, should be coming into reach. Even if this expectation is too optimistic, I would still contend that it is for this condition that we must strive, and for which we should do our planning. For it can hardly be doubted that any serious disturbance to our rate of progress would itself push the level of money wages, under conditions of full employment, in an upward direction. If this push is superimposed upon a wage-level that is otherwise stable, then (within broad limits) it can be borne; but if it is superimposed upon a wage-level that is already rising as fast as is tolerable, the additional strain of a more rapid rise must be very dangerous.

17

A Note on Wage-Differentials

This was published, as an appendix to the preceding essay, in the *Economic Journal* for September 1955.

What is said about differentials on pp. 202–7 of essay 16 above can be filled out a bit with the aid of a diagram. This diagram (Fig. 17.1) is of the conventional supply-and-demand type, but in order that it should give satisfactory results it must be interpreted in a somewhat special manner. In the first place, the wage-level which is measured on the vertical axis is the wage-level in the particular (skilled) trade

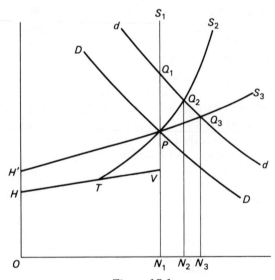

Figure 17.1

under consideration, deflated by an index of wages in comparable occupations; what it shows is the relative wage, in this sense, in the occupation we are considering. In the second place, the quantity of labour supplied is taken to be measured by the number of workers, having at least a certain prescribed efficiency in that trade, who are available for employment in it in the circumstances we are going to examine. Thirdly, when we speak of the labour supplied at a given wage, we imply that the given wage (the relative wage) is expected, so far as such things are expected, to be permanent; the effects of purely temporary differentials, which are felt to be abnormal, would require a different treatment.

With these understandings, a supply curve of labour to our trade can be constructed, but the form of the curve will still depend upon the time allowed for adjustment. We may speak of a short-period curve and a long-period curve; but it is better to think of a family of curves, varying continuously in form as more time is allowed. The shortest of the short-period curves will be sharply kinked at the actual number (ON_1) who happen to have the required capacity just at the moment; it will accordingly follow the course HVS_1 where the stretch VS_1 is vertical and the stretch HV may be nearly horizontal or rise quite gradually – the successive ordinates along HV measuring the wages at which successive existing employees would leave the trade, in order to seek less skilled but more remunerative employment elsewhere.

A rather less short-period curve would take the form $HTPS_2$. A wage which is between VN_1 and PN_1 will keep existing workers attached to the trade, but the supply of labour will nevertheless diminish by normal wastage, a wage at this level being insufficient to attract enough labour to fill the gaps. Above PN_1 there will be sufficient recruitment to fill the gaps, both from new entrants into employment and (at a suitable level) by transfer from occupations with neighbouring skills. On the whole, one would expect this recruitment to be more rapid, the higher the wage offered; but bottlenecks in training facilities will sometimes set a limit on the rate at which new labour can be absorbed. The curve HPS_2 may therefore become vertical after a certain point.

As more time is allowed, T will move to the left, S_2 to the right, so that the ultimate shape of the curve (in the *very long period*) will approach $H'PS_3$. In general, it would seem right to suppose that this long-period curve is upward-sloping, like the rest; but if the skill in question in such that almost anyone can acquire it if he is willing to undergo the necessary training, the upward slope will be very slight.

If, on the other hand, the skill cannot be successfully acquired unless one possesses the capacity to acquire it, even the long-period curve may slope upwards quite steeply. For it is then not merely necessary to offer a sufficient wage to induce a sufficient number of suitably gifted persons to enter the trade, as against the competition of other uses of these same gifts, it has also to be remembered that such a person will not know that he can acquire the skill successfully until he has endeavoured to acquire it, so that enough must be offered to make him willing to bear the risk of lack of success. Different people are bound to vary in the importance which they set upon such risks, so that this also is a factor making the long-period curve slope upwards.

Let us now start from a position in which the actual supply of qualified labour is ON_1, and the longer-run supply curves are as shown. If the demand curve for the labour were DD, *and* the wage were at PN_1, the existing labour would be fully employed, and there would be no tendency for supply to vary. If, while demand remained at DD, the wage were pushed above PN_1, some of the existing labour would be unable to get employment in this trade; and while the wage itself would attract more labour, the attraction would be offset by the difficulty of getting employment. Again, if the demand curve were at dd, the wage (of the existing labour) could be pushed up to Q_1N_1 without causing unemployment; if the labour is unionised, and the Union pursues an aggressively monopolistic policy, this is presumably the wage which it will try to fix. But neither of these is the case which I want primarily to consider. If wages are raised by competition among employers, they may well be reluctant to go so far as Q_1N_1, a wage at which they will have to abandon hope of drawing labour from outside, but are reduced to poaching from one another. I accordingly suggest that the wage which would be established by competition would be more in the nature of Q_2N_2; at this wage there is still a shortage of labour in the very short run, but it is a shortage that will be overcome if some more time is allowed. Nevertheless, even if the wage is at Q_2N_2, the time will come when the supply of labour, which could be available at that wage, will be greater than the demand for it; thus if the wage is *fixed* at Q_2N_2, the monopolistic situation (of Q_1N_1) will in time be repeated, though at a lower wage and a higher supply of labour. It is only if the wage is at the long-period equilibrium level Q_3N_3 that there is no tendency to monopolistic restriction; but if the wage is fixed at that level, and never rises above it, the shortage of labour may persist for a very long time.

What, then, is the economist to recommend? There is a certain sense in which the ideal solution is to begin with the short-period equilibrium wage and gradually to reduce it to the long-period level. But this would be bound to cause trouble in practice, if only because it means cheating the expectations of those who will have acquired the skill because the wage was at the higher level, and would not have done so if the wage had been lower. It does, however, seem that the economist could look with some satisfaction upon an arrangement by which basic agreed rates are kept in some relation with the differentials that are appropriate in the long period, while short-period scarcities are reflected in (no doubt relatively disorderly) bonuses above the agreed minima. This is far from being a perfect solution, but the problem is in its nature very difficult; it does not look as if it can admit of any simple way out. If relative wage-rates are to exercise their full influence upon the supply of labour, they ought to be steady and reliable; but steady differentials will not exercise a proper effect if demands (and supplies) are changing, as they must often be expected to change.

In an opening page of my *Theory of Wages* (1932) I committed myself to the foolish remark that these problems (of the distribution of labour among occupations) are 'one of the easiest parts of wage theory'. For this I was most properly rebuked by Gerald Shove in his admirable review of my book in the *Economic Journal*. On this, as on several other matters where he corrected me, I have come to know better.

Part IV
A New Start

18

Methods of Dynamic Analysis

PREFATORY NOTE

It is fortunate that I do have something which itself marks a turning-point with which to begin this fourth Part. MDA (as I shall call it) is, from my own point of view, one of my most important works. I already had behind me, when I wrote it, two substantial contributions to 'dynamic' theory: one was Parts III and IV of *Value and Capital* (1939) the other was *A Contribution to the Theory of the Trade Cycle* (1950). To these some more Keynesian writings, such as the *IS–LM* paper (essay 8 above), might well be added. These were all quite different; they seemed to have little contact with one another. I did not want to abandon any of them, though I was prepared to qualify them; so I had to find a way of fitting them together, before I could make further progress. It was in MDA that I found it, so that the 'muddle' (in which I have confessed[1] that I still found myself in the forties) was at last cleared up. At last I could go ahead.

That was, and is, my personal attitude towards this essay. But I have made things very difficult for my readers because it has until now remained so unavailable. It was originally published (by the Ekonomisk Tidschrift, Stockholm) in a volume in honour of Erik Lindahl, which was given the appalling title of *25 Economic Essays in English, German and Scandinavian Languages* – enough to frighten any librarian! I owed a great debt to Lindahl; but I should have known that to publish anything of importance in a *festschrift* is a sure way of burying it. It is true that I did not need to leave it so long in its obscurity; I could have found a way of reprinting it elsewhere. I did not do so because I was thinking of it as having the same relation to my *Capital and Growth* (1965) as the Harrod review (essay 15 above) had borne to *TC*. But the fact is that *CG* made less impression than *TC* had done; and I have since become convinced

---

[1] See essay 10 above, p. 129.

that one reason for this was that MDA was missing. It is a clearer and sharper statement of my new view than anything in *CG*. The later work did add some useful detail, but in adding the detail the main points were obscured.

Nevertheless, when I now go back to MDA, I feel that even there these points were not made sharply enough. I was still puzzling things out, and still did not sufficiently emphasise my conclusions. So it may well be that MDA itself will (now) be more intelligible if in the rest of this prefatory note I add some emphasis.

The key to clarification was classification. My 'methods' are classes of models. All models are simplifications of reality; they leave out things which are judged to be unimportant, for the purpose in hand, in order to make it possible to think more clearly about the things that are retained. What is to be left out, and what is to be retained, is to be chosen with reference to the problem in hand. It is perfectly proper to use one sort of model for one purpose, and another for another.

All of the models here considered are 'dynamic' models, in the sense that they are to be used for the analysis of a process. I have found that, if such an analysis is to be securely based, it must consider the process as taking place in a succession of periods, sub-periods or 'single-periods'. These must subsequently be strung together; but we have to begin with a model for the single period, which, of course, has a past behind it and a future in front. My classification is a classification of models for a single period.

I found that I could distinguish four classes, or 'methods'. They could be arranged in a 2×2 table, since there were two, quite distinct, lines of division. One line divided (1) *ex ante–ex post* models, formed (as I showed) on the analogy of government budgeting, from (2) stock-flow models, formed on the analogy of business accounts. The other divided (a) *P*-models, or, as I subsequently came to call them, flexprice models, from (b) *Q*-models (subsequently fixprice models). I could find instances, some 'macro', some 'micro', of each of the four (1a, 1b, 2a, 2b). But I could also find examples of hybrid models, in which one method was applied to one market (or part of the system considered) and another to another. The Keynes model, as I understood it, was the most distinguished of the hybrids.

It is highly inconvenient, for clear thinking, to begin with hybrids; that is why the logic of the Keynes theory has caused so much trouble. It is much better to get the pure types in proper shape first. A pure type must exhibit logical consistency, its own kind of logical consistency; so one can theorise about it in the way that economists are practised at doing. But this is entirely separate from the question of the applicability of the model to particular empirical data – whether, in relation to those data, it is a good model or not. It is indeed quite difficult when writing about them to keep these questions distinct from one another; but if one does not do so, one is heading for confusion. I claim that my classification, my 2×2 table, should make it a little easier to make these distinctions. By spreading out the alternatives, it shows up the responsibility, which is left to the user, of choosing one and not another.

Of my four pure types, it was probably (2b), stock-flow fixprice, which most needed some further explanation. When I returned to it in *CG*, I found that I needed at least two chapters (7–8) to say all that I had to say about it. These cannot be reproduced here, but an abstract of their contents is given in an addendum to this essay.

One of the greatest changes which has come over economic theory in the last thirty years is the transformation of economic dynamics from a pious aspiration into a respectable body of principles. It is, however, true that these principles do not quite fit together into a single coherent whole; they are still the fruits of different, though obviously related, lines of approach. What I propose to do in this paper is to make some examination of the relations which these approaches bear to one another.[2]

I

As was long ago discovered, it is impossible to make a study of method without saying something about scope. But what I have to say about scope can be kept brief and simple. For though the scope of economic dynamics has been defined in several ways, it turns out, on examination, that some of these definitions are in fact announce-

---

[2] My subject is one that has already been worked over by Erik Lindahl (see the first chapter of his *Studies in the Theory of Money and Capital*). My debt to that work (and to the corresponding parts of E. Lundberg's *Economic Expansion*) will be apparent as I proceed. But I may perhaps add at this point that since I have myself been led on different occasions (in the latter parts of *Value and Capital* on the one hand, and in my *Contribution to the Theory of the Trade Cycle* on the other) to approach dynamic theory by what look like quite different routes, one of my objects in writing has been to build a bridge between my own approaches.

ments of the *method* which the writer who advances them proposes
to use; while others are restrictive definitions, which define that part
of the general dynamic field on which the writer proposes to concentrate. If we look for a definition which shall define scope not
method, and which shall embrace the whole of the field which
practice treats as dynamic, the kind of definition to which we must
come is fairly obvious. I shall take it to be the theoretical analysis of
the *process of economic change*. So defined, the subject includes the
study of fluctuation as well as that of growth; it includes the study
of change in particular markets as well as in the whole economy; and
no commitment is made in advance about the method by which the
subject is to be examined. The question of method remains as a
separate question; but before we pass on to that question, there is
one consequence of this definition of scope which is worth a
mention in passing.

One of the advantages of defining dynamics as the study of the
process of change is that it does something to rehabilitate statics. For
dynamics is left as much less than the whole of economics. Dynamic
economists, who are (very properly) excited by what they are doing,
are often tempted to make excessive claims for it. Statics (they seem
to tell us) is a mere toy of the class-room, a mere introduction to
dynamics, which cannot possess of its own any direct relevance to
the real world. I do not believe that this is correct. There is no reason
why we should be so dogmatic about the stationariness of our static
models as to condemn them to hopeless unrealism. Static economics
is perfectly valid economics; only it is economics arranged for the
comparison of states, not for the analysis of processes. The one
purpose can be as realistic as the other.

Perhaps the clearest way of showing that the distinction between
statics and dynamics is not a distinction between abstraction and
realism is to observe that a similar distinction persists in the wholly
realistic field of economic history. One of the standard ways of
writing economic history (particularly practised by political
historians in their economic chapters) is to survey the *state* of the
economy under consideration, as it was in various historical periods,
comparing one state with another. This is the method of comparative
statics. It is when the economic historian tries to throw his work
into the form of a narrative that he becomes, in the theoretical
sense, dynamic. Any examination of the work of economic historians
will show what a difficult threshold has to be crossed at that point. It
is in fact exceedingly difficult to cast economic history into a
narrative form without becoming *more* abstract than one has to be

on the survey method; greater realism in the matter of time-sequence has to be purchased by a higher level of abstraction in most other respects. We are, I believe, in substantially the same case in economic theory. The historian is baffled by the problem of narrating in a single sequence events that occur successively and those that occur contemporaneously; and even in theory the analysis of a number of contemporary interacting processes soon proves to be beyond our powers. It is no accident that dynamic theory tends so largely to run in terms of simple aggregative models.

II

However much we simplify the processes which are to be studied, the mere notion of an economic process has complications in itself. It is of the essence of economic behaviour that it is purposive behaviour, directed towards the future, so that it always contains within itself a time-dimension of its own. It was the main contribution of the Böhm-Bawerkian movement that it emphasised the consequential time-structure of economic activity *even in a stationary state*. For it thereby indirectly threw up the central dynamic issue – how to superimpose the pattern of change, which is one time-pattern, upon the underlying pattern of capital-using production, which is another. Though there are ways of avoiding this issue, they are bound to result in depriving the behaviour under study of its purposive character, so that the economic system is reduced to a mere mechanism. If we are not to do violence to the essential nature of the problem, a way has to be found whereby this issue can be faced.

The vital discovery which made possible the analysis of a process of change, in properly economic terms, was the introduction of accounting procedure. While economists were fumbling around to find a set of categories by which they could make a formal analysis of economic change, other people were doing the job in a professional manner. In all its main forms, modern economic dynamics is an accounting theory. It borrows its leading concepts from the work which had previously been done by accountants (with singularly little help from economists); and it is in accordance with this that social accounting should be its main practical instrument of application.

So much, I believe, is generally realised; but it is not so often observed that there are several kinds of accounting structure which are relevant to economic analysis, so that the mere decision to utilise accounting concepts does not itself produce uniform results. There are indeed two major alternatives which, in the present context, I want to distinguish; for they lead, on the one hand, to the analysis in terms of plans and realisations which is especially to be associated with the name of Lindahl, and on the other to the kind of approach of which the Keynes theory is the most famous representative. I am going to maintain that it is the second approach which arises most naturally from the application to economics of the ordinary concepts of business accounting; while the first is to be similarly associated with the concepts of a special kind of accounting – that which operates in practice in the important field of Public Finance.

III

Government accounting has several peculiar features; two of them are of particular importance for our purposes. One is the fact that governments are not obliged by any company law to present balance-sheets; it is nearly always true that their only account is a 'running' or 'income and expenditure' account. Again, unlike businesses, governments do not merely present a running account for the year which is closed at the time the account is presented; they also present a quite formal *forward* account – of the expenditure planned, and the revenue expected, for the ensuing year. Both of these peculiarities persist in the corresponding theory; the balance-sheet drops into the background, but immense stress is laid upon the distinction between backward and forward accounts – *ex post* and *ex ante*.

This latter distinction is itself sufficient to enable the Lindahl theory to clear its first hurdle. It is made abundantly clear that economic dynamics is not only concerned with what happens; it is also concerned with what is planned, or intended, or expected to happen. We do not merely have to deal with one time-scale; time reduplicates itself as in a mirror, or in a series of mirrors. Parallel to the real events, which have one course in time, are constantly changing series of planned or expected events, with similar but distinct courses. The comparison of what does happen with what is expected to happen becomes a key-point of dynamic analysis.

A second thing follows from this. Dynamic analysis is not solely concerned with the comparison between what happens in successive periods, so as to build up a story in terms of these *actual* changes;

there is also a form, or phase, of dynamic analysis which concentrates attention upon a *single period* (or *accounting period*), being concerned with the difference between what happens in that period and what is planned (at the commencement of the period) to happen in it. These differences ('windfalls') may be due to exogenous causes (acts of God or of politicians); but the more interesting windfalls are those which are traceable to inconsistencies between the plans of the various individuals (and concerns) composing the economy – assuming that there is no omniscient planning authority.

Once this approach is accepted, the general dynamic problem falls into two parts. There is, in the first place, what we may call *single-period theory*, theory which is concerned with the determination of what happens in a single period in the above sense; and secondly what we may call *continuation theory*, which is concerned with the effect of the events of a first period upon the expectations and plans which themselves determine the events of its successors. Since we do not concern ourselves with changes in the rates of flow (of output or consumption, for instance) which occur *within* the single-period, single-period theory can make a good deal of use of static method; indeed it has often been described as 'quasi-static'. I do not myself care for this description, since I am convinced that single-period theory is a part, and indeed an essential part, of dynamic analysis; but I fully admit that it needs to be completed by some form of continuation theory if it is to do its properly dynamic job of analysing a process.

IV

The properties which I have been describing must, I think, be common to all theories which work in terms of plans and realisations; but now we come to a parting of the ways. There is one form of single-period theory (a classic description of it has been given by Lindahl[3]) in which it is assumed that prices are fixed at the commencement of the period – before it is seen whether plans are consistent; a failure to fulfil plans then results in an unwanted accumulation or decumulation of stocks (or perhaps in the appearance of 'negative stocks', in the sense of unfulfilled orders). It is accordingly characteristic of this model that demands and supplies are not necessarily equal; or rather, in the accepted terminology, that

[3] See the chapter of his *Studies* previously cited.

ex ante demands and supplies are not necessarily equal (*ex post* demands and supplies, being adjusted for the unintended accumulations and decumulations, are equal as an accounting identity.) This is the type of single-period theory which emerges if we think along this particular track; it implies that the determination of prices is held over to be a first step in continuation theory. Prices are determined, in each successive period, largely as a consequence of the discrepancies between supplies and demands which have appeared in the period before.

Now whatever we may think about this particular framework, it was clearly one which deserved to be tried out. It is relatively realistic, and it has performed great services in the clarification of thought. Its defect, if one may put it that way, is that it is not very *efficient*. This is because so little change is allowed to occur within the single period (where it is relatively manageable) and so much has to occur at the carry-over from one period to another (where it is much harder to manage). So long as the problem is that of analysing change in a particular market only, this defect is perhaps not very serious; but it becomes much more serious when one proceeds to analysis of the economy as a whole. I believe that it is this defect which has set economists looking for an alternative theory; and which will keep them looking for alternatives, even though experience has shown that the only alternatives which are available are bound to suffer from defects in other ways.

Of the various alternatives which have been explored, that which is nearest to the above is the one worked out in my *Value and Capital* (though it was developed from a study of Myrdal and of Lindahl himself.) The essential difference between this model and that just described is that I took prices to be flexible, so that there could be no unintentional carry-over of stocks; prices could vary within the *single-period*, but the movements of prices within the period (from one part of the period to another) were neglected. It was accordingly prices, not quantities, which were likely to turn out different from what had been expected. Demands (over the period) would always equal supplies (over the period) in terms of quantity; the windfall gaps between expectation and realisation were thrown over on to the price side. Since prices are then determined, within the single-period, by an adaptation of ordinary equilibrium analysis, the results which can be achieved within the single-period part of this theory are relatively rich. Though I did not myself pursue the corresponding continuation theory very far, that was partly because there is so much less, on this approach, for the continuation theory to do. I still believe that this is a coherent approach by which an instructive dynamic theory can be built up. It gives us a functioning dynamic model, which will answer the questions we put to it.

But these advantages are purchased at a cost. The trouble with the *Value and Capital* model is that it is not sufficiently realistic. In saying this I do not merely refer to its dependence upon the assumption of perfect competition, though that is related to the defect which I have in mind. Suppose that there were only two sorts of commodities that were traded: (1) perishable goods and personal services, which *could not* be carried over from one period to another; (2) speculatively traded commodities, stocks of which were held by merchants in order to make a profit on the difference between present and future prices; an economy which contained no other goods than these could be very adequately analysed on *Value and Capital* lines. But in fact there are good reasons (connected with the heterogeneity of products and the imperfection of competition) why most non-perishable goods are not traded on speculative markets. Both the manufacturer and the retailer are, for the most part, 'price-makers' rather than 'price-takers'; they fix their prices and let the quantities they sell be determined by demand. The prevalence of this latter type of market means that a model in which quantities bear the brunt of disequilibrium fits most of the facts distinctly better. Where the *Value and Capital* analysis goes wrong is that it treats an exceptional type of market as if it were the normal case.

We have now distinguished two types of *ex ante–ex post* analysis, which may be called the '*Q*', or quantity-disequilibrium, and the '*P*', or price-disequilibrium, types respectively. There does not seem to be any reason why it should be impossible to make a synthesis of these two types. But, so far, that does not seem to have been done.

V

It is time to turn to the main alternative route, which has its accounting analogue in the field of business accounting, not in that of public finance. It is characteristic of this route that it works much less explicitly in terms of plans and expectations. This difference does not, I think, spring from any less insistence on the purposive character of the activities that are being analysed; that is common ground on both approaches. But it is felt (and it is really quite proper to feel) that *explanations* which run so largely in terms of subjective factors (*quantified* subjective factors) are unsatisfactory, because they are so largely incapable of verification. A framework which lays less stress upon such variables keeps us closer to the facts.[4]

It seems to me that a pure theorist, who had simply set himself the task of analysing a process of economic change by using a framework of business accounts, in the way that the other approach uses government accounts, would produce a scheme of analysis which would differ from that which we have been considering in the following ways. In the first place, he would drop the emphasis upon *ex ante* budgeting. Businesses have too little control over their future operations to be able to present formal forward accounts; though they do of course make estimates and plans for their own purposes, those estimates are always affected by a high degree of uncertainty. But the forward-looking aspect of a business position is in fact reflected in formal accounts in another way; it is reflected in the balance-sheet of the business – the statement of its assets and liabilities at the moment for which its accounts are drawn up.

Thus what corresponds on this route to the *ex ante–ex post* distinction on the other route is the distinction between *stock* and *flow*. There will here be a study of *flow* variables (inputs and outputs, consumption and employment), admittedly determined in large measure by expectations, but with the expectational side relatively unstressed as compared with other determinants. There will be set against this a study of *stock* variables (the valuation of the existing stock of real capital, and the network of claims and obligations that are built upon it). It is in the determination of the stock variables that the expectational side will come into its own.

Stock-flow theories, like *ex ante–ex post* theories, could be of various sorts. There could, for instance, be a Q-sort and a P-sort (utilising the distinction made above); and there could be various sorts of hybrids. The Keynes theory, as we shall see, is a very special sort of hybrid. Just for that reason, it is not convenient for our

---

[4] It is true that the point should not be overstressed. Expectations and plans, though often shadowy, are not wholly intangible. The forward prices that rule upon future markets are reflections, though distorted reflections, of price-expectations; while business plans are nowadays often drawn up with such definiteness that statistics of them can be collected. But in spite of these qualifications, the point seems to retain a certain amount of validity.

Once again, the analogy from historiography is helpful. While political history, and especially diplomatic history, can be superbly written in terms of *ex ante* and *ex post*, of expectations and realisations, it is hardly possible to conceive of economic history being written in such terms. This is partly a matter of the factual material with which the economic historian has to work; but is partly due to the kinds of explanation for which he is looking being different.

purpose to begin with the Keynes theory. It is better to begin with a purer case; even though in practice stock-flow theorists have not been purists, but have mixed their methods, adjusting them to the particular conditions of particular markets.

If, instead of proceeding at once to the whole economy, we begin by considering the working of particular markets, the distinction between the Q-type and the P-type of stock-flow analysis becomes readily apparent. The stock-flow P-theory of a particular market is nothing else but the regular theory of price-determination in a speculative market (of which a particularly elegant statement is to be found in the early chapters of K. Boulding's *Economic Analysis*).[5] Here, at any given moment, there are in existence given stocks of the commodity; but, over a period, these stocks are being added to by production and being drawn upon by consumption. At a moment of time, or over any sufficiently short period of time, these additions and subtractions can be taken as negligible; price is therefore determined by the Liquidity Preference of the dealers, or, in other words, by their willingness to hold stocks. (This, of course, is governed in its turn by their expectations of the future state of the market.) Thus, at each moment, price is determined by the condition that demand to hold equals the available supply; but as soon as we look at a period of appreciable length, the inflow and outflow become significant. Even if the willingness to hold stocks remained unchanged (the Liquidity Preference curve remained constant in position), an excess of supply over demand, in the *flow* sense, would cause an addition to the stocks to be held with a consequential fall in price. Thus it is true that at any given moment, price is determined by *stock* demand and supply; but it is also true that price will only remain constant, even with unchanged willingness to hold stocks, if flow demand and supply are equal.

This is the stock-flow P-theory of a particular market; it would be on these lines that we should have to proceed if we sought to construct a corresponding theory for the whole economy. In any case, we must proceed on these lines so far as we desire to make use of the P-approach, even if we only apply it to certain parts of the economy, to those markets for which it is most suitable.

Let us turn to consider the corresponding Q-type of theory, again for the case of a particular market. In a market where stocks are held by producers (or retailers) price-movements may be relatively sluggish; it is possible to follow through a process of change

[5] Chapters 5–7 (any edition).

in production without assuming any price-changes. (Prices may indeed be set by some mechanism which has nothing to do with supply and demand, such as the 'full-cost principle'; they may even be set in accordance with some political sliding-scale.) If prices are taken to be for the time rigid, it is not necessary (as it was in the corresponding *P*-theory) that the market should be in *stock equilibrium* at every moment; it is perfectly possible that stocks may be larger, or smaller, than their holders would desire. But it is only when stocks are at their desired level that the condition of flow demand equalling flow supply will maintain a steady level of production. For the only means which is open to (say) a manufacturer who has surplus stocks and desires to reduce them is to cut down his production below his sales; the only means which is open to him to replenish a depleted stock is to raise his rate of production above his sales. It is this chain of causation, working from sales via stocks to inputs, which is the characteristic nexus of the type of theory to which we have now come.

Suppose that we start from a position of stock equilibrium (actual stock equals desired stock), and that demand then increases beyond the point where it can be met from current output, so that it has to be met in the first place out of stocks. Then, as is well known,[6] even if the rate of production is stepped up, at the moment when demand increases, to such a point that flow supply will ultimately be sufficient to match flow demand at the new level, stock equilibrium will not be maintained. If we compare the position when the increased output is ready for sale with the initial position, we shall find that stock has diminished, while *work in progress* has increased. Flow equilibrium has been restored, but only by a disturbance of stock equilibrium. In order to restore stock equilibrium, additional investment is required – 'induced investment'.

Strictly speaking, this must always be true; but it is possible to maintain that businesses do not in practice have very precise ideas about their 'desired stock'; they will be prepared to allow their stock to move some way away from a normal figure without taking any steps to right the position. If this is so, there will be a certain range over which demand can vary without inducing any investment (or disinvestment) in stocks; the only condition which will have to be observed is that flow demands and supplies should be kept (more or less) in balance, in order that stocks should not *go on* moving in the same direction. But it is only within this range (which may of course

---

[6] Cf. Lundberg, *op. cit.* ch. 4; and *TC*, ch. 4.

be wider or narrower in different circumstances) that it can be proper to concentrate attention exclusively on flows, so as to leave induced investment out of account.

VI

With these ideas in our minds, we can on the one hand get some idea of what a *complete* stock-flow theory of economic dynamics would be like; and on the other we can begin to appreciate the true nature of the Keynes theory, which is nothing else but a drastically, and most ingeniously, *simplified* stock-flow model.

A complete stock-flow theory would presumably proceed on *P*-lines when dealing with markets for which a *P*-approach was appropriate, and on *Q*-lines when dealing with markets for which a *Q*-approach was appropriate. It would show prices in the *P*-markets being *directly* determined by stock equations, with the flow relations affecting price-expectations which would react back on current prices. It would show quantities in the *Q*-markets primarily determined by the flow equations, but with stock relations reacting back on the flow equations by the generation of induced investment (or disinvestment). Thus in both sorts of markets both stock and flow relations would come into the picture, but their role would be different in the two cases.

In contrast to this *complete* theory, we can see what it was that Keynes did. In the first place, he used a *P*-approach for one market only (that for bonds); all other markets were dealt with on *Q*-lines. (This was a superb simplification, but the procedure was by no means perfectly realistic; a complete theory would surely have used *P*-methods for quite a number of different financial markets,[7] and for some commodity markets also.[8]) Next, so far as his one *P*-market was concerned, he concentrated attention almost entirely upon the stock equation, the flow aspect of that market being pushed right into the background. (He would, I think, have justified this procedure by reference to his doctrine of the *minimum* to the rate of interest, which – so far as it is valid – ensures that there are circumstances in which excess of flow demand or supply will not

---

[7] Much of this extension has in fact been made by Professor R. F. Kahn ('Notes on Liquidity Preference', *Manchester School*, 1954).

[8] Here, of course, one suspects that Keynes was influenced by a belief that in the course of historical evolution such markets were in fact on the way out.

disturb the stock equilibrium, though this justification can only be admitted if we agree that these particular circumstances do exist in fact, as they may have seemed to do in the thirties, but hardly today.) Thirdly, so far as all remaining markets (taken to be Q-markets) were concerned, he similarly concentrated attention on one side, this time on the flow side. (That, as we have seen, is only justifiable if we take it that businesses are prepared to allow their stock – and indeed the whole make-up of their asset structure – to vary a good way away from its normal relation with output without taking steps to right the relation.) These, so it now seems to me, are the central simplifications which are the basis of the so-called 'General Theory'.

It is unnecessary to emphasise what power these simplifications give. As all experience has shown, the Keynes theory is a highly efficient theory; it is easy to use, and the range of real problems to which it can be applied is very wide. That is why it has worked a 'revolution'. But though it is needless to dilate upon this strength, one of the reasons for it has a special relevance to the present discussion, but has not yet been mentioned. It is because Keynes reduced the whole theory of the Q-markets to their flow equations that he was able, in effect, to aggregate those markets, replacing them by a single market governed by a single relation – the Consumption Function. Thus he boiled down the whole economy into the one Q-market and one P-market, linked by a single price-link – the effect of the rate of interest on (otherwise autonomous) investment.[9]

If we look at the Keynes theory in this light, we can give it full credit for its virtues – without allowing it to bamboozle us.[10] The

[9] Even with all these simplifications, all that could be boiled in this way was the stage in stock-flow theory which corresponds to the *single-period* phase in the other approach, and the Keynes theory requires *continuation* quite as much as the other theories we have considered. But Keynes himself never faced the *continuation* question; this is the origin of the difficulties about the *marginal efficiency* and *marginal productivity* of capital which he left to others to clear up. This, too, is the origin of those prophetic extrapolations to a 'Day of Judgement' which have become so unfashionable. The substitution of Growth Economics for Eschatological Economics is for the most part a phenomenon of the oscillation between optimism and pessimism to which economists are subject like other mortals; it has nevertheless been the vehicle for some slight deepening in our understanding of the process of capital accumulation.

[10] That is, for one thing, we shall not waste time in trying to find in it a formal coherence, such as is beloved by General Equilibrium theorists, but which a hybrid (and a selective hybrid at that) cannot be expected to attain. A uniform dynamic theory, of whatever type, should exhibit coherence; but the Keynes theory is not uniform, because the equilibria of its different markets do not mean the same thing. For the miseries into

real stroke of genius that went to its making was Keynes's perception that the economic system of reality was moving into a shape which made it capable of this great simplification; so that a dynamic theory of exceptional efficacity had come, at least for the time being, into reach. But the Keynes theory was not merely the child of genius, it was also the heir of luck. The world of the thirties, which was Keynesian for one reason – because the working of the price-mechanism was so largely suspended by Depression – was succeeded by the world of the forties which was Keynesian for quite another reason – because the price-mechanism was superseded by controls. In both of these worlds the Keynesian model was at home. But one has a feeling that the world of the fifties is not Keynesian in either of these ways; it may be Keynesian in its policies, but it is not Keynesian in its working. If there is any simplification which is appropriate to our present problems, it must be a simplification of a somewhat different character.

But it is not inevitable that there should be any single simplification which is appropriate. Unless we can find means of constructing a really general theory which can be put into a usable form (and that is almost too much to hope), we are bound to be thrown back, at least on occasion, upon relatively *ad hoc* methods. We shall then waste much time upon unnecessary conflicts between these methods, unless we have at the back of our minds some rough outline of a structure into which they can be fitted. To make some contribution to the formation of that outline is what I have sought to do in this paper.

ADDENDUM ON FIXPRICE METHOD

I begin with a word on the length of the single-period. One is, of course, at liberty to make it any length one likes; but if one lengthens it or shortens it, one must take the consequences. If one makes it very long, say a decade, it may not be inappropriate, at least in some economies,[11] to work in flexprice terms – with flow demands

---

which men have been led in the search for a non-existent uniformity, see the Somers-Klein controversy in *Econometrica* (1949–50) and the long hunt which has been pursued through various journals after the hare started by D. Patinkin. (A recent bibliography is given in the article by F. Hahn in *EJ*, March 1955.) [This should be somewhat qualified in the light of the analysis given below in essay 23.]

[11] I do not say that it would be appropriate, even in this long-period sense, in every economy; for it may be that there are institutional arrangements which permit of supplies being held off the market, more or less indefinitely. That applies to the labour market, as to others. One does not have to go far to find examples.

equalling flow supplies, over the period as a whole, and prices, on some sort of average over the period as a whole, being such as can assure this equality. But that will not do for the study of a process, to be regarded as a chain in which the single-periods are links; where it belongs is in static, not in dynamic analysis. For the study of a process the single-periods should surely be much shorter.

Suppose we make them months. No one would claim that over a month the flow demand for any product (current sales) and flow supply (current output) must necessarily be equal – save for the case in which the product is perishable, so that there can be no carry-over.[12] Ordinarily, inequalities will arise, reflecting themselves in accumulations and decumulations of stocks, or in unfilled orders. This is, of course, admitted, on either method. What makes the difference is that on the flexprice method it is insisted that the producer will only accumulate stocks if he thinks that the price he will be able to get, by selling them in some future period, will be better (in spite of the costs of holding) than what he could get by selling now; so in this sense the accumulation of stocks is *voluntary*. If the behaviour of all markets is interpreted in this manner, the system is regarded as being *in equilibrium* all the time. Though flow demands and flow supplies are unequal, total demands and total supplies (including what are added to stocks or taken from stocks) will be equal all the time. The flexprice method is a *temporary equilibrium* method.

The fixprice method, by contrast, is a disequilibrium method. The carry-over of stocks is not (necessarily) regarded as voluntary – though it is not at all denied that some part may be voluntary. If flow demand is less than flow supply, stock will have to be carried over; we say here that it *has to be* carried over, for the alternative policy of cutting price so as to dispose of them *within the current month* is not seriously considered. (And is not that, very often, realistic?) Thus in a fixprice model, demands and supplies do not have to be equal; there is then no equation of demand and supply to determine prices. In describing this model as a fixprice model, it is *not* assumed that prices are unchanging over time, or from one single-period to its successor; only that they do not necessarily change whenever there is demand–supply disequilibrium. It is nevertheless true that when this possibility is envisaged, one is naturally led to attach particular importance to the working of a system in which

---

[12] I have dealt with the case of perishables in *CG*, pp. 79–82. It does not need repeating here.

demands and supplies are variable, but prices do not change; for this is the case which on the other method is excluded. Once we are clear about that, the model can be elaborated to admit of price-formation on a variety of *policies* – a simple cost-plus policy being naturally the easiest to manage.

Although the fixprice method is a disequilibrium method, it cannot dispense with a concept of equilibrium – which it needs, at the least, as a standard of reference. It needs both stock equilibrium and flow equilibrium. Flexprice theory can manage with flow equilibrium alone; but fixprice theory needs both, and it is stock equilibrium which is fundamental.

To say that a firm is in stock equilibrium must mean that the goods (and claims) that are listed on its balance-sheet are the best (or appear to be the best) out of a range of alternatives. What alternatives? This is a question that in flexprice theory is hard to answer; but in fixprice theory, where we most need it, it is answerable. 'The alternative balance-sheets are alternative forms in which the capital of the unit (or its 'net worth') might *apparently* be held. A change from one to another is an exchange of equal value (at the ruling prices) for equal value. But because the system is a disequilibrium system, such exchanges cannot necessarily be made. At the best they take time. The comparison between the alternatives is nevertheless significant. For if the situation of the unit is in this sense one of stock disequilibrium, we may assume that it will endeavour to get out of that disequilibrium, when and as it can.' (*CG*, p. 88.) So stock disequilibrium is the engine, or a part of the engine, by which the process that is under analysis is carried forward.

Though it must be that in general the switching of the capital stock from one form to another takes much time, there are clearly some special, but most important, cases where it can be much quicker and much easier. Take the case of a financial firm, nearly all of whose assets are marketable securities; it can change these assets from one form to another, almost at a moment's notice. So we should say that such a firm would be, nearly always, in stock equilibrium. In the study of the markets on which such firms operate flexprice analysis should thus be rather suitable. An industrial business, by contrast, must have a large proportion of its assets in forms which make them not at all readily marketable; and even if they could be sold, they could not be replaced in new forms in a hurry. We should therefore expect that an industrial firm will always be, to some extent, in a state of stock disequilibrium. Its endeavours, over time, to right that disequilibrium will be a major aspect of its

policy. They will determine the time-path of the induced investment (or disinvestment) that it will undertake.

Flow equilibrium is equilibrium over a period. 'If a unit is in stock
equilibrium at the beginning of the period, and is still in stock equilibrium at the end, we shall want to say that it is in flow equilibrium
during the period,' (*CG*, p. 89). So flow equilibrium can just be
regarded as a *maintenance* of stock equilibrium; that is quite
defensible, but it is not all that has to be said. For if stock equilibrium is to be maintained over the period, the end-stock equilibrium
must be consistent with what was envisaged at the beginning; if,
during the period, there had been a revision of expectations about
the further future, the passage from one to the other could not be
reduced to the flows that had occurred between them. This cuts both
ways. 'Even though we insist on defining flow equilibrium as a
maintenance of stock equilibrium, additional conditions are
necessary, in addition to the stock equilibrium conditions, in order
that stock equilibrium should be maintained. These conditions are
quite properly defined as *conditions of flow equilibrium.* But they
are necessary, not sufficient conditions. If they are satisfied, in
addition to the stock conditions, then we may safely say that there is
full equilibrium (or equilibrium over time). But if they are satisfied,
while the stock equilibrium conditions are not satisfied, it is hard to
justify describing the resulting situation as one of equilibrium at all.'
(*CG*, p. 90.)

With this behind me (including the other things which are set out
more fully in chapters 7–8 of *CG*) I found that I could go on to what
is in substance a re-statement of the central arguments of *TC* – a re-
statement which I now feel to be more defensible, partly indeed
because it is less ambitious. This will be found in the chapters 9–11
which there follow. The use which I felt inclined to make of it in
later years (as in the chapter on the Multiplier in *CKE*, and in essay
23 below) was even less ambitious; but there is still a link. In the
essays which follow immediately in this volume, I take up the
concept of stock equilibrium, in another way.

This is perhaps the place where I might make two further points.

First, I have often been tempted, in my later work, to suppose
that the dominance of flexprice methods in the work of the older
economists was a reflection of the kind of industrial organisation
which may well have been common in the nineteenth century, but
is surely much less common today. As I put it in the chapter on
Marshall in *CG* (pp. 55–6):

The standardised and branded goods, which are the typical consumers' goods of present-day economic organisation, had not then appeared, though (in Marshall's day) they were perhaps on the point of appearing. The modern economist takes it for granted that it is the manufacturer who fixes the price that the consumer is to pay; but in those days even manufactured goods usually passed along a chain of wholesalers and retailers, each of whom was likely to have some independent price-making opportunity. Nowadays, when demand increases, it is the manufacturer who decides whether (or when) to raise his price; when demand falls off, whether (or when) to lower it. In Marshall's day it will quite usually have been the case that he had no such choice.

An increase in demand would not be allowed to remain unsatisfied, or to run down stocks unduly. Price would rise, not because of any action by the manufacturer, nor by the ultimate consumer (who, then as now, would normally be a passive party); the initiative would come from the wholesaler or shopkeeper, who would offer higher prices in order to get the goods, which, even at a higher price, he could re-sell at a profit. Similarly, when demand fell, it would be the wholesaler who would offer a lower price.

I return to this matter in essays 21–4.

The other concerns what I now feel to be an error in *CG*. After the chapters (6–11) which correspond with MDA, I went on to a Part II, on Growth Equilibrium, or Steady State, which was represented as being a further 'method', an addition to those that had previously been discussed. I now feel that this was a mistake. Steady state models are not concerned with a process of change. They are concerned with conditions in which ratios, relative prices, and relative quantities, can remain unchanged; so, on a proper classification, they do not belong to dynamics, they belong to statics. They are just an extension of static theory – useful in the way that static theory can be useful, but no more than that. In *CG* they were misplaced.

19

The Foundations of Monetary Theory

PREFATORY NOTE

The four pieces that are here put together were written at different times, but I have put them together, because I think that they belong together. They are meant to represent the substance of my later work on monetary theory, work which is scattered over several books,[1] and of which, even here, I cannot present an entirely unified account. For my ideas have developed, and it is the purpose of the present volume to show their development. I doubt if even the later of these pieces represent a final version; they claim to do no more than show the direction in which my thought has been moving.

Part I, here called a 'Preliminary Reconsideration', is a somewhat abridged version of the Presidential Address, which I gave, as was my duty, to the Royal Economic Society in 1962. It was published in the *Economic Journal* of December of that year, and there just called 'Liquidity'. It was the first thing I had written on money (not just 'money and this' and 'money and that') since the 'Simplifying' paper of 1935 (essay 5 above), and it was not easy to recover the insights that I had then possessed. There is practically nothing in it about costs of making transactions – costs of switching assets from one form to another – costs, which as I myself was to say later, 'it is fatal to neglect when one's subject is money'. In the 1935 essay they had been given their proper place, but here they are missing. Even with that limitation there are some useful things that can be said; but as a discussion of liquidity it is seriously inadequate.

To part I, as originally published, there was added an appendix, in which the theory (the limited theory that had there been set out) was explored algebraically. Since I have done a good deal more work on this matter since 1962, I have suppressed that appendix, and also

---

[1] Chiefly in 'The Two Triads' (*CEMT*, essays 1–3), in *CKE* (especially chapter 2) and in *EP* (essays 3 and 8).

a long footnote (with a geometrical version) and have worked their substance into part II, which also incorporates a much later[2] 'second theorem', which I feel belongs. I would now attach much greater importance to the second theorem than to the first. There is something of it that survives when costs of transaction are taken into account, as not here until part III.

That, and part IV, have been newly written for this volume. My first intention, before I began to write them, was to do no more than give a summary of what is in the books, a summary which at this point did seem to be required. I would begin from the third of the 'Two Triads' papers,[3] which I still feel to be the most central of all those writings; and it did in fact prove to be a good place from which to start. But I found, when I got to work, that I had to do more than I had intended. So much has happened since 1967, when that paper was written; we have had to learn to live with seriously inflationary conditions, which even at that date seemed unlikely to be so permanent; one had to take account of these things when re-writing the theory, and when weight is given to them, the theory is transformed. One cannot now keep as close to Keynes as it was possible to do in 1967. He was writing for a world that was so very different from ours.

I nevertheless found, when I went over what I had written, that there was a strand in my thinking that was a help. It goes back to a supplementary chapter in *Capital and Growth* (1965) – a chapter that had little to do with the rest of the book. It is called 'Keynes after Growth Theory'; but I must have realised, before the book left my hands, that the title was inappropriate. For to the title I added a footnote 'Or Wicksell after Keynes, as it turns out'. That is indeed what it is. One is driven back, in the end (or in what so far has been the end) from Keynes to Wicksell.

A brief account of how this happens is given in part IV. I here sketch out the Wicksell-type model, which in my present view takes us furthest towards an understanding of the working of the monetary system, in these still strange conditions.[4]

---

[2] A first draft of this appeared in essay 8 of *EP* ('The Disaster Point in Risk Theory'). I am not contented with that version, which was only completed as the volume was going to the press, and was not by any means fully revised. The 'second theorem' here is meant to supersede it.

[3] *CEMT*, essay 3.

[4] I have also made use of the section on Wicksell in *EP* (pp. 61–72).

PART I.   A PRELIMINARY RECONSIDERATION

It is not easy for an economic theorist like myself to find a suitable subject on which to address the Royal Economic Society as President. If, like some of my predecessors, I was an expert on some particular practical problems, I could choose one of those problems, and there would be no difficulty. If, on the other hand, I was devoted to the defence of some particular kind of policy, I might be unable to resist the opportunity of championing that policy from the platform with which I am presented. In my case neither of these caps will fit. The practical subjects which I have got up, from time to time, have been rather miscellaneous; it was certainly not for anything which I have done in those ways that you did me the honour of electing me. I have not gone far in associating myself with the support of any particular policy; when I have ventured, even a little, on to that ground I have generally regretted it afterwards. Now, at least, I do not want to come out as a champion, not even of economics itself; indeed, I fancy that I would attach less importance to the economic aspects of society – to 'economic welfare' as a 'constituent of general welfare' – than would most of my fellow economists. I am, for instance, by no means convinced that we do our best for the community in which we live by trying to maximise its growth rate.

I am thus, you will see, in a rather sceptical frame of mind. And being in that frame of mind, I have to ask myself very seriously what justification I can offer for what I do – what function can economic theory (I do not say economics as a whole) perform? I do not say economics as a whole, for I have no doubt about the function of applied economics – the improvement of our knowledge and understanding of the world in which we live, a function just like that of any branch of science. Economic theory, however, cannot get off so easily. Evidently there is a relation of economic theory with some of the techniques of applied economics – economic statistics, econometrics and all that; and even with some techniques that reach outside economics – linear programming and operational research. I would not minimise the importance of these relations; but I do not believe that it is for the sake of its role as a mother (or should I say matrix?) of techniques that there is a general case for the study of economic principles or theory. There is, in any event, another function which is at least as important. This is the part which it can play in the communication of ideas, in clarifying them and criticising them; it is one particular instance of this which will be the main subject of this paper.

But before I go on to that particular instance there is another general point which I want to make. We used to be taught (it was a thing on which Marshall frequently insisted)[5] that economics has to operate mainly in terms of concepts drawn from 'everyday life' (or business practice); to these it must, for the sake of its own logic, give more precise meanings, while yet, for the sake of intelligibility, keeping in touch, as best it can, with the 'everyday' use. That, no doubt, was the situation in Marshall's time; but I should like to draw attention to the change which has occurred, in this respect, since then. It is not merely that economics has developed (as was no doubt inevitable) quite a bit of private language, or 'jargon'; it was indeed impossible for Marshall, in spite of his principle, not to do quite a bit of that himself. The interesting thing which has happened is that what was a one-way has become a two-way traffic. The private language of economists is not kept private to economists; other people overhear it, so that it gets out of the circle – into 'everyday life'. Only the other day one caught a Minister of the Crown talking – not in Parliament, but to a public meeting – about 'imperfect competition'. We have, I suggest, some responsibility for these animals, when they are so inclined to get loose.

You will now begin to see the point of view from which I propose to discuss Liquidity. It is, I believe, a leading example of the phenomenon which I have been describing. It is now so much at home in the 'outside world' that it is easy to get the idea that it belongs there; historically, however, that does not seem to be altogether true. If one looks at the older 'practical' books on money and finance it seems quite hard to find an example of the use of the word *liquidity*. (I have not done all the research on this that I should, but that is certainly the impression that one gets from a casual examination.) The point at which it seems to come in is in the early thirties, at the time of the Macmillan Report[6] and of the major works of Keynes. I would suggest that there is a good deal of evidence that it is a Keynesian word: that it would never have had the career that it has if if had not been for the use that Keynes made of it. It is one of the words that have come out of economic discussion into practical affairs.

I must not be misunderstood. I am not for a moment maintaining that there do not exist related words that have a long business history. It was centuries ago (so we are told by the *OED*) that the first firm went into *liquidation*. It was in the nineteenth century that

[5] See, for instance, A. Marshall, *Principles of Economics*, 8th edition, p. 55.
[6] Committee on Finance and Industry Report, 1931.

bankers were foolish enough to believe that bills were *self-liquidating*. But I doubt if it was before the thirties that bankers (and presumably accountants?) began to talk about *liquid assets*; and it certainly seems wonderful (now) how much monetary discussion could go on without the word *liquidity* ever being mentioned.

But turn to the Macmillan Report. Most of the discussion in that Report proceeds on the old lines, but there is one notable passage (pp. 150 *et seq.*) where *liquidity* and its congeners (*liquid resources, liquid assets*) begin to flow all over the vocabulary. Can one doubt who is responsible for that passage? There are many ways in which it has his hall-mark upon it. And then look back at the *Treatise on Money*, published a year earlier. The terminology of the *Treatise* is just a bit *too* liquid. There is a very important definition of *liquid assets* (written, it should be noticed, in quotes – the term is not supposed to be familiar); but there are also monstrosities like *liquid capital* (meaning inventories, not anything which anywhere else would be regarded as liquid) and even (I almost blush to mention it) *liquid output*. We are here, it can hardly be questioned, in at the birth. But *liquidity* is already showing its dangerous tendency to be slippery in meaning; the *Treatise*, wonderful work as it is in so many ways, is in this, as in some others, a warning.

All this before the *General Theory*, and *Liquidity Preference*. There are some obscurities about Liquidity even in the *General Theory*, but the dominant impression received by the reader is perfectly clear-cut; liquidity preference is the reason why ready money commands a premium over bills or bonds – is the cause, therefore, of the existence of a rate of interest. With the coming of Liquidity Preference, the term (for economists) was anchored; from that time on its meaning, for them, appeared to be established. It is nevertheless desirable that we economists should be more conscious than we usually are nowadays of that earlier history which I have been rehearsing. For Liquidity escaped to the outside world, not through the *General Theory*, but through the Macmillan Report, and hence through the Treatise; some of the slipperiness which belongs to that period it carried with it. Now (since Radcliffe)[7] that is a situation with which we economists can no longer refuse to reckon. And perhaps it will do us no harm to open our minds to some of the nuances which the strong music of the *General Theory* for a while almost blotted out.

[7] Committee on the Workings of the Monetary System (Radcliffe Report), 1959.

Let us accordingly turn back to the *Treatise*, and consider rather closely its key definition – the definition of 'liquid assets', to which I referred just now. Keynes is talking about bank portfolios – the balance sheet of a commercial bank. 'Bills and call loans are more *liquid* than investments, i.e. more certainly realisable at short notice without loss, and investments are more liquid than advances.'[8] *More certainly realisable at short notice without loss*. No further explanation is given; but the definition is a valuable one – every word in it deserves examination.

Let us begin at the end. 'Without loss.' Without loss relatively to what? There is one interpretation, which is perfectly possible if the definition is looked at *in vacuo*, but which can clearly be set aside, as having nothing to do with what Keynes can possibly have meant. This would compare the price at which the asset is expected to be sellable with the price at which it stands in the books of its proprietor (the price, maybe, at which it was purchased in the past). Some sorts of rule-of-thumb procedure would attach importance to that kind of comparison; but it has nothing to do with the intelligent behaviour which Keynes is (clearly) analysing. We may (I think) put it out of our minds straight off.

There is, however, another interpretation (but again, I think, not Keynes's) which is more appealing. An asset may be 'realisable *at short notice* without loss' in the sense that the price at which it is realisable at short notice is much the same as that at which it is realisable at longer notice. Or, more accurately, the length of the notice that is given does not in itself have any important effect on the price at which the asset can be sold.

The characteristic just described is an important characteristic which is related to liquidity, but it is not (I think) liquidity. Fortunately it has a name of its own. An asset which can be sold quickly just as well (apart from ups and downs of the market) as it can be sold after negotiation and perhaps advertising is a *marketable* asset. Evidently there are degrees of marketability. The sacrifice which one must expect to make, merely because one desires a quick sale, may be large or small. There is nevertheless an important contrast between the things for which this loss must be expected to be significant and those for which it does not have to be expected to be significant. There is a large class of assets which are traded in upon organised markets ('money markets' of various kinds, stock exchanges and commodity markets also – so far, in this latter case, as futures

---

[8] *Treatise on Money*, vol. II, p. 67.

contracts, but not the physical commodities themselves, are concerned); these things, to those persons who have access to the relevant markets, are perfectly marketable. But it is by no means the case that they are in consequence perfectly liquid. One thing is more liquid than another if it is '*more certainly* realisable at short notice without loss'. It is time that we look at the whole definition.

The comparison is between things, each of which is 'realisable at short notice', and concerns the terms on which they are so realisable. It does not concern the terms on which they may be realisable after negotiation. Now in the case of unmarketable (or imperfectly marketable) assets, the terms on which they can be realised at short notice are not, save in exceptional circumstances, relevant to conduct; they are not compared on that basis. But the perfectly marketable assets (which I was just describing) are compared on that basis; there is indeed no other basis on which they can be compared. We seem therefore to be entitled to say (as a fair gloss on the *Treatise* defintion) that liquidity is a characteristic which is *only* possessed by perfectly marketable assets; but that they do not possess that characteristic to the same extent. That is what I should now like to say; I think that if one does allow oneself to say it the matter is considerably clarified. I doubt, however, that Keynes himself can have drawn this deduction, for he talks (in the passage cited) about 'investments being more liquid than advances'. Advances, I should have thought, must be reckoned to be non-perfectly marketable; so that the passage can only be rescued, on my interpretation, if we say that non-perfectly marketable assets have a liquidity of zero. That is formally possible, but I do not now much care for that way of putting it.

Let us then, for the present, confine our attention to the perfectly marketable assets: those which, on the interpretation just given, can possess some degree of liquidity. They *are* 'realisable at short notice'; one is to be more liquid than another if it is 'more certainly so realisable without loss'. We are brought back to the meaning of without loss'. That question does not yet answer itself, but it has become a little easier to answer. For we have now limited the comparison to assets which have a market price in the present, and which are expected (with fair confidence) to continue to have a market price at any (relevant) future date. Further discussion must clearly run in terms of expectations of what those prices will be, and of the certainty with which those expectations are held.

If I were attempting a more complete analysis what I should want to do at this point would be to insert a formal theory of choice between perfectly marketable assets. This, of course, is by no means the occasion for such a statement. There are, however, a few points about such a theory to which I fear I must allude.

It would, I think, begin by considering the choices that confront a concern which *only* operates in perfectly marketable assets. This is indeed a very special case. In view of what I have said about advances, it is not a close fit even to the case of a commercial bank; we may perhaps think of an investment trust or of a discount house; the only assets that come into question (apart from cash) are marketable securities.

What directly matters to such a concern is not the certainty with which the outcome[9] of any individual investment is regarded, but the certainty of the value of its portfolio as a whole. This total value may be thought of as having a probability-distribution, which is a result-ant of the probability-distributions of the individual investments, weighted by the amounts invested in each. By changing the weights, making marginal adjustments between one investment and another, the probability-distribution of the whole may be varied. It could be taken to be a consequence of the marketability that the probability-distributions of the individual investments are outside the control of the investor (though they will, of course, be influenced by his read-ing of the facts on which his judgment of them is based). It can then be shown, without difficulty, that if he were to be insensitive to the certainty of the outcome of his whole portfolio (even though recog-nising that the individual outcomes are not certain) he would put his whole capital into that investment which, after allowing for risk, offers the best return; but that if he is sensitive to certainty he will normally distribute his capital over a number of investments, he will 'spread his risks', as investment trusts and such like bodies are observed to do. Spreading of risks, and sensitiveness to the certainty of the *whole* outcome, are tied up together.

What form, however, are we to suppose this sensitivity to take? Many forms have been suggested, and in a sense it does not much matter what form we use, for what is substantially the same theory could no doubt be expressed in various ways. What has long seemed to me to be the simplest method is just to take the regular method of summarising probability distributions familiar in elementary statistics. For if we use these statistical parameters we have available to us the well-established rules by which the parameters of an aggregate can be built up from those of its parts.

[9] I think of the 'outcome' of an investment in a liquid asset as being its expected value at the next moment at which a decision can be taken, e.g. at the next board meeting.

It would obviously be convenient if we could take just one measure of 'certainty'; the measure which would suggest itself, when thinking on these lines, is the standard deviation.[10] The chooser would then be supposed to be making his choice between different total outcomes on the basis of mean value (or 'expectation') and standard deviation only. A quite simple theory can be built up on that basis, and it yields few conclusions that do not make perfecty good sense. It may indeed be regarded as a straightforward generalisation of Keynesian Liquidity Preference. We would be interpreting Liquidity Preference as a willingness to sacrifice something in terms of mean value in order to diminish the expected variance (of the whole portfolio). Instead of looking simply at the single choice between money and bonds, we could introduce many sorts of securities and show the distribution between them determined on the same principle. It all works out very nicely, being indeed no more than a formalisation of an approach with which economists have been familiar since 1936 (or perhaps I may say 1935).[11]

And yet it will not quite do. We are still left with that puzzling clause in the old Keynes definition – the 'without loss'. There are still some depths in the matter that we have not fathomed.

A two-parameter theory of portfolio investment, running entirely in terms of mean value and variance, could be a satisfactory theory if either of two conditions were satisfied. It is possible, on the one hand, that the probability-distributions (of the whole portfolio), between which choice was made, might be such that they could be adequately described in terms of the two parameters. Or, on the other hand, the preferences of the choosers might be adequately described in terms of these same two parameters. It is not necessary that both of these conditions should hold; either would do.

In fact, these two conditions have quite different degrees of plausibility. It would not, I think, be at all surprising if there was a wide range of cases, in the field of portfolio investment, where the choice lay between probability-distributions (of the value of the whole portfolio) which were approximately normal, or at the least not differently biased to one side or the other. If this was so they would be alternatives that could be described, sufficiently for us to talk sense about them, in terms of the two parameters above-mentioned;

[10] It is better to take the standard deviation, which is a sum of money (so that it can be compared with the mean value, also a sum of money), than to take the variance, which has no economic meaning in itself, being a sum of money squared.

[11] Referring to my article 'A Suggestion for Simplifying the Theory of Money' (essay 5 above).

and that would account for the fact that a two-parameter theory does as well as it seems to do.

If we can do this we do not need to assume that *preferences* can be adequately described in terms of two parameters – that if a chooser were confronted with two probability-distributions of the same mean value and variance, but with quite different skewness (for instance) he would be indifferent between them. That, I feel sure, we do not want to assume. There is a very important reason why we should not assume it.

This is not the reason which has bulked so large in the literature: that a theory which neglects skewness cannot deal with gambling. I do not see why we should want to deal with gambling; or rather why we should be bothered with it in this sort of a theory. This is not because gambling is irrational (if it is irrational), but because it belongs to an altogether different field of conduct from that which we have been analysing. Decisions which run in terms of the probability distribution of a whole portfolio are difficult decisions, almost necessarily professional decisions. They are work; gambling is relaxation. To expect consistency in gambling is futile, for gambling is a rest from consistency. But the sort of conduct which we are analysing requires to be consistent if it is to be successful.

The reason why we should not expect this sort of chooser to be indifferent to skewness emerges clearly enough if we consider what he is doing all this for. We have indeed got ourselves into a bit of trouble at this point by our device of considering the liquid (the *more or less* liquid) part of the balance sheet in isolation. Even an investment trust or discount house has liabilities as well as assets; it is because of them that its attitude towards the chances of favourable or unfavourable outcomes cannot be symmetric. A worse than 'expected' outcome must be dreaded more than a better than 'expected' outcome is desired. This is not because of any abstract 'law of diminishing marginal utility'; it is because of the impact which such unfavourable outcomes may have upon the non-liquid elements in the situation (things that may happen on the side of liabilities or on the side of other, non-liquid, assets). Here is the motive force behind the desire for 'certainty'. It is this, I feel sure, which led Keynes to insert 'without loss' into the definition on which I have so extensively commented; it is this which makes the definition sound reasonable, as it clearly has sounded reasonable. It may nevertheless often be adequate, for the reason which I have explained, to define the degree of liquidity of a liquid asset solely in terms of the 'certainty' of its expected value; and so to say, in the manner described, that a rise in Liquidity

Preference is expressed in an increased valuation of 'certainty' relatively to 'expectation' (or mean value).

I now leave the Keynes definition of 'liquid assets', which (as will be seen) I wholly accept, at least when it is interpreted in the above manner; and turn to other uses of the term Liquidity. There is, in the first place (and especially in the light of what has just been said) no difficulty at all in giving a corresponding meaning to the Liquidity of a balance sheet as a whole; it is a judgment of the adequacy of the liquid assets that are comprised in it (expressed in terms of probability distribution of future value) to meet the claims, of whatever kinds, that may be made upon them. Liquidity, in this sense, is still a matter of degree. One state of a balance sheet may be judged to be more liquid than another, but there is no sense in saying that it is so much per cent more liquid. It is, however, perfectly natural that in the making of such judgments, and for the reconciling of different judgments, help should be sought from conventional rules (liquidity ratios and the like). Even so, we are not very ready to accept the statement that mere observance of such a rule would be sufficient, in all cases, to establish an acceptable standard of liquidity. We do, I think, always have some more qualitative concept of the liquidity of a balance sheet at the back of our minds.

There is nevertheless another sense (to which I now come) in which Liquidity may sometimes be quantified with greater propriety. I have been careful, hitherto, to insist that *liquid assets* must include both *more* and *less* liquid assets; an interpretation which is not only defensible (as I hope I have shown) on the ground of theoretical convenience, but keeps in line with what seems to have come to be common usage among accountants. There are, however, occasions on which we may be justified in drawing a firm line between those assets which are very liquid and those which are not so liquid; the term liquid asset may then be applied in a more restricted sense, only to the former. The Liquidity of a balance sheet may then be measurable (in this more restricted sense) by the *quantity* of such fully liquid assets (money and near-money, according to some suitable definition) which it contains. It is a short step from this to the popular use of Liquidity to mean practically the same thing as money: a usage to which the theory of Liquidity Preference (as it appears in Keynes's later work) does, I think, give some countenance. What I have said here is meant, on the whole, to be critical of that usage; it does not give us a *general* meaning of Liquidity, but I would nevertheless admit that there are occasions when it is very natural to fall into it.

Some further light can be thrown upon the matter by the theoretical apparatus which I have been describing. Suppose that there is a sharp line between *money*, the capital value of which is certain (in money terms), and 'risky securities', the capital value of which is quite uncertain. It does then follow quite strictly, if we accept the two-parameter theory, that there will be a range in which any desired combination of mean value and dispersion can be built up by a division of one's capital into so much money, on the one hand, and so much 'risky securities', on the other; the 'risky securities' being combined in such proportions as seem best for risk-spreading, proportions that have nothing to do with the amount of money that is being held. 'Liquidity Preference' then determines the proportions in which capital is divided between money and risky securities; it does not affect the proportions in which the risky securities are themselves combined. Within this range it is entirely proper to think of Liquidity Preference as determining the demand for money in Keynes's manner: money as against bonds (or securities) which, so far, can be lumped together.

It is, however, by no means necessary that the desired combination should lie within this range. The demand for money that has thus been determined is the liquidity demand for money; it does not necessarily account for the whole amount of money held at a particular moment, but only for that part of the demand for money which is deliberately planned. Much of the demand for money is not deliberately planned; so far as that part is concerned, the choice of 'money or securities' does not in practice arise. It is therefore entirely possible that the liquidity demand for money from a particular investor, or even from most investors, should be zero. If it is zero, liquidity preference cannot affect the demand for money, but it can then affect the demand for securities – for *more* or *less* liquid assets. The proportions in which these are combined will now be affected by the preferences of the investor and not only by his anticipations.

Situations of this latter kind (made more likely when interest rates are high, when investors are confident and when there are facilities for operating upon a continuous spectrum) make it dangerous to commit ourselves entirely to the identification of liquidity with the size of a money balance. That Keynes (in 1936) should have treated Liquidity Preference as a matter of the demand for money was appropriate, and may well at that time have been sufficient; but it is also appropriate that in 1959 the Radcliffe Committee should have found itself in need of something rather different. (I return to this matter in part III below.)

PART II.   TWO THEOREMS ON PORTFOLIO SELECTION

1.   I am here considering the behaviour of an operator who has a capital K, which he may hold in money form or in the form of some combination of n securities, or partly in one and partly in the other. His choice is to be made for a period, during which he cannot vary the choice that he has made; the period may however be as short as we like. I assume (throughout this second part) that *costs of investment and disinvestment are negligible.*[12] Thus he may just as well begin by having the whole capital K in money form (having realised anything which had been held, in the past, in other forms), and he may just as well be planning to realise it all, converting it all into money, at the end of the period. Thus his decision, for the period, is kept self-contained – which, of course, is a great simplification. It is important to notice that we are able to make that simplification because we are neglecting the costs of transactions.

His capital then is fixed in money terms, and the prices of the securities are also fixed in terms of money. We assume, that is, that he is operating on a perfect market, so that he cannot by his own actions affect the prices of the securities, as they are at the beginning of the period, at the time he makes his decision. But he does not know what these values will be at the end of the period, save in the case of money. where the value (in terms of money) must be the same at the end as at the beginning. I call the value of a security at the end of the period the *outcome* of investment in that security. The expected outcome from holding £1 in money form is thus certainly £1; but the outcome from investing £1 in a non-money security is uncertain. We shall, however, allow ourselves to suppose that it has a probability distribution, which can be described in one of the ways in which probability distributions are reckoned. I shall call this probability distribution the *prospect* of investing £1 in that security; it would seem to follow from our perfect market assumption that this prospect will be independent of the amount that is invested in the security.

2.   I assume that the operator is only concerned with the prospect of the whole portfolio; his investments in the individual securities are means to the end of making that as favourable as possible. This prospect will itself have a probability distribution. To describe it in all detail might well require quite a number of parameters (moments

[12] See above, p. 236.

and so on); but it does not seem unreasonable to suppose that a practical choice will be expressible in terms of two parameters – a most probable return and some index of uncertainty. Call these E and S respectively. I shall take it that for given S, a larger E is preferred to a smaller; and that for given E, a smaller S is preferred.[13] The behaviour of our operator can then be illustrated on a diagram (Fig. 19.1).

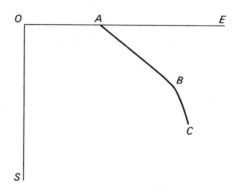

Figure 19.1

E is measured on the horizontal axis, S on the vertical (downwards). A position in which the whole portfolio is held in money form will then be represented by the point A on the horizontal axis, with $OA = K$ (for S must then be zero). If our operator requires a larger E than this, he will have to take some of the non-money securities, thus increasing S; so possible alternatives are represented by points to the 'south-east' of A on the diagram. But the best such alternative, giving minimum S for a gain in E, will lie on a particular line through A; and it would seem to follow from our perfect market assumption that the first stretch of this line (AB) will be *straight*. For it will not usually be a particular security, to be substituted for

[13] Thus I assume that our operator is a 'risk-averter'. Reasons for believing that this is the correct assumption to make in the present theory have been given above (p. 245). More will follow when we come to the Second Theorem.

It may indeed be objected that a security, or bundle of securities, the value of which is uncertain in terms of money, may yet have an outcome which is more certain than that of money itself, in terms of a basket of commodities which to the operator is more important. I shall here neglect that possibility because I regard its occurrence as an indication that the 'moneyness' of the money in question is breaking down. For a fully functioning money I think my assumption holds.

money, which will minimise S for a given gain in E; it will be better for the operator to spread his risks, choosing a bundle of securities the total outcome of which has the least uncertainty. What bundle it is that minimises uncertainty will depend upon the (unit) prospects of the individual securities; and we have taken it that these prospects are independent of the amounts of the securities taken. Thus it will be the *same* bundle that is substituted for money along the whole of the stretch AB. This should presumably mean that the marginal rate of substitution of E for S will be constant along AB, so the line AB will be straight.

At the point B, however, the whole of the capital has been put into securities; there is no more money to be substituted. It will then be impossible to get more E save by substituting another bundle of securities for the first; and since the first was that by which S could be traded for E on the most favourable terms, the new bundle must represent a trade which, at the margin, is less favourable. Thus after B the 'frontier' must curve round, as shown.

Thus, so long as some money is held, a greater or less willingness to bear risks will just be expressed in a simple substitution between money and a 'least risky' bundle of securities. It is only when the money holding is zero that it will take the form of substitution between less and more risky securities. This is my First Theorem.[14]

[14] I think that the demonstration of it, as just stated above, is fairly compelling; it may nevertheless be useful to set out a formal proof, for a simple case where such a proof is easy.

I here write x_0 for the money that is held, and x_j ($j = 1, 2, \ldots, n$) for the initial money value of what is held in the jth security. These xs must add up to K; so

$$x_0 + \Sigma x_j = K \tag{1}$$

may be regarded as the constraint under which the operator is working. (I here take it that all xs are non-negative; more will be said about that in note 19 on p. 255 below).

The additional assumptions that are needed for our special case are: first, that the probability distributions of the security-outcomes are *normal*, so that they can be fully described by the two classical parameters, mean value (e) and standard deviation (s); secondly, that those of the different securities are independent of one another; and thirdly, that the E and the S, a utility function of which the operator is maximising, can be identified with the mean value and standard deviation of the whole portfolio. If these are granted, we can use the regular statistical rules, which give

$$E = x_0 + \Sigma c_j x_j \tag{2}$$

and

$$S^2 = \Sigma s_j^2 x_j^2 \qquad (j = 1, 2, \ldots, n) \tag{3}$$

(for $e_0 = 1$ and $s_0 = 0$). Since all the coefficients in the constraint (equation 1 above) are unity, the condition for the maximisation of $U(E, S)$ is that

$$U_E E_j + U_S S_j$$

It is a property, as has been emphasised, of choice of portfolio *when transaction costs are negligible*.

3.   We have so far been considering how our operator would react if, while still having the same initial capital K, he had been more or less willing to bear uncertainty. But there is a further question. How would he have reacted if, while his expectations and safety-preference remained unchanged, his capital had been different?

I long supposed that there was little to be said on this matter. There would just be a 'wealth effect' (like the income effect of consumer theory); and about that, as in consumer theory, we could learn very little from a mere postulate of consistent behaviour. But I have later become convinced that in this case there is a way by which one can make some further progress.[15]

___

should be the same over all securities (including money) that are taken. (U_E, U_S are partial derivatives with respect to E and S; E_j, S_j are partials with respect to x_j.) U_E is positive, U_S negative; so $- (U_S/U_E)$, which I write as W, is the marginal rate of substitution between E and S. Thus the maximum condition may alternatively be written as saying that $A_j = M$ (a common value) where

$$A_j = E_j - WS_j \qquad (4)$$

Then, from (2) and (3), we have $E_j = e_j$ ($E_0 = 1$), and $SS_j = s_j^2 x_j$ ($S_0 = 0$). Thus $A_0 = 1$; so, if some money is taken, $M = 1$. If no money is taken, $M > 1$; for that is in fact the condition that no money should be taken.

In each of these cases, we have for each of the non-money securities (from $A_j = M$)

$$e_j - M = s_j^2 x_j (W/S) \qquad (5)$$

Thus if $M = 1$, the proportions in which the x_j are combined depend solely upon the e_j and the s_j, which are pure characteristics of the unit prospects of the securities, as stated in the text. But if $M > 1$, the proportions depend on M.

Now take each of the equations (5) – which hold for each of the non-money securities that are taken, multiply it by the corresponding x_j and add. We get

$$(E - x_0) - M(K - x_0) = WS$$

Now either $M = 1$, or $x_0 = 0$; so *in all cases*

$$E - MK = WS \qquad (6)$$

Since W is the slope of the frontier, this last equation has a clear interpretation geometrically. It tells us that the intercept of the tangent to the frontier, on the horizontal (E) axis, is equal to MK. This is equal to K, so long as $M = 1$, which establishes the linearity of AB, while it is clear that M will rise as risk-aversion diminishes so the curved part of the frontier (BC) must be curved outwards, as drawn.

It is shown in *CEMT*, pp. 112–13, that the same rules will hold even though the prospects of the securities are inter-correlated, so long as they are *normal*. I have no such proof of the more general form of the proposition that was given in the text; it rests, I am afraid, largely on 'intuition'.

[15] Here is where I draw on my 'Disaster Point' paper (*EP*, essay 8).

For there is no need, in the case of choice under uncertainty, to confine attention to ordinal preferences, as in consumer theory. Choice under uncertainty does involve comparisons between degrees of preference, as choices between consumption bundles do not.[16] We are thus at liberty to use the alternative scheme of maximisation (due ultimately to Bernouilli) according to which what the operator maximises is the expected value (or mathematical expectation) of the 'utility' which he derives from the outcome of his choice. Whether or not we find this procedure convincing (and I myself would have plenty of reservations about it) we shall find that it leads to an interesting proposition, which should be fairly generally acceptable, and which I shall dignify by the name of my Second Theorem.

We have to suppose that there are m eventualities, or 'states of the world', any of which may occur. The operator knows what will be the outcome, of the investment of £1 in each security, in each eventuality; but he does not know which eventuality will occur. (This just amounts to sweeping the knowns and unknowns into separate boxes.) Then, if a_{ij} is this known outcome, of a unit invested in the jth security in the ith eventuality, the total outcome of amounts $(x_0, x_1, \ldots, x_n)$ to be put into the various securities, including money, will, in the ith eventuality, be

$$y_i = \Sigma \, a_{ij} x_j \qquad (j = 0, 1, \ldots, n)$$

The Bernouillian assumption is that the operator maximises $\Sigma \, p_i u(y_i)$ over all eventualities – the ps being *given* probabilities, while $u(y)$ is a (total) utility function, with conventional properties.

4. This is a particularly interesting hypothesis for dealing with changes in K, since it enables us to give a definite answer to the question: is there any utility function $u(y)$ which will ensure that a rise in K will leave the proportions in which the securities (including money) are taken the same as they were before? It has sometimes been denied that there is any such function, which makes sense;[17] but I believe that it does exist, and is quite suggestive.

If all x_i (including money) were increased in the same proportion, all y_i would be increased in that same proportion (assuming, that is, that the a_{ij} are unchanged – our perfect market assumption again!). But if the operator were in a preferred position at the old y_i, there must have been a particular relation between their marginal utilities

---

[16] The classical demonstration is in Samuelson 'Probability, Utility and Independence' (*Econometrica*, 1952). See also R. G. D. Allen on independent goods, in Volume I of this Collection (pp. 49-53).

[17] As by K. Arrow, *Aspects of the Theory of Risk-bearing* (1965).

in the old position;[18] that relation will be unchanged when the y_i increase equi-proportionally, if the marginal utilities $u'(y_i)$ also change in equal proportions. Thus for a small change in K, the *elasticities* of the MU curves $u'(y_i)$ must be the same. But these are not different curves; the different y_i and their corresponding $u'(y_i)$ are just different points along the *same* curve. So what is being said is that the (single) MU curve $u'(y)$ is to have constant elasticity.

Now it is well-known that for any downward-sloping curve to have constant elasticity, its equation must be of a definite form. We must have $u'(y) = Ay^{-\alpha}$, where A is a constant, and α is the reciprocal of the Marshallian elasticity. Now if this curve is drawn out on a diagram (Fig. 19.2), it is *asymptotic to both axes*. What can that mean?

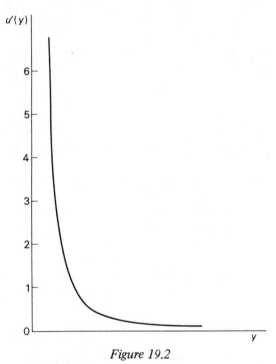

Figure 19.2

[18] For if $U = \Sigma p_i u(v_i)$, we have U_j (the marginal utility of investment in the *j*th security) = $\Sigma p_i u'(v_i) a_{ij}$ (over all *i*). In a preferred position, all U_j are equal. If the $u'(y_i)$ change in equal proportions the U_j will change in equal proportions; if they were equal before, they will still be equal.

Thus equal proportional changes in the $u'(y)$s are a sufficient condition for equal proportional changes in the *x*s. But, as is shown in a rather crabbed footnote on p. 176 of *EP*, it is not a necessary condition – if the number of eventualities is greater than the number of securities, as seems reasonable. But a sufficient condition is all we want.

The behaviour of the curve on the right looks easily acceptable. As wealth increases, its *MU* falls, but never falls to zero. There is always some gain from an increase in wealth, though it may be very small. That, I think, is what we should want to say; but what of the infinite *MU* on the left? If total utility, for positive y, is finite (as we should clearly like to make it), it will follow from the marginal utility at $y = 0$ being *plus* infinity that total utility at $y = 0$ is *minus* infinity. That is surprising, but I think it makes sense, in the present context.

There is no reason, in risk theory, why we should exclude the possibility of an outcome having a utility of minus infinity, for this would simply mean that the operator would *always* avoid such an outcome, if it were possible to avoid it. Now if the securities that are on offer are of the usual kinds (bills, bonds and equities carrying limited liability) the worst that can happen from any choice of such securities is total loss (of the whole portfolio); that is to say, $y = 0$. To put $u(0) = -$ infinity amounts to saying that a chance of such loss would always be avoided. If there was some security for which there was a finite chance of total loss, to put the whole capital into that security would be a choice that would always be avoided. For if in the ith eventuality, y_i were zero, so that $u(y_i)$ were minus infinity, $\Sigma p_i u(y_i)$ would be minus infinity, if p_i were finite. So what follows from the utility function we are examining is that the operator would never put the whole of his fortune into such an investment. He may put a part of his capital into such an investment; but so long as the rest is put into investments where there is no such possibility, he is not faced with a finite probability of total loss over his whole portfolio. The *minus infinity* of the utility function just means that that, obviously foolish, behaviour is excluded.

So we have shown that there is a quite intelligible utility function which (on Bernouillian principles) would account for the proportions in which all securities (including money) are held remaining unchanged when capital increases. But having got so far, we can easily go further.

5. Why should the disaster point, which is always to be avoided, be set at this purely arithmetical *total loss*? It only looks even apparently plausible that it should be set at that point, because we have been looking at the money-securities part of the balance-sheet in isolation, without regard to other items, the real goods on the assets side, and the liabilities. If the operator has liabilities as well as assets, or if he is carrying on a productive business which itself creates calls upon him, he may well face disaster, when the outcome of his invest-

ments in securities has fallen very low, even if it is not zero. His utility function $u(y)$ should then go to minus infinity at a positive value of y, which we will call c.

We can deal with this amendment rather easily. We have only to put $u'(y) = A(y - c)^{-\alpha}$, so that the whole MU curve is shifted to the right, becoming asymptotic to $y = c$.

The effect of this is quite simple. We have

$$y_i = \Sigma\, a_{ij}\, x_j \quad \text{and} \quad K = \Sigma\, x_j$$

(the sums being taken over all securities, including money). Thus

$$y_i - c = \Sigma \left(a_{ij} - \frac{c}{K}\right) x_j.$$

Thus maximisation is just the same as in the former case, save that all unit outcomes (of particular securities in particular eventualities) are written down by c/K. If K is large compared with c, the write-down is negligible; so the chosen portfolio will be practically the same as with the former function. But as K diminishes, relative to c, the write-down will take effect. Some of the $a_{ij} - c/K$ will then start to go negative. So the operator will then tend to avoid such securities – those which have a very low outcome in some eventualities. He will avoid such risky securities. He will 'play for safety' as he gets poorer, or as he gets nearer to his disaster point.[19]

Now, out of a large population of persons and businesses, who are managing portfolios of securities, there will surely be some who will know that they will come to grief if the value of their portfolio falls very low, even if does not fall to zero. And it is hard to see that there will be any (save perhaps some exceptional cases of which we do not need to take account) for whom total loss will not spell disaster. It will then follow that for the group as a whole there must be a positive wealth effect. That is to say, if we re-interpret Fig. 19.1 to represent a plotting of E/K against S/K – so that the frontier can remain unchanged when K changes – an increase in K, *with given commitments* will tend to move the chosen point along the frontier

[19] It is interesting to notice that with this amendment, we have changed the character of the disaster point. As originally stated, it appeared to be a characteristic of the securities on offer – that the worst that could happen from investment in any security was total loss. But now it becomes a characteristic of the preferences of the operator himself. This actually gives the theory a wider applicability, for we are now enabled to drop the assumption that the xs are non-negative. We can allow our operator to borrow, or to trade on margins; he can be a speculator, but he must not be a silly speculator. Of course, he may be wrong in his assessments; he may come to grief. But he must not *plan* for disaster.

to the right. This is my second theorem. It is very near to what I con-jectured, many years ago, in essay 5.[20] It was there no more than a conjecture; the Bernouillian analysis, here presented, gives it a little more substance. The qualification that it has introduced – that the bias in the wealth effect is a matter of the strength (or comfort) of the operator's position – will stand, whether or not we accept the Bernouillian approach; but without that approach, it would be hard to bring it out so clearly.

PART III.   SOLIDITY, FLUIDITY AND LIQUIDITY[21]

1.   It is generally recognised that the demand for money, to be held at any moment by any entity (person or business or other) should be analysed by the purpose for which the money is held. Keynes's three-way classification, into transactions, precautionary and speculative balances, is an example. I have myself come to the view that such a classification gains in richness (that is to say, it becomes applicable to a wider variety of situations) if we allow ourselves to observe that money is only one of the assets which may be held for corresponding purposes. I have therefore proposed[22] to make a corresponding classification of all assets in the balance-sheet, dividing them into what I call Running Assets, Reserve Assets and Investment Assets. (One advantage of this procedure is that we do not have to begin by deciding just what assets we are to reckon as *money*.)

Some assets are financial claims; others are property rights in real goods. This is a different classification from the first, but both are needed. So what results is a six-way table:

	Running	*Reserve*	*Investment*
Real	A	B	C
Financial	D	E	F

What kinds of asset should we put into each of these boxes?

We should not expect to find that in every balance-sheet there are instances of all six. A manufacturing firm will have real running assets (*A*) in the form of goods in process, and of plant and machinery in use. They are running assets because they are in active use, in the work on which the firm is engaged. It will probably have some real

---

[20] Pp. 59–60 above.

[21] For what is in effect a prefatory note to this paper, see above, p. 237.

[22] First in *CEMT*, essay 3; later in *CKE*, pp. 46–7.

reserve assets (*B*) in   the form of reserve stocks of materials, and perhaps some equipment, machines and such like, which will only come into use in the event of a need for repairs, or some similar emergency. It is not easy to see that there is the same need for such a firm to have real investment assets (*C*) though it may have. But clearly there are other entities which do have assets under (*C*); an obvious case, to the present writer, is land held by colleges *as an investment*. Land-holding is not the regular business of the college; the land is just held to get an income from it.

Real assets (*B*) that are held as reserves are already embodied in specific forms; so they are only useful as reserves in appropriate emergencies. But the kinds of emergency that may arise in the future can never be exactly foreseen; so a form of reserve that is not so tied down must in general be required. This is the function of the financial reserve assets (*E*) which we should thus expect to be very widely held. One is indeed tempted to say that any business, which is not in danger of collapse, must have some financial reserves. But this does not necessarily mean that it must have such reserves as assets, for there is a possible alternative. It may be that it is working on an overdraft arrangement, or on some equivalent which gives it assured borrowing power. We may perhaps reckon this as an 'invisible asset'. It does not appear on a formal balance-sheet, but it is so important nowadays that we must not forget it.[23]

Financial investment assets (*F*) are easily identified. They are a principal asset of the private capitalist, and of the Pension Fund or Charitable Trust. It is an essential characteristic of the assets in this compartment that they are held for the sake of their yield, of the interest or dividends that are to be derived from them.

There remain the financial running assets (*D*) which are clearly of major importance for monetary theory. For money, in some sense or other, in the till, in the pocket or in the bank account, is without doubt a leading financial running asset, for almost any entity. But before I come to that, I shall look further at (*E*) and (*F*).

2.   If (as Keynes often did) we regard it as an essential characteristic of money that it does not bear interest, it would seem at first sight

---

[23] A parallel analysis can be made for the personal sector, and it is quite instructive. Private persons who are utterly without reserves do in some emergencies just starve. Social conscience, from quite early times, has revolted against that, and has provided substitutes (invisible assets). They go back, in English history to the responsibility of the manorial lord for his dependents and to the charitable work of the Church. These were replaced (well or badly) by Poor Laws; then by the modern apparatus of social security. The ability of wider classes to call on consumer credit has been a contemporaneous development.

that no money should be held under (F). For these assets are held for their yield, for the income that is expected to be derived from them. Keynes nevertheless maintained that money could be held under (F), for his 'speculative motive'. This was quite a shock to some of his first readers, who had been thinking that an investor, who bought a security in order to derive an income from it, would be intending to hold it indefinitely. If he had that intention, there would be no point in holding 'barren money'. Keynes, however, was not thinking of that sort of investor, but of one who plans to *manage his portfolio*, selling and buying again as opportunity offers. I am myself convinced that both types are real types; neither should be overlooked. So we shall want names for them. 'Non-speculative' and 'speculative' is too clumsy; it will be neater to say that the one type invests *solid*, the other *fluid*.

There can be no doubt that there will be occasions when a fluid investor will act as a bear speculator. If he expects a fall in the prices of securities (a rise in rates of interest) he will sell and then (if his expectation is correct) buy back at the lower price. During the interval he will have held his funds idle, for a speculative motive. Even if he gets no interest on the funds held idle during the interval, he will still gain, even in income terms, in the longer run.[24] So one must accept that there is this case in which money may be held as an investment asset. But this, though so much attention has been paid to it, is by no means the chief way in which the solidity–fluidity distinction is important.

A solid investor, though he may choose his investment with care at the moment he makes it, can only do so in the light of what he knows at that moment. He denies himself the opportunity of changing his decision, in the light of further information available later. The fluid investor is not denied that opportunity; this to him is an advantage. Why should the former deny himself that advantage? The obvious answer is transaction costs. Every act of investment (and disinvestment) in securities must ordinarily involve some costs – which may be subjective, time and trouble involved, but may also be quite objective, stamp duties and brokerage charges in particular. If a portfolio is managed in a very fluid manner, these transaction costs

---

[24] I quote an example I have used elsewhere. 'Suppose it is expected that the rate of interest on a (long-term) bond will rise, from 4 to 5 per cent, within a year. £100 invested now will yield £4 per annum; if invested later, it looks like yielding £5 per annum; thus by delay there is a gain of £1 per annum, in perpetuity, against a loss of £4, at the most, in the period of delay. Considered in income terms this is quite a profitable investment. The *barren* money, properly accounted for, is not without yield.' (*CKE*, p. 26)

must pile up. They have to be deducted from the gains from fluidity if there is to be a net advantage of changing over to a fluid policy. It is therefore of the first importance that there are likely to be great differences in the transaction costs that are faced by investors of different sorts.

One can assert, with some confidence, that transaction costs, of most kinds, increase less than proportionately to the volume of funds to be invested, at least for large differences in volume. This is shown, if it needs showing, by the fact that when the portfolio is large, it pays to have specialised departments, or equivalent organisations, to do the managing; it does not pay when the portfolio is smaller. Thus it is essentially the large investor who can profitably pursue a fluid policy; it does not pay the small investor to do so. It is better for him to invest at least fairly solid.[25]

3.   It is indeed true, and of the greatest importance, that solidity (and fluidity) are matters of degree. Even the sleepiest investor may sometimes wake up; and the fluid investor, who must still pay some attention to transaction costs, is, as we shall see, the realistic case. For it may be doubted whether perfect fluidity is in practice attainable. Though, for a large investor, transaction costs may be small, in proportion to dealings, they do not seem to disappear. It is nevertheless convenient, for theoretical purposes, to keep perfect fluidity as a case to keep in mind. For this is the case to which the 'static' analysis of the preceding parts I and II most exactly applies.

If transaction costs can be wholly neglected, it is unnecessary for the operator to look further forward than the shortest period ahead. He can invest, in the most advantageous way, for week 1, being prepared to come back into cash at the end of the week; he would then invest in the most advantageous way for a second week, in the light of any new information that had come up by that date. So he need only attend to the probable outcomes of possible investments, as he expects them to be at the end of one week. So his behaviour can be fully analysed in terms of uncertainty theory, without reference to time. But, as soon as some attention has to be paid to transaction costs, considerations of timing come in.

They come in more obviously with funds that are held under (E) than with those held under (F). Reserve funds are held against emergencies, the extent of which is not exactly foreseen, nor is the

---

[25] The investment trust accordingly appears as a device by which small investors can get some of the advantages of fluidity, by combination.

date of their arising exactly foreseen. If the date when they will be required is completely uncertain – it may just as well be in the near future as further ahead – it will be essential that the funds should be held in a form which makes them realisable easily, at any moment. And this does not only mean that they must be held in securities that are readily marketable; it also means that they must be held in such a form that the value of the portfolio is not likely to vary too much over time. The value, at whatever date there is to be realisation, must be much the same. A particular asset which has this property, is surely what in practice is meant by a *liquid asset*.

This then is where we come to *liquidity*, not (I now think) earlier. I wanted a different name to distinguish between alternative *policies* that might be pursued for the management of funds, and *fluidity* was fortunately to hand. The ideal way of preserving the value of a portfolio is by keeping perfectly fluid, thus taking full advantage of every new piece of information that may come in; for that will preserve the value, as far as it is possible for it to be preserved, and will do so in the most profitable way. But if that way is closed – or if it is too expensive, in view of transaction costs, to make more than a limited use of it – the best way of preserving reliability, over time, is to hold a good part of the portfolio in liquid form. For the more that is held that way, the less will be the potential time-variability.

So this is where we come to the *spectrum of assets*. It has been shown, in parts I and II above, that if no attention is paid to the timing of outcomes, there is a sharp line between assets the expected outcome of which is certain, and those in which it is uncertain. So long as any amount of the certain asset is taken, the best policy is to combine the holdings of the uncertain assets in such proportions as give the best mean value (over the whole bundle) for given dispersion, and to hold to those proportions whatever is the amount of the certain asset that is taken. So there is just a two-way choice, how much to hold in the certain asset, and how much in the bundle. But as soon as timing is relevant, the expected outcomes get a new dimension; this causes the two-way choice to break down. If the emergency against which the funds are being held may occur at any time (it may just as well happen tomorrow as five years hence) it will be foolish not to hold a good part of the reserve in liquid form. If there is confidence that it is unlikely to occur for some time, it will seem safe to be relatively illiquid, as there should then be time to make readjustments to deal with it. Thus it is fair to say that with greater confidence (lower liquidity preference, in Keynesian terms) there will be a movement 'to the right' along the spectrum; this is so, whether anything is held in 'quite certain' form or not.

4.   All this is clearest with respect to reserve assets (E); but there is something of the same sort in the case of investment assets also. The manager of a pure investment fund does not have to attend to the value of his portfolio, as it may be in the event of some external emergency, arising at an uncertain date, as the manager of a reserve fund has to do. But he still needs to be in a position so that he can take advantage of opportunities for profitable investment, which cannot now be foreseen, but which may arise in the future. If he is illiquid, being tied up in securities, the value of which at an uncertain future date is uncertain, he may find that an opportunity arises, just at a moment when the value of his portfolio is *abnormally* low. The new opportunity would have been profitable, if there had not been this prospect of recovery, just from staying where he is; but when the expected gain from that is set against the expected gain from the new investment, the net gain vanishes. So he also has a need for liquidity, for having some part of his portfolio in relatively liquid assets.

I suppose that this need for liquidity under (F) corresponds to what Keynes called the *speculative motive*, while that under (E) corresponds to his *precautionary*. I have generalised these concepts a little, and when they are generalised they do not look so very different. The investment manager, when he pursues a fluid policy, is looking for gain; the reserve fund manager is seeking to avoid loss; but they are operating on similar spectra, and the motives that cause them to move in the directions of greater or less liquidity are much the same. Each of them, when he manages his portfolio in a fluid manner, is bound to *speculate*.

5.   I can get as far as this without having to specify what kinds of asset are liquid, to a greater or less extent. I have not even had to write out the conventional spectrum

cash   short loans   long loans   equities   real assets

in which it is assumed that cash does not bear interest, so that its money value is identically the same from one week to another, while the real assets, at the other end, are not even readily marketable. And it has been as well to hold this over, for the concept of liquidity, to which we have been coming, is essentially relative to the circumstances of the operator. I want to be able to say that a balance-sheet which from the point of view of one operator is very liquid may not be at all liquid from the point of view of another.

We would usually say that a portfolio, which consisted of nothing but cash, was perfectly liquid. But we would not want to say that a

British firm, trading with Argentina, which held all its assets in cash in Argentine pesos, was perfectly liquid. We would want to consider the claims against which the assets are held. If all that the firm could have to pay out, in relevant emergencies, were sums fixed in Argentine pesos, to keep its reserves in the form of pesos would give it liquidity; but if its probable outpayments were fixed in pounds, it would be sterling reserves that it would require for liquidity. This is, of course, a matter of much practical importance in these days of fluctuating exchanges; it is a very real trouble for 'multi-nationals'. And the conundrums which it is setting to Central Banks – what (now) just are the liquid reserves of a Central Bank? – is becoming notorious.

There is also another way in which the kind of business a firm is doing affects its liquidity requirement. There must be many businesses (or for that matter persons) who can *usually* be quite confident that no exceptional demands for cash payments will be made upon them, for which they will not have a certain amount of notice. To suppose that this notice will be at least for a week is surely very modest. But, if so, any funds that can be converted into cash at a foreseeable rate, at a week's notice, are, from the point of view of such a firm, perfectly liquid. So it is not necessary, for such a firm, to hold its liquid reserves in cash. It is more profitable, and quite safe, to hold them in the form of 'shorts', bills or interest-bearing deposits. Perfect liquidity, for a firm in this situation, can extend quite a long way along the spectrum.

But there are others who are not, or may not be, in this easy position. They are subject to demands which have to be met 'at sight'. The banks themselves are a leading example, but there are many finance houses which are 'quasi-banks', so that they fall into a similar category. The in-payments and out-payments, which go on all the time in the most settled conditions, require a certain cash holding to finance them, since they do not exactly fit; but the cash that is required for that purpose is surely to be reckoned as a running asset (under D), not as a reserve asset (under E). The amount that is required will depend upon the volume of business that the firm is doing; it would not seem that it should be significantly sensitive to liquidity shifts. It is only the cash that is held as a reserve asset, against emergencies, which would seem (in terms of our previous analysis) to be so subject.

6.　This leads on to an important issue, which is best treated historically. The reason which Keynes gave for his belief that there must always be some money that is held for a speculative motive was that, unless there were such funds, open-market operations by a monetary authority would be impossible.[26] By selling bonds, the Bank draws cash from the market; where is it to come from? Who are the people who are to be persuaded, by the offer of a higher rate of interest, to give up their holding of cash, and to hold the bonds instead?

I have come to believe that the peculiar view on this matter, which Keynes took in the thirties, is to be explained in terms of the peculiar conditions of the time when he was writing. From 1933–8 the market rate of discount in London was very sticky, and very low, at approximately two-thirds of one per cent. So short rates of interest were nearly negligible. It mattered little whether one interpreted *money* narrowly, as cash that does not bear interest, or widely, to include 'shorts'. What did matter was the gap between this negligible yield (zero to $\frac{2}{3}$ per cent) and the rate on long government bonds (which had then come back, after the 5 per cent at which it had stood in the twenties, to roundabout 3 per cent, where it had stood for so much of the nineteenth century). Keynes was much concerned that this gap should not widen; so it is this gap which figures in his theory as *the* rate of interest. But all that is very past history, which already, soon after 1950, had begun to seem far away.

When in the 1960s, I myself came to reconsider these matters,[27] I kept as close to Keynes as I could. I laid stress upon the position of those 'financiers', who would still need to keep some cash as a reserve asset; so in their response to changes in their preferences for liquidity (or to changes in the cost of obtaining liquidity) they would operate upon a wide spectrum, including non-interest-bearing money at its 'leftward' end. How far that was justified, at that date, I do not know. But I am sure that in the much more inflationary times that have followed it must have ceased to be justified.

When short rates of interest are in the range of 10–20 per cent, as we have learned to expect them to be, no prudent operator will hold his reserve in the form of cash, if he can find any way of avoiding doing so.[28] A firm which is not subject to claims 'at sight' will indeed have gone out of cash at much lower rates of interest. But the 'financier' also must surely endeavour to get out of cash, when rates are so high. It will be better for him to borrow, even at such high rates, when he needs to do so, than to sacrifice the yield which he

---

[26] *General Theory*, p. 197.

[27] In *CEMT*, especially essay 3.

[28] He may indeed be compelled by law to hold some 'reserves' in cash, but since these have been made inaccessible to liquidity shifts, they may here be left out of account.

could get from holding shorts, all the time, when immediate cash is not needed. The flight from cash, which already at lower rates (not the negligible rates of Keynes's time) would surely go far in the non-financial sector, must surely, at these high rates, affect the financial sector also.

What then, in this position, is the answer to Keynes's puzzle? I am convinced that (now) one must boldly say that there is no answer. Let us go to the extreme, as is always useful to bring out a point, and suppose that there are no reserve (or speculative) funds held in cash, in the system, at all. We cannot in fact be very far from that situation. What happens, then, if the Bank attempts to draw cash from the market, by selling long-term bonds in the traditional manner? The only way it can do it, or appear to do it, is by itself, in some indirect manner, providing the cash which it is purporting to soak up. Borrowing at one door, it must be lending at another. It is nevertheless true that it is open to the Bank to choose the terms on which it will lend, so that the impotence of 'open-market policy' does not deprive the Bank of some power of controlling rates of interest. If the Bank tries to avoid coming to the rescue, interest rates will shoot up; still, at some point, it will have to come to the rescue. I think one can see that this is in fact what happens.

So the focus goes back on to interest rates. What that means, in terms of monetary theory, is that Keynes, for us, is *too* monetarist. What we need, as a simplified version of the monetary system, which will stress the things which for us are important, is something which will pay *less* attention than Keynes did to the Quantity of Money. There have been some parts of my later writings in which I have tried to sketch out such a model. I shall give a brief account of them in part IV which follows. It means going back from Keynes (the Keynes of the *General Theory*) to the Keynes of the *Treatise* – and to Wicksell.

7.   I can get as far as this while saying scarcely anything about money under (*D*), money as a financial running asset. I could do so because I believe that in a sophisticated economy (in which, as I have explained, investment has become very fluid) this use of money – though still in a sense primary, since the economy, as organised, could not function without it – has lost a great deal of its former *causal* importance.

It is from its running assets that a firm makes its profits; but the individual running assets are a bundle of complements, not at all easily substitutable for one another, save by a change in technical methods, not usually practicable, to a great extent, in the short run. If we widen technical method to include organisational method, the same applies to the cash that the firm requires as a running asset.

This may, of course, vary over the week, and probably over longer cycles, but there will be a certain pattern of money holding which is implied in the way the firm does its job. The average volume of money that is held in this way may well bear a certain relation (not at all necessarily a fixed proportional relation) to the volume of its business, expressed in money terms. In normal times this may be rather dependable, in any but the shortest period; but it is not easy to see that there are any rules about the way in which it will react when conditions change, especially if they change sharply.

It is not to be denied that the pressure of high rates of interest will give an incentive for economising in money holding, here too. But the ways that are open for such economising, without drastic change in organisation (such as, to take the most obvious example, a change in the time-pattern of paying wages) are rather limited. The most important, probably, is to go over to an overdraft system, on which interest is *saved* on the part of the overdraft that is *not* used; so that a firm which entirely uses the overdraft system is in a similar position to one which held its running balance in shorts, so far as the effects at the margin is concerned. But whereas a balance held in shorts gives a greater gain when rates of interest rates are high, an overdraft is more burdensome. So this is only a partial way out.

A full way out could only be attained if running balances could be held in shorts, and those shorts were acceptable as a means of payment. It is conceivable that under great inflationary pressure we might come to that, and there may be some signs of it already. But, so far, the most obvious shorts are not means of payment; they have to be turned into cash to be so used. And that is vital.

For it is tempting to suppose that if money, in the narrow sense, had become confined to its use as a running asset, it would be sufficient to control the volume of money in that narrow sense and a direct effect on the value of output (or even on the Gross Domestic Product) could be obtained. But this is a chimera. For the separation between money, in the narrow sense, and the shorts (which are undoubtedly functioning as quasi-money), though it has come about through the pressure of high interest rates, is itself dependent upon the convertibility of the shorts into money. It is not at all easy to see how the volume of money, in the narrow sense, could be controlled, without damaging that convertibility. If the convertibility were lost, the quasi-monies would cease to be liquid; the liquidity crisis which would then develop could pass all bounds. The control through interest rates, which is still feasible, though (as we shall see) it has its own limitations, is better than that.[29]

PART IV.   THE CREDIT ECONOMY

1.   What I mean by a credit economy is one that contains no money that does not bear interest; so that the key instrument of monetary control must be the rate of interest, or the interest rates. Actual economies, as we have seen, are tending in that direction; so it need not surprise us to find that much may be learned about actual money by considering the pure type. It may indeed be claimed that we get from it a grasp of essentials more quickly and more easily than in any other way.

If there is no money that does not bear interest, what is money? We have to go back to the function of money as a means of payment; money is what is acceptable in the payment of debts. But what is the payment of a debt? When I pay my tradesman with a cheque that will be honoured (for otherwise there is no payment) he is exchanging my debt to him for a debt from my bank to him, while the bank has less of a debt to me (assuming that there is a surplus in my bank account). If I am working on an overdraft, I have more of a debt to the bank. The payment of a debt is an exchange of debts.

We regard it as a payment because the debts have different *quality*. It is different quality from the point of view of the creditor which is what matters. I may be quite sure that I am going to pay, but my creditor has to face the risk that I may have gone away for a holiday, just as his bill comes in. The debt to him from the bank is more reliable.

In what way is it more reliable? It is not just that he knows the hours when the bank will be open, so that the cheque can be cashed. For notes (and indeed coins) are no more than tokens; they are themselves to be regarded as debts of the banking system; all that happens when one cashes a cheque is that one exchanges one form of debt for another. Even if the bank cashiers go on strike, the debt from the bank does not lose its quality; it can still be used, though with some inconvenience.

---

[29] It should be emphasised that what has just been said relates to instruments of monetary control, not to targets. Whether one definition of money supply is a more suitable target than another is a separate question.

Suppose that the creditor, to whom I pay my debt, keeps his account at a different bank from that on which my cheque is drawn. He still accepts it as a money payment, since he knows that his bank will accept it as a money payment; debts from the one bank, and from the other, have (from the points of view of all concerned) equal reliability. We normally expect that that will be the case; but if I had drawn my cheque on a bank of which he had never heard, and which (so far as he could tell) might be purely imaginary, he would not have accepted it as a payment.

2. One can construct, in the light of these reflections, two pure models of a credit economy, each of which has its uses. I call them the *monocentric* and *polycentric* respectively.

It is characteristic of a monocentric model that it has just one 'central' entity, promises to pay by which have superior quality (in that they are more widely acceptable) than promises by any other entity. The continuance of that superiority is taken for granted, so that there is just this one 'monetary authority'. The polycentric model has no such single centre. But there will still be differences in the qualities of promises by different entities; so there will be some, at any particular moment, which have highest quality. If there is just one which at the moment has the highest quality, it acts, for the moment, like a monocentre; but there is no certainty that it will retain that position. It may be, on the other hand, that there are several that have established an equal reliability, each maintaining a willingness to convert its promises, at a fixed rate, into those of the others. If there is perfect convertibility, each has some of the properties of a monocentre; but there is no single 'monetary authority'.

It will surely be noticed that a monocentric model is likely to be most relevant to the problems of a national economy, especially when the international aspects of that economy – external trade and capital movements – are being left out of account. The monocentre can then be identified with the Central Bank (or may be with Government including central bank); or, in some cases, with the whole of the banking system, when commercial banks are closely controlled by the central bank and Government). The polycentric model has most relevance to international problems.

3. I begin with the simplest type of monocentric model, a type which may fairly be described as the Wicksellian type. There is just one bank, providing credit money, the only money there is; and there are no other financial bodies. The only form in which savings can be

held is as deposits in the bank, and it is only from the bank that those undertaking investment can borrow. The only means of control that is available to the bank is the rate of interest which it pays (and charges). We call this the *money rate* of interest.

It is tempting to say that a system such as this would be *in equilibrium*, over a period, if the net increase in the volume of loans being made by the bank was equal to the net increase in the volume of deposits. For this would mean that the volume of money that was circulating outside the bank would be remaining unchanged over the period. Wicksell himself was sometimes inclined to this interpretation of equilibrium; but there is really no reason, in general, why it should be useful. The volume of money that was in circulation might be constant and yet, in other directions to which importance might reasonably be atributed, the system might fail to be in what we should want to call an equilibrium. So there is another criterion, which also makes it appearance in Wicksell's work, according to which the system is in equilibrium if the price-level is remaining constant. Then the equilibrium rate of interest is that which maintains constant prices. This is not the same thing, and it is perhaps more appealing.

But we need not stop there.[30] There are after all many indices of prices, which do not always move together; so that there should be an equilibrium rate of interest corresponding to each. One of them is a wage-index, so there should be an equilibrium rate which would keep the wage-level constant. Or, if wages are *sticky*, it could be interpreted as a rate which would give a desired level of employment (à la Keynes). And if it is not the wage-level which has become sticky, but a conventional rate of rise in the wage-level which has become sticky, there could be an equilibrium rate of interest which (in the same sense) would fit that rate of rise in the wage-level. To keep the money rate at that 'equilibrium' level would not cure inflation; all it could do would be to ensure (by being high enough) that monetary policy was not, in itself, aggravating inflation – and (by being low enough) that the activity of the economy was not being depressed by monetary policy.[31] All these things, which I need not remark have become very topical things, are already in sight of the simple Wicksellian model.

[30] It was the achievement of G. Myrdal's *Monetary Equilibrium* (see essay 4 above) to have made this clear.

[31] If the rate of inflation, that is set by this wage-behaviour, is itself regarded as intolerable, there may be a case for keeping the money rate above the equilibrium that is set by this behaviour, to bring pressure to bear upon the 'stickiness'. That is not ruled out.

4.   Still it is not good enough. For what about uncertainty, and the cost of making transactions, which I have repeatedly emphasised are at the heart of monetary problems? They have got left out. Let us try to put them back, and see what happens.

Not much needs to happen on the side of the savers. Their deposits in the bank are certain; they can deposit what they like, and will get the rate of interest which the bank is offering, to all alike. But on the side of the bank's advances it is a different story. We must no longer think of the bank just fixing a rate of interest at which it is willing to lend, and letting anyone who is prepared to pay that rate have the money. The bank will have to attend to the prospects of particular borrowers and to their character; so whether, in its judgement, they can be relied upon to repay. This is a question of the information which is available to the bank.

One can conceive of a situation when the bank would be receiving deposits but was finding it difficult to find suitable borrowers. It would thus be withdrawing money from circulation; and this could go on on such a scale that, in none of the senses that have been distinguished, could there be an equilibrium. Should one then say that the money rate is too high? That would only make sense if a way out could be found by lowering it. But to lower the rate which the bank was charging to borrowers would not necessarily help it to find new borrowers; it does not in itself provide a better way of finding them. To lower the rate that it paid on deposits might indeed do something to discourage deposits; but, when we remember that the savings may in large measure be planned as reserves (and, at the point to which we have now come, it is right to give some weight to that), even a zero rate on deposits might well fail to choke them off to the extent required.

We are thus, already, in sight of the famous crux – an excess of 'saving' over 'investment' that by interest policy cannot be righted. But it is much too soon to push on to fanciful remedies (negative rates of interest or money dropped from helicopters) which so readily suggest themselves when the issue is looked at in these simple terms. We should first consider if we have not been placing too great a responsibility upon our myopic bank.

5.   To insist, as in this First Version of the model we have been doing, that all borrowing and lending must take place through the bank, is quite unnecessary. If the bank is unable to search out suitable borrowers, why should not some of the savers search them out for themselves? There is no reason why we should deny them the

possibility of making more direct contacts. In so far as they do this, they will have less to deposit with the bank; so the surplus of funds, which we have been supposing to be going into the bank, will be moderated. It should, however, be noticed that since the alternative of depositing with the bank remains open to the savers, and the liquidity of their lendings to the firms (as it will now be convenient to call them) must be less than that of their deposits with the bank, the rate of interest that is offered by the firms[32] must be greater than the deposit rate of the bank. This will still act as a minimum to the system of interest rates which in this Second Version begins to develop.

It is indeed this deposit rate which acts as the king-pin of the system, playing much the same part as was played by *the* money rate in our original Wicksellian model. For the alternative of depositing, at the fixed deposit rate of the bank, is always open to the savers, while the alternative of borrowing directly from the bank is not so regularly open to the firms. We are not excluding the possibility of the bank doing some direct lending to the firms – at a rate which (we should now say) would be somewhat higher than the rate it was paying on deposits. For the model is now to allow for transaction costs; the bank will have costs of administration, and these must be covered. The firms will get what they can at this rate (which we may fairly suppose will be lower than what they pay on direct loans from the savers); but they want more than that, and it can be got from the savers.

It will be noticed that in this Second Version the bank is less important than it was in the First; but it still retains some power of control, through its deposit rate.

6. The solution that has so far been found for the information problem is very imperfect; it has really added nothing more than an opportunity for the firms to raise some part of the funds which they require by borrowing from their friends. A modern economy does not rely much on that, though there have been times in history when it has been important. Its place has largely been taken by an alternative of much greater potency – the introduction of financial intermediaries, which make a direct attack on the information problem.

---

[32] Or its equivalent, in terms of prospect offered, if the direct lending to the firms takes the form of subscription to equities.

The financial intermediary can prosper[33] if it can make use of specialised knowledge about the prospects of particular kinds of real investment so that it can make advances to firms, or investments in the securities of firms, which the bank would not know were sound investments; and if it can acquire resources which enable it to make those financial investments at a less loss of liquidity than they would entail upon the private saver. But it cannot prosper unless it makes a profit; this implies that it must borrow at a lower rate than that in which it lends, there being a sufficient difference to cover its administrative expenses, and to compensate it for the additional risk with which it (in its turn) is involved in every extension of its operations.

Thus its 'in-rate' (as we may call it – the rate at which it borrows) and also its 'out-rate' will have to be fitted into the structure of rates, which had already appeared in our Second Version. It is not necessary that the in-rate of the financial intermediary should be higher than the rate which is paid by the firms (directly) to the bank, or by the firms (directly) to the savers; for it may be expected that the intermediary may be able to attract funds from the bank and from the savers, by offering a greater degree of security (by pooling of risks) than the firms could do directly. And it need not necessarily charge a lower out-rate than is charged by the bank, since it will be willing to do business with the firms which the bank would not do. It is however clear that its in-rate must be appreciably higher than the bank's deposit rate, and its out-rate must be higher than its in-rate, if it is to function at all.

It will surely be granted in this Third Version of it that our Wicksellian model has taken a big step towards reality. The particular institutions, which play the parts I have ascribed to the 'bank' and to the 'intermediaries', will no doubt differ from country to country, and from time to time. But that some bodies will be found which play something like the parts in question can hardly be doubted. We have made room for many sorts of lending, between our four sectors – savers and bank, intermediaries and firms – and account could be taken of flows of funds within the sectors without much difficulty. We could have gone on to introduce a Government, as a privileged borrower, offering high security (in money terms) and, if it likes, high liquidity;

---

[33] I here borrow a passage from *CG* (pp. 266–7), which I can fit, with very little alteration, into the present context.

thus being a strong competitor for bank funds, if it chooses to be. Alternatively, we might treat the Government as belonging, in some measure, to each of the four sectors; thus establishing a special route for flow of funds between them.

7.   This is no place for enlarging upon such applications; there yet remains a vital question about the Third Version, which I cannot avoid. How much is left (when we allow for risks, and for the growth of financial institutions to deal with those risks) of the original Wicksell construction – the money rate and the equilibrium rate, in one or other of the senses we have found ourselves giving to the latter? We can still identify the money rate with the deposit rate of the bank, which still stands as the *base* of the interest rate system. But what has happened to the equilibrium rate, which we were to set against it?

Let us simplify a little (I think it is only a little) by supposing that marginal funds – those required for a marginal increase in the value of its investment programme – will always be raised by the firms from the intermediaries, and by the intermediaries from the bank. There is then a straightforward sequence. The savers deposit in the bank at an interest rate r_0; the bank lends to the intermediaries at interest r_1; the intermediaries to the firms at r_2. r_1 must exceed r_0 to cover the administrative costs of the bank; r_2 must exceed r_1 not only because of administrative costs, but also to provide a liquidity premium. So r_2 exceeds r_0 by two margins, those of the bank and of the intermediaries.

And having gone so far, we may allow ourselves to go further. Let us suppose that there is a rate R, which will stand for the return which the firms expect to get from marginal investment; this will have to exceed r_2 by another liquidity premium. We could then say that it would be R which, from the point of view of the Wicksell construction, would need to be kept at an equilibrium level, the level which would be appropriate to the kind of equilibrium which it was sought to attain.

To get as far as that one has had to simplify, simplify drastically; still we have come into sight of an essential point. There is bound to be a gap (depending on liquidity preferences, in a broad sense, and on transaction costs) between anything that can be directly controlled by an interest rate policy *of the bank*, and the yield on investment (R) which is the key to equilibrium. If the gap is narrow, and can be relied upon to be narrow, interest policy can be quite effective; but if the gap is wide, and undependable, there is a formidable obstacle in its way.

Let us, however, remember that the problem is an information problem. In order to make wise decisions on the big issues that are here in question, many sorts of information need to be gathered; they can hardly be gathered without having many listening points. The financial intermediaries are listening points; the question is one of transmission, from those points to the centre. We have so far been supposing that the only means of communication between the bank at the centre and the intermediaries on the circumference are rates of interest charged (or offered); though these could be generalised into 'terms of lending' without much difficulty. All dealing, that is to say, is 'at arm's length'. There have undoubtedly existed financial systems which have worked in this manner; but it is by no means inevitable that a system should work in this manner. When the intermediaries are well established, the relations between them and the centre can be much closer. It seems to follow from the preceding analysis that it is desirable that they should be closer. Control must have power if it is to be effective. Whatever we think about monopoly and competition, in the rest of the economic system, there are good reasons, in this monetary sphere, for not being afraid of some concentration.

Whatever the links between the centre and the intermediaries, the collection of information, the information required, can never be perfect. The system will still be subject to shocks; things will happen which no one (who was in a position to take action) had foreseen. It is a system which is based upon arrangements for risk-taking, in the face of an uncertain future; as such it is bound to be fragile. An arm's length system is particularly fragile. A serious blow to one part can have wide repercussions. Closer association, by making it easier to find a 'lender of last resort' reduces the fragility.

8.   That is all that I shall say here about the monocentric model, which I recognise to be no more than a part of the monetary theory which on this line of thought is required. It should evidently be matched by a similar analysis of polycentric models; but I can offer no more than the beginnings of that.

One can distinguish (at least) two pure types of polycentric model. The first is that in which there are separate centres, but they are providing (or seeking to provide) what is in effect a common money. It makes no difference if the monies provided are given different names; what is essential is the fixity of the rates of exchange between them. Each of the banks, that is, declares itself ready to exchange its promise to pay for that of any other, at this fixed rate of exchange. There is perfect convertibility at the fixed rates.

It is at once apparent that it will be impossible to maintain this convertibility (except momentarily) unless the deposit rates of all the banks are the same; for if any bank held to a deposit rate which was lower than that which was being paid by the other banks, it would find itself losing its deposits. And this means that it will be impossible for any bank, acting singly, to force a reduction in the common deposit rate; but it will be possible for a single bank, acting alone, to force a rise in the common rate – for by raising its rate, it can force the others to follow its example. So such a system, as is beginning to be understood, has a natural deflationary bias. This can indeed be overcome if there is some bank which is so much stronger than the others that it can face a withdrawal of funds with equanimity; or if it has some other way than interest policy of 'giving a lead' to the others, thus bringing about some sort of agreement on common action. But in any of these cases the system is moving in the direction of monocentricity. It is even more apparent here than it was in our monocentric analysis, that a system in which all transactions are 'at arm's length' will not work.

The second type will readily be recognised as that of non-fixed exchanges. Convertibility at fixed rates is abandoned, but convertibility, on the market, is maintained. Does this restore, for the individual centres, their interest-rate autonomy? It seems often to be supposed that it does so; but the answer surely is, not very much. Suppose that there is just one bank (the bank of country X) which abandons the fixed rate of exchange. It is then possible for it to reduce its deposit rate below the common rate maintained by the others; but only if its X-currency depreciates in terms of the others, and if the depreciation is expected to be *temporary*. For if it is expected to be temporary, a depositor at the X bank, though he gets a lower rate of interest, in terms of X-currency, than he could get elsewhere, in terms of other currencies, can expect to make up the difference, in terms of other currencies, when the X-currency recovers. Thus he need not lose anything, in terms of the other currencies, by holding his deposit at the X-bank.

This is indeed what was noticed by Keynes, in the twenties, when he advocated a 'widening of the gold points', as a means of increasing the national bank's autonomy, giving it at least a little more elbow-room. And it was this which led Hawtrey to develop the argument as a general argument in favour of exchange fluctuation, *about a fixed parity*.[34] The fixed parity is essential. An exchange depreciation,

---

[34] See my paper on Hawtrey, in *EP*, pp. 128–9.

which is not expected to be temporary, does nothing to hold the funds that are capable of movement.

The moral, it will no doubt be said, is that convertibility, *at any rate of exchange*, should be abandoned. That some degree of impediment to convertibility, in a world of sovereign states, is necessary to make the international monetary system workable, does seem probable. But this is a slippery slope; to find impediments that do not themselves do great damage cannot be an easy matter. I myself regard it as part of a more general issue – that which I posed at the end of my first considered work on monetary theory, in 1935.[35] A monetary system – a sophisticated monetary system, with much 'fluidity' – is inherently unstable; it needs to have frictions imposed upon it to make it work. They will be frictions from the point of view of the arm's length 'price-mechanism', which I do not at all deny has a part – a great part – to play. From that point of view they are a nuisance. Still we need them.

[35] Essay 5 above.

20

The Costs of Inflation[1]

Inflation, we all say, is a bad thing; but just why? It is surely the duty of economists to make up their minds on that question; for they will not make wise recommendations about policy for dealing with it unless they have done so. I can, however, distinguish three quite different cases against inflation which have been presented by economists; they seem to lead in quite different directions.

I begin with the oldest argument. There is a clear statement of it by Dennis Robertson, which I quote.

Our economic order is largely based upon the institution of contract – on the fact, that is, that people enter into binding agreements with one another to perform certain actions at a future date, for a remuneration which is fixed here and now in terms of money. A violent or prolonged change in the value of money saps the confidence with which people make or accept undertakings of this nature.[2]

It is easy to see why Robertson, writing in the 1920s, thought that this was the point to emphasise. He was thinking of an inflation that had started up, after a state of affairs in which prices had been stable, or fairly stable. Contracts had been made on expectation of stable prices, and those expectations were cheated by the inflation. There can be no doubt that in those conditions his emphasis is correct. But his point has much less weight when inflation has been continuous, so that people have had time to adjust themselves to it. It may indeed be said that his argument is not an argument for constant

---

[1] The theme of this little note is one that has repeatedly come up in my later work. Part has been reprinted elsewhere ('Expected Inflation', in *EP*, pp. 108–17). The main thing which has not been reprinted is a review (*EJ*, Dec. 1970) of M. Friedman, *The Optimum Quantity of Money* (1969). That hardly stands by itself, so I have thought it better to work its substance into a more connected treatment.

[2] *Money* (1928 edition), p. 13.

prices; it is an argument for reliability. Once inflation has become established, it is indeed an argument against acceleration of inflation; but cannot it then be stood on its head, and used as an argument against deceleration? To impose a condition of constant prices upon an economy which had become adjusted to rising prices would surely, as in these latter days we have had much cause to suspect, be quite as much, or even more, of an upset.

I next turn to an argument which does assume the continuance of inflation, at a constant rate, so that there is no lack of reliability, in the sense of Robertson. The inflation is fully foreseen, and to it there is perfect adjustment. Is it then of any importance what the rate of inflation is? Is an 'inflationary equilibrium' at 10 per cent per annum any worse than one at 2 per cent per annum? Whether it is possible to get that full adjustment is one of the questions, as we shall see; but supposing that it is attainable, does the *rate* of inflation matter?

The chief remaining cost that has been distinguished concerns the use of money as a means of payment, or (in my terminology)[3] money as a running asset. It is taken for granted that this money does not bear interest; yet it is held, if only temporarily. There must then, it is urged, be an advantage from holding it, though there is a loss of interest in holding it. What is the advantage to be set against this loss of interest? This is a question which monetary theorists have long been willing to answer in terms of convenience.[4] To get the interest which could be earned on the money – which, it must be insisted, is only temporarily available – is not worth the bother. The transaction cost is too high.

Nevertheless, when the issue is looked at in this manner, there is a choice, at the margin, between holding money, even as a running asset, and investing it, however temporarily, in a way that does yield interest. So one would expect that, when interest rates were low, the convenience motive would nearly always be dominant; but, at higher rates of interest (such as must accompany an 'inflationary equilibrium'), it would become too expensive to indulge it. It would become worth while to accept the inconvenience, in order to avoid the cost.

It is easier to see this in the case when the cost in question is not just an opportunity forgone, but an actual expense. It is more important to keep a watch upon an overdraft when the rate that is

---

[3] Above, p. 256.

[4] They would have said 'convenience and security'; but security is a matter of money that is held as a reserve asset; that is not here in question.

charged upon it becomes higher; it will be worth while to take measures, which themselves are costly, to keep the overdraft down. And the point becomes even clearer when we remember that cash is by no means the only non-interest-bearing asset which is normally to be found on a balance-sheet. There will also be debts on which interest is not being charged. If one asks why it is that a firm should 'give credit' in this way, the answer surely is that it is a matter of convenience, just like the motive for holding the money. A debt that is due from a regular customer is not regarded in isolation; it is a part of the regular relation between customer and supplier, which it is in the interest of both to maintain in a way that is convenient to both. On this, as on the money holding, inflation exericises a pressure. It becomes profitable to take more trouble in collecting debts promptly, exerting pressure on debtors which would otherwise not need to be exerted. There is a real loss, measurable in labour time, in exerting such pressure. And since the debtor himself has a similar incentive to delay payment, it may surely be that the loss is quite considerable.

One can satisfy oneself in these ways that this Friedman point (as I think it is fair to call it)[5] is perfectly valid; the Friedman margin does exist, and it can be important. It can be that at high rates of interest it becomes too expensive to purchase a convenience, which still is valuable. But I think it is a mistake to suppose that people will be alike in their sensitiveness to this margin. In these matters the 'representative individual' is a snare. There must surely, in any economy, be many people who have limited opportunities for economising in their use of money; the convenience which they get from a marginal unit of money holding is far in excess of any return which they could get from lending it out (and from taking the trouble to do so). The fact that from them there is no *equality* at the margin does not mean that there is any loss. I would therefore suggest that we get a better picture if we think of the people (and firms) who compose the economy as being arrangeable in orders of (potential) sensitivity. There will be some who will be sensitive even at low rates of interest; others would become sensitive at higher rates; and it is not to be excluded that at very high rates (those to be associated with hyperinflation) the mass of the public would

---

[5] It is here that I draw upon my review of the Friedman book above cited. I praise his insight in perceiving that the conventional theory of welfare economics has a bearing on the problem; but it does not follow from that theory that there must be a social loss whenever 'utility' and cost, at the margin, are not exactly matched. The increment of surplus is of the form of the area of a triangle $\frac{1}{2}\delta p \, \delta q$; it is zero if δq is zero whatever δp.

become sensitive. This is the 'flight from the currency' which has to be fitted in. The Friedman cost, on this interpretation, is an increasing function of the rate of inflation. In the band of interest rates that is consistent with stable prices, or moderately stable prices, the sensitive sector is small, and the inconvenience that they inflict upon themselves is inconsiderable. At the rates of interest to which most countries have become accustomed in the seventies it becomes noticeable. In hyperinflation it is overwhelming. That, in my view, is what emerges from the Friedman point.

Of course, it is clear why Friedman has attached such particular importance to it. It is perfectly possible, in his view, to keep the rate of price-rise constant; by following his monetarist prescription it will be done. But it is surely much easier for it to be done (and, what is essential, to establish a general conviction that it will be done) in a country which is fairly well insulated from external shocks, and which has a government which is strong enough to resist the internal pressures that may be exerted upon it. If these conditions are not satisfied, and there must be many countries (including my own) where they are clearly not satisfied, it must be hard to give the assurance required. Even if a target rate of price-rise is stated, there is always a risk, a considerable risk, that the target will not be hit.

Inflation is expected, but the rate of inflation is quite uncertain. That adds to risks (so one comes back to the Robertson point, in another form), but it does more than that. One must distinguish between the effects on different kinds of markets. A perfectly competitive market, such as economists delight to use in their models, need be no more damaged by inflation than in the Robertson way, and in the Friedman way, of which we have already taken account. Dealers can allow for the risks in their dealings; they can make adjustments. But the principal actual markets which approximate to this type are the financial markets, where there is no doubt that allowance is made, the behaviour of interest rates being a leading example. It is not so simple a matter with the imperfect markets, which are characteristic of much of the rest of the economy. On imperfect markets prices have to be 'made'; they are not just determined by demand and supply. It is much easier to make them, in a way which seems satisfactory (because it seems fair) to the parties concerned, if substantial use can be made of precedent; if one can start with the supposition that what was acceptable before is very likely to be acceptable again. When prices in general are fairly stable, that is often rather easy. The particular prices which result from such bargains may not be ideal from the point of view of the economist; but the time and trouble which would be involved in improving them is simply not worth while. To be obliged to make them anew, and to go on making then anew, as one is obliged to do in continuing inflation, involves direct economic loss, and (very often) loss of temper as well.

It is, of course, in the labour market that such considerations are of particular importance; but it is by no means only to the labour market that they apply. Any system of prices (a system of railway fares, just like a system of wage-rates) has to satisfy canons of economic efficiency and canons of fairness – canons which it is very difficult to make compatible. It is bound to work more easily if it is allowed to acquire, to some degree, the sanction of custom – if it is not, at frequent intervals, being torn up by the roots.

This then is the cost of inflation to which I myself would attach the greatest importance, being influenced, no doubt, by British experience, but not recent experience only.[6] I have long been convinced that a *system* of relative wages, if it is to be maintained without excessive friction, must not only satisfy economic criteria, but must also be felt to be fair, at least tolerably fair. It is possible for such a system to be maintained, but only so long as the 'economic' relativities are fairly stable; but when they change, if they change at all sharply, there is bound to be trouble. The sharp rise in oil prices, in 1973–4, raised the marginal product of British coal miners, the producers of a major oil substitute; thus what was required, for an economic adjustment, was a sharp rise in miners' wages relative to the wages paid in other occupations. This was resisted, by the then government, in the interest of maintaining the social relativities; but the pressure was too much for them. The miners had to be given their rise, upsetting the social relativities – but that position was not tenable either. Other wages followed, so that a wage–price spiral developed. No monetary means could have prevented it; all that could be done, by such means, was to slow it down, at the expense of inducing an 'inflationary depression'. That had to be done in order to prevent a complete explosion. The restriction which becomes necessary, in order to prevent an inflation of this type running away, is the deepest way in which my third cost shows itself.

It is clear, from this angle, why indexation is no answer. If one simply looks at the problem as one of maintaining socially acceptable

[6] See essay 15 above.

relativities, indexation (tying all wages, and ultimately all prices, to a general price-index) looks like being the solution. But how, in the first place, is such an acceptable system of relativities to be established? It is inevitable that at any particular moment in an inflationary process, there should be grave disparities, both social and economic. Are these to be frozen? If not, how are they to be mended? And, even if that first step could be successfully taken, the indexed system would still show up its fragility in the face of the new shocks, which would surely be to be expected. Reactions, having been made automatic, would be so much quicker. One can readily point to examples of countries which have experimented with formal indexation (such as Australia and Italy) and have found out how dangerous it is.

When inflation is uncontrolled, it is destructive. A loss of 'convenience' is too mild a word for what happens in all-out inflations. There are nevertheless cases, as in the major inflations after the two World Wars, when a money has been destroyed, but has risen from its ashes. The old money is gone, but a new money succeeds it. But I think it will be found that, whenever there has been a successful 'monetary reform', some new *real* factor has emerged; so that there is reason to believe that the pressures which fed the old inflation have somehow passed away. After the inflations which had been incidents in post-war recovery, that could readily happen. But, so long as the old pressures persist, the prospects for a new money would be no better than for the old. If one has to look forward to a continuance of those pressures, there is nothing for it but to resist inflation, and to face the costs of resisting it.

21

Time in Economics

This was a lecture given in 1975 at Vanderbilt University (Nashville, Tennessee) in honour of Nicholas Georgescu-Roegen, and subsequently published in a festschrift for him, *Evolution, Welfare and Time in Economics* edited by A. M. Tang *et al.* (1976). He is one of the most original thinkers among my economist contemporaries; though in this paper I am largely summarising my own work, I was helped to find essential points in it when I looked at it in the light of his.

I should like to draw attention to the correspondence between the *economics in time*, of which I speak in this paper, and the *sequential causality*, which is the subject of chapter 7 of my *Causality in Economics* (1979). There is perhaps a better balance in the later book between this and the 'equilibrism', which there figures as *contemporaneous causality*, or even as *static causality*. Perhaps I was too hard on it here; it has its uses, though I still want to press on beyond it. I return to the same point, in another context, in essay 23 below.

Two years ago I published a book called *Capital and Time*. You might reasonably expect that in the present lecture I should just be going on with what I did in that book. This is in fact one of the things to which I shall be coming; but such continuation is only one of the things which I have in mind. My subject here is much broader. It concerns a principle which has come up, in several ways, in the work of Professor Georgescu; so it should be a suitable topic for a paper that is being written for him. It has also come up, sometimes in similar ways, more often in different ways, in much of my own work. I have not always been faithful to it, but when I have departed from it I have found myself coming back to it. It is clearly his principle; but I think I can claim that on the whole it has been mine as well.

It is a very simple principle: the irreversibility of time. In space we can move either way, or any way; but time just goes on, never goes back. We represent time on our diagrams by a spatial coordinate; but that representation is never a complete representation; it always leaves something out. And it is not only in simple diagrams that we represent time by space; there are highly sophisticated models which, in effect, do the same thing. It is quite hard to get away, in any part of our thinking, from the spatial representation. We represent time by a 'trend variable'; but that is again the same thing; it does not fully show time going on.

One of the principal consequences of the irreversibility of time is that past and future are different. Not just different as front and back are different; you cannot turn past into future, or future into past, as by turning round you can turn back into front. The past is past, over and done with; it is there and cannot be changed. 'Not heaven itself upon the past hath power' – the line of Dryden which I was already quoting, on nearly the first occasion when I came to grips with the issue, in *Value and Capital* (1939).[1] The past, however, has this virtue that we can have knowledge of it, knowledge of fact. The knowledge that we have, or can have, of the past is different in kind from what we can know of the future; for the latter, at best, is no more than a knowledge of probabilities. This may happen, or that may happen. But it is something quite definite which *has* happened.

It is true that our knowledge of the past is incomplete. All we know is what has been remembered, or recorded; or perhaps it has left some mark upon the present world from which we can deduce what happened, probably what happened. Thus even our knowledge of the past is largely a matter of probabilities. But these probabilities are different from probabilities about the future. Past populations, for instance, are recorded at census dates; if we want a figure for population between census dates we have to estimate it. Yet the estimation of population in 1885, when populations in 1880 and in 1890 alone are recorded, is a matter of getting as near as we can to a *right* figure. The country did have a population in 1885; by using more and more of relevant information available to us now we can in this (no doubt favourable) case be fairly sure that we cannot be far wrong. With estimates of the future, the situation is quite different. There is no *right* figure for population in 2000, no right figure *now*. There will be a right figure when 2000 comes, but only when that date is passing into the past.

[1] *VC*, p. 130. The poem from which I took the quotation purports to be a translation from Horace, but the correspondence with its 'original' is far from close.

It is already apparent from this simple example how complicated these time-relations can be; how easy it is to slip into ways of thinking which treat past and future alike. How easy it is to forget, when we contemplate the past, that much of what is now past was then future. Action is always directed towards the future; but past actions, when we contemplate them in their places in the stream of past events, lose that orientation toward the future which they undoubtedly possessed at the time when they were taken. We arrange past data in time-series, but our time-series are not fully in time. The relation of year 9 to year 10 looks like its relation to year 8; but in year 9 year 10 was future while year 8 was past. The actions of year 9 were based, or could be based, upon knowledge of year 8; but not on knowledge of year 10, only on guesses about year 10. For in year 9 the knowledge that we have about year 10 did not yet exist.

What I have been saying, so far, must sound very obvious. But its consequences for economics are quite far reaching.

One application, which I shall do no more than mention, is to Social Accounting. We are tempted to say that the net investment of a year is the difference between opening and closing stock – the difference between the value of the capital stock at the end of the year and at the beginning. We know that we must correct, for inflation or deflation, changes in the value of money which may have occurred within the year. But this does not get to the root of the matter. The value that is set upon the opening stock depends in part upon the value which is expected, at the beginning of the year, for the closing stock; but that was then future, while at the end of the year it is already present (or past). There may be things which were included in the opening stock because, in the light of information then available, they seem to be valuable; but at the end of the year it is clear that they are not valuable, so they have to be excluded. Such revisions, due to new information, may occur at any time. Suppose that information comes in during year 2 which makes it clear that the capital stock at the end of year 1 was over-valued. This may well mean that the net investment of year 1, calculated at the end of year 1, was over-valued – at least it seems to be over-valued from the standpoint of the end of year 2. It needs to be written down for its mistakes – mistakes which only in the course of time have become revealed.[2]

---

[2] See *CT* pp. 164–6. Also a paper entitled 'The Concept of Income in relation to taxation and to business management' which was given at a meeting of the International Institute of Public Finance in 1979 and will be reprinted in Volume III of this Collection.

I leave that on one side, and pass to other applications, of which the first is a simple application to consumer theory. The point is very simple; yet it is one which in most presentations (including some for which I have been personally responsible) gets most blatantly left out. It is immensely convenient, in economics, to suppose that 'the consumer' (as we call him) has a fully formed scale of preferences, by which all the choices that are available to him on the market can be ordered. I am still of the opinion that there are many purposes (including, very probably, the most important purposes) for which that assumption can be justified. But it is itself a very odd assumption; to take it, as many economists do, as being justifiable for all purposes, must, I now believe, be wrong.

The picture which is called to mind by this conventional assumption is that of the consumer (or his wife) paying a weekly visit to the super-market, having been given just so much to spend out of the family income. She picks up goods from the shelves; then, as she adds up the cost in her mind, she finds that it comes to more than her allowance. So she has to give up some of the things she wanted to buy, or has to substitute something cheaper. She juggles things about until she finds the collection which is within her budget and which suits her best.

Such a consumer I would agree, 'reveals her preferences'. But consider the case of another consumer decision, a decision of what car to buy, or whether to buy a new car. If it is asked how that decision is made it is surely a matter of deciding *what one can afford*. I can afford this; I cannot afford that. But what is meant by not being able to afford it? The conventional answer, by the economist, is to say that if the car is acquired, something else will have to be given up; and that 'something else' is more desired than the car. That is to say, the consumer is supposed to re-think his whole budget, identifying the collection of goods which would have to be given up if the car was purchased. Now it may sometimes happen that a consumer proceeds in that way, but it seems unlikely that it will often happen. It seems much more likely that he proceeds with some idea, based upon previous experience, of what he can afford. He judges whether or not to buy a car, not by re-thinking his whole budget, but by a single test.

From this point of view the replacement of the old consumer theory – the marginal utility theory – by the modern theory of ordinal preferences (a replacement in which I myself have played a part) was not so clear an advance as is usually supposed. Marshall's consumer, who decides on his purchases by comparing the marginal utility of what is to be bought with the marginal utility of the money he will have to pay for it, is more like an actual consumer, at least so far as some important purchases are concerned, than Samuelson's consumer, who 'reveals his preferences'. The marginal utility of money, on which Marshall relies, is much more than the mere Lagrange multiplier, the role to which it has been degraded. It is the means by which the consumer is enabled to make his separate decisions, and to make them fairly rationally, without being obliged to take the trouble to weigh all conceivable alternatives. It is the means by which he decides *what he can afford.*

But his estimate of the marginal utility of money, to him, is based upon his past experience. It is by experience that he learns the standard by which his desires for the things he would like to buy are to be judged. In static conditions, when income is steady (or fairly steady) and prices are steady (or fairly steady), it is a reliable standard; and it was of course in terms of such conditions that Marshall's theory was originally set out. But when income is changing (or when many prices are changing) it becomes less reliable. It is based on the past; when the present is seriously unlike the past it becomes a less reliable guide. The *lags* with which consumption responds to a change in real income, though they are partly a matter of constraints set by commitments (including as commitments the possession of durable goods), must also be a matter of the time which is taken for the marginal utility of money, as it appears to the consumer, to respond to the change. To make fully rational decisions in fundamentally new conditions is by no means easy.

The matter is probably of greater importance in times of inflation than it is in more settled conditions. I believe that we miss the point about inflation when we look at it, as we so usually do, in terms of index-numbers. In terms of index-numbers there has always been some inflation (or deflation); an index-number of prices hardly ever stays quite constant from year to year. Yet there have been conditions in which there has been no inflation, in a highly significant sense. This is when there are many prices which are not changing, or changing very little. So long as that condition holds, the standard which the consumer makes for himself, out of his past experience, is a reliable standard; so he can make his decisions, deciding what he can afford fairly rationally. This is to be contrasted with the condition that is now being experienced in so many countries, when all prices, or nearly all prices, have broken loose from their moorings. That is true inflation; apart from its other costs (which are more familiar) there is this other cost – that rational decisions, even within the field of consumption, become so much harder to make.

That is all I have to say on this particular matter. I turn to wider questions. The parts of economics where the distinction with which I began is of greatest importance are the theory of capital and (as we shall see) the theory of markets.

As far as capital theory is concerned, the story goes back a long way. It appears, very strikingly, in the history of the Austrian school, a group of economists who (as everyone knows) were particularly concerned about the relations of capital and time. The two progenitors of the Austrian school were Menger and Böhm-Bawerk (Wieser, at this time of day, seems very secondary; while Schumpeter and Hayek belong to later generations). At a casual reading, Menger and Böhm appear to be saying much the same thing; so it is something of a shock when one discovers that in the view of Menger (as recorded by Schumpeter)[3] Böhm-Bawerk's theory was 'one of the greatest errors ever committed'. What was it in Böhm that so annoyed Menger? I believe it is simply that in Menger time is unidirectional. Menger's theory is an economics *in* time but Böhm's is an economics *of* time, in which time is no more than a mathematical parameter – a parameter of what we should now call capital-intensity. (Of course, there are passages in which Böhm gets closer to Menger than he does in the structure of his theory; but to say that in Böhm time is just a parameter of capital-intensity is not so far wrong.) In Menger time is much more than that.

I do not suppose that Menger ever read Wicksell; but if he had read Wicksell's version of Böhm's theory (the version which has become more familiar to most economists) he would have found that his judgment was amply confirmed. For he would have found that in the hands of Wicksell the theory became no more than a theory of a stationary state, no more than that. In a stationary state one moment of time is just like another. The stationary state is out of time; time has stood still. In Menger, time never stood still.

I do not claim that Menger had more than the beginnings of a theory of an economy *in* time. But he did have that; a clear indication is his theory of liquidity.[4] What Menger had to say on liquidity

---

[3] *History of Economic Analysis* (1954), p. 847.

[4] *Grundsätze der Volkswirtschaftslehre* (translated by Dingwall and Hoselitz as *Principles of Economics*), chapters 7 and 8. There can be no doubt that Menger would have been on the side of Marshall, rather than on that of Pareto, with respect to the point about consumer theory discussed above, and essentially for the reason given. I owe the beginnings of my understanding of this to conversations with Professor Rosenstein-Rodan.

is deeper than what was said by anyone else before Keynes; indeed I think it is deeper than what is in Keynes. I know that I had to go on thinking about liquidity for many years after Keynes before I realised that I had got to a point which Menger had reached, in effect, nearly a hundred years before. For Menger had grasped, already, that the holding of liquid reserves, in money or near-money, is only one aspect (though no doubt the most important aspect) of a much more general kind of behaviour. It is a matter of provision against an uncertain future – not passive provision (like insurance) but active provision, providing oneself with the ability to take action to meet emergencies which may arise in the future, and which are such that their particular shape cannot be accurately foreseen. Obviously, then, there can be no question of liquidity, in either the wide or the narrow sense, in a stationary state. Liquidity is a problem of the economy *in* time.

I have begun with this old story because it presents the issue so sharply. In later work, it has been thoroughly muddled. The man who began the muddling was Keynes.

Keynes's theory has one leg which is *in* time, but another which is not. It is a hybrid. I am not blaming him for this; he was looking for a theory which would be effective, and he found it. I am quite prepared to believe that effective theories always will be hybrids – they cannot afford to bother about difficulties which are not important for the problem in hand. Complications (and for a simple theory the flow of time is a complication) must be allowed for when they have to be allowed for; but if there is any place where we can avoid them, avoid them we will. In facing the world that may well be good policy; but when a hybrid theory is subjected to classroom criticism, places are bound to be exposed which are not easy to defend.

There are many passages – many famous passages – in which Keynes proclaims his theory to be *in* time; he makes quite a fuss about it. 'The dark forces of time and ignorance which envelop our future'[5] – everyone knows them. Take these passages at their face value, as they are so often taken, and one would suppose that Keynes was actually producing a full theory of economics *in* time – the theory which Menger had adumbrated but had certainly not carried through. Yet that is not so; there is only a part of the Keynes theory which is *in* time. He has (very skilfully) divided his theory into two parts. There is one, that concerned with the Marginal Efficiency of

---

[5] *The General Theory of Employment, Interest and Money*, p. 155.

Capital and with Liquidity Preference, which is unquestionably *in* time; it is basically forward-looking; time and uncertainty are written all over it. But there is another, the multiplier theory (and indeed the whole theory of production and prices which is – somehow – wrapped up in the multiplier theory) which is out of time. It runs in terms of demand curves, and supply curves and cost curves – just the old tools of equilibrium economics. A state of equilibrium, by definition, is a state in which something, something relevant, is *not* changing, so the use of an equilibrium concept is a signal that time, in some respect at least, has been put to one side.

For Keynes's own purpose, I have insisted, this was justifiable; but what a muddle he made for his successors! The 'Keynesian revolution' went off at half-cock; so the line, which I believe to be a vital line, was smudged over. The equilibrists, therefore, did not know that they were beaten; or rather (for I am not claiming that they had been altogether beaten) they did not know that they had been challenged. They thought that what Keynes had said could be absorbed into their equilibrium systems; all that was needed was that the scope of their equilibrium systems should be extended. As we know, there has been a lot of extension, a vast amount of extension; what I am saying is that it has never quite got to the point.[6]

I shall make no attempt in what follows to work through the whole of what has happened; that would be a vast job, and I much doubt if I am capable of doing it. What I can do, and am perhaps well fitted to do, is to look over my own work, since 1935, and to show how some aspects of the struggle, and the muddle, are reflected in it. I can at least explain how it has been that, in one way after another, I have found myself facing the issue, and (very often) being baffled by it.

I begin (as I am sure you will want me to begin) with the old *IS–LM* (or *SI–LL*) diagram, which appeared in a paper I gave to the Econometric Society within a few months of the publication of the *General Theory*.[7] The letter which Keynes wrote me about that paper has now been published.[8] I think I am justified in concluding from that letter that Keynes did not wholly disapprove of what I had made of him. All the same, I must say that that diagram is now much

[6] I make no claim that I am the first to say this; it seems to me to be in substance the main point which emerges from the influential book by Axel Leijonhufvud, *On Keynesian Economics and the Economics of Keynes* (1968).

[7] Essay 8 above. See also essay 23 which follows.

[8] In Keynes, *Collected Writings*, vol. 14, p. 79; also in my *EP*, p. 144.

less popular with me than I think it still is with many other people. It reduces the *General Theory* to equilibrium economics; it is not really *in* time. That, of course, is why it has done so well.

Much more to the point is *Value and Capital* (1939). A good deal of that book was written before I saw the *General Theory*; though Keynes came in at the end, even the so-called 'dynamic' part was begun under the influence of Lindahl. Lindahl, it is surely fair to say, was most decidedly *not* an equilibrist; the distinction between past and future (*ex ante* and *ex post*) was at the centre of his work. Thus, even before I read Keynes, I was finding myself confronted with a parallel problem: how to build a bridge between equilibrium economics and an economics which should be securely *in* time. (Since the first part of my book was very thoroughgoing, quite static, equilibrium economics, the problem came up in my work even more sharply than it did in Keynes's.) I built a kind of a bridge, but, as I now see very well, it was a very imperfect bridge, not so very unlike the imperfect bridge that had been built by Keynes. My theory also was divided; there was a part that was *in* time and a part that was not. But we did not divide in the same place. While Keynes had relegated the whole theory of production and prices to equilibrium economics, I tried to keep production *in* time, just leaving *prices* to be determined in an equilibrium manner. I wanted, that is, to go further than Keynes, keeping closer to Lindahl. But I could only do so by an artificial device, my 'week', which was such that all prices could be fixed up in what would now be called a 'neo-Walrasian' or 'neo-classical' manner, on the 'Monday'; then, on the basis of these predetermined prices, production *in* time could proceed. It was quite an interesting exercise; it did bring out some points – even some practically important points – fairly well; but I have become abundantly conscious how artificial it was. Much too much had to happen on that 'Monday'! And, even if that was overlooked (as it should not have been overlooked) I was really at a loss how to deal with the further problem of how to string my 'weeks' and my 'Mondays' together.

In *Value and Capital* terms, there were these two problems left over; they correspond fairly well, though not precisely, with what could be expressed in Keynesian (or Marshallian) language. Keynes (he would no doubt have admitted) had been mainly concerned with constructing a general theory of Marshall's *short period*. All he had said about the things included in Marshall's long period had been pretty sketchy; and, except in relation to financial markets, the things with which Marshall had been concerned in his theory of exchange (or barter) had got quite left out. Whether one prefers that statement, or my statement (as just given), does not much matter. What does matter is that the Keynes theory and the *Value and Capital* theory were weak in corresponding ways. They both lacked, at one end, a satisfactory theory of *markets*; and at the other end, they lacked a satisfactory theory of *growth.*

Since these deficiencies were so different, it is scarcely surprising that what has come out of them has been very different. I shall have to take them quite separately.

Growth theory, say since Harrod and Domar (or perhaps since von Neumann), has been the scene of a tremendous come-back of equilibrism. Trying to push on beyond Keynes it has slipped back behind him. What made this possible was the discovery of the Regularly Progressive Economy, or 'steady state'. A stationary state, as found in the Classics or in Wicksell, was a very poor instrument for the study of saving and investment, even in the long-run; for in a Stationary State both net saving and net investment must by definition equal zero. The Steady State, with its constant growth rate, admitted positive saving, so it looked much better. It could be tidied up, on equilibrium lines, just as well as the Stationary State; for though the quantities of inputs and outputs did not remain unchanged over time, their ratios did. In ratio terms, the Steady State was still quite stationary. Thus, so long as attention was fixed on ratios (and the growth rate itself is a ratio), the Steady State could be absorbed into full-brown equilibrium economics, in which one point of time is just like another. It was just as much 'out of time' as the Stationary State itself.

I shall not say much about Steady State economics; for in spite of all that it has meant for the economics of the fifties and sixties, it is my own opinion that it has been rather a curse. I do not merely mean that the impression that has been given to non-economists (through the mediation of statisticians) that there is something natural about a constant growth rate has been a curse. That is obvious; maybe it will be one of the (few) advantages of the present economic crisis that it will teach us to get over it. I also mean that it has encouraged economists to waste their time upon constructions that are often of great intellectual complexity but which are so much out of time, and out of history, as to be practically futile and indeed misleading. It has many bad marks to be set against it.

I must, however, admit that I have myself spent much time on steady state economics – the Harrod type, the Joan Robinson type, the Kaldor type, the von Neumann type, the Solow type – one after

another. I felt that I had to learn them, and the best way to learn
them is to write out one's own version. But in the successive versions
which I have produced, I have always been making some effort to get
away.

Thus in my *Trade Cycle* book (1950) I began with my version of
Harrod. I am not particularly proud of that book, but it does have
the virtue that it makes some attempts to get back *into* time. One is
by introducing lags, though that is a device which is more appropriate
in econometrics than in economic theory. By making *present*
behaviour depend upon *past* experience, one does something to re-
introduce the flow of time; but, I fully admit, not very much.
Another route of escape was my concept of Autonomous Investment
– a concept which equilibrists, very naturally, have found hard to
swallow. As first introduced, it looks like a piece of steady state
economics; and there, admittedly, it is out of place. But I did go on,
in the later parts of the book (which have received much less
attention) to allow Autonomous Investment to change autono-
mously. I believe that at that point my model did become less
deterministic, and so less equilibrist.

The next stage in the story, so far as I personally am concerned,
was my *Capital and Growth* (1965), written fifteen years later. It is a
long gap, and, of course, it is true that during these years much that is
relevant had been done by others. A large part of *Capital and Growth*
is just a survey of what they had been doing. They had taken the
capital stock of the Harrodian steady state – much too 'macro' in
its original form – and had broken it down into its components:
capital goods of different specifications, different durabilities, and
different 'vintages'. They had been able to do this by a massive
injection of matrix algebra. I had to learn the matrix algebra, which
had come into fashion since the days of my mathematical education
– and it took me quite a time! They had also developed a new kind
of 'dynamic equilibrium' in which not even ratios are kept constant;
a plan, a consistent plan, is nevertheless developed between time 1
and time 2. (This goes back to von Neumann and to Ramsey and
includes much work descended from them: turnpike theorems,
optimum saving theorems and the like.) Though these are not steady
state theories, they are nevertheless equilibrium theories. One point
of time is not like another, even in the ratio sense; yet the whole of
the plan is looked at together. The plan is mutually determined;
there is no movement from past to future, except in the sense that
there is also a movement from future to past. There is no room for
the unexpected.

I had to learn these things; and a great part of *Capital and Growth* is occupied with setting out my version of them. But there are some signs, even in *Capital and Growth*, that I was trying to get away. There are many of them in the opening chapters (which are chiefly of a critical character); and there are some, even in the latter part of the book, though that is mainly concerned with the steady state, or with the other kind of 'dynamic equilibrium'. There is the monetary chapter (23); but that really belongs to the theory of markets, to which I shall be coming later. There is a funny chapter on 'Interest and Growth' (22), which tries to break away; but it is an unsuccessful break-out since it is still using the tools of steady state economics, which are obviously unsuitable. Most important is the chapter called 'Traverse' (16). This was a first attempt at a formal theory of an economy which is not in a steady state, not in 'Growth Equilibrium' – an economy which has a history, so that things actually happen. Since it is a system in which the actors do not know what is going to happen next, it at once appears that flexibility (which disappears from sight in the steady state) is a matter of major importance. The method that is used in that chapter is not, as I have since become convinced, very suitable; but I do not regret having made the attempt. Some quite interesting things did come out. I was able, in particular, to throw some new light (or what to me was new light) upon the *role* of prices – to show how different it is in an uncertain world from what it appears to be in equilibrium economics.[9]

So we come to *Capital and Time* (1973), as I promised. People, I can see from reviews, have not known quite what to make of it; it probably needed a preface (such as I have been giving, in fact, in this essay) so that it could be explained. The whole of the second part of *Capital and Time* is called 'Traverse'; it corresponds to that single chapter in *Capital and Growth*. It is in fact the case that the chief (almost the whole) purpose of the latter book is to seek a better way of doing what I was trying to do in the former 'Traverse' chapter. In that former chapter I was trying to build a theory which should at least be rather more *in time*, while using a fairly conventional steady state model as a basis. It did not do. So I tried, in the later book, to build my 'Traverse' on a different steady state model, which I hoped, and I think I showed, could get one just a little further. But this new steady state model (descended from Böhm-Bawerk through one of the less read chapters of *Value and Capital*)[10] would, I knew, be

[9] *CG*, esp. pp. 194–7.
[10] *VC*, ch. 17.

unfamiliar to most of my readers. So the whole (or nearly the whole) of the first part of *Capital and Time* is taken up with explaining it.

But this first part is *not* the important part. Taken by itself, its conclusions are quite negative. It just shows that you get the same steady state results in my model as in other models, a thing which was to be expected *a priori* but needed to be demonstrated in detail. The results come out rather neatly, so it may be that it will be found (even by equilibrists) to be quite useful, if only for teaching purposes. But that is all.

Even in Part II, I had to start very slowly. If I had started with a fine set of plausible assumptions, drawn from the real world, I am sure I should have got nowhere. I had to build up my model bit by bit. I began from a steady state (but that was simply because I had to have something firm, which I thought I understood, from which to start), but the point of the steady state (in Part II) is that it is to be *disturbed*. I made a lot of use – perhaps too much use – of what I called a Simple Profile, a production plan which admitted the construction of a plant and then its utilisation, but not much else. It is not surprising that some of the results which I got with the Simple Profile were much the same as those which others have got by more conventional methods. I am again not ashamed of my 'fixwage' hypothesis, with which I still think it was proper to begin; I did indeed push on quite a long way beyond it. Nor am I ashamed of the 'static expectation' assumption, which made firms choose their plans on the basis of today's prices, or rather price ratios; that again I think was the right way to begin. Though I did not do much to modify this assumption, I don't think it would be hard to modify it. But this is no place to discuss these matters in detail. What I want to emphasise is that in Part II I was trying to build something up. It ends with a chapter called 'Ways Ahead'; that was meant as a signal that I was sure I had not finished the job.

Most of my critics have been (and no doubt will be) equilibrists; but there is one, for whom I have great respect, who has opened fire from the other flank. Professor Ludwig Lachmann, of the University of Johannesburg, South Africa, is (like Professor Hayek) a chief survivor of what I distinguished as the Mengerian sect of the Austrian school. It is clear that his view of me is like Menger's view of Böhm-Bawerk. He cannot, of course, abide the steady state.[11] Even the modest uses of it which I have made (and perhaps, until now, I have not sufficiently emphasised that they are meant to be very modest

[11] See his review of *CT* in the *South African Journal of Economics* (September 1973).

uses), even these fill him with dismay. Even the explanations which I have now been giving (and which are meant, incidentally, to assure him that I am more on his side than on the other) will, I fear, fail to placate him. His ideal economics is not so far away from my own ideal economics, but I regard it as a target set up in heaven. We cannot hope to reach it; we must just get as near to it as we can.

There is one further thing I want to say about *Capital and Time*. I was trying in Part II to analyse a growth process *sequentially*; there were things which emerged almost as soon as one tried to do that, even if one was not succeeding in doing it very well or very completely. I began, for instance, to understand why there had been so much trouble with that old distinction between autonomous and induced inventions, a distinction for which I must admit I had myself some responsibility in days gone by.[12] It is a static distinction, quite out of time, though it concerns a matter where some time-reference is essential. When one puts it back *into time*, it looks quite different.

As I said in the book:

> *the* technology, and the technological frontier, now become suspect....The notion of a technology, as a collection of techniques, laid up in a library to be taken down from their shelves as required, is a caricature of the inventive process....Why should we not say that every change in technique is an invention, which may be large or small? It certainly partakes, to some degree, of the character of an invention; for it requires, for its application, some new knowledge, or some new expertise. There is no firm line, on the score of novelty, between shifts that change the technology and shifts that do not.[13]

One can say that, and still admit a distinction between autonomous and induced invention, but the distinction must now be of a more dynamic character. An induced invention is a change in technique that is made as a consequence of a change in prices (or, in general, scarcities); if the change in prices had not occurred, the change in technique would not have been made. I now like to think of a major technical change (one that we may agree to regard as autonomous, since, for anything that we are concerned with, it comes in from outside) as setting up what I now call an Impulse. If the autonomous change is an invention which widens the range of technical possibilities, it must begin by raising profitability and inducing expansion; but the expansion encounters scarcities, which act as a brake. Some of the scarcities may be just temporary bottle-necks which in time can be removed; some, however, may be irremovable. Yet it is

[12] See *TW*, ch. 6.
[13] *CT*, p. 120.

possible to adjust to either kind of scarcity by further changes in technical methods; it is these that are the true *induced inventions*. The whole story, when it is looked at in this way, is *in time*, and can be in history; it can be worked out much further, and can, I believe, be applied.[14]

That is rather a mouthful; it deserves a lecture to itself; but there I must leave it. For I have still to say something (it cannot, at this stage, be very much) about the other 'deficiency' which, as I explained, was left unfilled in the thirties. I must turn, that is, to the theory of *markets*.

How – just how – are prices determined? In *Value and Capital* (even in the 'dynamic' part of *Value and Capital*) I had been content to be what is now called neo-Walrasian; prices were just determined by an equilibrium of demand and supply. And I am afraid that for many years I got no further, or very little further. When I was asked to review Patinkin's book, which really raised the issue, I quite failed to see the point.[15] It was only by slow degrees that it began to sink in.

Walras himself, it is true, had been much less obtuse. He had seen that for a market to work in his way (the way in which so many others have followed him) some market *structure* was necessary. But the market structure which he posited was very special. One would be tempted to think that it was invented by Walras just to give the right result if there were not some evidence that there did exist examples of markets which did work in much this way, and could well have been familiar to him.[16] One, in fact, may have been the Paris Bourse itself!

---

[14] I have tried to draw some more practical consequences in a paper entitled 'Industrialism' (*EP*, pp. 20–44).

[15] 'A Rehabilitation of "Classical" Economics' (*EJ*, June 1957).

[16] So I was told by Keynes himself. I had sent him the article on Walras which I had published, entitled 'Leon Walras' (*Econometrica*, 1934). I have a letter from him about it dated 9 December of that year. The substantial part of the letter is as follows: 'There is one small point which perhaps I may be able to clear up.... You enquire whether or not Walras was supposing that exchanges actually take place at the prices originally proposed when these prices are not equilibrium prices. The footnote which you quote [p. 345 of my paper, p. 44 of the 4th French edition of the *Elements* which I was using] convinces me that he assuredly supposed that they did not take place except at the equilibrium prices. For that is the actual method by which the opening price is fixed on the Paris Bourse even today. His footnote suggests that he was aware that the Agents de Change used this method and he regarded that as the ideal system or exchange to which others were approximations. As a matter of fact, this is also the method by which opening prices are fixed on Wall Street. It is unfamiliar to us because the only London example which I can think of is the daily 'fixing' of silver by the bullion brokers. In all these cases there is an application of Edge-

These, however, would be very sophisticated markets, requiring a lot of organisation; for who is to pay the official who is to 'cry' the prices, or (as Clower would call him) the 'auctioneer'?[17] There must be a prior agreement among the parties to play the game according to these rules; but how is such an agreement to come about? A proper theory of markets must clearly include the Walras-type market as a particular case; but I think it needs to start much further back.

The simplest form of exchange is barter; and (since Edgeworth) we know how that works. One might begin with a market (or pre-market) – a sort of village fair – in which all transactions were barter transactions between a pair of individuals, each giving up something which he wants relatively less in exchange for something which he wants relatively more. But such simple barter, as the textbooks have long been telling us, is bound to leave some opportunities for advantageous trading unexploited; so one must go on from that to introduce some form of triangular trade. At that point, two things happen. One is the evolution of some form of money; in a more complete account than I can offer here, that would have to be fitted in.[18] The other is that there arises an opportunity for the development of specialised merchanting – a merchant being defined as one who buys not for his own use but in order to sell again. It is easy to see that once the market has passed a certain size, so that problems of communication become important, there will have to be specialised merchants (or, perhaps, some substitute for them).

I am very convinced that for the purpose in hand, the specialised merchant is the key figure. When Gerschenkron reviewed my *Theory of Economic History*, he entitled his review 'Mercator Gloriosus'[19] – indicating that from his point of view, the point of view of the historian, I had made too much of the merchant. I dare say that he is right. But I am sure that from the point of view of economic understanding I was right. The role of the merchant in the development of market organisation is crucial.

---

worth's principle of re-contract, all those present disclosing their dispositions to trade and the price which will equate offers and demands is arrived at by an independent person, known in New York as the specialist.'

It is much to be desired that the methods of trading on organised markets, in different countries and at different times, should be studied systematically.

[17] Robert Clower and Axel Leijonhufvud, 'The Coordination of Economic Activities: A Keynesian Perspective' (*The American Economic Review* May 1975).

[18] I started the job in the first lecture of 'The Two Triads' (*CEMT*). See also *TEH*, ch. 3.

[19] *EHR* (November 1971).

Once merchants exist there are three kinds of dealings to be distinguished: (1) dealings between merchants, (2) dealings between merchants and non-merchants, and (3) direct dealings between non-merchants, which in some particular cases may still survive. The most obvious example of direct dealings between non-merchants, surviving into otherwise sophisticated economies, is the market in private dwelling-houses. We rarely find house-merchants holding stocks of dwelling-houses (for rather obvious reasons); but there remains a problem of communication, which is dealt with in another way. This is by the appearance of house agents, a particular kind of commission agent, who has the function of bringing buyer and seller together, and consequently of advising them of the price at which they should trade. He charges a commission to cover the cost of his services (which may formally be paid by the buyer or by the seller, but the price is in fact so adjusted that it falls to some extent on both). In a complete theory of markets, the commission agent would have to find a place.

The market for dwelling-houses is a notoriously 'imperfect' market; the most perfectly organised markets are at the other end – the markets on which specialised traders trade with one another. It is here that we should look for the Walras-type market and for other sophisticated types. For when merchants habitually trade together, they develop needs for assurance about the carrying-through of their dealings – needs for legal assurances about property and contract, and other related matters – and it is worth their while to pay something in order to get these rules policed and enforced. All this is very important, but it is just one end of the spectrum of market structures.

At the centre, however, is what remains: dealings between merchants and non-merchants. It is here that we meet the shop-keeper and the wholesaler. They buy to sell again, so must buy before they sell, so they must hold stocks. The holding of unsold stocks is expensive, so their appearance is again an indication that information is imperfect. They are giving those who buy from them the service that they can buy the things they want when they want them. The provision of that service is expensive; for the costs that they incur in providing it they properly charge.

In this sort of market, with sharply specialised merchants, there is no question who fixes prices; it is the merchant himself. When he finds his stock running down, so that he is in danger of failing to meet the demands that they be made upon him, he will first try to get more from other merchants; if they have ample stocks, all is well;

but if their stocks also are running down, he will have to offer higher prices, to the other merchants or to outside producers, in order to get more stock. Then he will charge a higher price to consumers in order to cover the rise in his costs. Such a market may well be quite similar, in many ways, to the textbook competitive market; but until we take uncertainty and costs of information into account we cannot show how it works.[20]

I believe that there was a stage in the development of capitalism when a market such as I have been describing was the typical market – for consumers' goods, and for many sorts of producers' goods also. But I greatly doubt if it can still be regarded as the typical market. What has upset it is the taking over of the mercantile function by the producers themselves. The manufacturers do it directly, the primary producers indirectly, through the formation of their own associations or by selling organisations equipped with political power. This is, of course, the point at which the question of monopoly becomes so important. But that, again cannot in general be understood unless we look at it *in time*, as an aspect of the evolutionary process we have been considering. Why is it that the theory of monopolistic competition, or imperfect competition, to which so much attention was paid in the thirties, now looks so faded? Because it is quite shockingly *out of time*.[21]

There is a practical conclusion from what I have just been saying to which I should like to draw attention. You have a long tradition in in the United States of anti-monopoly action; and in my own country, in recent years, it has been ineffectively imitated. I do not think it has been much of a success, even with you. On the line of thought I have been sketching out, one can see why. It is an attempt to go back from the late stage of capitalism – the producer-dominated stage – to the earlier stage, before the producers took over. But this earlier stage depended for its functioning upon a merchant class, an independent merchant class; and that cannot be raised from the dead by a stroke of the pen, or by an Act of Congress. It would have to grow up; to bring it back would be quite a job.

One final salute – to Georgescu. He has chosen a cosmic way of demonstrating the irreversibility of time.[22] Since he was addressing himself to a science-based culture, that (I am sure) was a good way of going about it. For my part, I am very ignorant of science; though

---

[20] See my chapter on 'The Method of Marshall' (*CG*, ch. 5).

[21] I made an attempt to start the business of bringing it back into time in 'The Process of Imperfect Competition' (*OEP*, February 1954); but I do not pretend that I got very far.

[22] Georgescu-Roegen, *The Entropy Law and the Economic Process* (1971).

I have dabbled in mathematics my spiritual home is in the Humanities. It is because I want to make economics more human that I want to make it more time-conscious; and since I am approaching the task from that end I am content with a more earthy way of going about it. We are nevertheless, I believe, on the same side. We are both of us evolutionists, but not straight-line, or 'exponential', evolutionists. It is the *new* things that humanity has discovered which makes its history exciting; and the new things that may be found in the future, before humanity blows itself up, or settles down to some ghastly 'equilibrium', make a future worth praying for, and worth working for.

22

Must Stimulating Demand
Stimulate Inflation?

This was a lecture given at the University of Sydney, in April 1976 and subsequently published in the Australian journal *Economic Record* in December of that year. It was naturally prompted by the state of the world at that time, not long after the first Oil Shock; but I do not think that what I said in it has seriously dated.

Another version of the same argument, using similar diagrams, appears in the section entitled 'Ourselves' in a paper that was published in 1979 in *EP*, pp. 86–107. I would not claim that this later version is much improvement on its predecessor, and it is probably less readable. I did, however, take greater care on some critical points. Most important was the insistence that the points on my curves are 'alternative equilibria (relatively long-run equilibria, of Wicksell–Myrdal type, not short-run equilibria like Keynes's). Thus nothing is shown on the diagram about the passage from one of these equilibria to another. What are shown are alternative possibilities' (pp. 89–90). This, as will be noticed by readers of the present volume, is the same point that comes up in the essays (21 and 23) which precede and follow this. (See especially pp. 327–8 below.) The use of 'relatively long-run equilibria' for analysis of this sort is evidently tricky; but I think it is shown here that it has its uses, though it must always be kept under some suspicion.

The question which I have put as a title to this paper is one which, I think, many people would like to have answered. How much more clearly we could see out way forward if we knew the answer to it! I am afraid I am not going to answer it, certainly not to give the straight answer 'yes' or 'no'. I shall take the proper academic attitude to it – 'it all depends'.

It is clear, in the first place, that a general 'no' is impossible; there are certainly some occasions when the answer must be 'yes'. One has only to look at war-time experience, in many countries, in both of the Great Wars of this century, to find examples. You can't explain them away.

The other end, admittedly, is more tricky. There are economists, even now, who would say that the answer must always be 'yes'; that it is practically impossible to find cases in which one could rightly say 'no'.

A casual reading of Keynes's *General Theory* (and even a not so casual reading of the many popularisations and textbooks that have followed from it) might, however, give the impression that Keynes thought conditions in which the answer is 'no' to be quite common. He seems to distinguish between conditions of Full Employment of labour, when an increase in effective demand will indeed be inflationary, and conditions of less than Full Employment when up to a point it will not. That is to say, in Full Employment the effect will be on prices; but with less than Full Employment the effect is not on prices, but on output. Thus if (as most people would do, and I certainly would do) we regard inflation as an evil, and unemployment as an evil, the effect is good in the one case and bad in the other. So we have just to decide which state we are in, and we have the answer.

That is primitive Keynesianism. It is a step forward; there are some circumstances which it suits, but in general it is not good enough. I am pretty sure that Keynes himself would have expected that there would be conditions in which it would not be good enough. I don't think that there is much doubt that such conditions are with us today.

So we have got to push on, as Keynes himself would surely have wished us to do. We have got to push on quite a way, so it will be best to proceed by steps. I am going to represent the steps on a diagram, just to make it easier to remember them.

What I shall draw on the diagram is a kind of supply curve. But it is not the ordinary supply curve of the textbooks, which relates the quantity of output to the price at which it is offered. Mine relates rate of change in the price-level (the rate of inflation) to rate of change in output (what is ordinarily called the growth rate of the economy). The former I shall call p, the latter q. Both my p and my q are rates of change.

I measure p on the vertical axis, q on the horizontal. Points on the vertical axis, where q is zero, are positions of zero growth; points on the horizontal axis, where p is zero, are positions of no inflation. I shall need another vertical line, marked as FF', to indicate the maximum growth that is possible at Full Employment. It may indeed be that a still higher growth rate could be attained by some re-organisation, which is not just the result of an increase in demand; but I shall not deal with that here. I shall suppose that *FF'* sets a limit to the real growth that is possible, at a particular time.

You can see how what I called Primitive Keynesianism would be represented on this diagram (Fig. 22.1). The only positions which the economy could occupy would be either along *OF* or along *FF'*. So the 'supply curve' would be like an L turned backwards, *OFF'*. There could not at the same time, be inflation and unemployment.

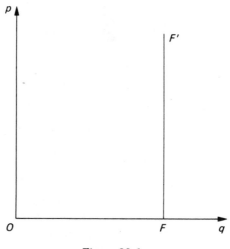

Figure 22.1

It was, of course, realised, quite early on, by sensible people, that that was much too simple. As the point first came up, attention was drawn to the fact that in hardly any country is the labour force homogeneous. Workers are specialised into occupations, so there may be a scarcity of labour in some occupations (leading, it was then supposed, to rising labour costs, and so rising prices), while there are others in which labour is still unemployed. Once this was recognised, the 'corner' in the 'L' had to be given up. It had to be rounded off, as shown in the curve *OAF'* in Fig. 22.2.

This already, as you will see, makes a substantial difference. For it interposes between the two simple states of Fig. 22.1 a mixed state – a state in which increasing demand has *both* effects. It both

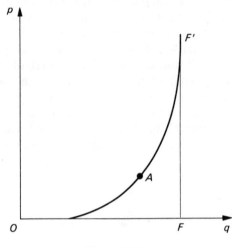

Figure 22.2

increases output, diminishing unemployment, and raises prices. So one has to decide how much unemployment is worth so much inflation. There is, as the Americans say, a 'trade-off' between them. Not at all an easy trade-off; one on which different people may have very different opinions.

There was a considerable period in the fifties and sixties during which the picture that many economists had in their minds corresponded to my Fig. 22.2. At that time it seemed to make sense. There was some inflation (not much inflation, as compared with what we have all of us more recently experienced, but some inflation none the less). And there was, often at least, a significant amount of unemployment. So it seemed to make sense to suppose that we were somewhere on the 'bend'.

The explanation that was favoured for being in that situation was nevertheless significantly different in different countries. I take UK and US as examples. In Britain we have a very well articulated labour force, most of it rather rigidly specialised into particular occupations (that is one reason why we have such strong Trade Unions); so the explanation I began by giving, in terms of labour specialisation, seemed in Britain to be very acceptable. I myself find it hard to believe that there is not something of that in the US also, but clearly there is less of it; so the Americans, when confronted with the same phenomenon of simultaneous inflation and unemployment, were often inclined to explain it another way. They thought of their unemployed as being typically in process of changing jobs; and indeed of their employed workers as continually looking over their shoulders to see if they could find a better job. On this basis they worked out quite elaborate 'search' theories, which showed that shortage of labour, making for rising money wages (essentially on simple supply-demand lines) could be consistent with considerable unemployment; the unemployment being ultimately due to imperfect knowledge of jobs, and of applicants for jobs, by the worker on the one side and by the employer on the other.

I shall not discuss these 'search' theories in detail since I myself find it hard to believe that the phenomenon on which they concentrate is, even in America, of decisive importance. (I do not think they are as much in fashion even there as they were.) I have, however, found it desirable to allude to them, since they illustrate a point which I do believe to be of importance. The labour markets of different countries are by no means exactly similar. The view which we take of inflation and of how it works, depends to a considerable extent upon the nature of the labour market with which we have to deal.

And not of the labour market alone. As we shall see, there are other variations, between one country and another, which need to be brought in. But let us, for the moment, go on with our diagram – and with its adventures!

The mere rounding off, that was shown in Fig. 22.2, is enough to account for the co-existence of inflation and unemployment. Even if there is a lot of inflation and a lot of unemployment, you can say there is more rounding-off; it does not necessarily upset the whole idea. But if a situation like that lasts a long time, so that we have to expect that the economy under study will usually be 'on the bend', further questions come up. What about that horizontal stretch, which we took over from Keynes (or from primitive Keynesianism)? Has it any business to be there at all?

The only justification for any such horizontal stretch must be the belief that in the absence of labour scarcity (any labour scarcity) wages would be constant. That I think, is the 'primitive' view; wages rise when there is scarcity of labour, but when labour is abundant, they do not fall. But even that does not justify the horizontal stretch on our diagram. If productivity is increasing, while money wages are constant, prices should be falling. So if there is a horizontal stretch, it should not be drawn at zero price-inflation ($p = 0$) but some way below the horizontal axis (p moderately negative), as in Fig. 22.3.

Though I do not want to stay at this version, it will be well to

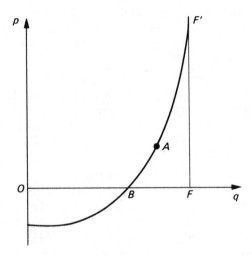

Figure 22.3

look at it for a moment, since it (or something like it) does seem to describe the view which many people (especially those who call themselves monetarists) have in their minds. By a sufficient degree of monetary restraint (however it is exercised) the system can be pushed back from an inflationary position A to a zero-inflation point B. B, it will be noticed, is a position in which wages are rising – but only just enough to offset the rise in productivity.

But let us look a little more closely at just what, in a position such as B, is supposed to happen. If productivity was increasing at the same rate in all industries, all would be well; but that in practice never occurs. It is always the case that a productivity rise is concentrated upon some activities, while there are others where no increase, or no measurable increase, is possible. It is obviously desirable, both socially and economically desirable, that the rise in productivity, though it is confined to a part of the economy, should be reflected in a rise in wages that is spread over the whole economy, indeed, if this does not occur, at least to some extent, the rise in productivity will not be absorbed – it will itself lead to unemployment. Nevertheless the direct effect is on wages in the industries where the rise in productivity occurs; it may well raise them so as (roughly) to match the rise in productivity. If that happens, and nothing else, there is no spreading; the people in the other industries do not get their share. It is not just the case that customary differentials are upset; they are upset in a way which is economically inefficient also. If on the other hand, wages in the other industries are raised, while wages in the 'advancing' industries have risen by the full extent of the rise in productivity, the *average* level of wages will rise by *more* than the *average* increase in productivity. So a position such as our *B* will not be reached. What will be reached is a position somewhat above it – a position in which the level of prices is tending, at least to some extent, to rise.

One can readily point to cases where a mechanism of this sort seems to have been at work. An outstanding example is that of Japan in the 1960s, an outstanding example because the rate of growth in productivity was exceptionally high. But it was by no means uniform; it was concentrated on particular industries, here export industries. Wages in those industries rose very rapidly; and because of the rise in productivity, they could do so without raising the cost of production of the exports. But then the wage-rise communicated itself to other industries, producing for the home market, where there was no comparable increase in productivity. Accordingly, though the prices of Japanese exports could be kept from rising, the general price-level in Japan did rise, very markedly. The rise in consumer prices, in Japan, during the middle sixties, was as great as that in any of the major industrial countries, and greater than in most. Yet these years, in Japan, were years of extraordinary prosperity.

If this interpretation is correct (and it seems to make sense) the Japanese 'inflation' (if we so call it) was not to any important extent a demand inflation; though it was a phenomenon of an expanding economy, it worked on the cost side, not on the side of demand. It was indeed a condition for it that the Japanese could sell their exports rather easily, without having to cut their prices; thus it may be said that the 'inflation' in Japan was an echo of the inflation, or at least of the expansion, taking place in the outside world. It could no doubt have been prevented, or at least moderated, by a sufficient appreciation of the yen relatively to other currencies. That would have damped down the Japanese expansion; wages would have risen less, and prices would have risen less. But if the rate of exchange was not to be altered, a more restrictive (monetary or fiscal) policy on the part of the Japanese government would not, in my view, have had much effect on inflation within Japan; it would doubtless have improved the Japanese balance of payments, already favourable – and so would have been a nuisance to other countries – but that would have been its main effect.

If we are to represent a condition of this kind on our diagram, we should (I suppose) allow our curve to have a horizontal (or nearly horizontal) stretch, as before; but now it would be *above* the horizontal axis (Fig. 22.4). A restrictive policy, causing the position of the economy to move to the left along the 'curve', would not prevent inflation, or would not altogether prevent it.

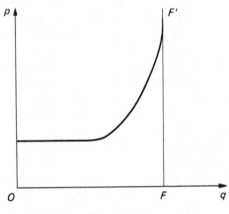

Figure 22.4

The case which I have just been describing (illustrated by Japanese experience in the sixties) is by no means the only case in which something like Fig. 22.4 could occur. There are others – indeed there are several others – which at the present time are more to the point.

One, rather obviously, is that in which the cause of inflation is an independent wage-push by Trade Unions – independent in the sense that the causes of the wage-push are social or political rather than economic. I do not doubt that this can happen, but I do find it hard to believe that it can go on for long without getting mixed up with other things. For even if the process starts by strong Trade Unions forcing a rise in wages, and then going on forcing a rise in wages, at so much per annum (in excess of the rise in productivity), it is quite certain that they will not be able to do this without bringing about rises in the prices of the things on which the wages are spent. I cannot believe that this will not react back on the wage-claim. It is after all real wages, not money wages, in which people are really interested.

And once this is admitted one has to face the question of the other things, other things than wages and productivity, which may affect the level of prices. That there are such other things, and that they are very important, seems to me to have been abundantly demonstrated by what has happened since 1972.

Everywhere, in every continent (save perhaps in some communist countries which have opted out of the international trading system) there has been since that date a large rise in prices. There had indeed been a general tendency towards rising prices throughout that trading area going much further back (twenty years further back); but in many countries, perhaps the majority of countries, it was in those days quite moderate, 2 or 3 per cent per annum or even less. Since 1972 it has sharply accelerated. The rise in consumer prices in Australia from the beginning of 1972 to the middle of 1975 was nearly 50 per cent, more than 10 per cent per annum. This was in no way exceptional; there are many countries which have had a similar experience. Even the best behaved countries (best behaved, that is, from the price point of view) such as Germany and the United States – countries which in the sixties had had very modest increases, usually not much over 1 per cent per annum, jumped to 5 per cent per annum. It was a world-wide experience.

It is very hard to believe that so general a phenomenon can be explained in terms of 'wage-push', to an 'independent' wage-push; that is, a wage-push which is to be ascribed to social or political causes. For why should the experience of so many countries, with exceedingly different social and political structures, have been so similar?

The root cause must surely be a common cause, and it is not hard to see what it has been. Some of its manifestations, at least, are easy to recognise. But if we are to understand them, we must begin a bit further back.

In order to do this, I must draw upon some ideas which were already beginning to come up in my Helsinki lectures, *The Crisis in Keynesian Economics.* These lectures were given early in 1973 and, of course, were written a little before that. I do not pretend that when I was writing I foresaw what was going to happen, or even that I understood what was beginning to happen. But even then I saw that the Keynesian model, which had been so familiar over many years (and on which the diagrams I have been using in this lecture were based) needed substantial amendment.

It was altogether too 'macro'. It had its sectors, consumption and investment sectors, and (when applied to a national economy) a separate sector for foreign trade. But it did not make a distinction which already appeared to be increasingly relevant. This was nothing else than the old distinction, which had sometimes come up as a distinction between industry and agriculture, sometimes as a distinction between secondary and primary production, sometimes as a distinction between diminishing cost and increasing cost industries. The last was possibly the most fundamental. Keynes could have got it from Marshall, but it was always regarded as the devil of Marshallian economics; Marshallians, if they could, forgot about it. But it is very unsafe to forget about it. There is no doubt about the fact. Firms, in industry, do produce under diminishing cost, and do survive.

How do they survive? By fixing their selling prices so as to yield a 'reasonable' profit in a 'normal' condition of the market, but then letting the market determine what, at any time, it will actually buy. If demand is higher than 'normal' then (with diminishing cost) profit will be very high; but if demand is abnormally low, profit will be very low (or negative). But profit cannot be made higher by cutting prices in times of bad trade, nor is there much incentive to raise prices in times of good trade, when profits are high – anyhow. So in diminishing cost industries, where competition is necessarily 'imperfect', but may nevertheless be very real, there is a strong tendency to keep prices stable against fluctuations in demand, so long as those changes in demand do not lead to other changes.

In my Helsinki lectures I called the markets which work in this way *fixprice* markets. By that, as I said, I did not mean that in these markets prices did not change; only that they did not change as a direct consequence of an imbalance between demand and supply. I was then thinking primarily of storable goods, goods of which sellers are likely to keep stocks. If demand goes up, stocks will fall; but the fall in stocks itself gives a signal for increase in production. The change in demand itself changes supply; it is carried through, without it being necessary for there to be a change in price for it to be carried through. A market can work that way.

Since I wrote, the argument which I advanced has been developed further. In an important paper, published last summer,[1] Arthur Okun has extended the argument from the stockholding stage, the stage on which I had concentrated, to the flow of production (short period theory in Marshallian economics). He thinks of his typical firm, in *his* fixprice sector, as being largely concerned with the maintenance of steady relations with regular customers. It wants to keep, not just its share of the market, in an arithmetical sense, but a

[1] A. M. Okun, 'Inflation: its mechanics and welfare costs', *Brookings Papers* (1975:2).

continual relation with particular customers, customers whom it has satisfied sufficiently well to limit their incentive to sample what is offered by its rivals. As he shows, a firm which sets that as its objective will seek to ensure that its prices are 'reasonable'; thus it will be reluctant to raise its selling prices unless it can give a reason for doing so, a reason which it can hope that its customers will accept. A change in costs, considered in these terms, is a presentable reason for a change in prices; but a change in demand is not a presentable reason. To say that price has been raised because demand has gone up amounts to saying to the customer 'I am charging you more because I can get more out of you'. That would not make for good relations! So one can understand that a firm of this sort will maintain steady prices, *except when costs change.*

Okun sometimes writes as if he thought this kind of behaviour to be universal throughout the manufacturing or (even more generally) the *secondary* sector. I would not myself go so far as that. I am sure there are exceptions. Sometimes the exceptions are important. Statutory monopolies, like the British nationalised industries, clearly do not work that way. When demand falls off, their costs (per unit of output) rise, so they say that they must raise their prices, and for that reason alone they sometimes do so. If one were writing about the UK one would have to take that into account. More generally it must be an exception. One cannot see that a firm which was subject to potential competition, even to competition some time in the future, could possibly act that way.

Doubtless there are other exceptions. And doubtless even if the Okun model is accepted, as reasonably representative short-period behaviour, it leaves, when applied to the longer run, quite a lot to be explained. Still, for the purpose of analysing inflation, it is short-run behaviour which matters.

But what now of the primary sector? There are several (perhaps many) agricultural and extractive products which are so tied up with cartel arrangements that their markets work, at least apparently, in a manner which is not altogether different from what has been described. Yet they do not really succeed in relating prices to costs in the way that industry does, though they may attempt to do so. The markets for primary commodities work much more in the textbook (or neo-classical) manner, prices rising when there is an excess of demand, falling when there is an excess of supply. There are indeed some speculative elements to be considered, but they are fairly well understood, and I do not need to emphasise them here. So if we want a simple model for the problems of inflation (a model which will give us the main points without fussing us with detail) a two-sector model, with industry working on a fixprice, or normal cost, basis, while the price of primary commodities are determined in their familiar supply-and-demand manner, seems to be the answer.

What then about wages? We have only to allow that rises in prices, of the things on which wages are spent, will react back on wages, and the model is complete. And that there should be this reaction (a reaction of which in the earlier part of this lecture I already took account) will now fit in perfectly. The firm which seeks to maintain a *regular* relation with its customers will surely also seek to maintain a *regular* relation with the workers whom it employs. It cannot expect to do that unless it pays them what they regard as fair wages.

The simple 'independent' wage-push will now fit in, if we want it. A rise in wages (in the secondary sector) will raise costs, and (by what has been said) a rise in prices will follow. Not perhaps at once; there may be a lag. During the lag profits will be depressed, and therefore (in all probability) industry will be depressed. It is just the regular wage-price spiral.

What will also fit in (and this is more interesting) is the possibility of a disturbance which originates in the flexprice, or primary product, markets, but communicates itself to the others. Suppose, for instance, that there is a reduction in the supply of important primary commodities, or simply a check to the rate of growth to which the system has become accustomed. The prices of these commodities rise, as we should expect, on the flexprice markets; and since they enter into the costs of production of some of the secondary products, the prices of those products will rise too. There is thus, in terms of statistical averages, a general rise in prices; if it is of sufficient magnitude, it will react back on wages, producing an inflationary spiral, just as would have happened if the original cause had been an independent wage-push. It works in the same way, even though in this case the original cause is external to the labour market.

It is very possible that the accelerated rise in prices, throughout the trading world, during the last four years, has been of something like this type. Some of it can be traced, on these lines, to the harvest failures of 1972; though it was the supply of food which by these was most directly affected, we should remember that food, by the time it reaches the consumer, has been involved in costs that are non-agricultural (distribution costs at the very least) so that it should be reckoned as a secondary, not as a primary product. More important, no doubt, was the oil squeeze of 1973, a clear case of a sharp rise in the price of a primary product, affecting the costs of production of secondary products almost universally. Though the immediate cause of the rise was cartellisation, not physical shortage, one can understand that it would work in essentially the same way.

That may well be the main answer; but it is arguable that there was something else as well. A case can be made for the view that the initial disturbance was on the demand side, not on the side of supply. For there was another change in the state of the trading world, between the sixties and the seventies, not so far mentioned. This was the floating of major exchanges, which followed upon the dollar crisis of 1971.

It was not just that in the sixties exchange rates were relatively stable. It is even more important that the policies of governments were very generally directed towards trying to keep them stable. This in itself put a brake on expansion, a brake which caused much annoyance at the time, but which (I think one can now see) was on the whole salutary. However that may be, after 1971 it was taken off.

The first result was a very general boom. Everyone bounded ahead. Governments everywhere whatever their political complexion, they all fell into the same trap. For it was a trap. The boom was very considerable, and very general; but it was very short-lived, lasting hardly more than a year. It was killed by lack of the primary commodities which were needed to feed it.

It is indeed remarkable, when one looks back, that the very great expansion in world production, during the fifties and sixties – it was indeed an enormous expansion – should have been possible without there being more strain on the primary production side. One might have expected more signs of diminishing returns. It may be that what has happened is simply that a check, which might always have been expected but was long postponed as a result of new discovery and technical innovation, has arrived at last. But it may be, on the other hand, that the exceptional expansion in industrial activity in 1972–3 was so out of line with what had preceded it that it was more than the primary sector could take. Either view is possible, and it is probably too soon to decide between them.

Whichever is the explanation, the immediate effect would be much the same. Let us begin by looking at it on our diagram. We have already seen that independent wage-push would raise the horizontal limb of our backward L (as in Fig. 22.4); now we have to take account of a primary product squeeze which moves the other limb to the left, through the operation of a constraint which appears well short of the Full Employment of labour. The whole of the L is thus displaced in a 'north-west' direction (Fig. 22.5). There is still (perhaps) a 'trade-off' between unemployment and inflation, but it is a very disadvantageous trade-off. No alternative is open which does not leave quite a lot of both.

That is one useful way of looking at what has happened. But there are several ways in which it is too simple, and some of them show it to be too pessimistic. I began with one of these.

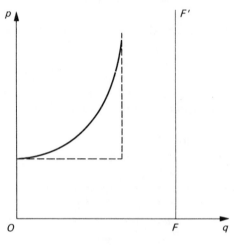

Figure 22.5

One may think of labour and primary products as inputs into 'industry'. In the short run, the proportions in which these inputs are required are not very easily variable. The rate of expansion of 'industry' will thus be limited by one *or* the other. If it is the supply of labour which is increasing less rapidly, labour will be the effective constraint, so in this case we have a Full Employment ceiling; but if it is the supply of primary products which is increasing less rapidly, then that will be the effective ceiling, so labour cannot be fully absorbed.

When the impasse is stated in that way, one can see that *in time* there are several possible ways out. For one thing, it may be that in time the supply of primary products will resume its growth; the check may have been only temporary. There is quite a chance of that; but it would be impossible to say anything useful about it without going into details, most of which are beyond my competence. Secondly, it may be that ways will be found of changing the input-proportions by suitable inventions; but these must usually require new sorts of capital equipment; the devising and installation of such equipment will take time, probably quite a lot of time. Thirdly, it is possible that the proportions might effectively be changed by a lowering of real wages, or at least by a check to their rate of growth; for this would reduce the volume of primary products that would be needed to satisfy demands arising from the spending of those wages. It would thus enable employment to be maintained with a smaller absorption of primary products than would otherwise be necessary. That runs straight into the obstacle, that the inflation has resulted from the determined effort to maintain real wages. But something has to give somewhere and that, sometimes at least, may be it.

One gets some way by looking at the issue like this; but one is still over-simplifying. We cannot really think of 'policy' selecting a point on our curve, as (in all my diagrams) I have been appearing to do. For the trading world does not have a single government, with a single policy. It has many governments, acting, to a considerable extent, independently. They affect each other; they are subject, in total, to the same construction; but they are affected by the constraints in different ways.

Obviously one must distinguish between those countries which are predominantly exporters of primary products and those which are predominantly importers – or rather, to be more precise, of those particular primary products which have proved to be in short supply. Let us, for short, call the former just exporters and the latter just importers (not forgetting that there are some very important countries, in particular the United States, which come in on both sides). The crisis begins with a relative rise in the prices of the scarce primary products, a change which in itself is clearly to the advantage of the exporters and to the disadvantage of the importers. Let us look at them in turn, taking the exporters first.

Unless the fall in supply is very great, it is likely (at the first round) that the exporters will experience a rise in the value of their exports without the value of their imports being much affected; a favourable movement in the balance of payments. This, in itself, is expansionary; so activity, in these exporting countries, will tend to increase. It will increase, even though no particular steps are taken by government; if government takes the opportunity to engage on an additional expansionary programme the expansion will be greater but the favourable movement in balance of payments will soon be absorbed. (This, I suppose, is what happened in Australia at the corresponding stage of the recent story.) The effect of an expansion of this sort by a single country may, however, not be great, so far as the level of prices is concerned; the main effect is on its balance of payments.

There is, however, another effect on prices. It is to be supposed that the exporting country itself consumes at home some of the primary goods which it exports. Their prices will rise on the home market as well as on the export markets. This rise, we should now expect, will react on wages, so that the rise in internal prices will be generalised. Inflation of this sort could only be prevented by restricting exports; but so far as that is done, more of the strain is left to be borne by the importing countries.

They must, in any case, be severely hit. For the balance-of-payments effect, in their case, is adverse; and at the same time they have cost inflation, due to the rise in the price of imports. How are they to react? It is very difficult for them to react except in ways that reduce activity, and hence employment.

For this is not the kind of balance-of-payments crisis where exchange depreciation is much help. Exchange depreciation will raise the prices of imports, in domestic currency, still further; and that is likely to aggravate the cost inflation. But the rise in internal prices (and hence in money incomes) prevents the depreciation from restoring equilibrium in the balance of payments. So depreciation is not at all an easy way out.

In fact, as we have seen from recent experience, there has to be a cut-back in the importing countries. But if they cut back, separately, they aggravate the trouble; for not only do they bring about the contraction, which is necessary in order that their imports from the exporting countries should be reduced to what they can pay for; they contract more than that, reducing their imports from each other, and hence their exports to each other. They have indeed, in the recent case been aware of this danger; they have therefore been willing to lend to one another on quite a massive scale, in order to check this further contraction. But even so it has not been enough. There has thus been the depression, which we have seen, in the importing countries, taken together.

That has indeed diminished their demand for imports from the primary producers. So, on the whole, the prices of primary products have come down, at least relatively. But, at least so far, this has just been a consequence of the depression. It does not, at least yet, give a firm indication that the shortage, which caused all the trouble, has been relieved.

It will, of course, be understood that, among the various importing countries, the severity of the shock has varied a good deal. It has been more severe for Britain and for Japan (dependent on imports for food as well as for supplies for industry) than it has been for Germany (not much dependent on food imports) and for the US (an exporter as well as importer of primary products). But even the latter have been forced to contract, and still at this time have severe unemployment.

I turn back, in conclusion, to the problem from which I started. Must stimulating demand stimulate inflation? You will already have gathered, from what I said about the case of Australia, that my answer is not an unqualified 'yes'. There is indeed in all cases a point beyond which it must do so; all-out stimulation must, in the end, run into shortages, of one kind or another. That is always true. But when, as today, there are in so many countries exceptional amounts of unemployed resources, it is not so clear that moderate stimulation must have this effect. The fact that nearly everywhere the unemployment is accompanied by inflation does not necessarily mean that stimulus to employment must make inflation worse. Even though the general situation may be such as is represented by my gloomy Fig. 22.5, it is possible that one may be on a fairly flat part of the curve – on the left.

But that diagram, as I have insisted, refers to the world situation, not to that of a single country. In the case of a single country, the chief *direct* effect of demand stimulation is on the balance of payments, not on the level of prices. So the optimistic view, that stimulation will not make inflation worse, depends on the balance of payments being able to take it. If it can, well and good; but if it cannot, if the result of stimulation is exchange depreciation, that will indeed make inflation worse.

That is as far as I can get, thinking in these very general terms. Beyond that one must indeed hand over to the writers of memoranda, using all the knowledge that they can get from current statistics, and using their best assessments of current states of mind, not only economic but also social, and political.

23

IS–LM – an Explanation

A first version of this paper was given at the Marshall Society, Cambridge, in November 1979; a later version at a symposium at the European University Institute, Florence, in the following May. It underwent considerable changes, as the result of discussions that took place on these occasions, before it appeared in the *Journal of Post Keynesian Economics* (Winter 1980-1). No further changes, of any substance, have been made in what follows, except that two footnotes have been transferred to the prefatory note to essay 8 above, which was the place where in the present volume they seemed to belong.

The *IS–LM* diagram, which is widely, though not universally, accepted as a convenient synopsis of Keynesian theory, is a thing for which I cannot deny that I have some responsibility. For it first saw the light (though there it was given different lettering) in my own paper 'Mr Keynes and the Classics' [essay 8 above]. And this is not my only connection with it; I also made use of it in some chapters (11-12) of my *Contribution to the Theory of the Trade Cycle* (1950) and again in a paper which appears as 'The Classics Again' in *Critical Essays in Monetary Theory*.[1] I have, however, not concealed that, as time has gone on, I have myself become dissatisfied with it. 'That diagram', I said in 1975, 'is now much less popular with me than I think it still is with many other people.'[2] In the reconstruction of Keynesian theory which I published at much the same time (*The Crisis in Keynesian Economics*, 1974) it is not to be found. But I have not explained the reasons for this change of opinion, or of attitude. Here I shall try to do so.

---

[1] I still believe that the use I made of it in the latter paper is perfectly legitimate. I am much less sure about the version in *TC*.

[2] Above, pp. 289-90.

I

It will be well to begin by showing how it was that I came across this method of exposition. The clue is to be found in 'Wages and Interest: the Dynamic Problem' [essay 6 above], the last of the relevant papers which I wrote before I saw the *General Theory*, published in 1936. It is a first sketch for what was to become the 'dynamic' model of *Value and Capital*. It shows (I think conclusively) that that model was already in my mind before I met that of Keynes.

When I did read him, I recognised at once that my model and Keynes's had some things in common. Both of us fixed our attention on the behaviour of an economy *during a period* – a period that had a past, which nothing that was done during the period could alter, and a future, which during the period was unknown. Expectations of the future would nevertheless affect what happened during the period. Neither of us made any assumption about 'rational expectations'; expectations, in our models, were strictly exogenous. (Keynes made much more fuss over that than I did, but there is the same implication in my model also.) Subject to these *data* – the given equipment carried over from the past, the production possibilities within the period, the preference schedules, and the given expectations – the actual performance of the economy within the period was supposed to be determined, or determinable. It would be determined as an equilibrium performance, with respect to these data.

There was all this in common between my model and Keynes's; it was enough to make me recognise, as soon as I saw the *General Theory*, that his model was a relation of mine and, as such, one which I could warmly welcome. There were, however, two differences, on which (as we shall see) much depends.

The more obvious difference was that mine was a flexprice model, a perfect competition model, in which all prices were flexible, while in Keynes's the level of money wages (at least) was exogenously determined. So Keynes's was a model that was consistent with unemployment, while mine, in his terms, was a full employment model. I shall have much to say about this difference, but I may as well note, at the start, that I do not think it matters much. I did not think, even in 1936, that it mattered much. *IS–LM* was in fact a translation of Keynes's non-flexprice model into my terms. It seemed to me already that that could be done; but how it is done requires explanation.

The other difference is more fundamantal; it concerns the length of the *period*. Keynes's (he said) was a 'short-period', a term with connotations derived from Marshall; we shall not go far wrong if we think of it as a year. Mine was an 'ultra-short-period'; I called it a week. Much more can happen in a year than in a week; Keynes has to allow for quite a lot of things to happen. I wanted to avoid so much happening, so that my (flexprice) markets could reflect propensities (and expectations) as they are at a moment. So it was that I made my markets open only on a Monday; what actually happened during the ensuing week was not to affect them. This was a very artificial device, not (I would think now) much to be recommended. But the point of it was to exclude the things which might happen, and must disturb the markets, during a period of finite length; and this, as we shall see, is a very real trouble in Keynes.

In the rest of this article, I shall take these two issues separately, beginning with the fixprice–flexprice question, which is the easier.

II

It will readily be understood, in the light of what I have been saying, that the idea of the *IS–LM* diagram came to me as a result of the work I had been doing on three-way exchange, conceived in a Walrasian manner. I had already found a way of representing three-way exchange on a two-dimensional diagram (to appear in due course in chapter 5 of *Value and Capital*). As it appears there, it is a piece of statics, but it was essential to my approach (as already appears in 'Wages and Interest: the Dynamic Problem' [essay 6 above]) that static analysis of this sort could be carried over to 'dynamics' by redefinition of terms. So it was natural for me to think that a similar device could be used for the Keynes theory.

Keynes had three elements in his theory: the marginal efficiency of capital, the consumption function, and liquidity preference. The market for goods, the market for bonds, and the market for money: could they not be regarded in my manner as a model of three-way exchange? In my three-way exchange I had two independent price parameters: the price of A in terms of C and the price of B in terms of C (for the price of A in terms of B followed from them). These two parameters were determined by the equilibrium of two markets, the market for A and the market for B. If these two markets were in equilibrium, the third must be also.

Keynes also appeared to have two parameters – his Y (income *in terms of wage units*) and r, the rate of interest. He made investment depend on r and saving on Y; so for each value of r there should be a value of Y which would keep saving equal to invest-ment – excess demand on the market for goods then being zero. This gave a relation between r and Y which I expressed as the *IS* curve. The demand for money depended on Y (transactions balances) and on r (liquidity preference). So for any given supply of money (*in terms of wage units*) there should be a relation between r and Y which would keep the money 'market' in equilibrium. One did not have to bother about the market for 'loanable funds', since it appeared, on the Walras analogy, that if these two 'markets' were in equilibrium, the third must be also. So I concluded that the intersection of *IS* and *LM* determined the equilibrium of the system as a whole.

Now this was really, at that stage, no more than a conjecture, for I had not properly shown that the Walras analogy would fit. In Walras, all markets are cleared; but in *IS–LM* (following Keynes) the labour market is not cleared; there is excess supply of labour. Does this, by itself, upset the Walras model? I think that by now it is generally accepted that it does not. It will nevertheless be useful, for what follows, to check the matter over in detail.

In strictness, we now need four markets, since labour and goods will have to be distinguished. But before giving them those names, let us look at the matter in terms of a general Walrasian four-goods model.

We then say that commodities A, B, C and X are being traded, with X as standard (*numéraire*). Prices p_a, p_b, p_c are reckoned in terms of the standard; $p_x = 1$. Demands and supplies on the ABC markets are functions of the three prices. The three equations $S_a = D_a$ and so on are sufficient to determine the three prices. Further, since

$$S_x = p_a D_a + p_b D_b + p_c D_c, \qquad D_x = p_a S_a + p_b S_b + p_c S_c,$$

when the supply and demand equations are satisfied for ABC, that for X follows automatically.

There is just this one identical relation between the four equations. We could use it to eliminate the X equation, as just shown, or to eliminate any one of the other equations, while retaining the X equation. Thus the system of three prices for ABC can be regarded as determined by equations for ABC, or by equations for BCX, CAX or ABX.

Thus far Walras. But now suppose that one of the commodities is sold on a fixprice market, where the price is fixed in terms of the standard, but where the equation of supply and demand does not have to hold. The actual amount sold will be equal to the demand or to the supply, whichever is the lower. So let p_a be fixed, with the equation $D_a = S_a$ removed. The remaining (variable) prices can still be determined from the equations $S_b = D_b$, $S_c = D_c$, for the p_a which appears as a parameter in these equations is now a constant. If it turns out that at these prices $S_a > D_a$, it is only D_a that can actually be traded. When calculating S_x and D_x, we must use this *actual* D_a for both D_a and S_a. With that substitution, we have $S_x = D_x$, as before.

And it is still possible, using this construction, to let the equation for the standard, $S_x = D_x$, replace one of the equations otherwise used, as could be done in the all-round flexprice case. For with D_a substituted for S_a, $p_a(S_a - D_a) = 0$ is an identity. The only terms in $S_x - D_x$ that survive, on application of this identity, are those which relate to the flexprice commodities B and C. The subsystem of BCX will then work in the regular Walrasian manner. We can determine p_b and p_c from any pair of the three equations that are left.

In this way, the Walrasian analogy gets over its first hurdle; but there is another, close behind it, which may be considered more serious. We have so far been making demands and supplies depend only on prices; and for the pure case of multiple exchange with flexible prices, that may probably be accepted. But as soon as a fixprice market is introduced, it ceases to be acceptable. It must be supposed that the demands and supplies for B and C will be affected by what happens in the market for A. That can no longer be represented by the price, so it must be represented by the quantity sold. Assuming, as before, that there is excess supply in the A market, this is D_a. So demands and supplies for B and C will be functions of p_b, p_c and D_a. The BCX subsystem would then *not* be complete in itself; but the whole system, with D_a included as a parameter, would still work in the way that has been described.

We would then have three variables to be determined, p_b, p_c and D_a – and four equations. They are the demand–supply equations for BCX (the X equation being constructed with the *actual* D_a, as before); and there is also the demand equation for D_a, which makes D_a a function of p_b and p_c. As before, any one of the BCX equations can be eliminated. The system is determined, whichever equation we choose to eliminate.

The model is still very formal; but now it is the same kind of model as the *IS–LM* model. We could represent that as a three-way (ABX) model, in which there is just on price (p_b, which becomes the rate of interest) that is determined on a flexprice market, and one quantity (Y) which plays the part of D_a. I have deliberately taken a case which in the same formal terms is slightly more complicated, since I have admitted two flexprice markets, for B and for C. It may indeed be useful to show that there is, in principle, no difficulty in introducing a second flexprice market – or, for that matter, introducing several. It could be useful, even for macro-economic purposes, to introduce a second flexprice market – for instance, a market for foreign exchange.

But that is not the reason I have introduced the extra market. The important use of a four-way model, in this connection, is that it enables us to consider the market for goods and the market for labour separately. And when we take them separately, quite interesting things happen.

One could construct a model in which only the market for labour was a fixprice market, and not only the rate of interest but also the price (or price level) of finished products was flexible. That would fit very exactly into the scheme which has just been outlined. with demand–supply equations determining D_a (employment) and the two flexible prices p_b, p_c. It is possible that Keynes himself sometimes thought in terms of that sort of model (see, for example, *General Theory*, ch. 21); but it cannot be this which *IS–LM* is supposed to represent. For Y is taken to be an index not only of employment, but also of output, so the prices of products also are supposed to be fixed in terms of the standard; and it is hard to see how that can be justified unless the prices of products are derived from the wage of labour by some markup rule. But if that is so, we have not one, but two, fixprice markets.

Say that A and B are fixprice markets, while C is flexprice. As long as we follow the Walrasian practice of working entirely in terms of price parameters, there is no trouble. p_a and p_b are then fixed, so that all demands and supplies are functions of the single variable p_c. p_c is determined on the market for C (or, equivalently, on the market for X) as before. And the actual amounts of A and B that are traded are D_a or S_a, D_b or S_b – whichever, at the equilibrium p_c, turns out to be the lower.

But now suppose that, as before, we change the parameters, making demands and supplies functions of D_a and D_b (assuming that there is excess supply in both markets), not of p_c only. One would at first say that at a (provisionally given) p_c, D_a would be a function of D_b and D_b of D_a; and there need be nothing circular about that. There are just these two 'curves' in the $(D_a D_b)$ plane (like supply and demand curves); at their intersection, the equilibrium is determined.

It must be this which, in the *IS–LM* model, is supposed to happen. We are now to take *A* to be the labour market, *C* the market for loanable funds (as before), and *B* the market for finished products (consumption goods and investment goods not being, so far, distinguished). p_a is the fixed money wage; p_b, the fixed price level of the finished products; p_c, the rate of interest, the only price that is left to be determined on a flexprice market.

How, then, do we identify the 'curves'? One, which makes D_b (effective demand for products) a function of D_a (employment) is easy to find in Keynes. D_b depends on D_a, since the consumption component of D_b increases when employment increases (the consumption function), while the investment component depends on the rate of interest, provisionally given. There is no trouble about that. But what of the other 'curve' – the dependence of D_a on D_b, of employment on effective demand? Keynes took it for granted that they must go together, but the matter needs looking into. For it is here that there is a danger of going seriously wrong by neglecting time.

III

It is not true, of course, that time has been wholly neglected. As I said at the beginning, all the prices and quantities that have figured in the analysis must belong to a period; the past (before the period) and the future (beyond the period) have always been playing their regular parts. What has been neglected is the flow of time within the period. It is here that the length of the period is important.

In my own version [essay 6 above or *VC*], the period ('week') was kept very short, so that little could happen within it. The actual outputs of products and (probably also) the actual input of labour would be largely predetermined. What could vary, considerably, would be prices. So for the study of price formation on flexprice markets, the 'week' had something to be said for it.[3] But that was not what Keynes was interested in; so he had to have a longer period.

It is not unreasonable to suppose that the prices which are established in flexprice markets, during a 'week' (or even at a point of time) do reflect the expectations of traders, their liquidity

---

[3] No more than something. I have myself become pretty critical of the *VC* temporary equilibrium method when applied to flow markets. (I do not question its validity for the analysis of markets in stocks.) See ch. 6 of *CG*.

positions, and so on. That is to say (it is equivalent to saying), we may fairly reckon that these markets, with respect to these data, are in equilibrium. And one could go on, as we have in fact been seeing, even while maintaining the 'week' interpretation, to admit that there are some markets which are fixprice markets, in which demands and supplies do not have to be equal. Then it is only to the markets which are flexprice markets that the equilibrium rule applies. Now it would be quite hard to say, in terms of such a model, that effective demand would determine employment. It is so tempting to say that there can be no output without labour input, so that an increase in demand must increase employment (as Keynes effectively did). But the question is not one of the relation between input and output, in general; it is a question of the relation between current demand and current input, both in the current period. It is at once shown, on the 'week' interpretation, that current output is largely predetermined; while, if the price of output is fixed, current demand may be greater or less than current output (stocks being decumulated or accumulated). How, then, is current input to be determined? We can only make it determinate, as a function of current demand, if we can bring ourselves to introduce some *rule*, according to which the extent of excess demand (or supply) in the current period will affect the employment that is offered, again in the current period. If we have such a rule, we can complete the circle, and show, in the current period, effective demand and employment simultaneously determined.

It is quite a question whether we would be justified, in general, in imposing such a rule.[4] For the effect on current input of excess demand or supply in the product market is surely a matter of the way in which the excess is interpreted by decision makers. An excess which is expected to be quite temporary may have no effect on input; it is not only the current excess but the expectation of its future which determines action. It may be useful, on occasion, to suspend these doubts, and so to make models in which current input depends on excess demands (or supplies) in the product markets according to some rule. But one can hardly get a plausible rule while confining attention to what happens within a single period. So it would seem that the proper place for such a proceeding is in

---

[4] My mind goes back to a conversation I had, a few years ago, with a distinguished economist, who might at an earlier date have been reckoned to be a Keynesian. I was saying to him that I had come to regard J. S. Mill as the most undervalued economist of the nineteenth century. He said, 'Yes, I think I understand. *Demand for commodities is not demand for labour*. It is true, after all.'

sequential models, composed of a succession of periods, in each of which the relevant parameters have to be determined; there is then room for linkages between the periods, and so for lags. I have myself made some attempts at the construction of such models.[5] I think they have their uses, but they are not much like *IS–LM*.

If one is to make sense of the *IS–LM* model, while paying proper attention to time, one must, I think, insist on two things: (1) that the period in question is a relatively long period, a 'year' rather than a 'week'; and (2) that, because the behaviour of the economy over that 'year'[6] is to be *determined* by propensities, and suchlike data, it must be assumed to be, in an appropriate sense, *in equilibrium*. This clearly must not imply that it is an all-round flexprice system; the exogenously fixed money wage, and (as we have seen) the exogenously fixed prices of products must still be retained. But it is not only the market for funds, but also the product market, which must be assumed to be in equilibrium.

Though the prices of products are fixed, it is not necessary to suppose that there is disequilibrium in the product market. Even at the fixed price and fixed wage, when these are maintained over the relatively long period, it will pay producers to adjust supply to demand, as far as they can. For a loss is incurred in producing output that cannot be sold, and a profit is forgone when output that could profitably be sold is not produced. There are problems of adjustment, of which sequential analysis can take account; but there may be purposes for which it is legitimate to leave them to one side. We should then assume that the product markets, during the 'year', are in equilibrium and remain in equilibrium. And since it is to be continuing equilibrium, maintained throughout the 'year', this must mean that plans (so far as they relate to the proceedings of the year) are being carried through without being disturbed.

It is not, I think, inconsistent to suppose that the product markets are in equilibrium, while the labour market is not in equilibrium. For although there are some possibilities for adjusting supply to demand in the case of unemployment on the labour market (even while prices and wages remain unchanged), as by withdrawal of elderly labour from the market, or by departure of migrants, they are surely less than the corresponding possibilities in the market for products. A model which permits excess supply in the labour market, but no product market disequilibrium, is not inconsistent.

---

[5] In particular, in *CG* (chs. 7–10).

[6] The *year* must clearly be long enough for the firm to be 'free to revise its decisions as to how much employment to offer' (Keynes, *General Theory*, p. 47, n. 1).

Once we allow ourselves to assume that product markets remain in equilibrium, things become easier. For once we assume that production plans, during the period, are carried through consistently, we have the relation between current input, during the period, and current output, during the period (which has been made equal to effective demand within the period) for which we have been looking. There are some difficulties about production processes which were begun before the commencement of the period, and others which will not be completed at the end of the period, but these, perhaps, may be overlooked. We can then proceed to the two 'curves' in the (D_aD_b) plane, by which employment and effective demand are simultaneously determined.

The goal is reached, but at a considerable price. For how, after all, can this equilibrium assumption be justified? I do not think it can be justified for all purposes, maybe not for the most important purposes, but I have come to think that there is one purpose for which it may sometimes be justified. I have described this purpose in chapter 6 of my book *Causality in Economics* (1979); an abstract of the argument of that chapter may be given here.

We are to confine attention to the problem of explaining the past, a less exacting application than prediction of what will happen or prescription of what should happen, but surely one that comes first. If we are unable to explain the past, what right have we to attempt to predict the future? I find that concentration on explanation of the past is quite illuminating.

We have, then, facts before us; we know or can find out what, in terms of the things in which we are interested, did actually happen in some past year (say, the year 1975). In order to explain what happened, we must confront these facts with what we think would have happened if something (some alleged cause) had been different. About that, since it did not happen, we can have no factual information; we can only deduce it with the aid of a theory, or model. And since the theory is to tell us what would have happened, the variables in the model must be determined. And that would seem to mean that the model, in some sense, must be in equilibrium.

Applying these notions to the *IS–LM* construction, it is only the point of intersection of the curves which makes any claim to representing what actually happened (in our '1975'). Other points on either of the curves – say, the *IS* curve – surely do not represent, make no claim to represent, what actually happened. They are theoretical constructions, which are supposed to indicate what *would have happened* if the rate of interest had been different. It does not seem farfetched to suppose that these positions are equilibrium positions, representing the equilibrium which corresponds to a different rate of interest. If we cannot take them to be equilibrium positions, we cannot say much about them. But, as the diagram is drawn, the *IS* curve passes through the point of intersection; so the point of intersection appears to be a point on the curve; thus it also is an equilibrium position. That, surely, is quite hard to take. We know that in 1975 the system was not in equilibrium. There were plans which failed to be carried through as intended; there were surprises. We have to suppose that, for the purpose of the analysis on which we are engaged, these things do not matter. It is sufficient to treat the economy, as it actually was in the year in question, as if it were in equilibrium. Or, what is perhaps equivalent, it is permissible to regard the departures from equilibrium, which we admit to have existed, as being random. There are plenty of instances in applied economics, not only in the application of *IS-LM* analysis, where we are accustomed to permitting ourselves this way out. But it is dangerous. Though there may well have been some periods of history, some 'years', for which it is quite acceptable, it is just at the turning points, at the most interesting 'years', where it is hardest to accept it.

What I have been saying applies, most directly, to the *IS* curve; what of the other?

In elementary presentations of the *IS-LM* model, the *LM* curve is supposed to be drawn up on the assumption of a given stock of money (the extension to a stock of money given in terms of wage units comes in only when the level of money wages is allowed to vary, so I shall leave it to one side). It is, however, unnecessary to raise those puzzling questions of the definition of money, which in these monetarist days have become so pressing. For I may allow myself to point out that it was already observed in 'Mr Keynes and the Classics' [essay 8 above] that we do not need to suppose that the curve is drawn up on the assumption of a given stock of money. It is sufficient to suppose that there is (as I said)

a given monetary system – that up to a point, but only up to a point, monetary authorities will prefer to create new money rather than allow interest rates to rise. Such a generalised (*LM*) curve will then slope upwards only gradually – the elasticity of the curve depending on the elasticity of the monetary system (in the ordinary monetary sense).[7]

---

[7] P. 113 above.

That is good as far as it goes, but it does not go far enough. For here, again, there is a question of time reference; and it is a very tricky question. The relation which is expressed in the *IS* curve is a flow relation, which (as we have seen) must refer to a period, such as the year we have been discussing. But the relation expressed in the *LM* curve is, or should be, a stock relation, a balance-sheet relation (as Keynes so rightly insisted). It must therefore refer to a point of time, not to a period. How are the two to be fitted together?

It might appear, at first sight, that we must proceed by converting the stock relation into a relation which is to hold for the period – treating it, in some way, as an average of balance-sheet relations over the period. But this has to be rejected, not merely because it is clumsy, but because it does not get to the point. It has been shown that, if we adopt the equilibrium interpretation, on the *IS* side, the economy must be treated *as if* it were in equilibrium over the period; that means, on the *IS* side, that the economy must remain in flow equilibrium, with demands and supplies for the flows of outputs remaining in balance. It would be logical to maintain that on the *LM* side the economy must be treated similarly. There must be a *maintenance* of stock equilibrium.

I have examined the relation between stock equilibrium and flow equilibrium in chapter 8 of my *Capital and Growth* (1965), where I have shown that the maintenance of stock equilibrium over the period implies the maintenance of flow equilibrium over the period; so it is a sufficient condition for the maintenance of equilibrium over time, in the fullest sense. A key passage is the following:

Equilibrium over time requires the maintenance of stock equilibrium; this should be interpreted as meaning that there is stock equilibrium, not only at the beginning and end of the period, but throughout its course. Thus when we regard a 'long' period as a sequence of 'short' periods, the 'long' period can only be in equilibrium over time if every 'short' period within it is in equilibrium over time. Expectations must be kept self-consistent; so there can be no revision of expectations at the junction between one 'short' period and its successor. The system is in stock equilibrium at each of these junctions; and is in stock equilibrium with respect to these consistent expectations. That can only be possible if expectations – with respect to demands that accrue within the 'long' period – are *right*. Equilibrium over time thus implies consistency between expectations and realisations within the period. It is only expectations of the further future that are arbitrary (exogenous) as they must be.[8]

---

[8] Pp. 92–3. I have made a few minor alterations in wording to make it possible to extract the passage quoted from the rest of the chapter.

That is the formal concept of full equilibrium over time; I do not see how it is to be avoided. But for the purpose of generating an *LM* surve, which is to represent liquidity preference, it will not do without amendment. For there is no sense in liquidity, unless expectations are uncertain. But how is an uncertain expectation to be realised? When the moment arrives to which the expectation refers, what replaces it is fact, fact which is not uncertain.

I have suggested, in my most recent book (*Causality in Economics*), a way of cutting the knot, but I do not have much faith in it.

We must evidently refrain from supposing that the expectations as they were before April (some data in the middle of the 'year') of what is to happen after April, were precise expectations, single-valued expectations; for in a model with single-valued expectations, there can be no question of liquidity. And we must also refrain from the conventional representation of uncertain expectations in terms of mean and variance, since that makes them different in kind from the experiences which are to replace them. There is, however, a third alternative. Suppose we make them expectations that the values that are expected, of the variables affecting decisions, will fall within a particular range. This leaves room for liquidity, since there are no certain expectations of what is going to happen; but it also makes it possible for there to be an equilibrium, in the sense that what happens falls within the expected range. A state of equilibrium is a state in which there are no surprises. What happens (during the period) falls sufficiently within the range of what is expected for no revision of expectations to be necessary. (p. 85.)

As far as I can see, that is the only concept of equilibrium over time[9] which leaves room for liquidity.

IV

I accordingly conclude that the only way in which *IS–LM* analysis usefully survives – as anything more than a classroom gadget, to be superseded, later on, by something better – is in application to a particular kind of causal analysis, where the use of equilibrium methods, even a drastic use of equilibrium methods, is not inappropriate. I have deliberately interpreted the equilibrium concept, to be used in such analysis, in a very stringent manner (some would say a pedantic manner) not because I want to tell the

[9] I should here make an acknowledgement to G. L. S. Shackle, who in much of his work has been feeling in this direction.

applied economist, who uses such methods, that he is in fact committing himself to anything which must appear to him to be so ridiculous, but because I want to ask him to try to assure himself that the divergences between reality and the theoretical model, which he is using the explain it, are no more than divergencies which he is entitled to overlook. I am quite prepared to believe that there are cases where he is entitled to overlook them. But the issue is one which needs to be faced in each case.

When one turns to questions of policy, looking towards the future instead of the past, the use of equilibrium methods is still more suspect. For one cannot prescribe policy without considering at least the possibility that policy may be changed. There can be no change of policy if everything is to go on as expected – if the economy is to remain in what (however approximately) may be regarded as its *existing* equilibrium. It may be hoped that, after the change in policy, the economy will somehow, at some time in the future, settle into what may be regarded, in the same sense, as a new equilibrium; but there must necessarily be a stage before that equilibrium is reached. There must always be a problem of traverse. For the study of a traverse, one has to have recourse to sequential methods of one kind or another.

24

Are there Economic Cycles?

This is a slightly amended version of a lecture that was given at the University of Stirling, Scotland, in October 1981, as the first of a series in honour of Lionel Robbins, who had played a large part in the foundation of that University, and had been its first Chancellor. I naturally began from the standpoint of the years when I worked with him in London, as have been described, from my own viewpoint, in the first of the essays in this volume.

Those of us who were already economists, at the time of the Great Depression of the thirties, used to take it for granted that what we were witnessing was a major example of a long-familiar type of disturbance, which was called the Trade Cycle, or Business Cycle. Already, before 1929, it had a considerable literature, going back, as we were well aware, to the famous story of Jevons and his sunspots. His sunspot theory of cycles[1] was, of course, a fiasco; yet it retains some importance on account of the belief, on which it was based, that something had been happening which was sufficiently repetitive to warrant analysis by some sort of scientific method. It is nevertheless not surprising that in the days of Marshall and Edgeworth his example in this respect was not followed. One may probably conclude that the British economists of that time had a good deal of scepticism about the cyclical character of the phenomenon.[2] The main work on cycles that was done in those early days was in other languages than English.[3]

[1] Advanced in papers written between 1874 and 1877.

[2] It is significant that Dennis Robertson, whose *Study in Industrial Fluctuations* (1915) is the most notable of the work on cycles that was written under Marshall's influence, spoke in his sub-title of the 'so-called cyclical movements'.

[3] C. Juglar, in French, 1862; K. Marx, the second volume of *Das Kapital*, in German, 1885; M. Tugan-Baranovssky, in Russian, 1894; J. Lescure, in French, 1906; A. Aftalion, also in French, 1909.

It was after the famous trade crisis of 1907 that in Britain, and in America, things began to change. Here we have Hawtrey, Pigou and Robertson; in America Mitchell.[4] All of these continued to work on cycles in the twenties – the crisis of 1920 providing another stimulus. Indeed by 1922 there was another Cambridge economist, Lavington, who had no compunction about entitling his book *The Trade Cycle*. I am tempted to quote the first sentences of that excellent work, for it set a keynote for much that was to follow,

The late autumn of 1921 finds the greater part of the civilised world in an economic condition which, if it were not so tragic, might justly be described as absurd. In their situation as consumers the people of two continents stand in urgent need, in varying but more than common degree, not only of their customary comforts but even of their daily bread. Simultaneously in their situation as producers they stand, again in varying but more than common degree, in most unwilling idleness.

Certainly, even before 1929, the problem had already been posed. The idea of the Cycle was becoming established.

And so it went on. The record of the thirties, in major works on cycles is outstanding, as was to be expected. I rather doubt whether Keynes's *General Theory* is to be put on the list; but there is no doubt about Harrod, and Haberler, and Schumpeter, and, of course, Hayek.[5] And so it goes on, not perhaps so strikingly, but sufficiently, through the forties and fifties. When the American Economic Association asked Gordon and Klein, in 1965, to compile a volume of *Readings on Business Cycles*, they had no difficulty in filling it with work that was fairly contemporary. But I think one can notice, even in glancing at that volume, that the papers that are latest in date are the least cyclical. The stream seems to be drying up.

And surely, if one looks at the last twenty years as a whole, it has dried up. It would nowadays be a very old-fashioned department of economics, in any university, which would put on a course of lectures on The Trade Cycle, as we used to do, and as I myself have done in my younger days. And yet – what is it that we are seeing? It looks like a Depression. If not, what is it?

There is something here that needs explaining. I do not claim that I can explain it, at least not fully. But perhaps it will be useful to start some thinking about it.

[4] R. Hawtrey, *Good and Bad Trade* (1911); A. C. Pigou, work on fluctuations that is included in *Wealth and Welfare* (1912); W. C. Mitchell, *Business Cycles* (1915).

[5] R. F. Harrod, *The Trade Cycle* (1936); G. Haberler, *Prosperity and Depression* (1937); J. A. Schumpeter, *Business Cycles* (1939); F. A. Hayek, *Prices and Production* (1931).

You will see that I have, already, been posing the issue historically. It will soon be one hundred years since the death of Jevons; he had just fifty or sixty years of cyclical experience on which to do his thinking; we still have those years, and also another century. Over a century and a half the world has changed, quite a lot. One of the ways in which it has changed is a vast increase in statistical information. We actually have much greater statistical knowledge about Jevons's half-century (the Jevonian period, I shall venture to call it) than was available to Jevons, or to his contemporaries; when it comes to later periods, we have enormously more information. Much of this information can be set out in the form of time-series. There were very few economic variables for which Jevons had time-series, now there are many.

Any time-series, of any variable (economic or other) is likely to exhibit fluctuations. The current observation is greater or less than its predecessor; the series is going up, or going down. A single rise (or fall) is, we admit, not significant; but the statisticians have been busy in giving us tests of significance, which largely consist in the fitting of the observations into a cyclical pattern. Mere continuance of a motion in the same direction gives a crude test of significance – as when the market analysts say that a fall in an index, going on for three quarters, may be called a *recession*. But we do not want a rise that starts from a low point, and never succeeds in getting far from that low point, to have the same significance as one that starts high. What, however, is 'high' or 'low'? It must be with respect to some norm, or standard. One can construct a norm by purely statistical methods, fitting a trend, and judging the actuals by reference to the trend. Most economic variables do not jump about very much from one observation to the next; so when there is a deviation from trend which is at all considerable it will usually last for a succession of observations. There will be sequences of pluses and sequences of minuses; and it is easy for these to begin to look something like a cycle.

It should, however, be noticed that the trend itself is computed from past observations; it belongs to the past, and it is quite an act of faith to maintain that that past is still relevant. It is a bigger act of faith the longer the period from which the trend is derived. So there is an assumption that is involved in the use of such purely statistical methods; it is taken for granted that there is some underlying uniformity, which can be relied upon to remain intact. I do not at all deny that it is often useful to make such an assumption, but we should realise that it is dangerous. History does move on.

In a century and a half it has had much time to move on. The world was pretty different in the Jevonian period (when, as we have seen, the image of a Cycle first took shape) from what it has become in this late twentieth century. Some of the differences, as we shall see, are to the point.

I am sure that when Jevons, and his contemporaries, talked about cycles, they were not thinking of statistical cycles; the statistical apparatus of trend-fitting was indeed not yet available to them. They were thinking of something which to them was quite obvious. They were thinking of the remarkable sequence of trade crises, 1825, 1847, 1857, 1867 – which, with a somewhat mysterious gap in the thirties, looked so like a ten-year regularity.[6] Now these were clearly financial crises; the pattern which repeated itself (at least in those aspects which to the knowledge of that time most clearly repeated themselves) was financial. There was a boom, with rising prices and then rising interest rates, it led to a crisis, with a wave of bankruptcies. (The unemployment which followed was a consequence of the bankruptcies, or of attempts to avoid them.) After the crisis prices fell; rates of interest then came down. That was a first step towards recovery.

It was already apparent to contemporaries how this could happen. A general rise in prices – many prices rising, without others falling – did not necessarily require an increased supply of money to finance it. It could be financed by credit, not (at first) even bank credit, just trade credit – a promise to pay by the buyer, so that he got the goods at the expense of an increase in his debts. (Or, what comes to the same thing, an increase in the velocity of circulation.) But trade credit though expansible would not be indefinitely expansible; the time would come when some of the extended trade would have to be financed by something more solid. Recourse would then be had to the banking system, and there would be an expansion of bank money. But bank money (then) was not ultimately solid enough; so there would be an increased demand for the really solid money, the gold coins, which (we must remember) were then in common circulation. The custodian of the gold reserve was the Bank of England; it had a reserve but it was strictly limited. So when the time came that the Bank was in sight of the point when it would be unable to

---

[6] The gap, in so far as it is a gap, has been largely cleared up by Robin Matthews, in his *Study in Trade Cycle History* (1954), a work which I am proud to say was begun when he was working with me in Oxford.

exchange its notes for gold, it had to take action, to enforce a restriction on borrowing. That was the crisis. The rising interest rates which preceded the crisis were a signal that it was approaching.

In the crisis weak positions were uncovered, and there were failures. But the Bank itself survived, and most of the banks survived. The pressure then relaxed, and interest rates, being a symptom of the pressure, came down. When the debris had been cleared up, a new equilibrium would be restored. But it would be unstable. Once settling down was complete, the whole process could re-start, all over again.

Of course, there were differences from one cycle to another; but that is in outline what the cycle looked like, in the Jevonian period. It has left a deep mark upon our thinking from that day to this. We are still inclined to think of it as the standard pattern of a Trade Cycle. It may nevertheless be questioned whether in these latter days it has continued to fit.

For there are two quite special characteristics of the Jevonian period which need to be noticed. One is that this was the time when Britain beyond question was the economic centre of the world. So it is perfectly proper to treat the British experience as *the* experience; much of what happened in other countries in the way of fluctuations just followed from it. The other is that in this period the Gold Standard was sacred: in Britain it was sacred. There was no question (and it was known that there was no question) that the convertibility of Bank of England notes into gold must be maintained. It was this that in the end provided a firm ceiling on expansion, a monetary ceiling. It was known that the expansion could not go on indefinitely; and so, as the boom developed, people began to take precautions. Wise men had battened down the hatches before the storm broke.

I now pass on to a second period, which I will reckon as running from about 1870 to 1914. It is characteristic of this period that the regular cycle, the Jevonian cycle which I have just been describing, almost disappeared. Of course, there were ups and downs – in Britain, to begin with, more downs than ups – but it is quite a job to fit them into the previous pattern. Only at the end was there an old-style trade crisis, in 1907. But its centre was not in London; it was in New York. I think that that is significant.

For already in this period the primacy that Britain had held was passing. The 1880s, in Britain, were regarded as a time of depression; but there was no such depression in Germany or in the United States. It is not at all surprising that in a country where industry is lagging there should be depression – especially when it and its competitors are on a common standard. This was not a cyclical phenomenon, in the old sense, at all. It was something that was present, all the time, throughout this period.

Yet there were fluctuations; one year was better than another, even in Britain. How were these fluctuations to be explained? If one persisted in trying to fit them into something like the old pattern, one would have to argue like this. One would have to say that because of its relative weakness, as compared with the past, the British economy could not let itself go, as in former booms; the monetary brake would have to be applied much sooner. There would then be no need for a sharp change of direction; there need be no crisis, leaving a mess which remained to be cleaned up. Depression, though long lasting, could be rather stable.

There was some evidence that pointed that way; but it was not very conclusive. Booms were checked at an early stage, there was no doubt about that, but a monetary cause for the check was not always evident. Was it not possible that a weak boom could just peter out by itself?

This directed attention to possible *real*, non-monetary, causes of fluctuations. Thus it is here, towards the end of my second period, that we find the beginnings of a *real* theory of fluctuations, which was later to be of such importance. It took many years before that theory was fully developed, and then, perhaps it was over-developed. For there is no reason why a real theory and a monetary theory should be inconsistent with one another. Each may have a part to play.

It may be that the main deduction which could have been drawn from the experience of weak booms petering out was not so much the need for a real theory as the need for the different parts of the old-style cycle – the boom, the crisis, the depression, the recovery – to be looked at more separately. Did one necessarily lead to the next? There could really be no question that the crises which had been experienced in the past (and that which was experienced in 1907 in the United States) were monetary phenomena; but if a boom could just peter out without leading to a crisis, the causes of such a boom did not look like being monetary. The monetary system must be permissive enough to allow the boom to occur; but at no point in the weak cycle, with the boom just petering out, followed by (usually) mild depression, did monetary authorities have to take positive action. So it did seem as if the weak cycle should be explained in terms of non-monetary causes. But, if that were so, might it not be that the ·more violent booms, which did end in monetary crises should be explained in terms of similar causes, here of greater strength? This does seem to me to have been an intelligent way, even at that time, of looking at the problem.

The real causes which could lead to booms could be quite various. Technical progress, leading to new opportunities for productive investment, is perhaps the easiest to understand. (The railway, in the Jevonian period, would be a major example.) One would nevertheless expect that such inventions, though naturally stimulating a boom in a part of the economy, would not easily have the general effect which we should want to ascribe to them, unless there were some mechanism by which the stimulus would spread. Later work on real causes was much concerned with such mechanisms for spreading. The cycle models which became so fashionable in the forties and fifties, and to which I myself made a 'contribution' (*TC*), were largely concerned with mechanisms for spreading.

I shall have a little more to say about that later; it is enough for the present to have made the main distinction, between the causes of booms, which may be accepted to have been for the most part real causes, and the causes of the crisis (if there is a crisis) which I would accept to have been, at least so far, essentially monetary. With this in mind, let us pass on to a third period, the inter-war period, 1919–39.

A word to begin with on 1920–2; the post-war boom, very violent but short-lived, and the depression, also violent but not long-lasting (at least in America), which followed. When economists had to make up their minds about this experience, the two approaches, real and monetary, are clearly distinguishable in their work. There was a monetary approach that was championed by Hawtrey, and a real approach, by Pigou. My own view [see essay 13 above] would be that it is right to attribute that boom to real causes – the urgent need for new construction to make up for war losses, and the shortage of materials, and of finished consumption goods, to meet the demands which the attempts at new construction generated. But it also seems to me to be right to attribute the crisis (it undoubtedly was a crisis) to monetary restriction, designed to preventing the boom becoming all-out inflation.

When one comes to 1929–34, the issue is still more complex. There was not just one crisis, indeed there was a succession of crises. And was there a boom preceding? Some of the symptoms of boom were undoubtedly there, in aggravated form; but there were others, such as a general rise in the prices of finished goods, which appeared to be missing. It is thus quite intelligible that the American authorities did not know what to do about it; a selective restraint, such as later experience would suggest should have been called for, was probably outside their powers. So in the end they imposed a general monetary restraint, very drastically.

Since it had not been clear that what had preceded had been a boom, the crisis was unexpected; preparations to ward off its perils had not been made. In the old-style crisis, much of the financial system was prepared, so it did stand firm; thus within a few months of the onset of the crisis, the skies began to clear. So it was quite soon after the original onset that interest rates came down. What followed was indeed a depression – a depression marked by bad trade and by unemployment – but at least it was clear that it had a bottom. It soon became apparent that things would not get worse; and that was a first step towards their getting better.

But in 1930 the threat to the financial system – indeed to the international financial system – was much more general. It was not only the American banks that were in trouble; the European banks were in trouble also. The European countries had quite recently returned to a Gold Standard, a very fragile Gold Standard, supported in many ways, both direct and indirect, by American credit. As long as the Gold Standard was taken for granted, as the old Gold Standard had been, and as it was hoped that the new would be, there was nothing for it but to shore up the weaker parts of the financial system, the international financial system, by advances from the stronger parts; but the making of those advances to borrowers of uncertain solvency weakened those who made them. So, being themselves in trouble, they restricted credit whenever they could. This went on for many months. So there was not just a single crisis as in former times rather quickly cleared up. There was a long *agony*, as it will be useful to call it – a continuation of crisis in the old sense of crisis. In the end something had to snap; when it snapped there was an end to that agony.

But it did not happen all at once. From the point of view of a devaluing country, such as Britain, 'going off the Gold Standard' was a release; the agony was ended. Although what followed was indeed a Depression, with unemployment persisting, the monetary restraint was removed, as the fall in interest rates made evident. So it was possible to begin preparations for recovery. But it is useful to remember that from the point of view of other countries the fall in the pound looked very different; it made their position harder. I remember being told, many years later, by an American (a professor of economics at one of their great universities) that it was Britain that caused the Depression! I was astounded, and it took me some time to reconstruct what he meant. He was not thinking of the story as a whole, from 1929 onwards; the first part, I am sure he would have reckoned, was an American business, with which America, if she had been on her own, could have coped. *The* Depression, for him, was the second part, the grimmest year of all, 1932. And there was a case for saying that that was caused by what must have appeared to him as the British default in 1931.

Nevertheless, by the time of our conversation, that had become very old-fashioned; for in 1933 the dollar also had been devalued in terms of gold, and by 1935, in terms of the dollar, sterling had recovered. By that time, what had essentially happened, in monetary terms, was that the gold reserves of the central banks, all central banks together, had been greatly increased in terms of their own currencies. Of course, that made things easier; it brought the agony to an end. But what had been done once could be done again. The dollar was still on gold, though at a reduced value; but the sanctity which had been attached to its value in terms of gold, the supply of which was not under the control of any single government, was at least somewhat damaged. In the end, as we know, it has not just been damaged; it has been destroyed.

It took a long time before this became fully apparent; but already by the middle thirties it was clear that less faith than before could be put in a monetary ceiling. It had done too badly for it to be able to resume its old authority. So it was quite appropriate, from that time onwards, that the attention of economists should be directed towards the question of what would happen if it were wholly removed. If there were just a weak boom, it might peter out, as before; but what if there were a strong boom, and no monetary ceiling? Would there just be a monetary explosion, or would there still be a cycle? Might there be a *real* ceiling, which would bring the boom to an end, without monetary action?

I am not suggesting that this was the cause of the shift in attention, among economists, which one can detect at this point; only that it explains why it came to make sense. That there should have been a revival of interest in the *real* causes of fluctuations, is easy to understand; the real (non-monetary) aspects of the Depression (in particular the unemployment) had been so shattering. It was natural, then, to turn one's attention to changes in inputs and outputs (about which, by that time, there was much more information) instead of the old concentration on prices and interest rates.

The shift in attention, in the work of Keynes, is well known; from the *Treatise* of 1930, which in essence was a theory of prices, or price-levels, to the *General Theory* of 1936, which was a theory of employment. It is not so well known that it is matched by a movement from Hayek to Harrod. I once asked Harrod what had put him on to the construction of his so-called 'dynamic' theory; he said, to my surprise, that it was thinking about Hayek. Hayek, of course, had been thinking in terms of prices and interest rates; but his special concern had been with the effects of changes in these on the *real* 'structure of production'. What I think Harrod meant was that Hayek had started him thinking about the structure of production, and its bearing on fluctuations. This had happened while he himself had been deeply under the influence of Keynes; so he had to fit something about the structure of production into an otherwise Keynesian theory.

It had been Keynes's contention that an increase in investment (expenditure, that is, which is directed towards increasing the capital equipment of the economy) would raise effective demand by more than the increase in investment itself, so that (output responding to effective demand) the increase in output would be greater than the increase in investment. That, in Keynes's view, was consistent with the attainment of a new equilibrium, with investment and output, and employment, all increased. But (said Harrod) what if there is a backwash of the increase in output on investment? In addition to the original increase in investment (what we might call the autonomous increase) there would be a secondary or induced increase, and that would have a further (multiplier) effect in increasing output. It is not obvious that when the induced investment is also taken into account, there can be established a new equilibrium, in Keynes's manner.

In the way that Harrod first stated his model, all these reactions were very fast, and the inducement of investment was very large. So any upward disturbance would produce a large expansion. This would go on until it was checked by a Full Employment ceiling (as in the Keynes model also an expansion would be checked). But – and here is the difference – the Harrod model would not stay on its ceiling, for, when the expansion was stopped by the ceiling, the Induced Investment would go into reverse. The model seemed then to be set for an irreversible decline. So there would be a slump, *in real terms*, though nothing had been said about a monetary ceiling.

That begins to look like, quite horribly like, some more recent experience; but how does one explain, in these terms, or in anything like these terms, the good performance of the economy (the world economy) in the 'Bretton Woods period', as it is commonly called, the fifties and the sixties of this century? First of all, the avoidance of a post-war crisis and slump – the absence, in the late forties, of anything like the events of 1919–22? This is commonly attributed to the more resolute maintenance of war-time controls; and that, I suppose, is largely right. What had gone wrong at the end of the First World War was the restoration of free markets, before the most immediate post-war shortages had been overcome; after the Second War, they were restored, but not until the productive process was ready for them. So one could put what happened into the form of saying that the economy (I still mean the international economy) was rather skilfully steered into what was in effect a new equilibrium, on, or nearly on, its full employment ceiling; and there is nothing in Harrodian principles which would say that such an equilibrium, if it were once reached, and there was a fairly good adjustment to it, could not be maintained. It is a violent change of direction, such as will occur when an expansionary path which has been followed in a boom encounters a real ceiling, so that it can no longer be followed, which is responsible for Harrod's slump.

That can, of course, be no more than a bird's eye view. It is not to be denied that in the Bretton Woods period there were fluctuations; the remarkable thing was that they passed off so easily. That may partly be explained by the pliability of the dollar standard; there still was a monetary ceiling, which kept the full employment path from generating an all-out inflation, but avoided the sharp collisions such as had marked the trade crises of former years. (The cost of that pliability, already, was a general upward drift of prices.) The monetary authorities of individual countries had to pay attention to their balances of payments, and that imposed a monetary constraint; but it was known that a continued strain on the balance of payments would lead to devaluation. That was expected, so when it came the disruption was remarkably small.

There may, however, be another reason why fluctuations in the Bretton Woods period were limited. I have said that in the Harrod model, as originally stated, the Induced Investment effect was violent. One of the reasons for this was that he supposed (quite reasonably, when first constructing his model) that all kinds of investment were affected. Every kind of concern had a *desired* capital outfit, which might be greater or less than that which was actually possessed. If actual capital was less than this desired capital, positive investment would be undertaken; if actual capital was surplus to what was desired, it would be allowed to run down. And the desired capital was supposed to respond, quite quickly, to current demand – to the way, that is, that current activity was moving.

Now there can be no question that, so far as working capital is concerned, the case for supposing it to react in this sort of way is a strong one. It is easy to recognise the reaction in the 'de-stocking' and 're-stocking' of which we hear so much. But if the only induced investment was of this character, though it could result in 'inventory cycles', the rather mild cycles, of a few months' duration, which have long been recognisable, it could not do more than that. These are definitely not what used to be meant by *The* Trade Cycle.

If there are to be more serious cycles, coming about through Induced Investment, the Induced Investment must go deeper; it must affect fixed capital also. Now it is characteristic of much investment in fixed capital that it takes quite a time to complete, and is then quite long-lasting, so the profitability, and even the usefulness, of such investment has to be judged by an assessment of what needs will be quite some way ahead. The discovery that at the moment it would be nice to have a larger capacity does not in itself give an incentive to add to capacity; there is nothing that can be done by investment in fixed capital to meet a current shortage. So what is important is an assessment of what will be required in the future, over quite a long future. As long as there is confidence that on the whole, over that future, the additional equipment will be wanted, it will still be sensible to go ahead with it, whatever at the moment is the state of trade.

Now to make good guesses about the state of trade five to ten years hence, or ten to twenty years, requires a lot of information; and during most of the century and a half, on which I have been commenting, such information was surely quite scarce. Thus it is understandable that the current state of trade, as being a chief thing on which there was information, should have had more effect upon investment, even in fixed capital, than one might think to be rational. That could be one thing which made the old cycles work in a rather Harrod-type manner.

But if this was true in the days of the old cycles, it must be much less true today, or even yesterday. Information, or what purports to be information, about what is to be expected in the future has become so much more abundant; one cannot believe that investment plans are now, to an over-riding extent, based on the current state of trade. That could make them more stable, and perhaps in the Bretton Woods period they were more stable; but it does not necessarily work that way.

For one thing, there is now a political instability that is added. The part played by the State in economic life has become so much more important; the ways in which governments can affect economic activity have become more various and more powerful. It can hardly be doubted that the turning-points in most of the fluctuations which have occurred in particular countries, say since 1960, have been reflections of changes in government policy, under political pressure. Sometimes it is the pressure of unemployment, which forces a government to take expansionary measures; sometimes it is a threat to the balance of payments, or of runaway inflation, which impels restriction. The stages at which such changes occur depend on political factors, such as the dates of elections; the timing of elections is by a political calendar that has nothing to do with economics. Nevertheless, if this were all, there would be a kind of stability, not so unlike the stability which did after all underlie the old cycles, as we have seen. The great difference, however, between these political cycles and the old Jevonian cycles with which I began is that the political cycles are less calculable; so that it is harder to plan long-term investment across them, as was possible with the old cycles, at least to some extent.

But this is by no means all. There is a further complication, a major complication, which nevertheless can still be analysed in the terms I have been using. It has been thought, in the fifties and sixties, the golden age to which we now look back with nostalgia, that the full employment of labour ceiling was the only *real* ceiling which set a limit on the expansion of the world economy. So to keep it moving along that ceiling (with advances in real income due to advances in productivity) was all that had to be done. All that was needed was to ensure that no monetary ceiling stood in its way. The great change which came in the seventies was an encounter with another *real* ceiling, the existence of which had been quite overlooked.

The new ceiling was a natural resources ceiling – or more particularly an energy ceiling – the ceiling that was revealed, so suddenly, in the oil crisis of 1973. The 'good' years that had preceded had been marked by a great increase in the productivity of labour, an increase which can be seen in retrospect to have largely consisted in a substitution of mineral sources of energy for human (and animal) sources. That path could no longer be followed in a carefree manner. Though new fuels could be found, they would take time to develop, and there seemed little prospect of their ever becoming as abundant as used to be supposed. Thus the maximum rate at which the economy could expand was lower than had generally been supposed. The agony that has followed (in *real* respects not so unlike the agony of the thirties) has been a matter of difficulty of adjustment to the new more modest growth rate which is all that has become possible. It is singularly difficult since the adjustment to the old growth path had been so complete. Not just the structure of industry, but also that of the public sector and of labour relations, are called into question.

It is a *real* crisis (or agony) so Harrod's analysis should apply to it. I think it does. What Harrod showed was that an encounter with a real ceiling, if it was at all sharp, would lead to a fall in activity *below* that which would be attainable on the ceiling. If the ceiling was a labour ceiling, the shortage of labour, which made it impossible to continue on the old growth path, would lead to unemployment. When the ceiling is an energy ceiling there will again be stages at which the energy that is available will not be fully used.

The sudden intervention of this new ceiling, at a point when monetary restraint had been almost fully discarded, would lead, as indeed it did, to an acceleration of inflation. Pure cost inflation this time – a desperate attempt to retain the real wages, and the rate of growth of real wages, experience of which, along the old growth path, had become so deep-rooted. The inflation, however, is no more than a symptom of the malady; it is not the malady itself.

It is nevertheless not surprising that attempts should be made to find a way out by the restoration of a monetary ceiling; but the search for a monetary ceiling, which should be able to impose something like the authority of the old Gold Standard, has, at least so far, proved abortive. There is, of course, no doubt that a monetary restriction can be imposed; but it works through interest rates, not through the Quantity of Money (in any sense) with which the rate of interest has proved to have no reliable connection. But, though high rates of interest do damp down the activity of industry (as if that needed to be damped further!), their effect on prices is nowadays often perverse. The old route by which they lowered prices is so largely blocked up. The large monopolistic, or quasi-monopolistic, concerns, whether in public or private ownership, feel a rise in interest as a rise in their costs (they even feel a fall in demand as a rise in their costs) and they react to either by *raising* their prices. The one way which is open by which a rise in interest reduces prices is that it strengthens the external value of the currency; that does tend to lower prices, or to check their increase, but again at the expense of aggravating depression.

In a country such as Britain these forces are particularly strong; they largely explain why the depression has failed to exercise very much of the therapeutic effects, which in former times it did exercise, thus paving the way to recovery. So this is not at all the old sort of cycle. The agony continues; some way out of it must be found. But there is no easy way out. It will not come of itself.

Index